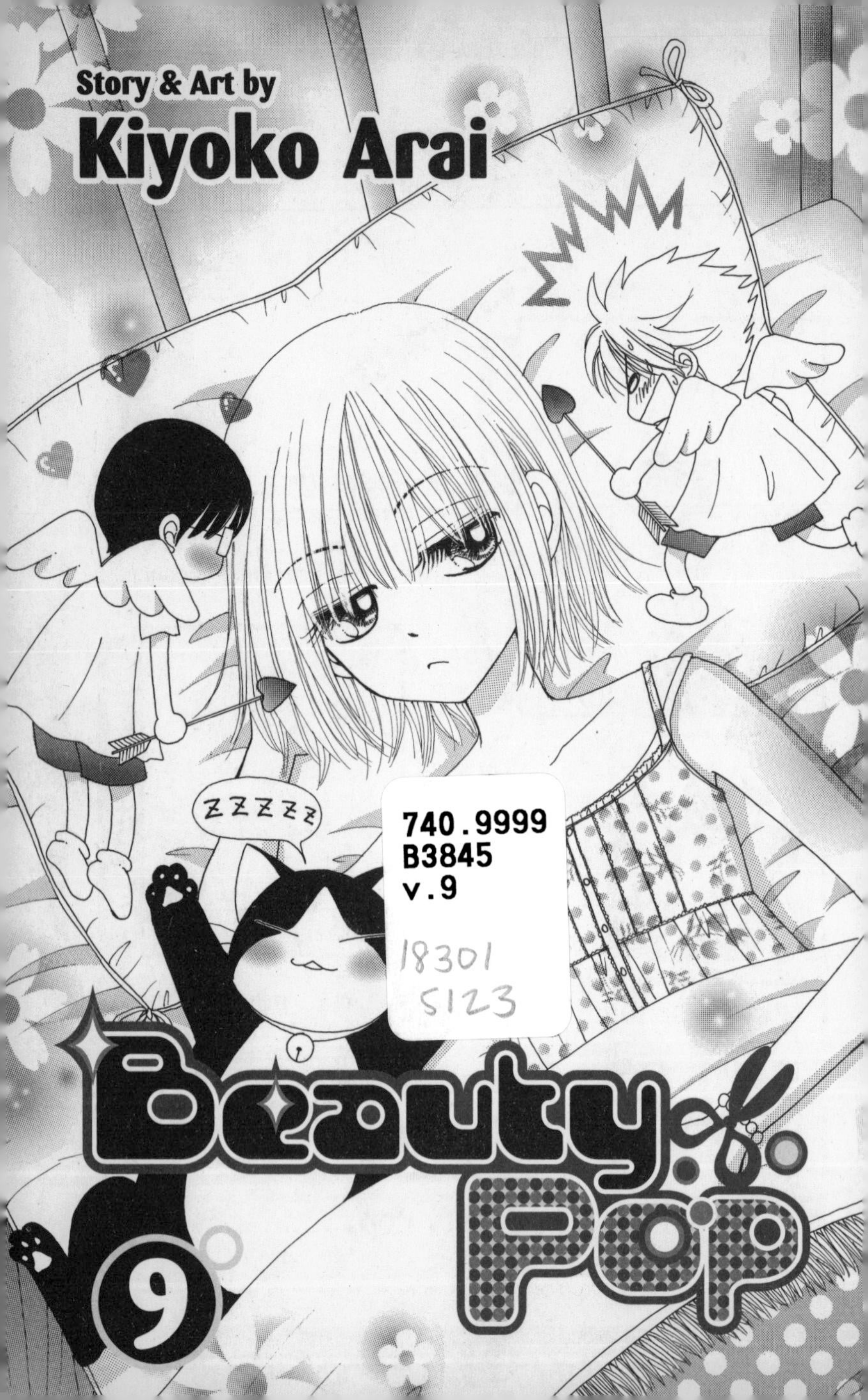
Story & Art by
Kiyoko Arai
ZZZZZ
Beauty Pop
9

Beauty Pop

Characters 9

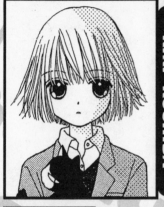

KIRI KOSHIBA

◀ She's absentminded and seems self-centered, but she really cares for her friends. Kiri has exceptional haircutting techniques.

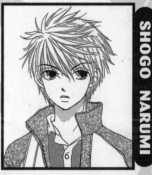

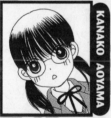

KANAKO AOYAMA

◀ She's Kiri's best friend. She likes Ochiai.

SHOGO NARUMI

▲ Narumi is aiming to be the top beautician in Japan. He's short-tempered and women freak him out.

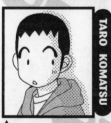

TARO KOMATSU

▲ He's Kiri's friend. He's adept at collecting information.

CONTENTS

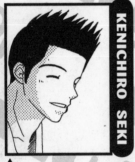

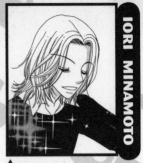

IORI MINAMOTO

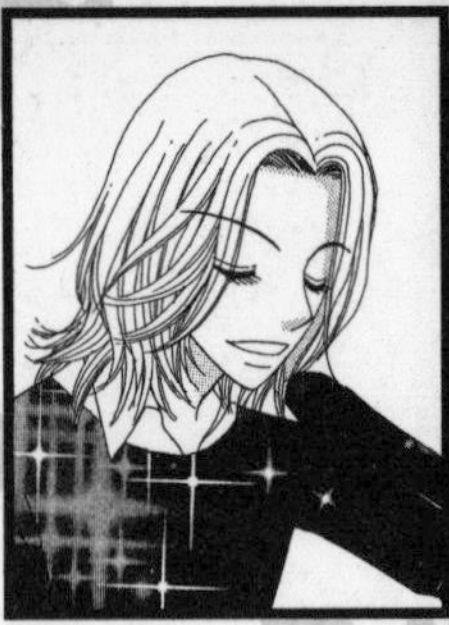

A narcissistic aromatherapist, he is Kiri's childhood friend who recently returned from N.Y.

KAZUHIKO OCHIAI

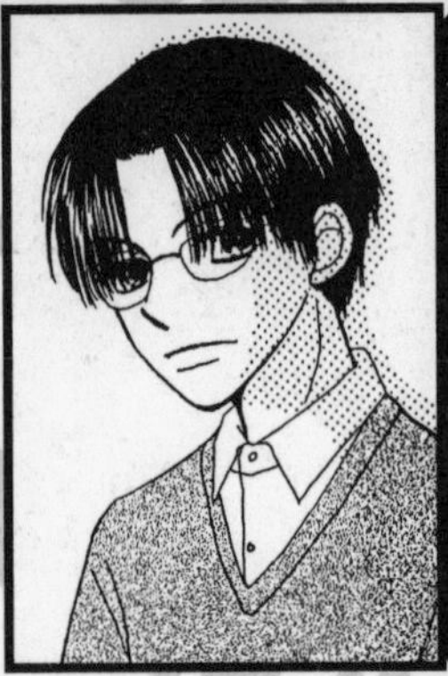

He's the respected president of the Scissors Project. Lately he can't stop thinking about Kiri.

KEI MINAMI

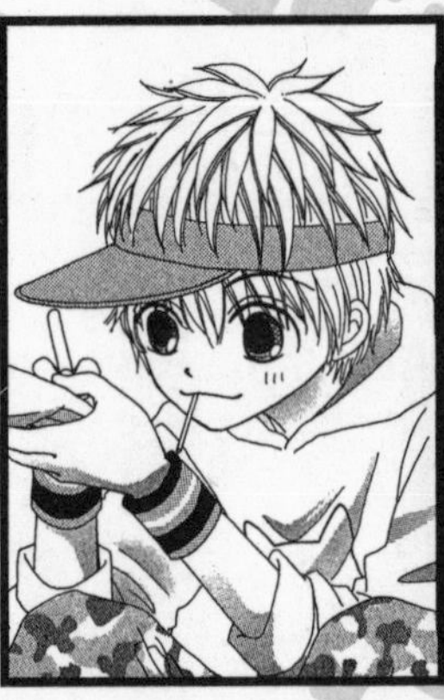

Childlike Kei loves to eat snacks. But his nail art is outstanding!

KENICHIRO SEKI

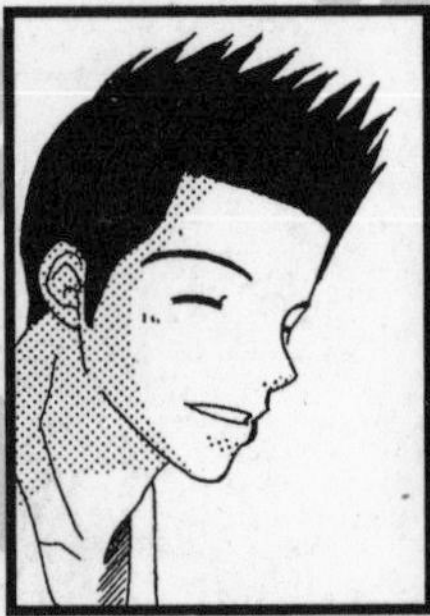

Another one of Kiri's childhood friends. He's very shy, but his shiatsu skills are top-notch.

BILLY IKETANI

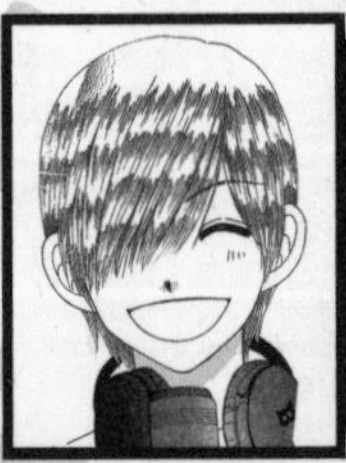

He's a genius hairstylist who is making a name for himself in Hollywood.

Story So Far

The Scissors Project has entered the All-Japan Beauty Tournament. In the first preliminary round, an opposing team bumps into Kiri and Narumi on purpose, making them fall down. Their lips touch and...?!

Beauty Pop

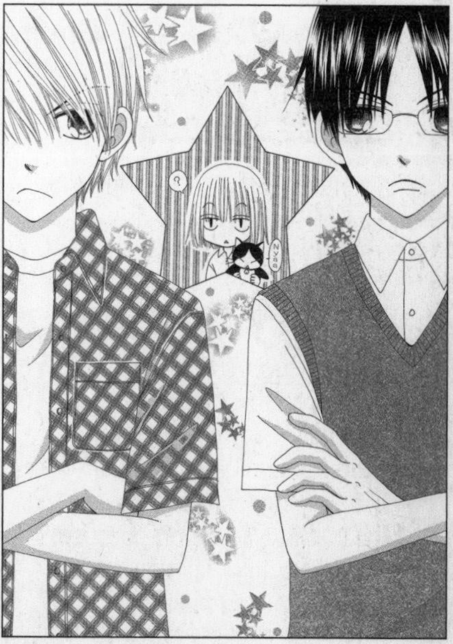
?
Nyaa

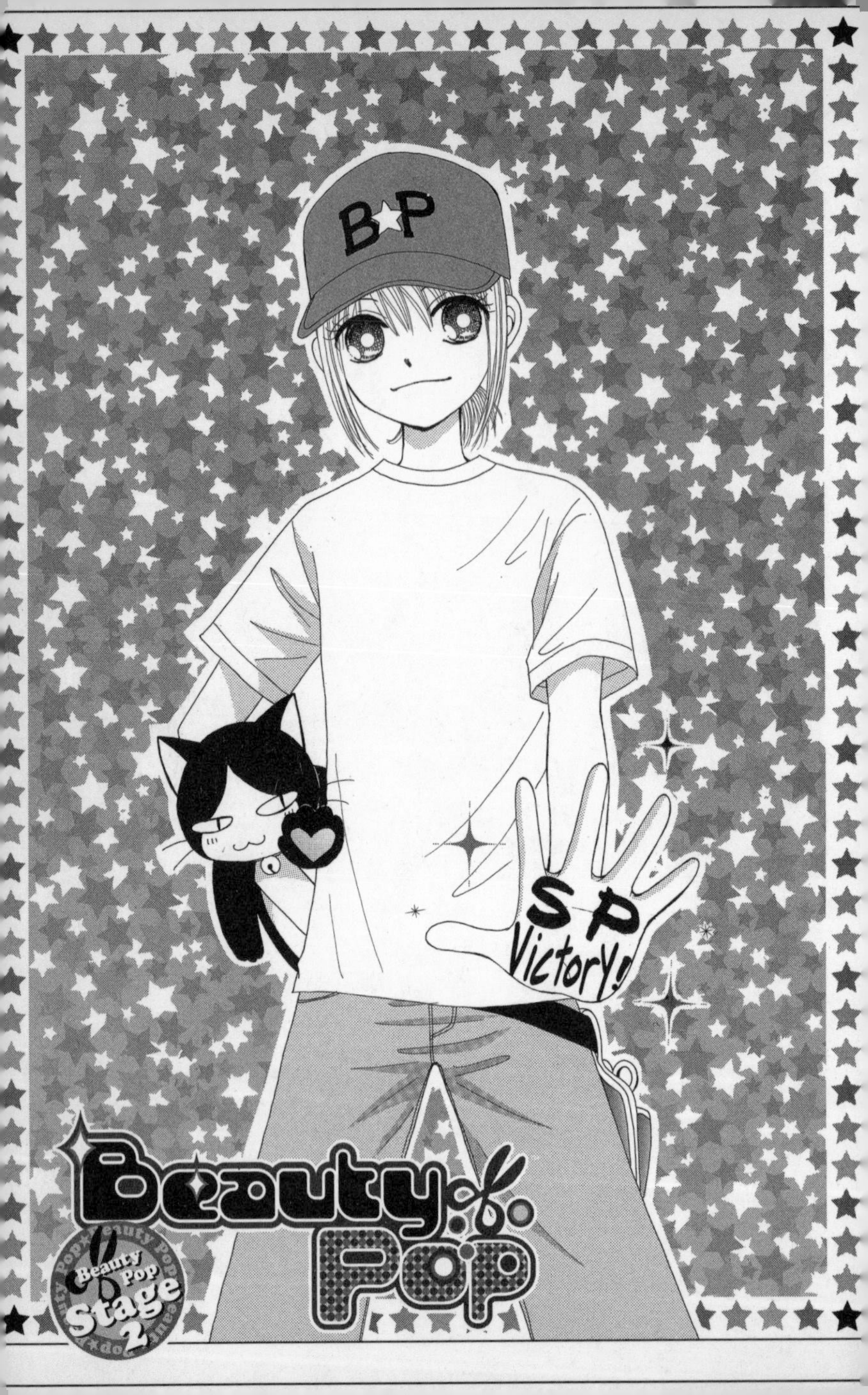
B★P
SP
Victory!
Beauty Pop
Beauty Pop
Stage 2

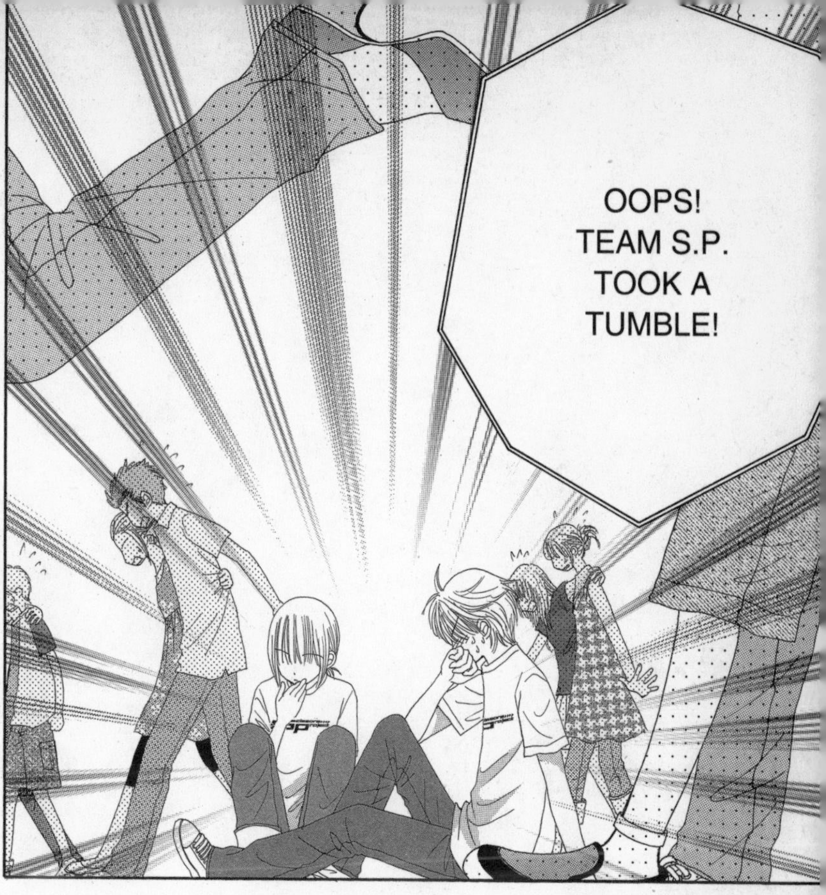
OOPS! TEAM S.P. TOOK A TUMBLE!

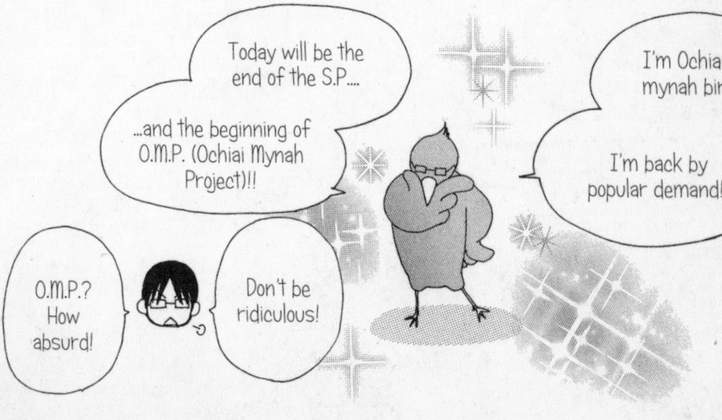
I'm Ochiai's mynah bird.
I'm back by popular demand!!
Today will be the end of the S.P....
...and the beginning of O.M.P. (Ochiai Mynah Project)!!
Don't be ridiculous!
O.M.P.? How absurd!

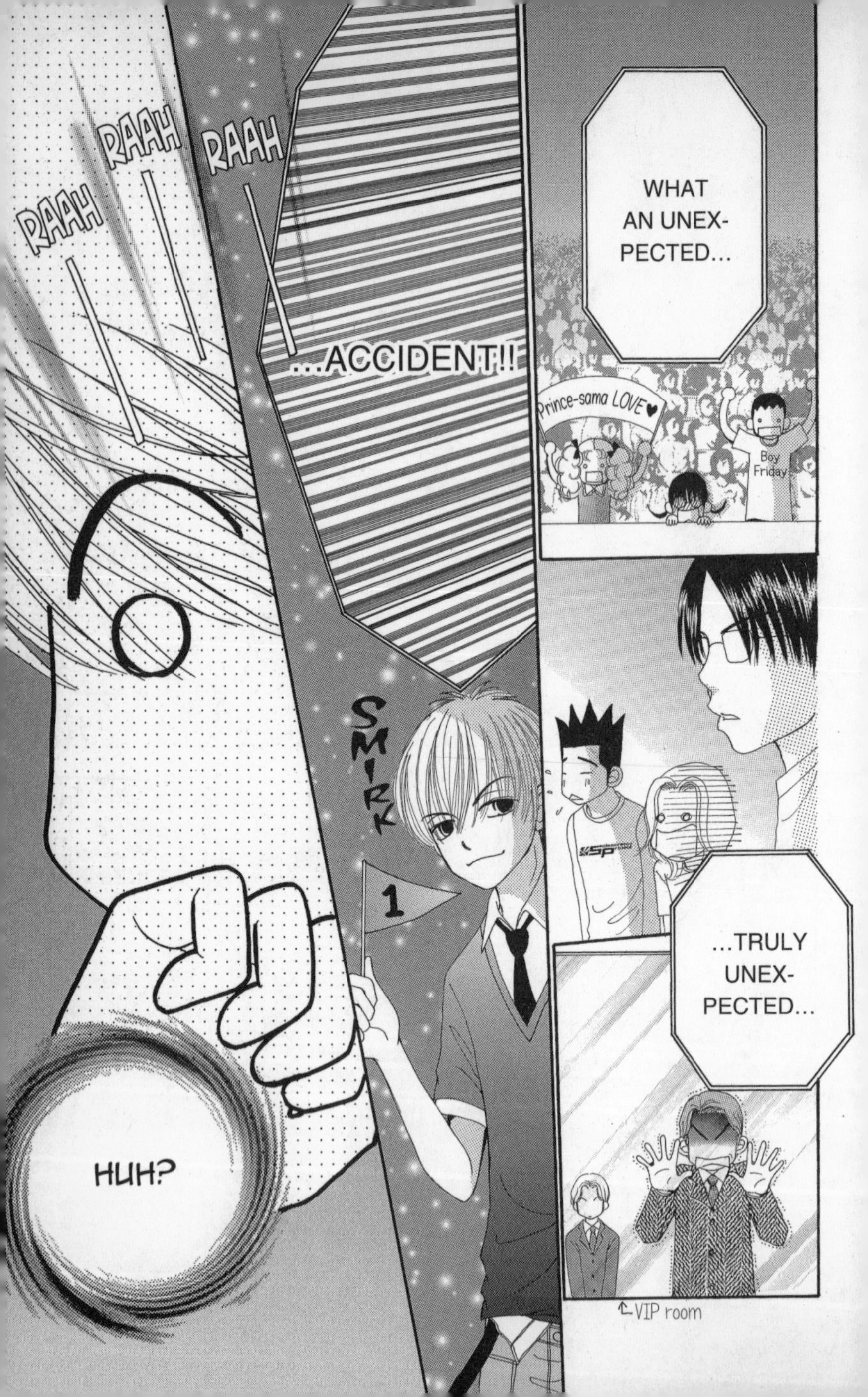
WHAT AN UNEX-PECTED...
Prince-sama LOVE♥
Boy Friday
...TRULY UNEX-PECTED...
↖VIP room
RAAH
RAAH
RAAH
...ACCIDENT!!
SMIRK
1
HUH?

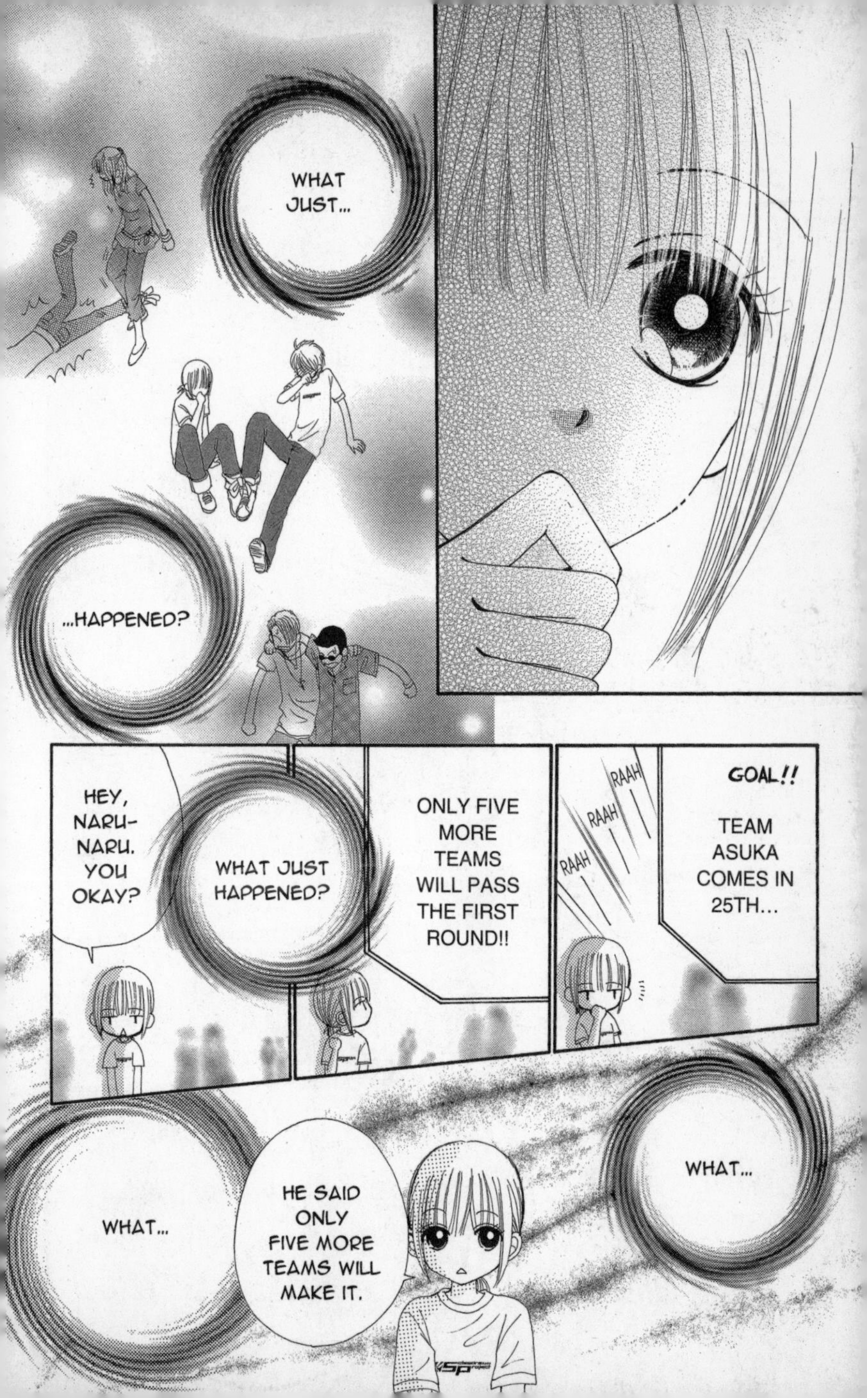
WHAT JUST...
...HAPPENED?
GOAL!!
TEAM ASUKA COMES IN 25TH...
RAAH RAAH RAAH
ONLY FIVE MORE TEAMS WILL PASS THE FIRST ROUND!!
WHAT JUST HAPPENED?
HEY, NARU-NARU. YOU OKAY?
WHAT...
HE SAID ONLY FIVE MORE TEAMS WILL MAKE IT.
WHAT...

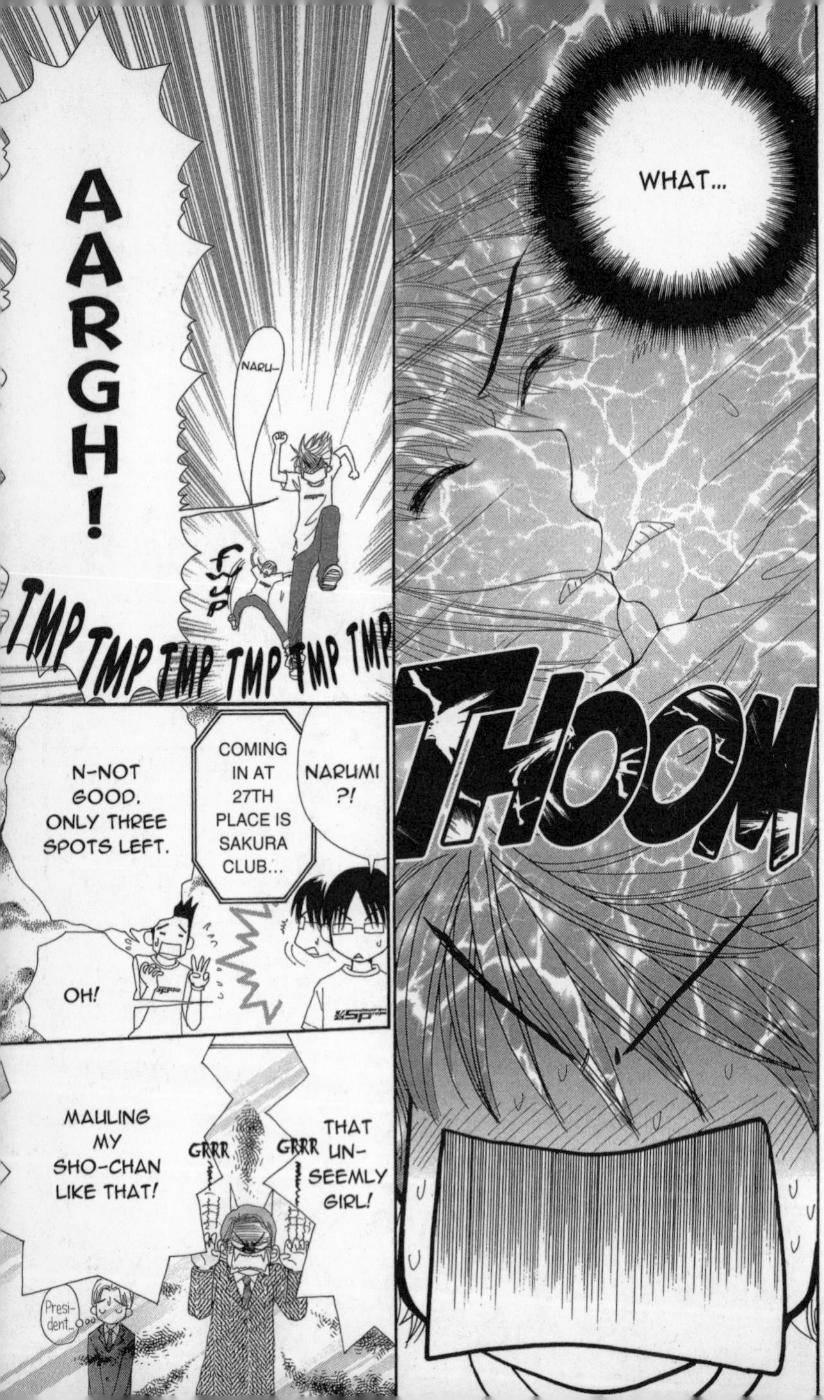
WHAT...
THOOM
AARGH!
NARU—
FWUP
TMP TMP TMP TMP TMP TMP
NARUMI ?!
COMING IN AT 27TH PLACE IS SAKURA CLUB...
N-NOT GOOD. ONLY THREE SPOTS LEFT.
OH!
THAT UN-SEEMLY GIRL!
GRRR
GRRR
MAULING MY SHO-CHAN LIKE THAT!
President...

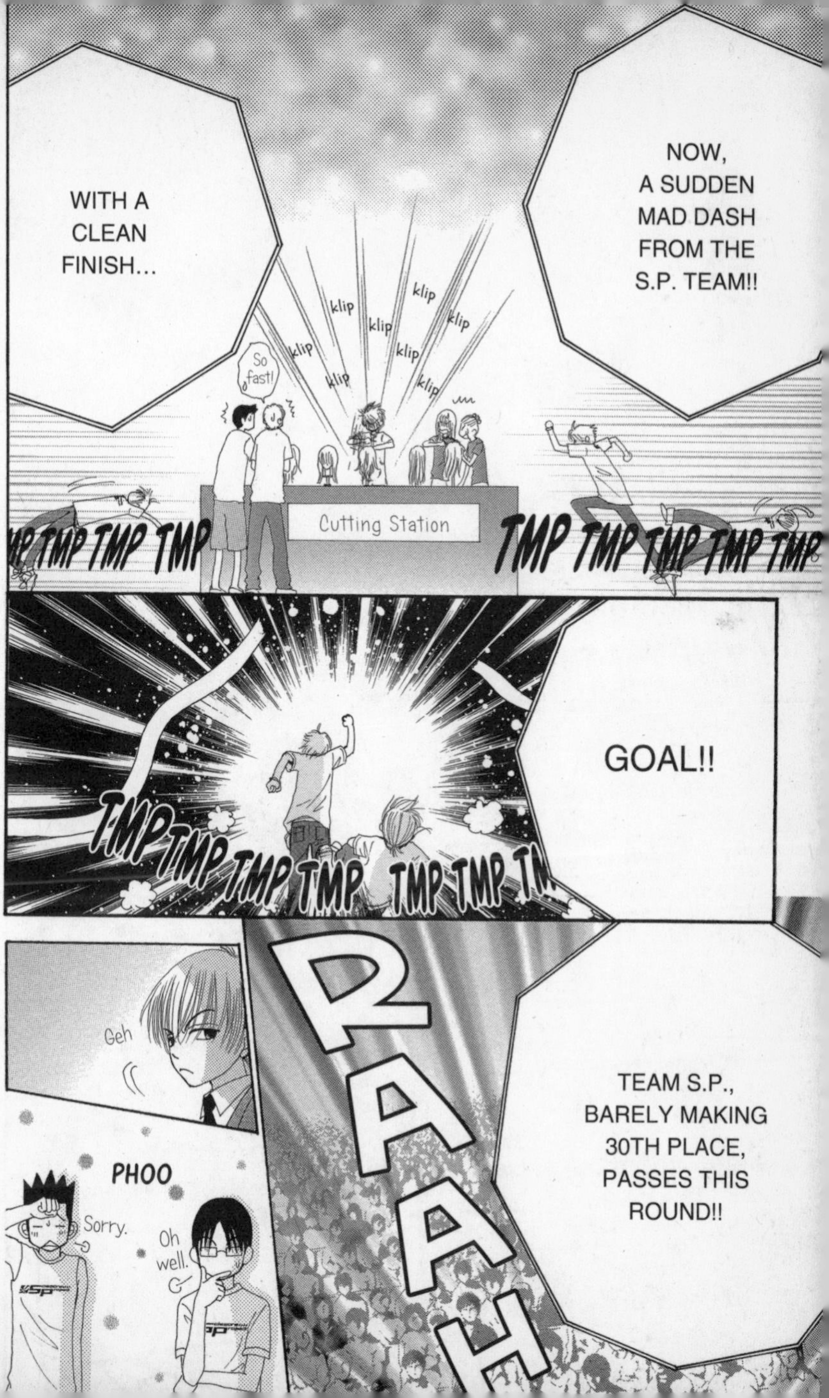
NOW, A SUDDEN MAD DASH FROM THE S.P. TEAM!!
WITH A CLEAN FINISH…
klip klip klip klip klip klip klip klip
So fast!
Cutting Station
TMP TMP TMP TMP TMP
TMP TMP TMP TMP
GOAL!!
TMP TMP TMP TMP TMP TMP TM
TEAM S.P., BARELY MAKING 30TH PLACE, PASSES THIS ROUND!!
RAAH
Geh
PHOO
Sorry.
Oh well.

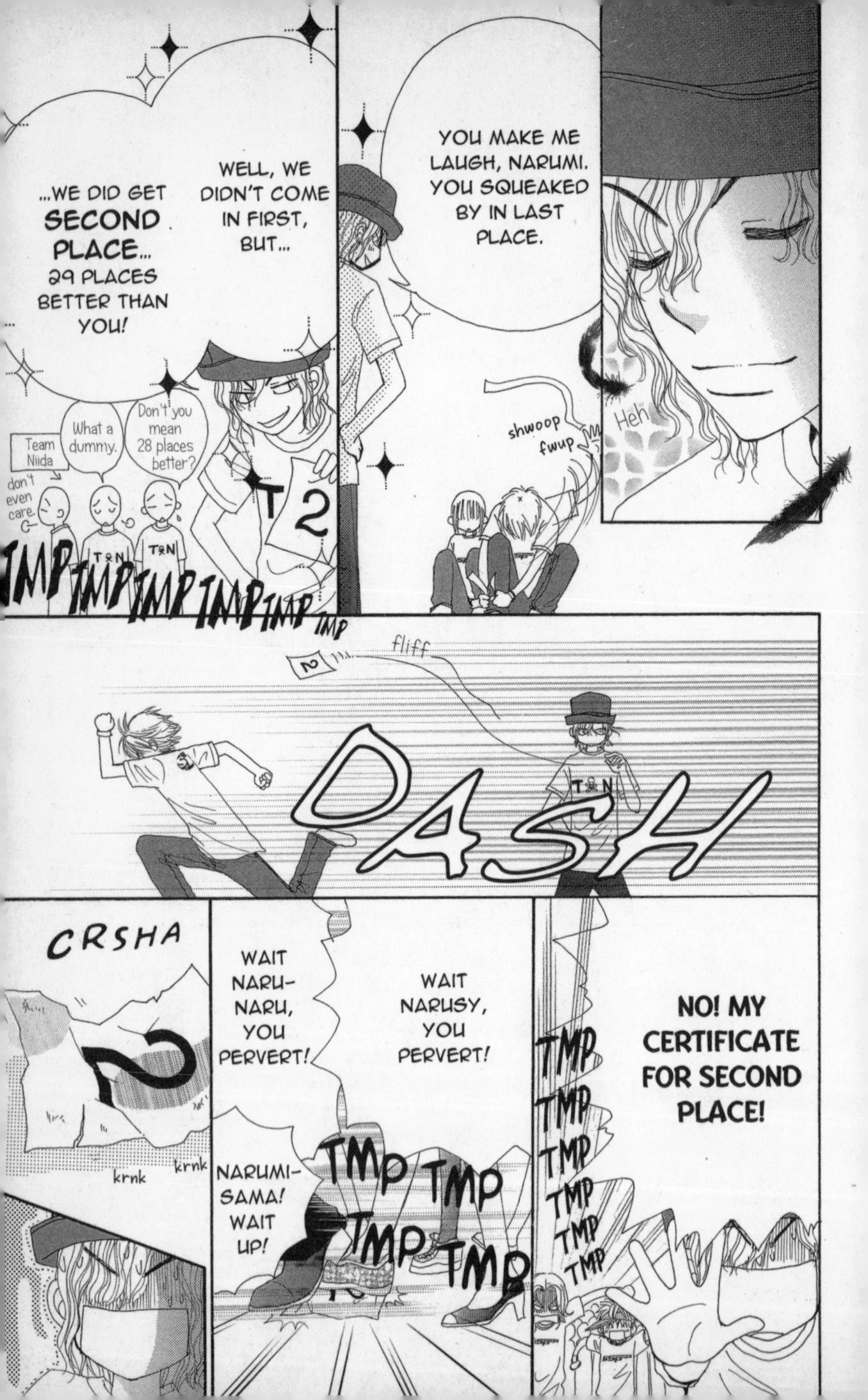
Heh
YOU MAKE ME LAUGH, NARUMI. YOU SQUEAKED BY IN LAST PLACE.
shwoop
fwup
WELL, WE DIDN'T COME IN FIRST, BUT...
...WE DID GET SECOND PLACE... 29 PLACES BETTER THAN YOU!
Don't you mean 28 places better?
What a dummy.
Team Niida don't even care.
TMP TMP TMP TMP TMP TMP
fliff
DASH
NO! MY CERTIFICATE FOR SECOND PLACE!
TMP TMP TMP TMP TMP TMP
WAIT NARUSY, YOU PERVERT!
WAIT NARU-NARU, YOU PERVERT!
NARUMI-SAMA! WAIT UP!
TMP TMP TMP TMP
CRSHA
krnk krnk

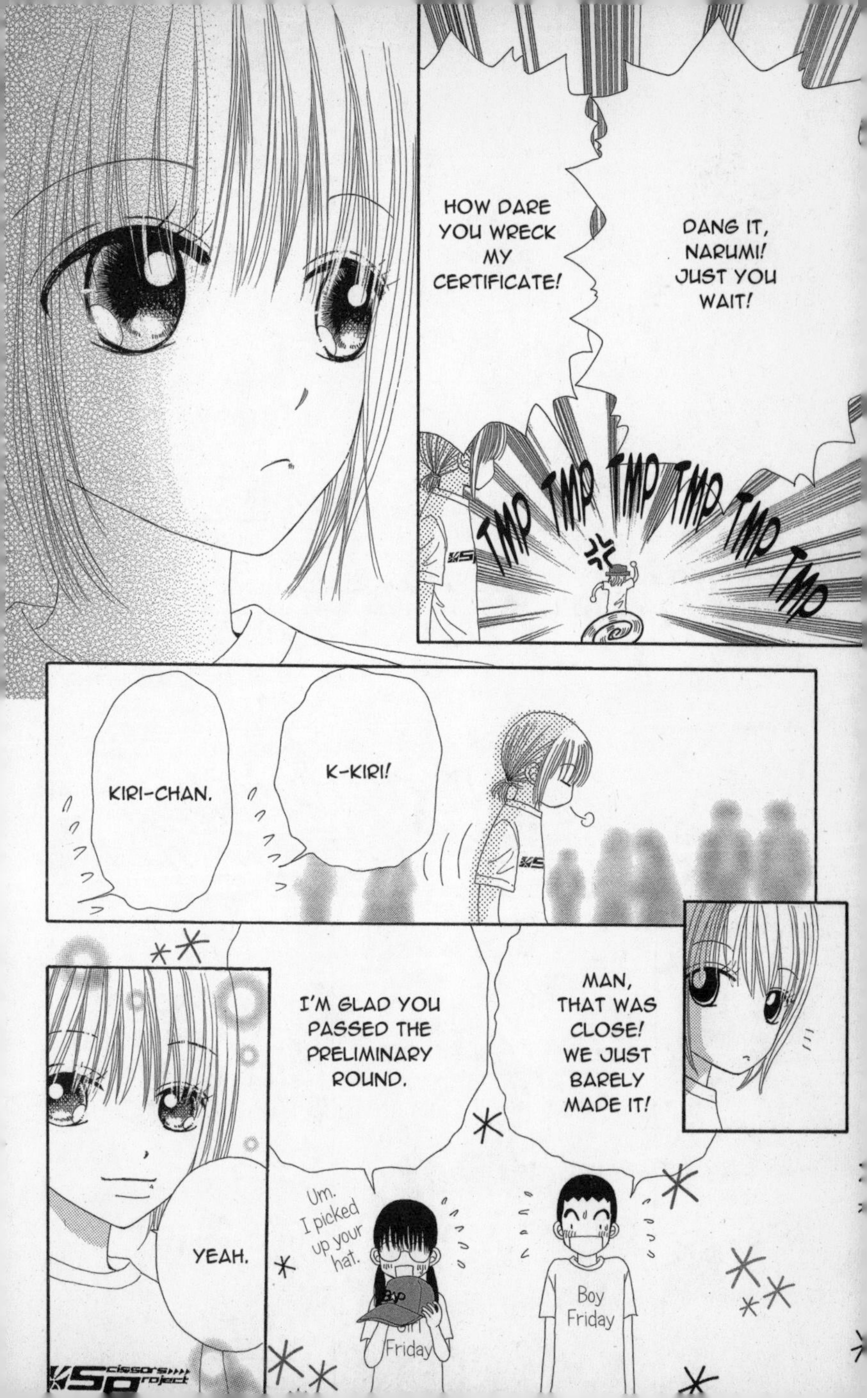
DANG IT, NARUMI! JUST YOU WAIT!
HOW DARE YOU WRECK MY CERTIFICATE!
TMP TMP TMP TMP TMP TMP
K-KIRI!
KIRI-CHAN.
MAN, THAT WAS CLOSE! WE JUST BARELY MADE IT!
I'M GLAD YOU PASSED THE PRELIMINARY ROUND.
Boy Friday
Um. I picked up your hat.
YEAH.

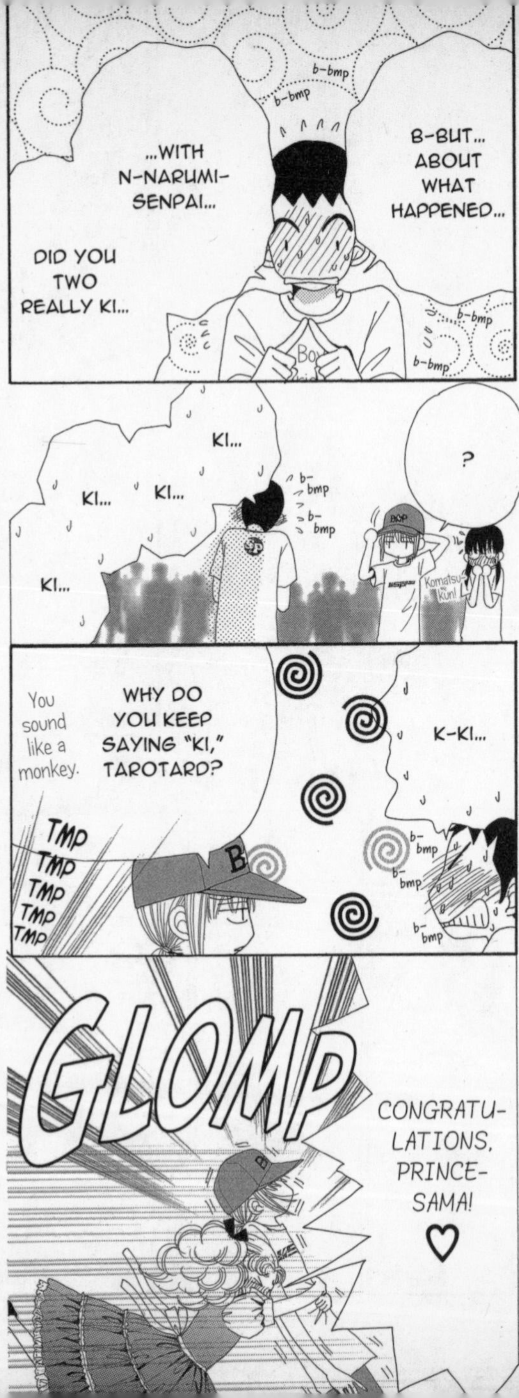
b-bmp
b-bmp
B-BUT... ABOUT WHAT HAPPENED...
...WITH N-NARUMI-SENPAI...
DID YOU TWO REALLY KI...
b-bmp
b-bmp
Bo
?
KI...
b-bmp
b-bmp
KI...
KI...
BOP
Komatsu-kun!
KI...
K-KI...
WHY DO YOU KEEP SAYING "KI," TAROTARD?
You sound like a monkey.
b-bmp
b-bmp
b-bmp
B
TMP TMP TMP TMP TMP
CONGRATULATIONS, PRINCE-SAMA! ♡
GLOMP

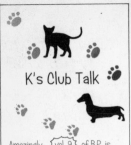

K's Club Talk

Amazingly, vol. 9 of B.P. is already here!! Incredible! (teary-eyed) And, as usual, I thoroughly agonized over what to do for the front cover. I finally decided to go with Occhi and Kiri. For Occhi, it's his 1st romantic shot with Kiri!! I'm sure Occhi is happy about it.

By the way, speaking of Ochiai, I had originally planned his character to be quite different. I wanted him to be a heartless jerk who made money by secretly selling cosmetics to upperclass ladies... He was meant to be somewhat like a gigolo or boy toy! A coldhearted person who profited from things like trading stock over the Internet and selling Narumi's personal belongings in online auctions... Someone who was horrifyingly obsessed with money and considered all women to be cash cows... But then he'd fall for Kiri and he'd shower her with presents no matter how much they cost. That's the kind of Ochiai I wanted to make. Aah! I really wanted to draw a heartless Ochiai like that!! But a character who makes money by selling his body would never be allowed in *Ciao* magazine, as you know.

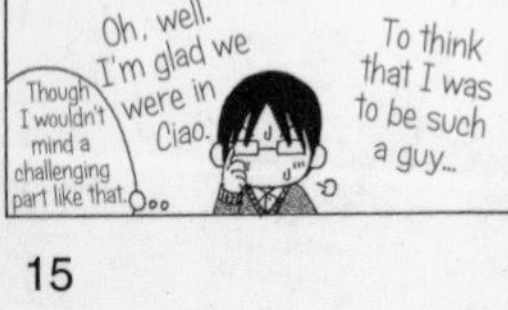
To think that I was to be such a guy...
Oh, well. I'm glad we were in Ciao.
Though I wouldn't mind a challenging part like that.

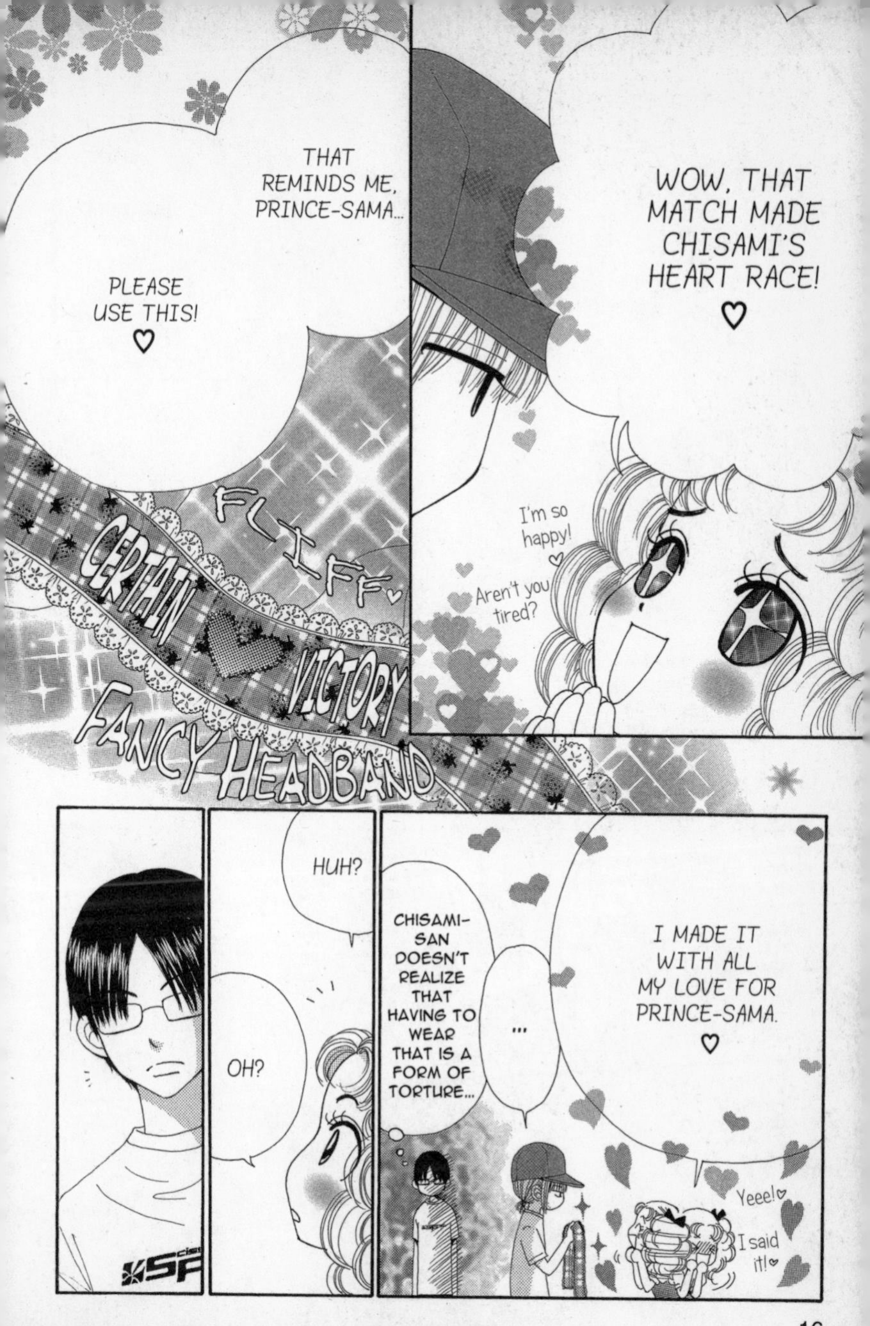
WOW, THAT MATCH MADE CHISAMI'S HEART RACE! ♡
I'm so happy! ♡
Aren't you tired?
THAT REMINDS ME, PRINCE-SAMA...
PLEASE USE THIS! ♡
FLIFFF♡
CERTAIN ♥ VICTORY FANCY HEADBAND
I MADE IT WITH ALL MY LOVE FOR PRINCE-SAMA. ♡
Yeee!♡
I said it!♡
...
CHISAMI-SAN DOESN'T REALIZE THAT HAVING TO WEAR THAT IS A FORM OF TORTURE...
HUH?
OH?

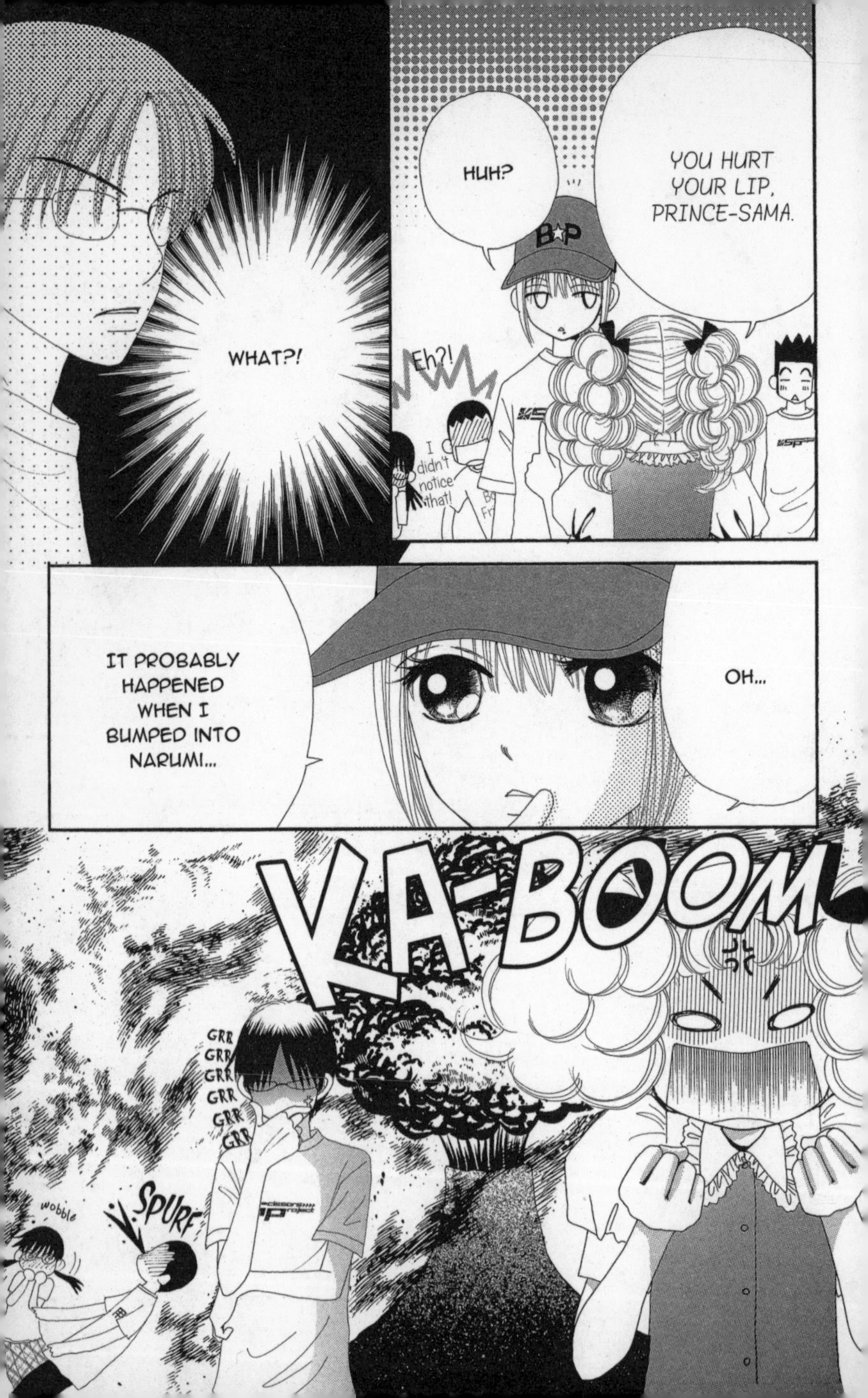

YOU HURT YOUR LIP, PRINCE-SAMA.
HUH?
Eh?!
I didn't notice that!
WHAT?!
OH...
IT PROBABLY HAPPENED WHEN I BUMPED INTO NARUMI...
KA-BOOM
GRR GRR GRR GRR GRR GRR
SPURF
wobble

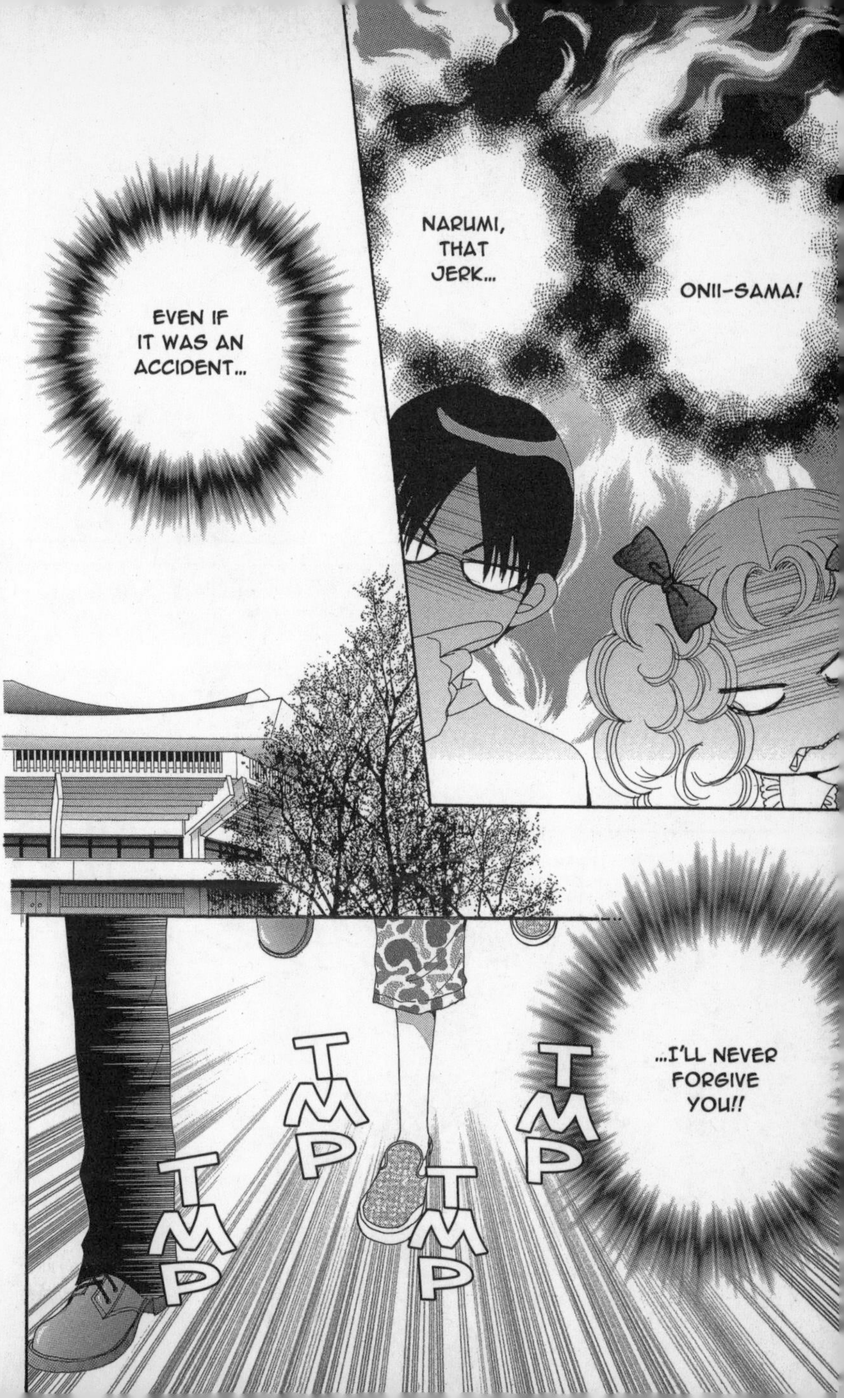
ONII-SAMA!
NARUMI, THAT JERK...
EVEN IF IT WAS AN ACCIDENT...
...I'LL NEVER FORGIVE YOU!!
TMP
TMP
TMP
TMP

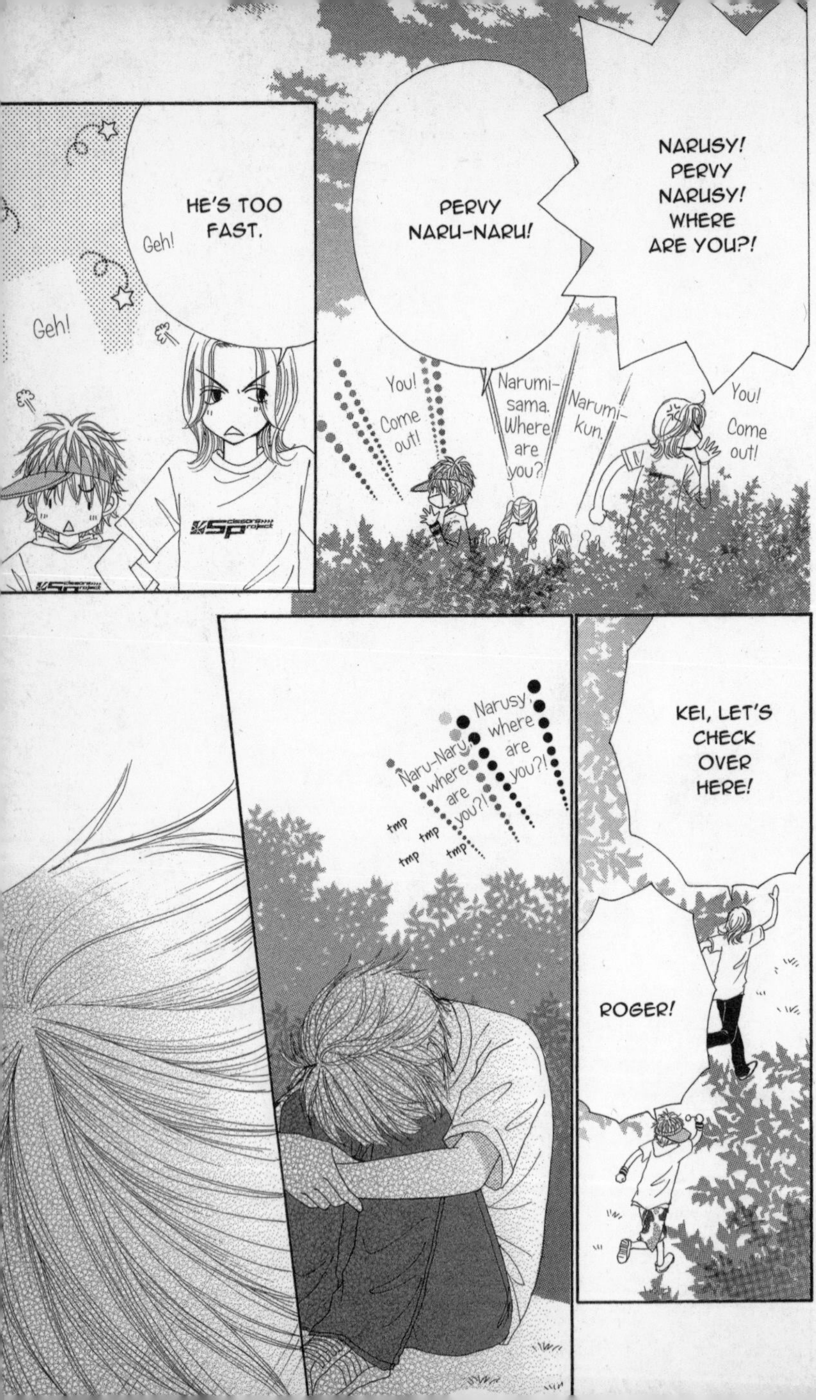
NARUSY! PERVY NARUSY! WHERE ARE YOU?!
PERVY NARU-NARU!
You! Come out!
Narumi-kun.
Narumi-sama. Where are you?
You! Come out!
HE'S TOO FAST.
Geh!
Geh!
KEI, LET'S CHECK OVER HERE!
ROGER!
Narusy, where are you?!
Naru-Naru, where are you?!
tmp
tmp
tmp
tmp

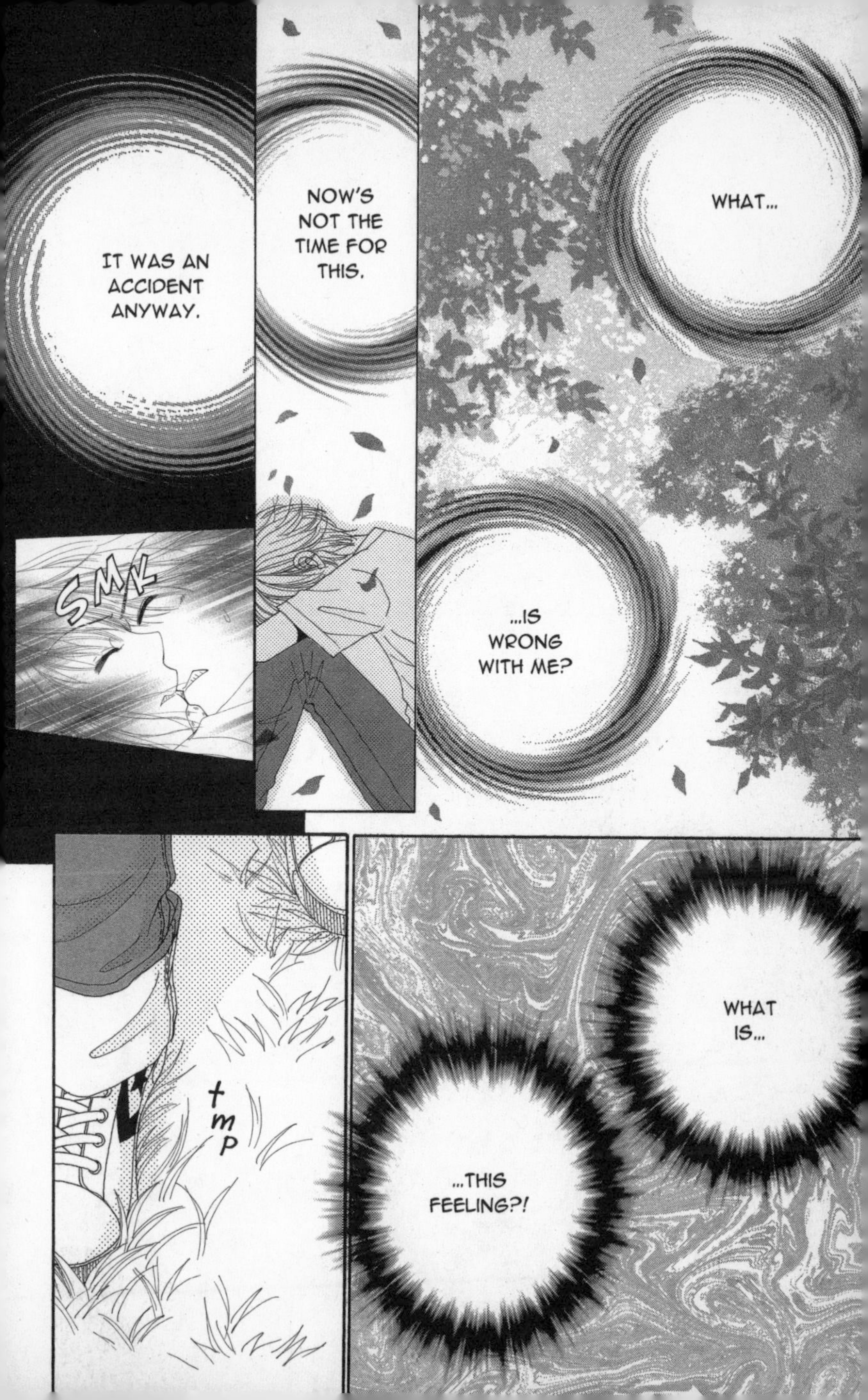
WHAT...
...IS WRONG WITH ME?
NOW'S NOT THE TIME FOR THIS.
IT WAS AN ACCIDENT ANYWAY.
SMK
WHAT IS...
...THIS FEELING?!
tmp

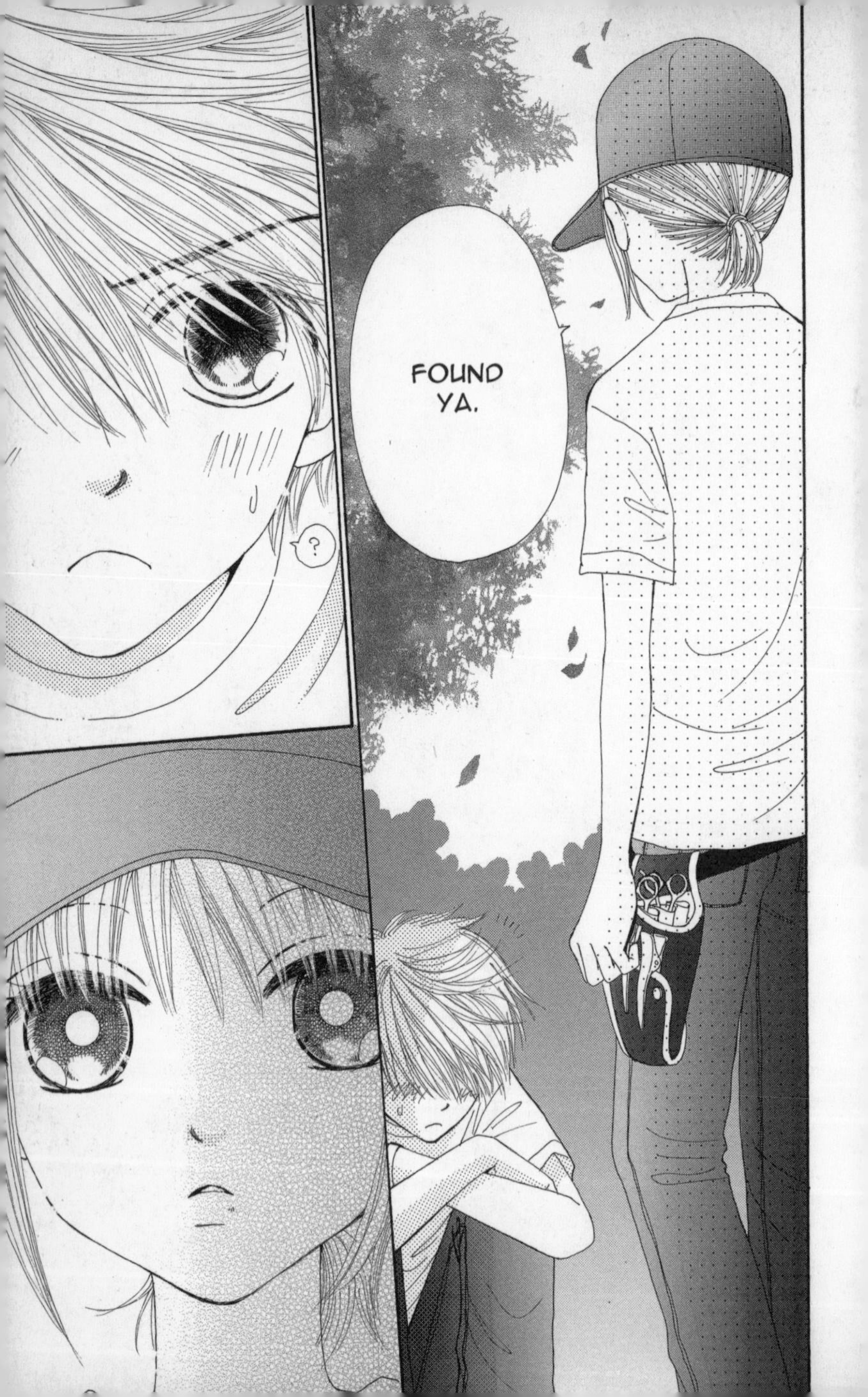
FOUND YA.
?

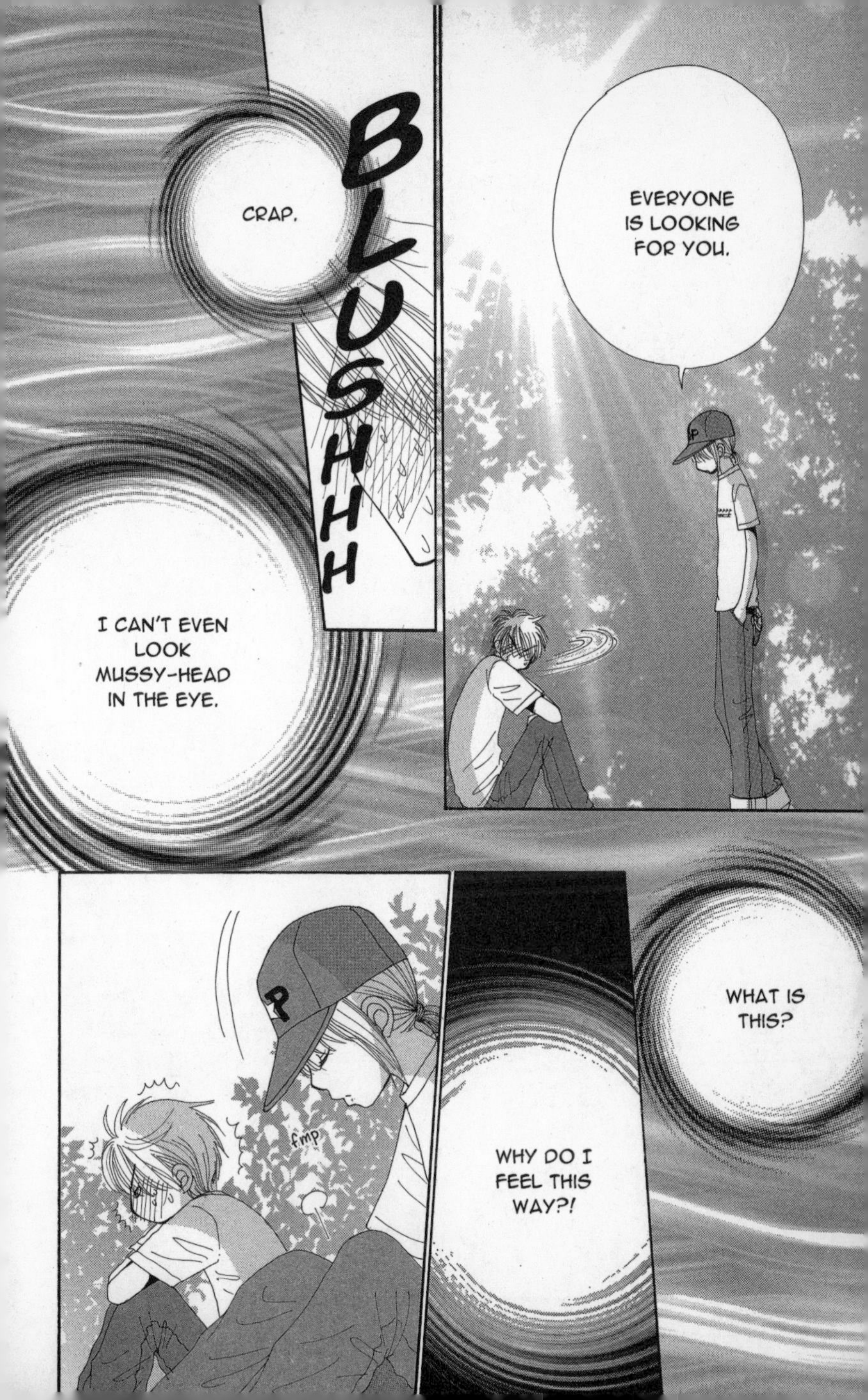
EVERYONE IS LOOKING FOR YOU.
CRAP.
BLUSHHH
I CAN'T EVEN LOOK MUSSY-HEAD IN THE EYE.
WHAT IS THIS?
WHY DO I FEEL THIS WAY?!
fmp

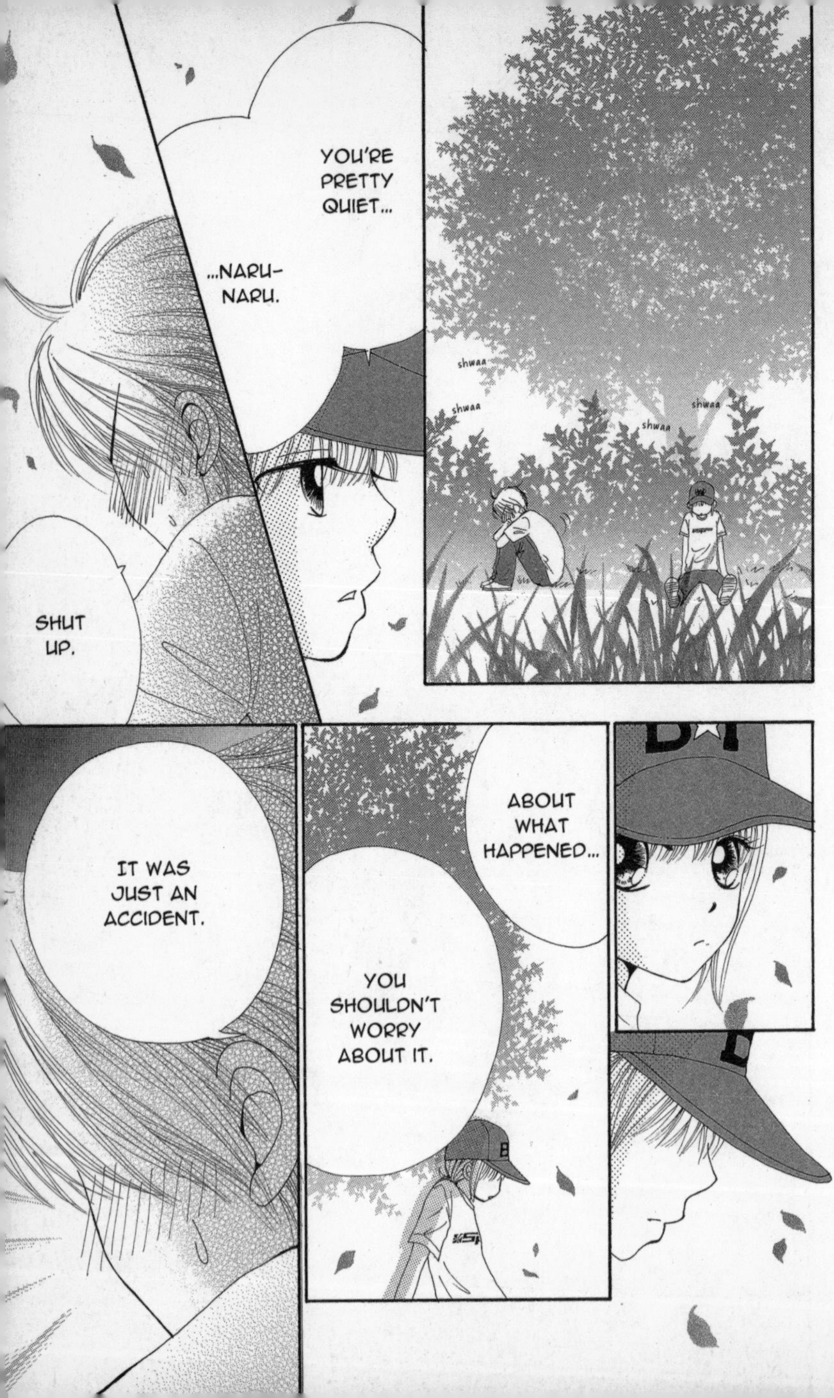
shwaa
shwaa
shwaa
shwaa
YOU'RE PRETTY QUIET...
...NARU-NARU.
SHUT UP.
ABOUT WHAT HAPPENED...
YOU SHOULDN'T WORRY ABOUT IT.
IT WAS JUST AN ACCIDENT.

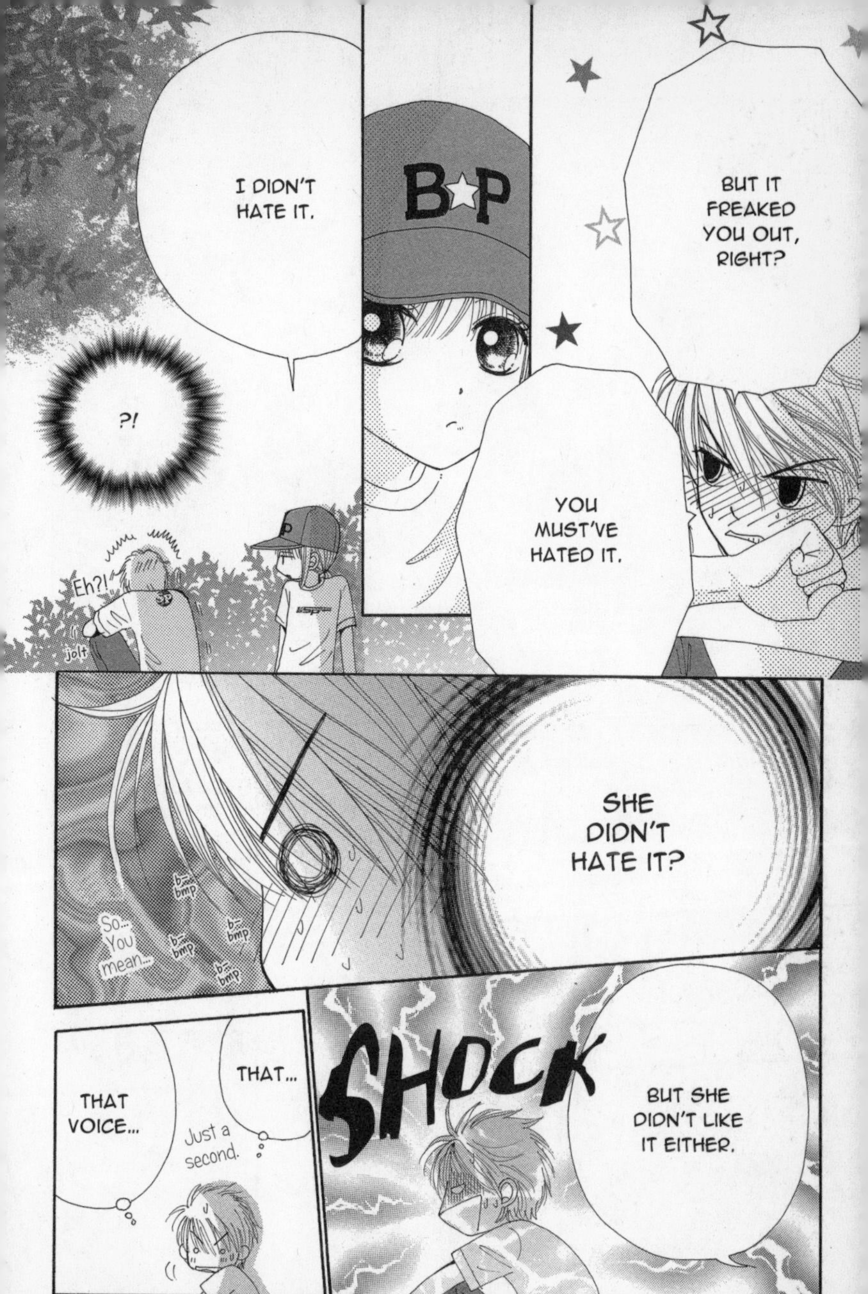
BUT IT FREAKED YOU OUT, RIGHT?
YOU MUST'VE HATED IT.
B★P
I DIDN'T HATE IT.
?!
Eh?!
jolt
SHE DIDN'T HATE IT?
b-bmp
b-bmp
So... You mean...
b-bmp
b-bmp
SHOCK
BUT SHE DIDN'T LIKE IT EITHER.
THAT...
Just a second.
THAT VOICE...

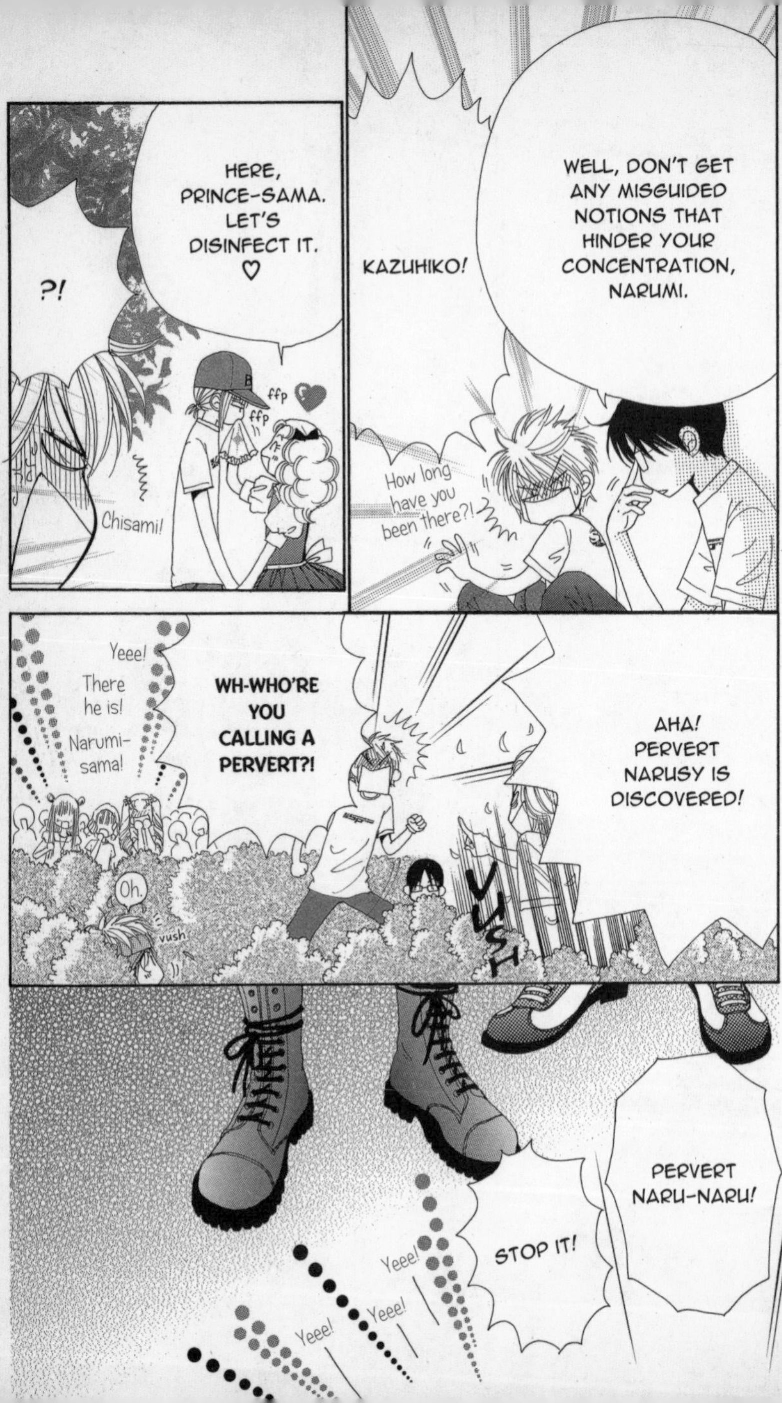
WELL, DON'T GET ANY MISGUIDED NOTIONS THAT HINDER YOUR CONCENTRATION, NARUMI.
KAZUHIKO!
How long have you been there?!
HERE, PRINCE-SAMA. LET'S DISINFECT IT. ♡
?!
ffp
ffp
Chisami!
AHA! PERVERT NARUSY IS DISCOVERED!
WH-WHO'RE YOU CALLING A PERVERT?!
Yeee!
There he is!
Narumi-sama!
VUSH
Oh.
vush
PERVERT NARU-NARU!
STOP IT!
Yeee!
Yeee!
Yeee!

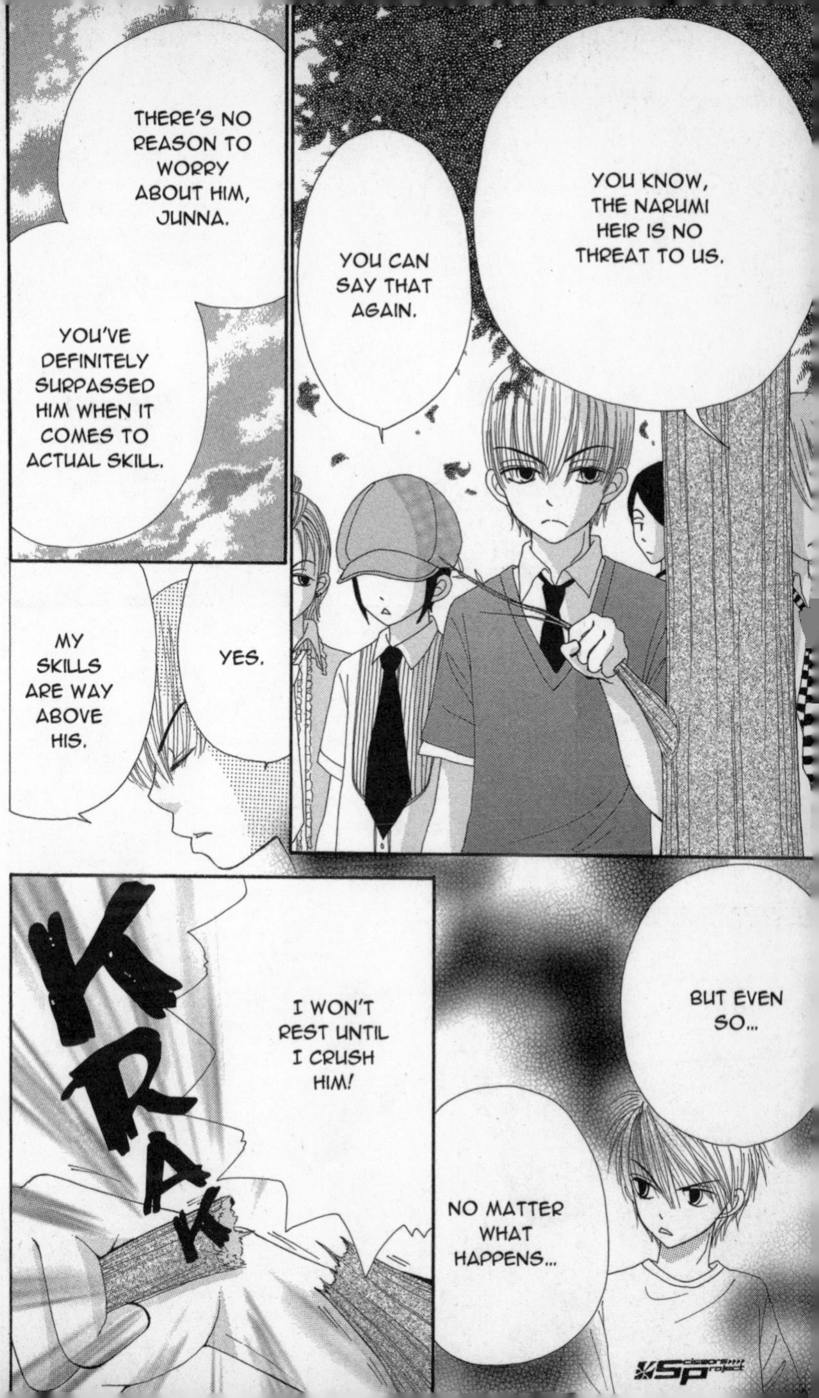
YOU KNOW, THE NARUMI HEIR IS NO THREAT TO US.
YOU CAN SAY THAT AGAIN.
THERE'S NO REASON TO WORRY ABOUT HIM, JUNNA.
YOU'VE DEFINITELY SURPASSED HIM WHEN IT COMES TO ACTUAL SKILL.
YES.
MY SKILLS ARE WAY ABOVE HIS.
BUT EVEN SO...
NO MATTER WHAT HAPPENS...
I WON'T REST UNTIL I CRUSH HIM!
KRAK

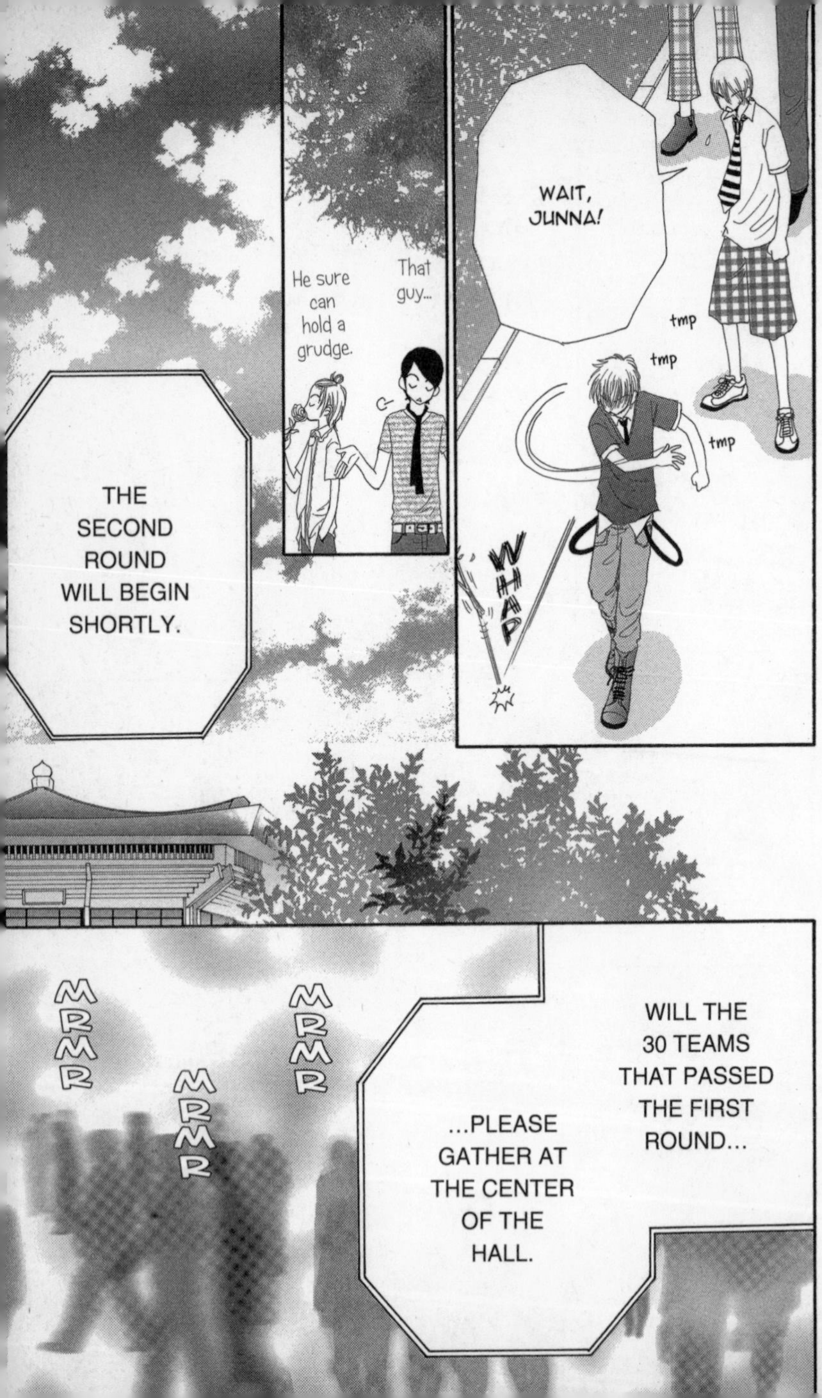
WAIT, JUNNA!
tmp
tmp
tmp
WHAP
That guy...
He sure can hold a grudge.
THE SECOND ROUND WILL BEGIN SHORTLY.
WILL THE 30 TEAMS THAT PASSED THE FIRST ROUND...
...PLEASE GATHER AT THE CENTER OF THE HALL.
MRMR
MRMR
MRMR

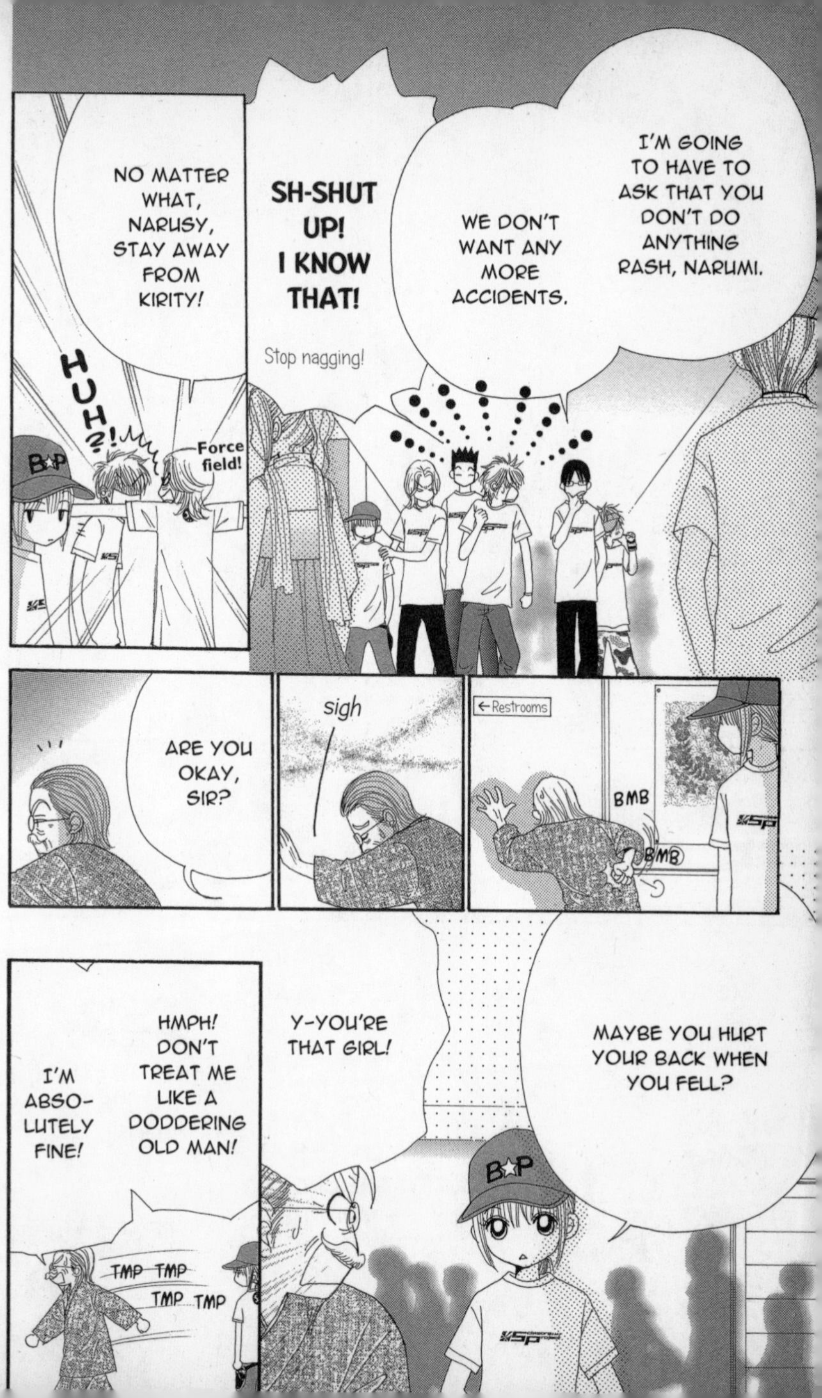
I'M GOING TO HAVE TO ASK THAT YOU DON'T DO ANYTHING RASH, NARUMI.
WE DON'T WANT ANY MORE ACCIDENTS.
SH-SHUT UP! I KNOW THAT!
Stop nagging!
NO MATTER WHAT, NARUSY, STAY AWAY FROM KIRITY!
HUH?!
Force field!
← Restrooms
BMB
BMB
sigh
ARE YOU OKAY, SIR?
MAYBE YOU HURT YOUR BACK WHEN YOU FELL?
Y-YOU'RE THAT GIRL!
HMPH! DON'T TREAT ME LIKE A DODDERING OLD MAN!
I'M ABSO-LUTELY FINE!
TMP TMP
TMP TMP

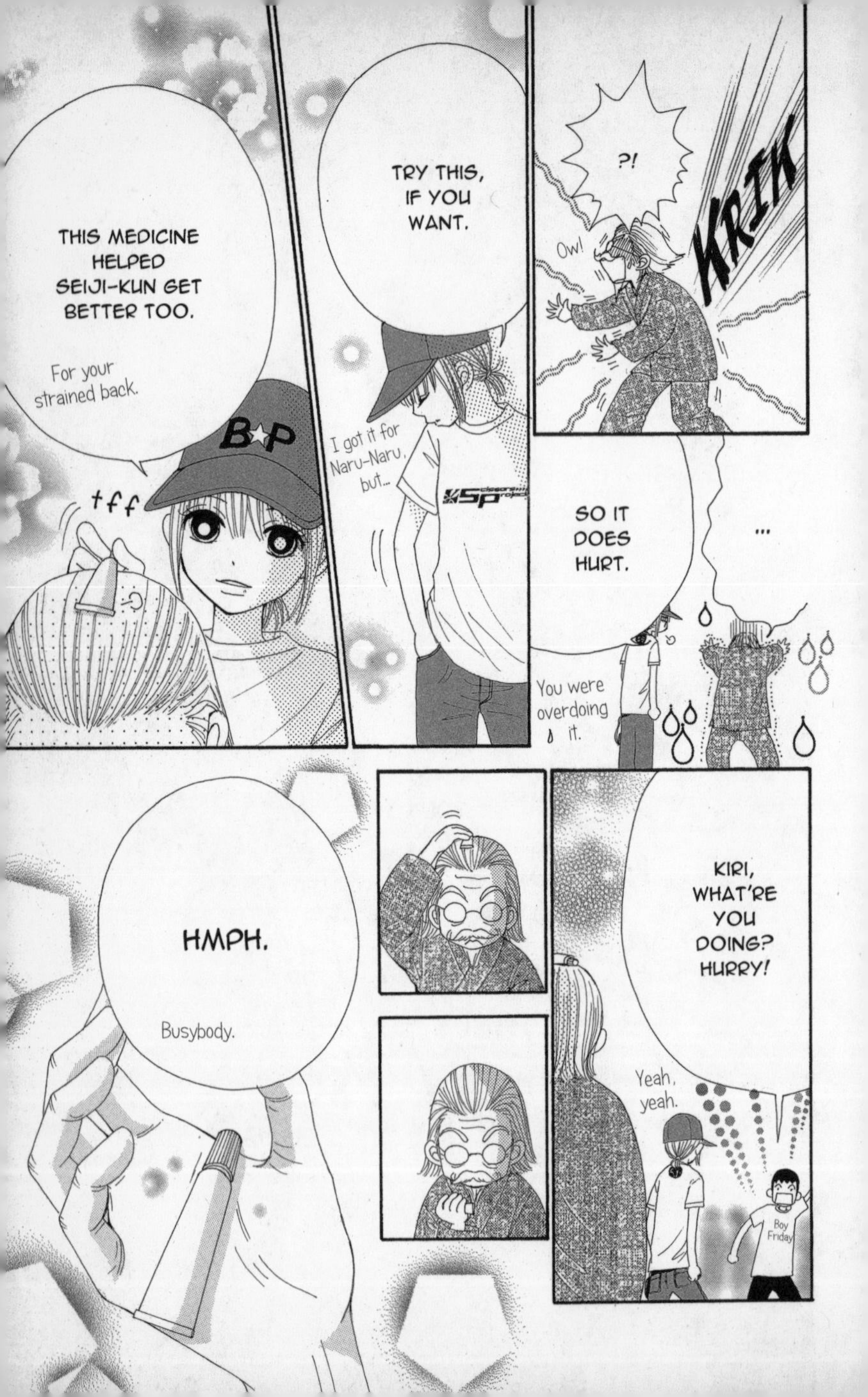
KRIK
?!
Ow!
...
SO IT DOES HURT.
You were overdoing it.
TRY THIS, IF YOU WANT.
I got it for Naru-Naru, but...
THIS MEDICINE HELPED SEIJI-KUN GET BETTER TOO.
For your strained back.
tff
KIRI, WHAT'RE YOU DOING? HURRY!
Yeah, yeah.
Boy Friday
HMPH.
Busybody.

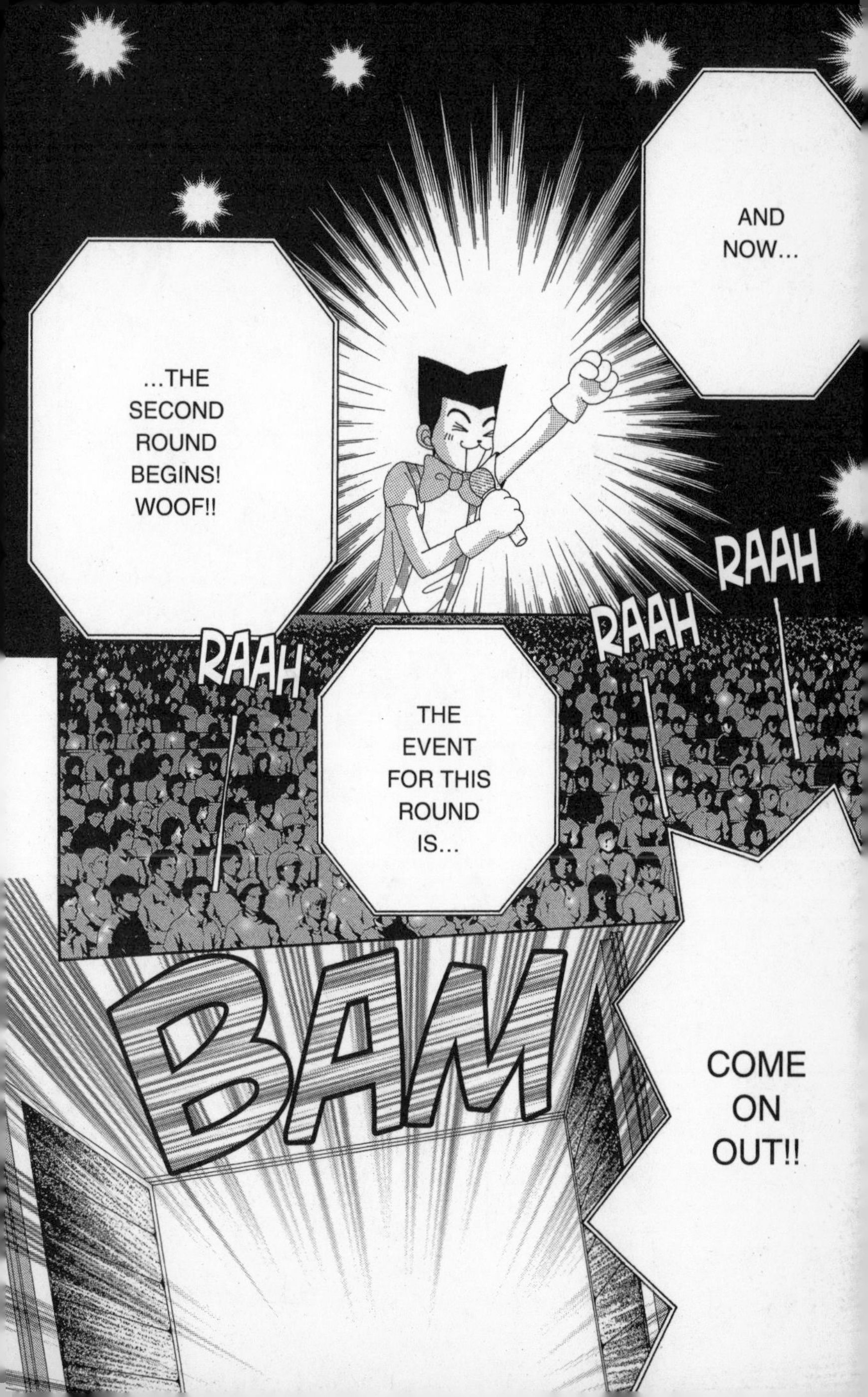
AND NOW...
...THE SECOND ROUND BEGINS! WOOF!!
RAAH
RAAH
RAAH
THE EVENT FOR THIS ROUND IS...
BAM
COME ON OUT!!

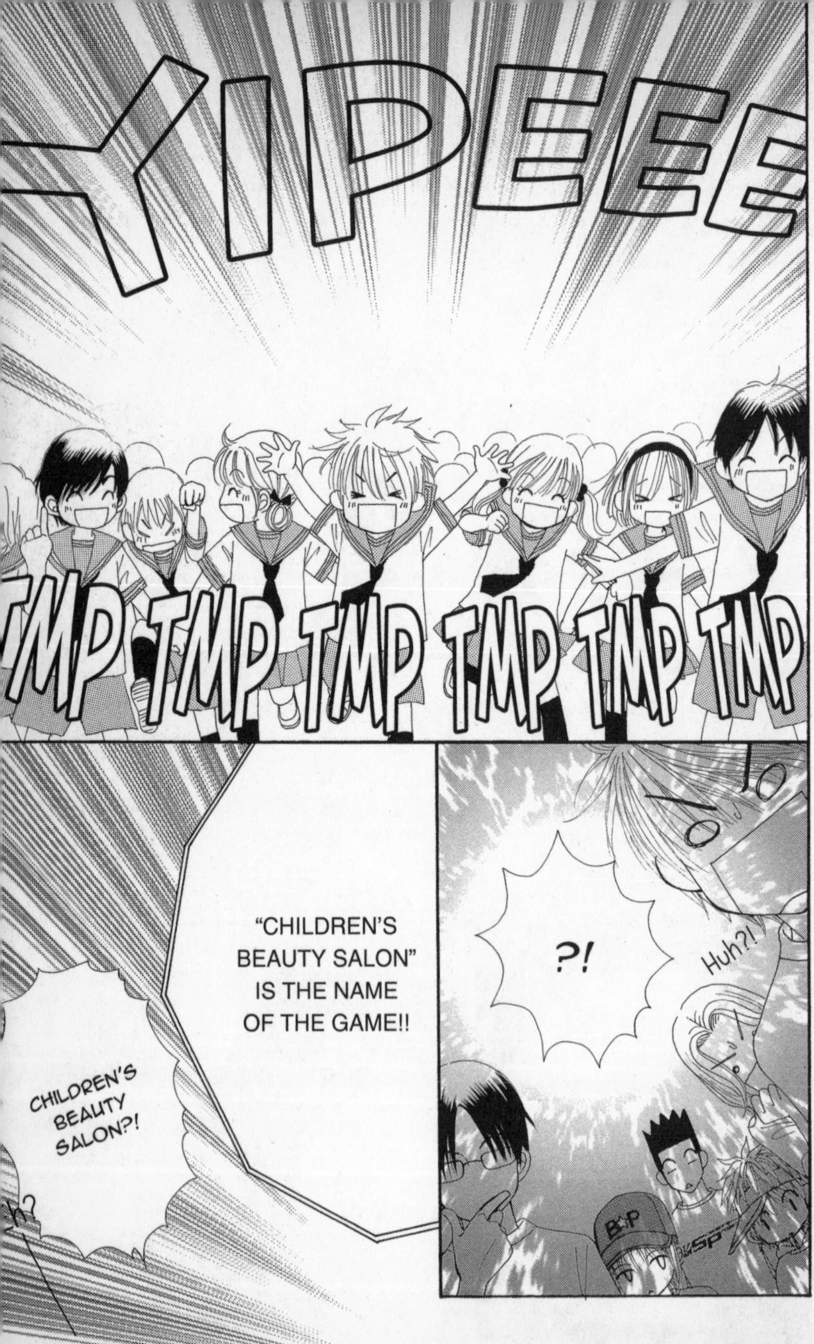
YIPEEE
TMP TMP TMP TMP TMP TMP
?!
Huh?!
"CHILDREN'S BEAUTY SALON" IS THE NAME OF THE GAME!!
CHILDREN'S BEAUTY SALON?!

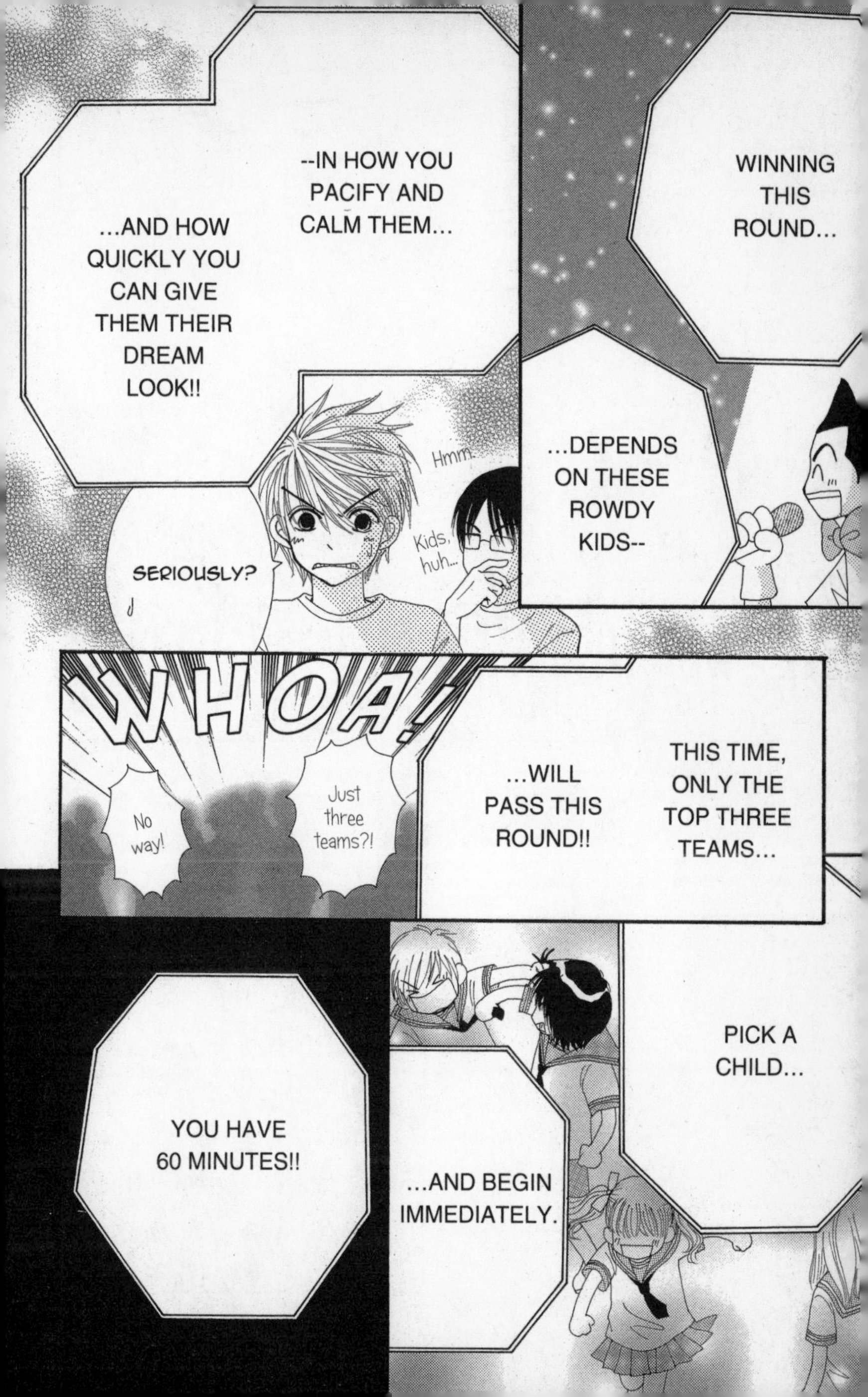
WINNING THIS ROUND...
...DEPENDS ON THESE ROWDY KIDS--
--IN HOW YOU PACIFY AND CALM THEM...
...AND HOW QUICKLY YOU CAN GIVE THEM THEIR DREAM LOOK!!
Hmm.
Kids, huh...
SERIOUSLY?
THIS TIME, ONLY THE TOP THREE TEAMS...
...WILL PASS THIS ROUND!!
WHOA!
Just three teams?!
No way!
PICK A CHILD...
...AND BEGIN IMMEDIATELY.
YOU HAVE 60 MINUTES!!

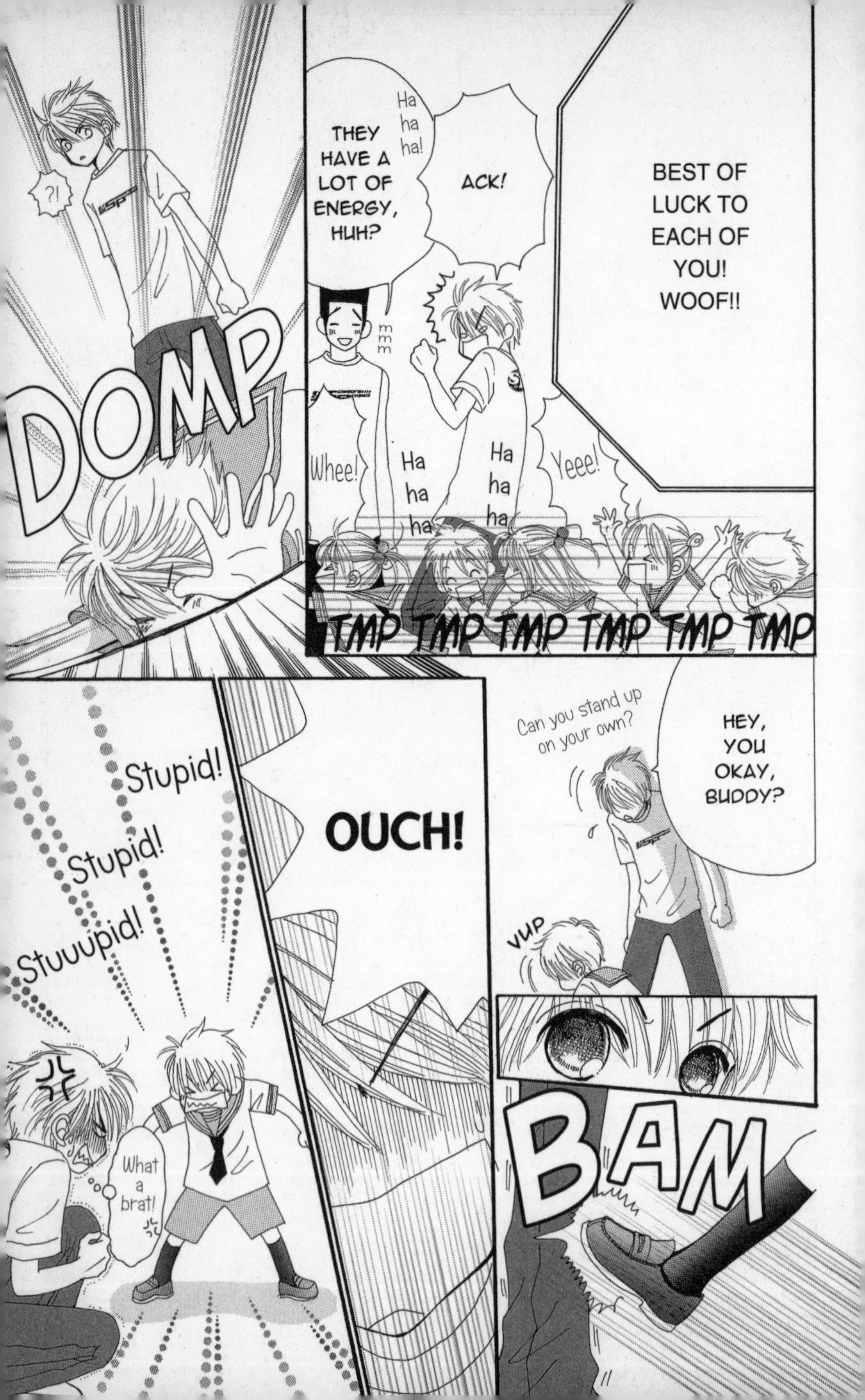
BEST OF LUCK TO EACH OF YOU! WOOF!!
ACK!
Ha ha ha!
THEY HAVE A LOT OF ENERGY, HUH?
mmm
Yeee!
Ha ha ha
Ha ha ha
Whee!
TMP TMP TMP TMP TMP TMP
?!
DOMP
HEY, YOU OKAY, BUDDY?
Can you stand up on your own?
VUP
BAM
OUCH!
Stupid!
Stupid!
Stuuupid!
What a brat!

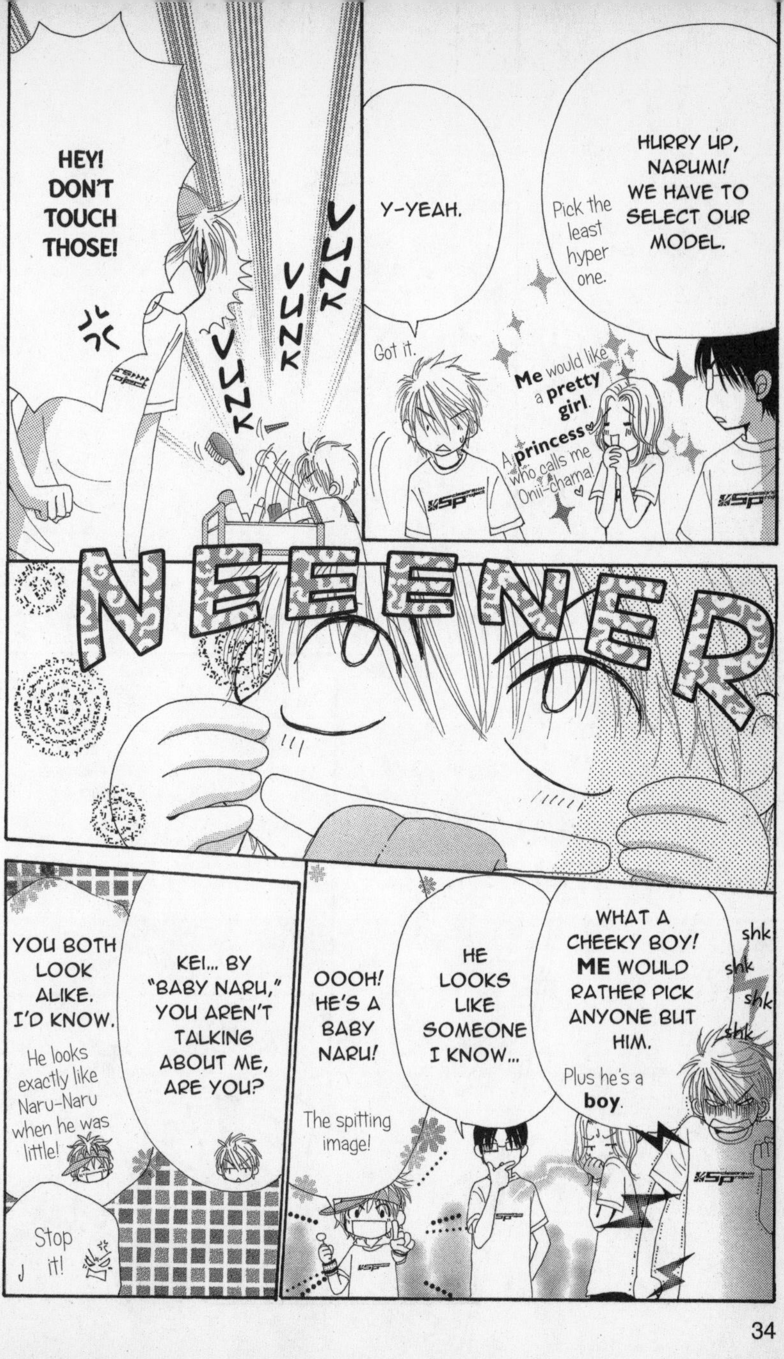
HURRY UP, NARUMI! WE HAVE TO SELECT OUR MODEL.
Pick the least hyper one.
Y-YEAH.
Got it.
Me would like a pretty girl.
A princess who calls me Onii-chama!♡
VUNK
VUNK
VUNK
HEY! DON'T TOUCH THOSE!
NEEENER
shk shk shk shk
WHAT A CHEEKY BOY! ME WOULD RATHER PICK ANYONE BUT HIM.
Plus he's a boy.
HE LOOKS LIKE SOMEONE I KNOW...
OOOH! HE'S A BABY NARU!
The spitting image!
KEI... BY "BABY NARU," YOU AREN'T TALKING ABOUT ME, ARE YOU?
YOU BOTH LOOK ALIKE. I'D KNOW.
He looks exactly like Naru-Naru when he was little!
Stop it!

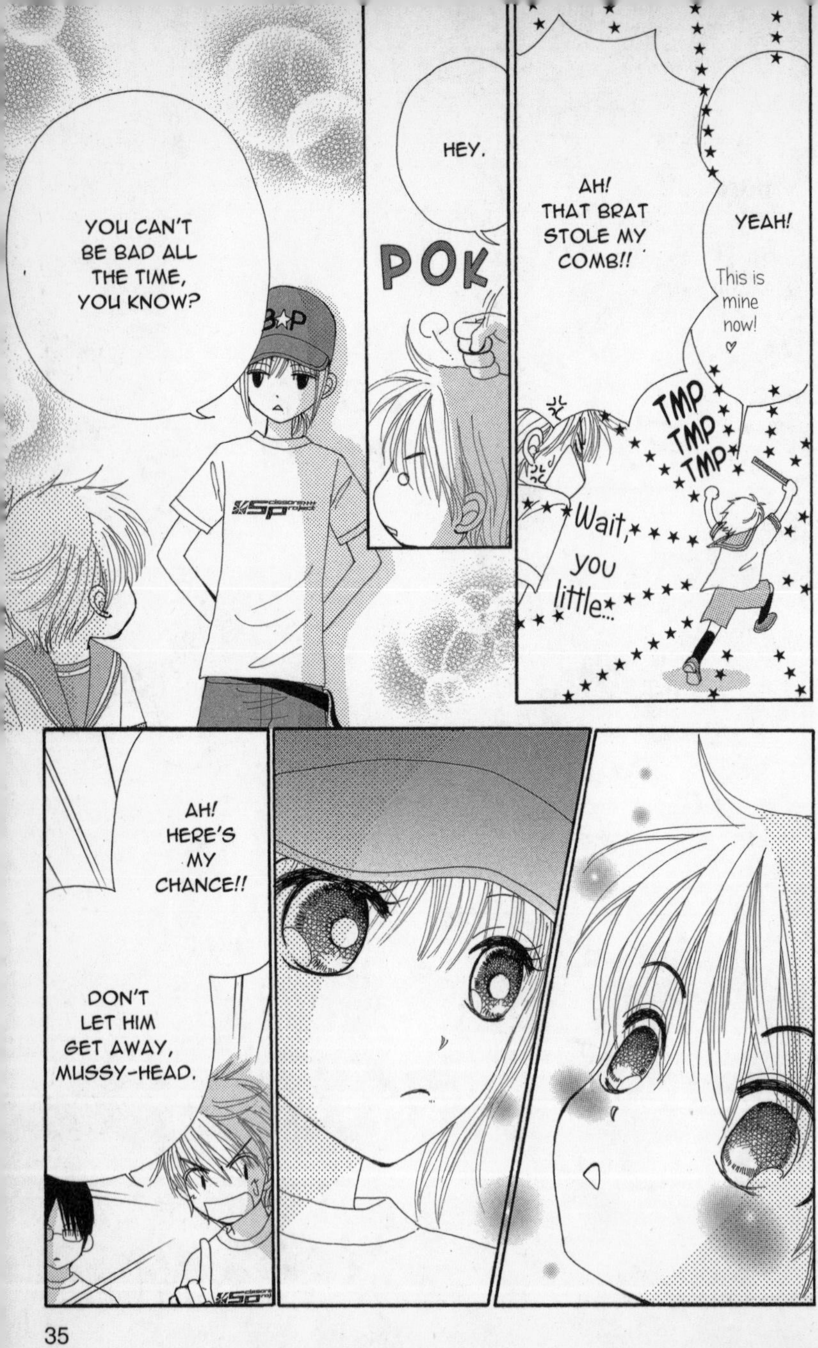
YEAH!
This is mine now! ♡
AH! THAT BRAT STOLE MY COMB!!
TMP TMP TMP
Wait, you little...
HEY.
POK
YOU CAN'T BE BAD ALL THE TIME, YOU KNOW?
AH! HERE'S MY CHANCE!!
DON'T LET HIM GET AWAY, MUSSY-HEAD.

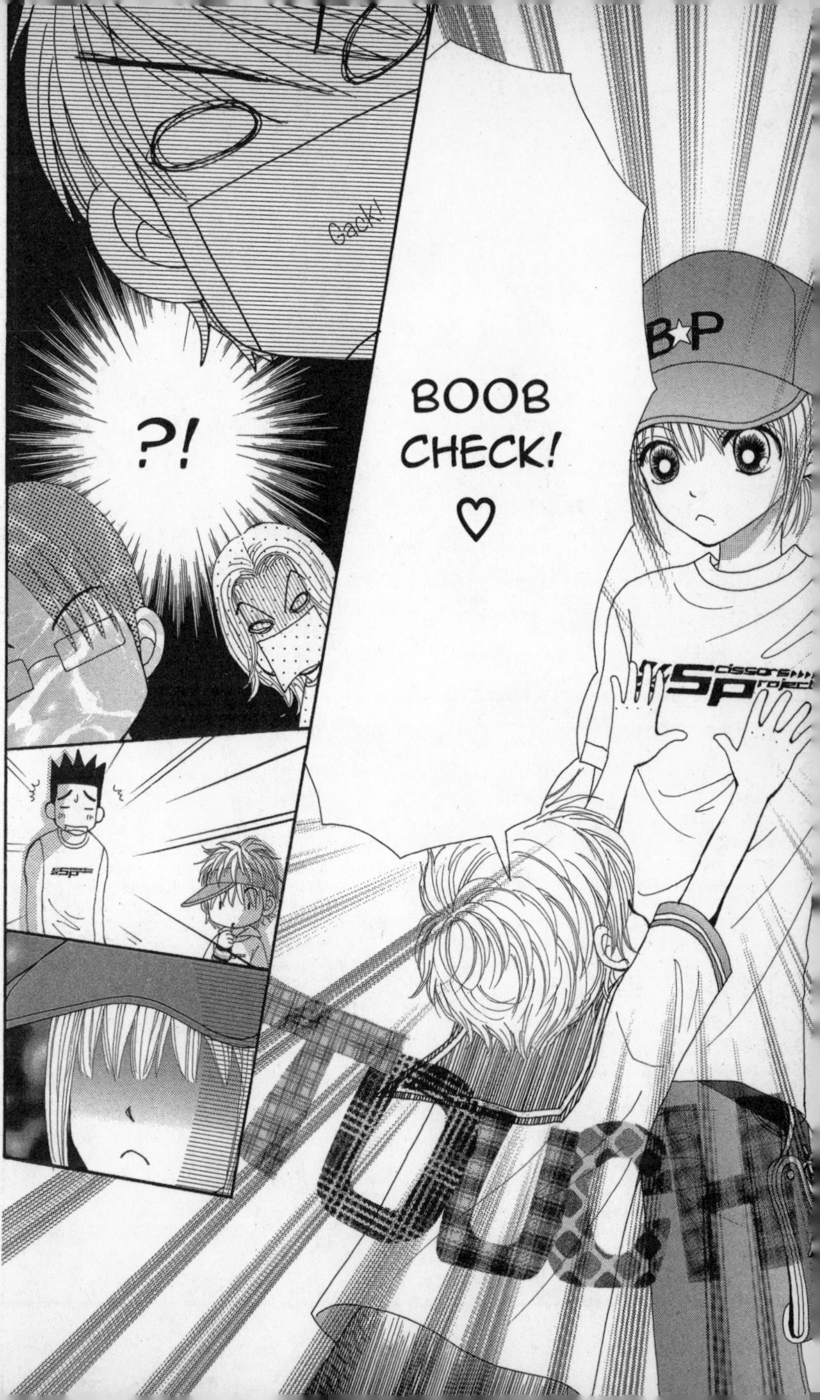
BOOB CHECK! ♡
Gack!
?!

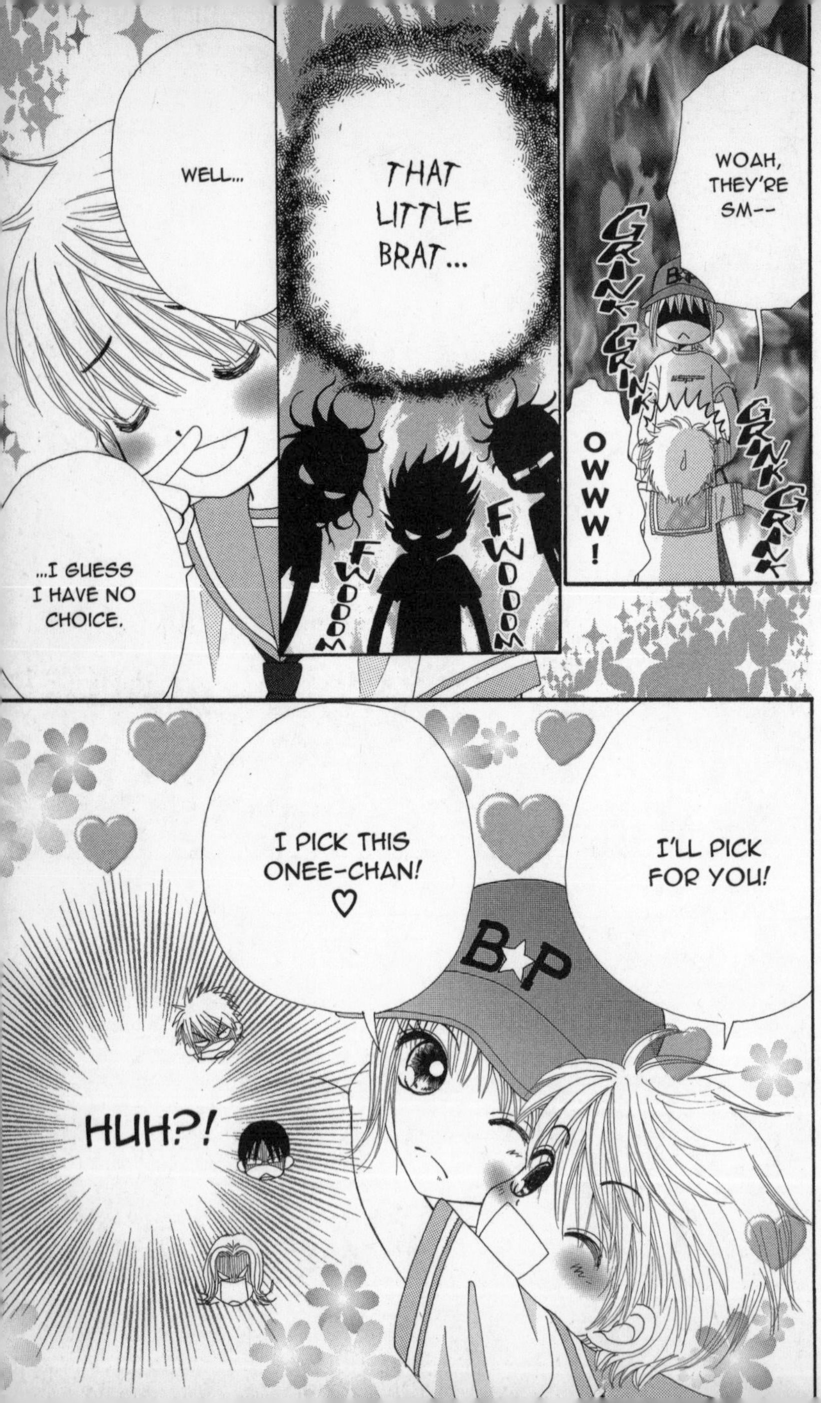
WOAH, THEY'RE SM--
GRINK GRINK
OWWW!
GRINK GRINK
THAT LITTLE BRAT...
FWOOOM
FWOOOM
WELL...
...I GUESS I HAVE NO CHOICE.
I'LL PICK FOR YOU!
I PICK THIS ONEE-CHAN! ♡
HUH?!

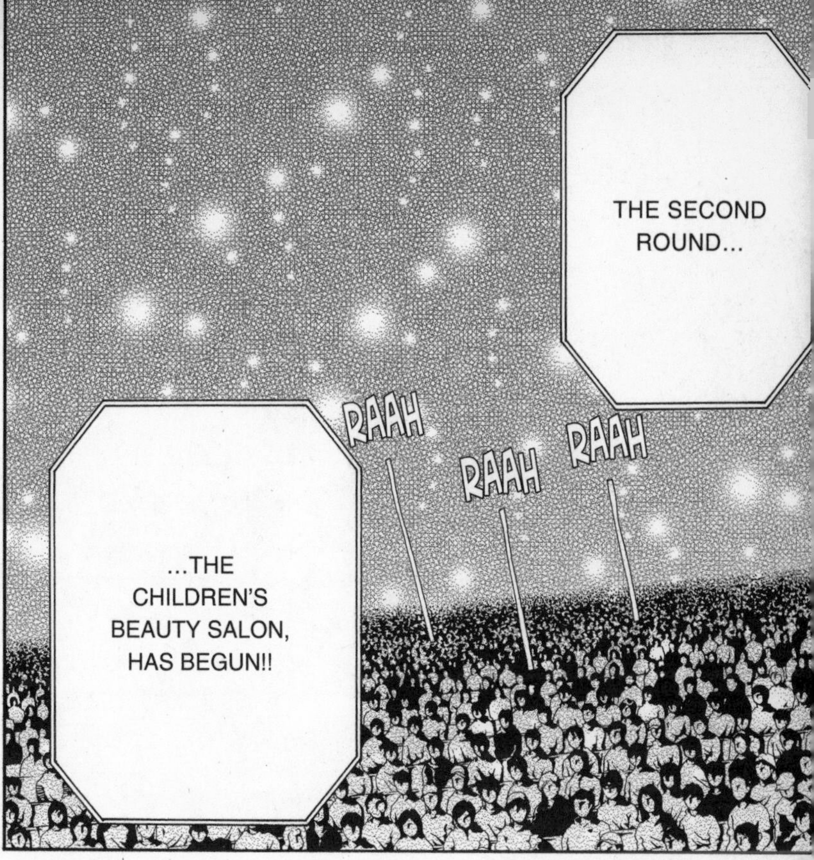
THE SECOND ROUND...
RAAH
RAAH
RAAH
...THE CHILDREN'S BEAUTY SALON, HAS BEGUN!!

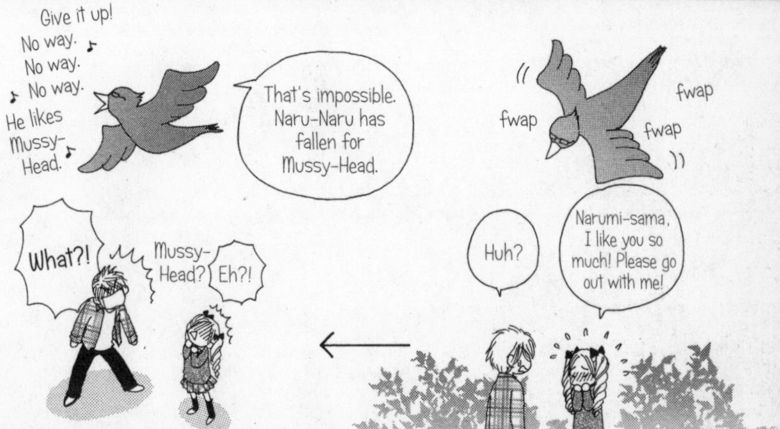
fwap
fwap
fwap
Narumi-sama, I like you so much! Please go out with me!
Huh?
Give it up! No way. No way. No way. He likes Mussy-Head.
That's impossible. Naru-Naru has fallen for Mussy-Head.
What?!
Mussy-Head?
Eh?!

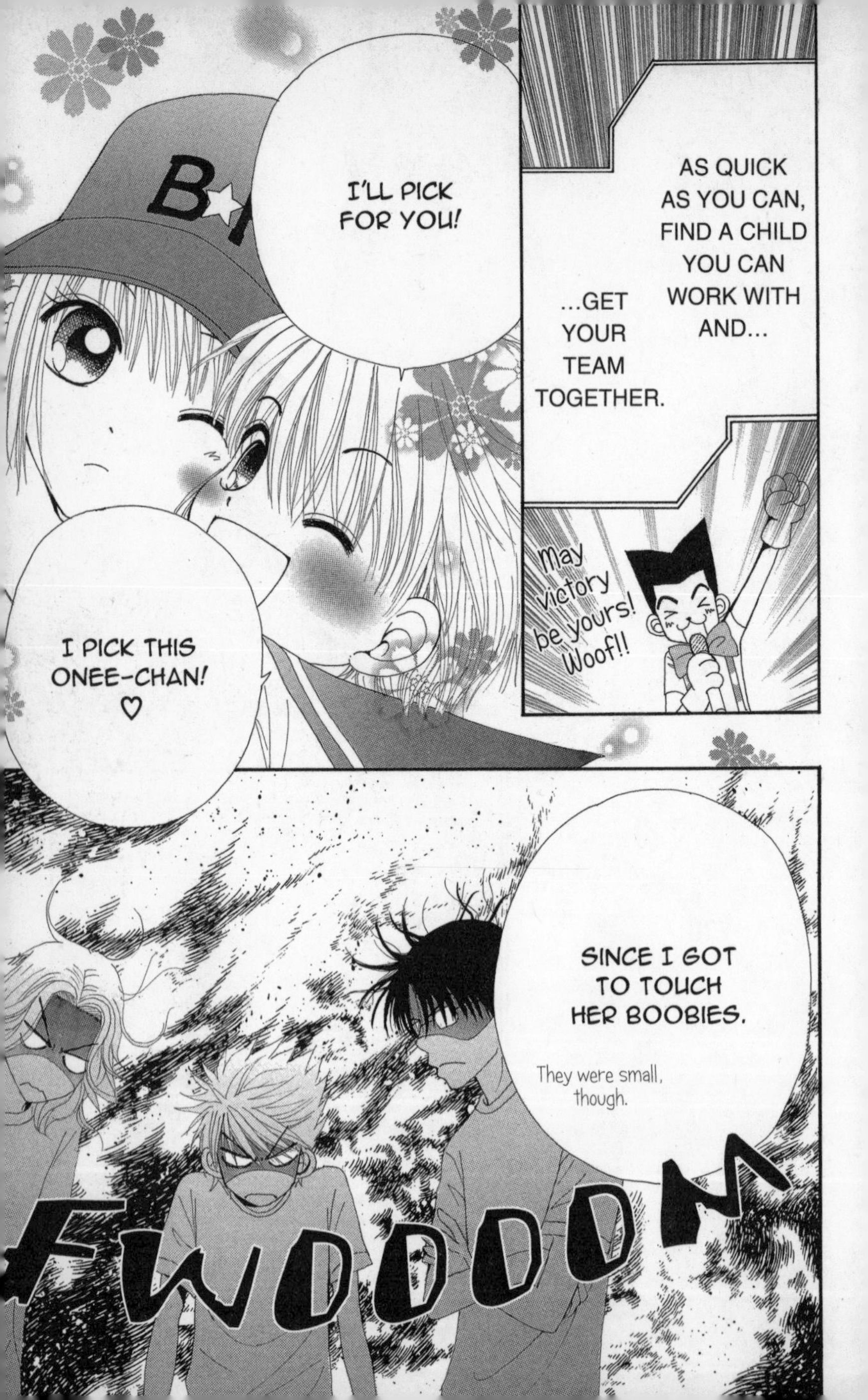
AS QUICK AS YOU CAN, FIND A CHILD YOU CAN WORK WITH AND...
...GET YOUR TEAM TOGETHER.
May victory be yours! Woof!!
I'LL PICK FOR YOU!
I PICK THIS ONEE-CHAN! ♡
SINCE I GOT TO TOUCH HER BOOBIES.
They were small, though.
FWOOOOM

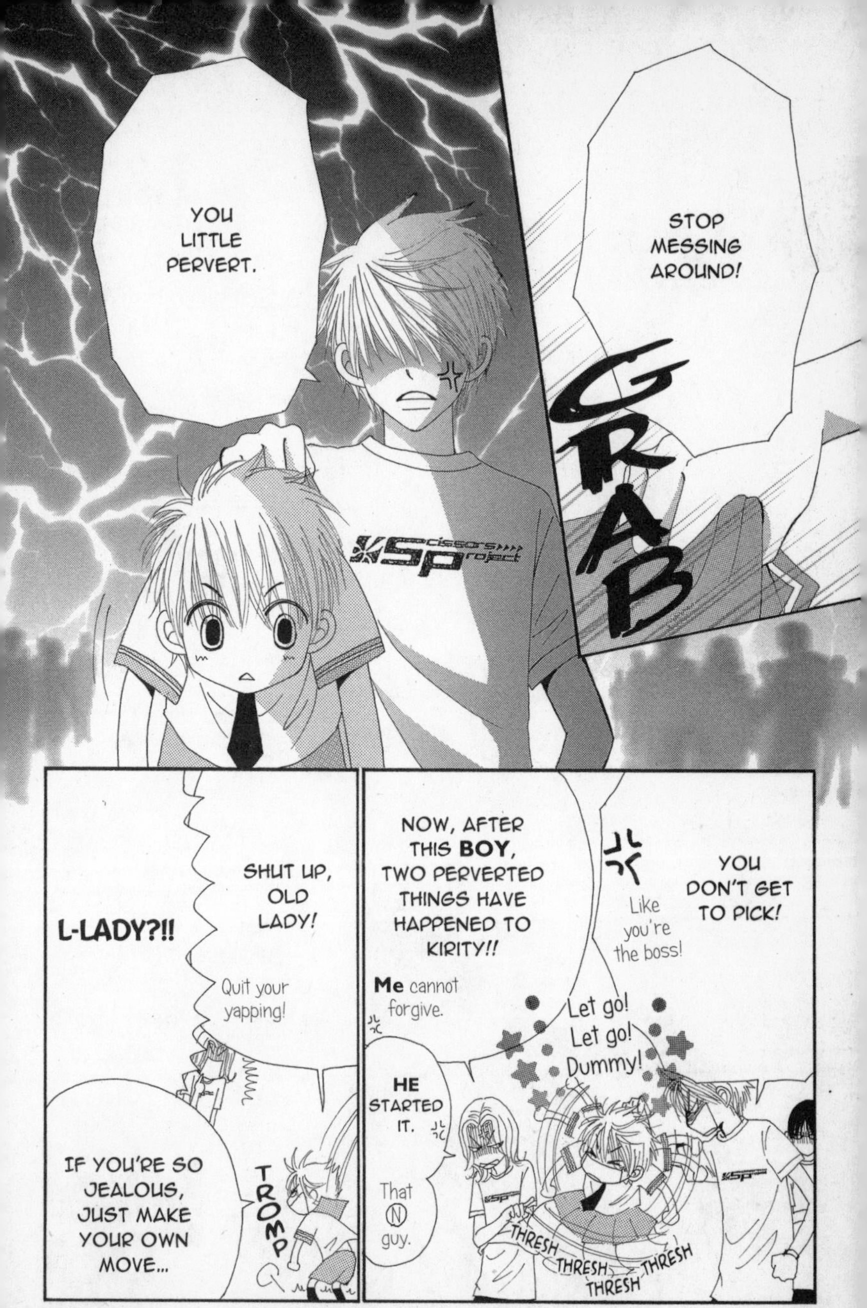
STOP MESSING AROUND!
GRAB
YOU LITTLE PERVERT.
YOU DON'T GET TO PICK!
Like you're the boss!
NOW, AFTER THIS **BOY**, TWO PERVERTED THINGS HAVE HAPPENED TO KIRITY!!
Me cannot forgive.
Let go! Let go! Dummy!
HE STARTED IT.
That Ⓝ guy.
THRESH THRESH THRESH THRESH
SHUT UP, OLD LADY!
L-LADY?!!
Quit your yapping!
IF YOU'RE SO JEALOUS, JUST MAKE YOUR OWN MOVE...
TROMP

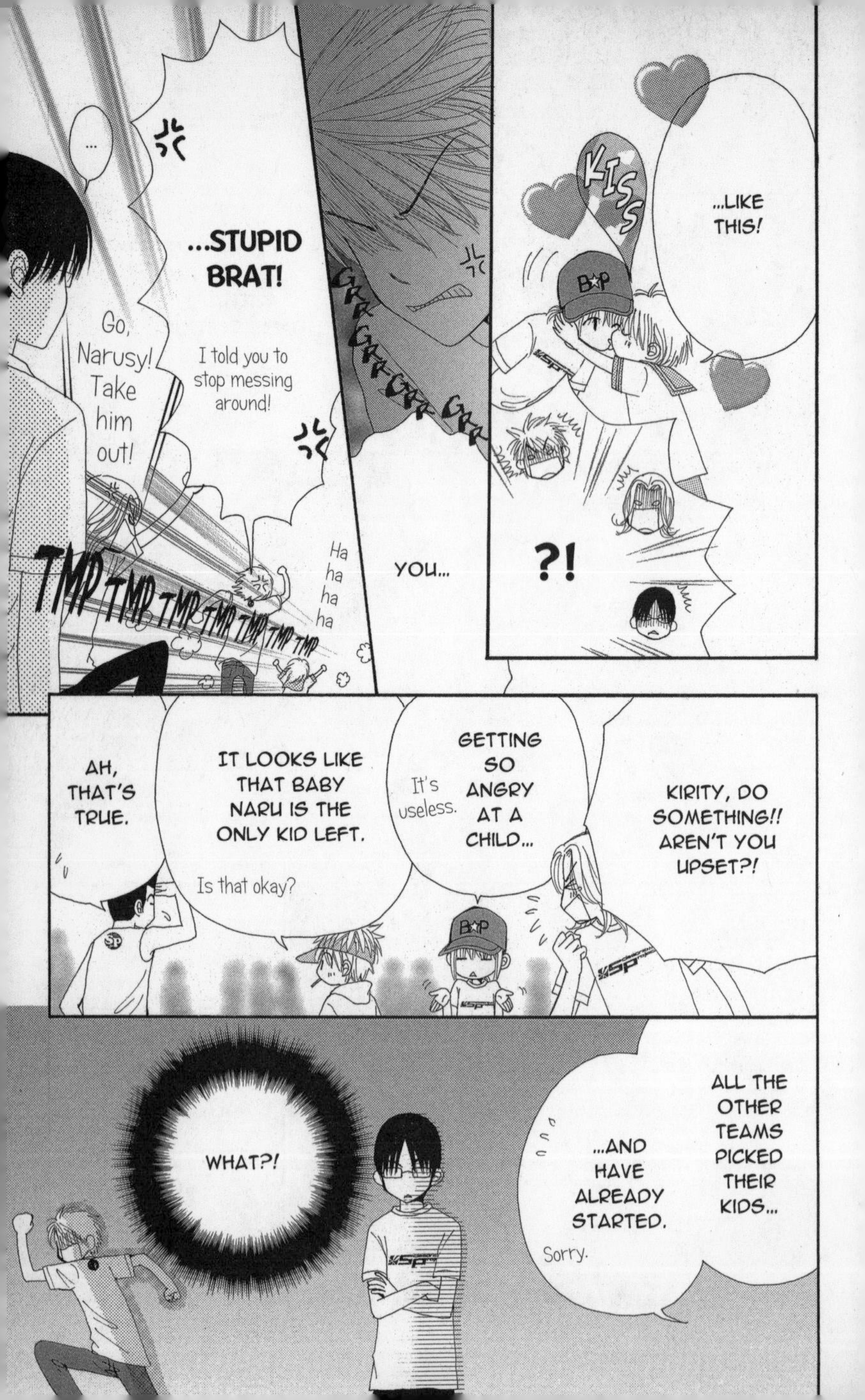
KISS
...LIKE THIS!
?!
GRR GRR GRR GRR
YOU...
...
...STUPID BRAT!
I told you to stop messing around!
Go, Narusy! Take him out!
Ha ha ha ha
TMP TMP TMP TMP TMP TMP TMP
KIRITY, DO SOMETHING!! AREN'T YOU UPSET?!
GETTING SO ANGRY AT A CHILD...
It's useless.
IT LOOKS LIKE THAT BABY NARU IS THE ONLY KID LEFT.
Is that okay?
AH, THAT'S TRUE.
ALL THE OTHER TEAMS PICKED THEIR KIDS...
...AND HAVE ALREADY STARTED.
Sorry.
WHAT?!

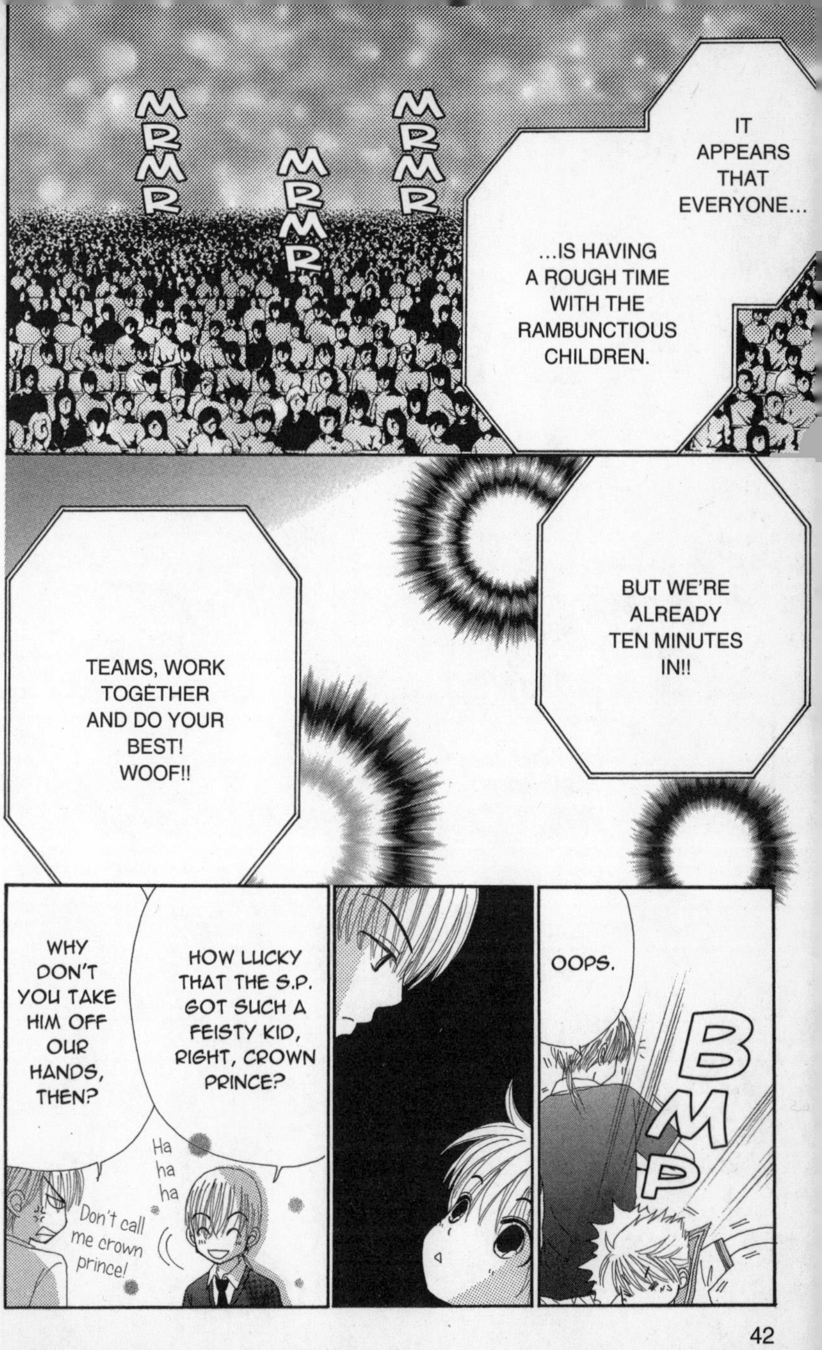
MRMR
MRMR
MRMR
IT APPEARS THAT EVERYONE...
...IS HAVING A ROUGH TIME WITH THE RAMBUNCTIOUS CHILDREN.
BUT WE'RE ALREADY TEN MINUTES IN!!
TEAMS, WORK TOGETHER AND DO YOUR BEST! WOOF!!
OOPS.
BMP
HOW LUCKY THAT THE S.P. GOT SUCH A FEISTY KID, RIGHT, CROWN PRINCE?
WHY DON'T YOU TAKE HIM OFF OUR HANDS, THEN?
Ha ha ha
Don't call me crown prince!

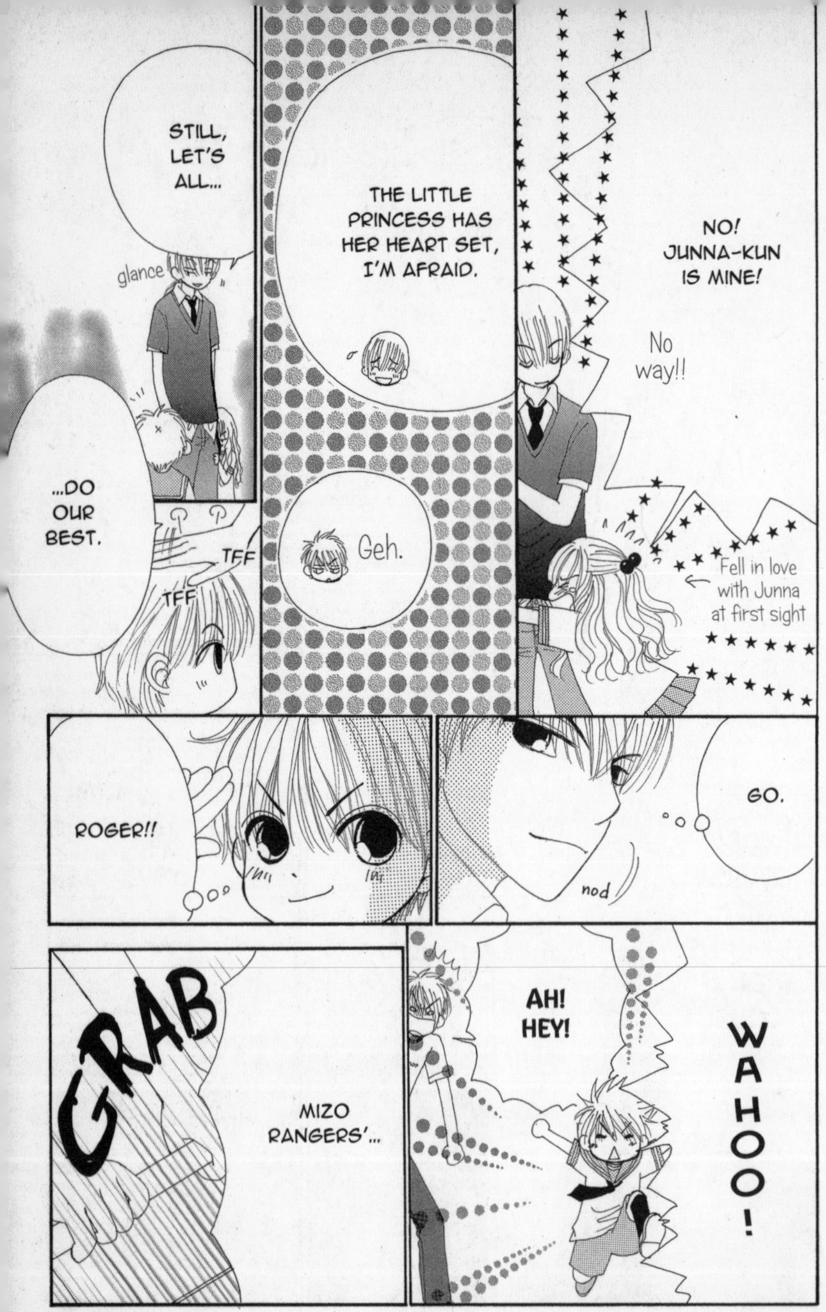
NO! JUNNA-KUN IS MINE!
No way!!
Fell in love with Junna at first sight
THE LITTLE PRINCESS HAS HER HEART SET, I'M AFRAID.
Geh.
STILL, LET'S ALL...
glance
...DO OUR BEST.
TFF
TFF
GO.
nod
ROGER!!
AH! HEY!
WAHOO!
MIZO RANGERS'...
GRAB

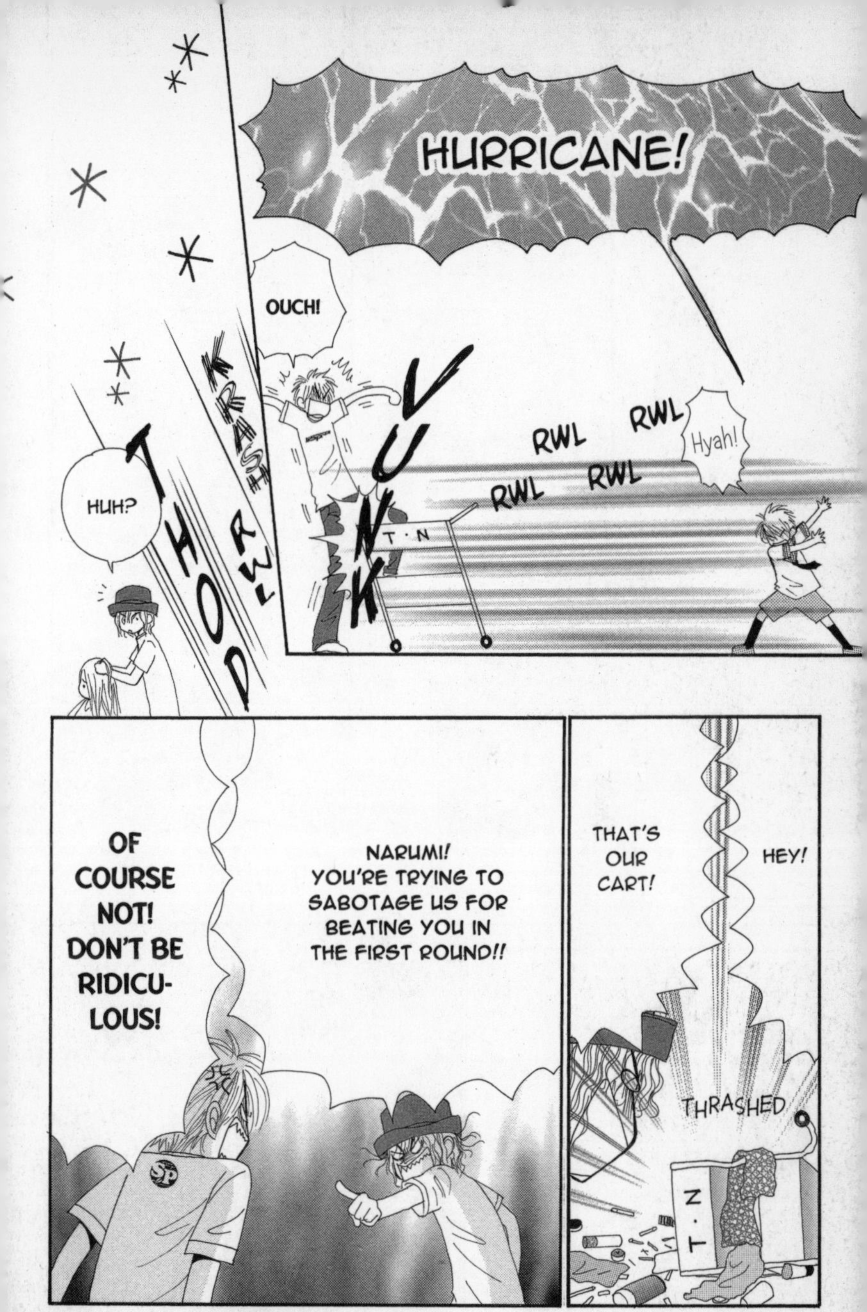
HURRICANE!
Hyah!
RWL RWL
RWL RWL
OUCH!
VUNK
KRASH
RWL
THOOD
HUH?
HEY!
THAT'S OUR CART!
THRASHED
NARUMI! YOU'RE TRYING TO SABOTAGE US FOR BEATING YOU IN THE FIRST ROUND!!
OF COURSE NOT! DON'T BE RIDICU-LOUS!

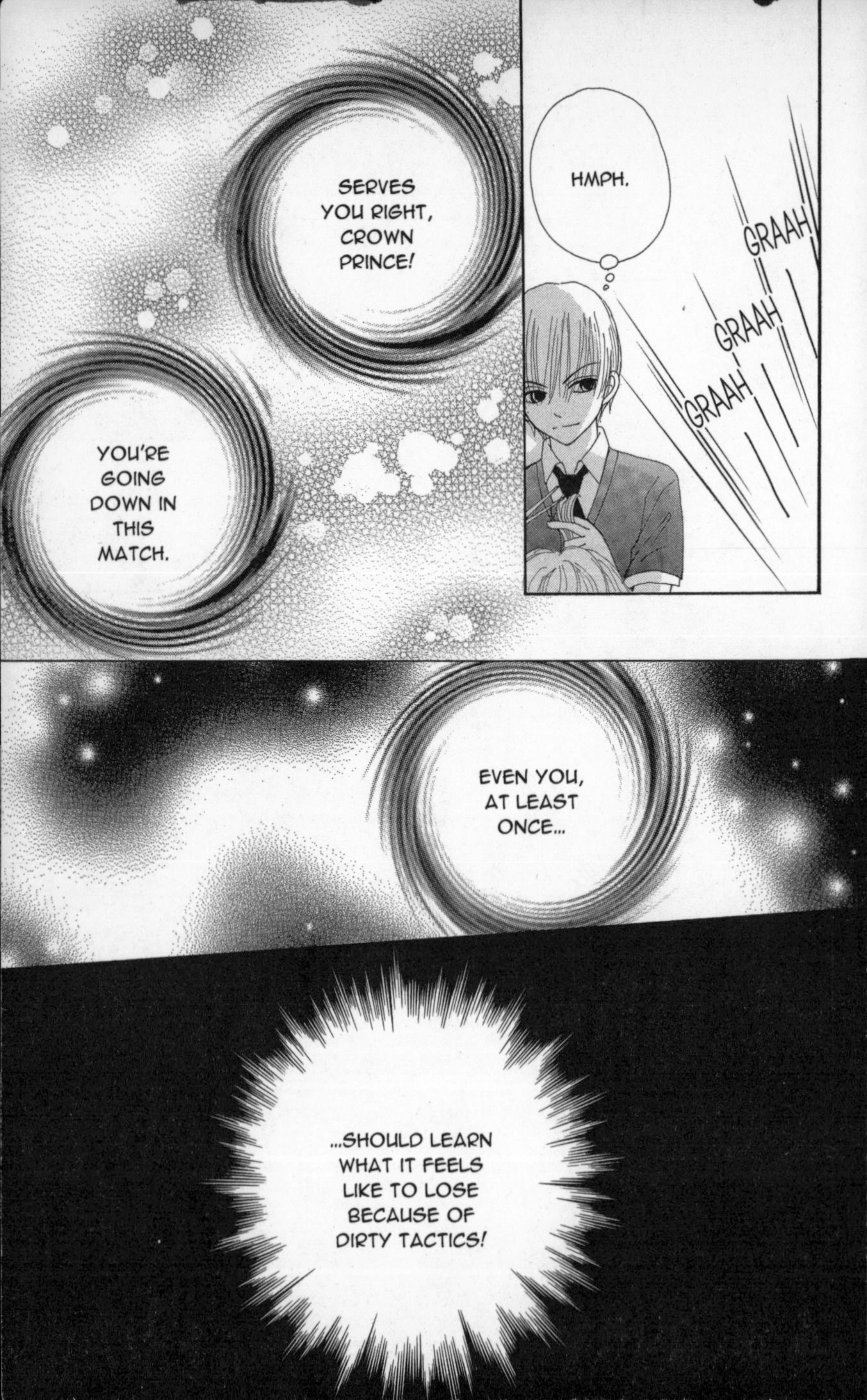
HMPH.
GRAAH
GRAAH
GRAAH
SERVES YOU RIGHT, CROWN PRINCE!
YOU'RE GOING DOWN IN THIS MATCH.
EVEN YOU, AT LEAST ONCE...
...SHOULD LEARN WHAT IT FEELS LIKE TO LOSE BECAUSE OF DIRTY TACTICS!

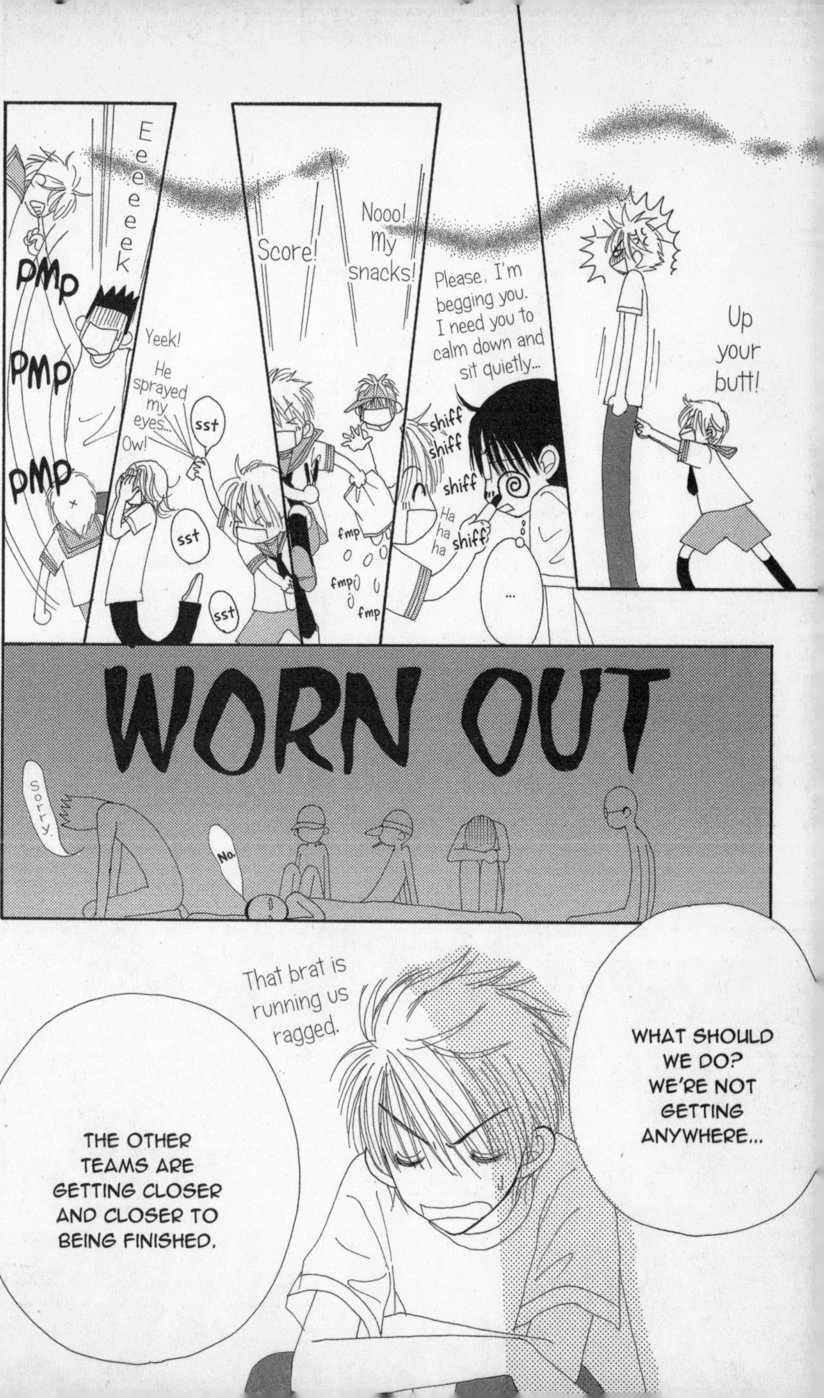
Up your butt!
Please, I'm begging you. I need you to calm down and sit quietly...
shiff shiff
shiff
shiff
Ha ha ha
...
Nooo! My snacks!
Score!
fmp
fmp
fmp
Eeeeeek
PMP
PMP
PMP
Yeek!
He sprayed my eyes... Ow!
sst
sst
sst
WORN OUT
Sorry.
No.
WHAT SHOULD WE DO? WE'RE NOT GETTING ANYWHERE...
That brat is running us ragged.
THE OTHER TEAMS ARE GETTING CLOSER AND CLOSER TO BEING FINISHED.

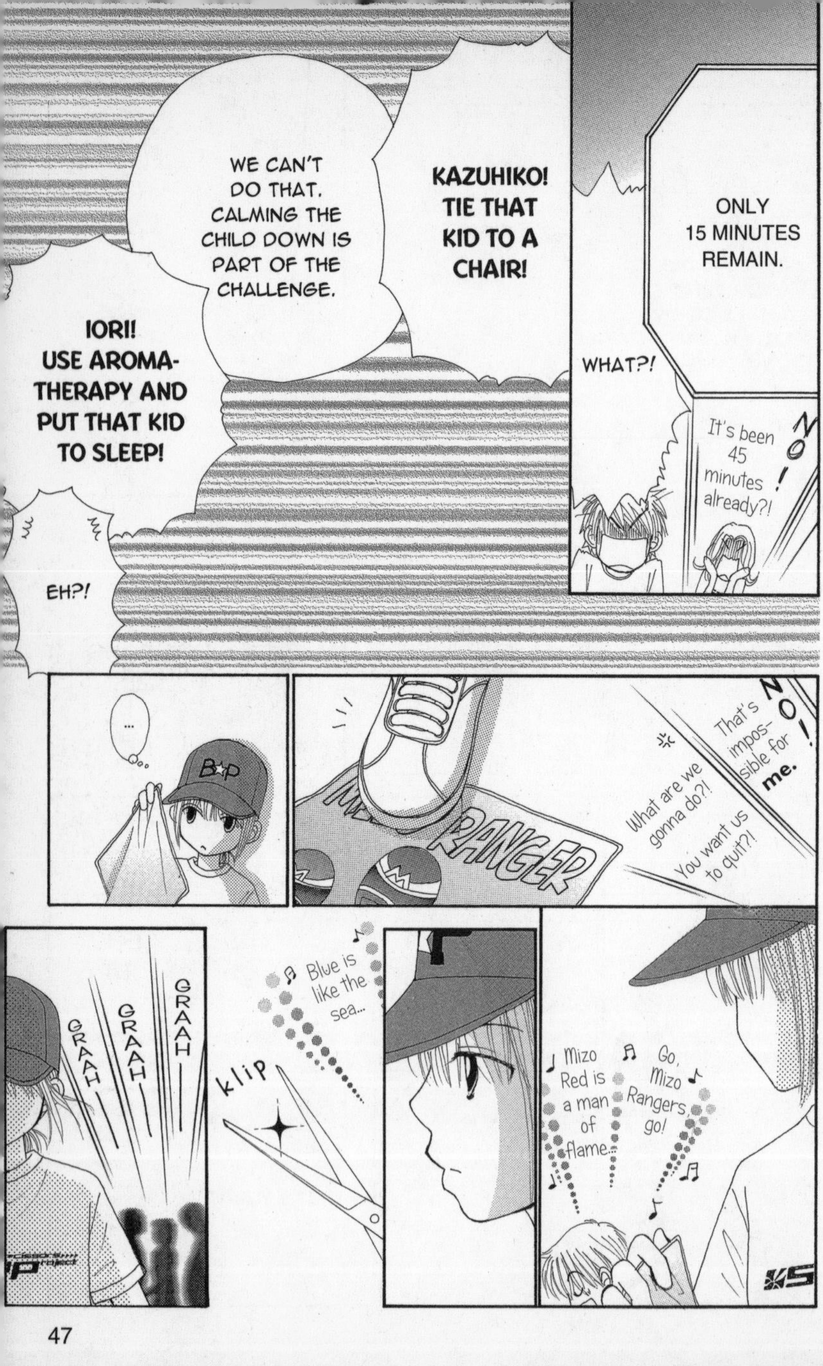
ONLY 15 MINUTES REMAIN.
WHAT?!
It's been 45 minutes already?!
NO!
KAZUHIKO! TIE THAT KID TO A CHAIR!
WE CAN'T DO THAT. CALMING THE CHILD DOWN IS PART OF THE CHALLENGE.
IORI! USE AROMA-THERAPY AND PUT THAT KID TO SLEEP!
EH?!
NO!
That's impos-sible for me.
What are we gonna do?!
You want us to quit?!
RANGER
...
Go, Mizo Rangers go!
Mizo Red is a man of flame...
Blue is like the sea...
klip
GRAAH
GRAAH
GRAAH

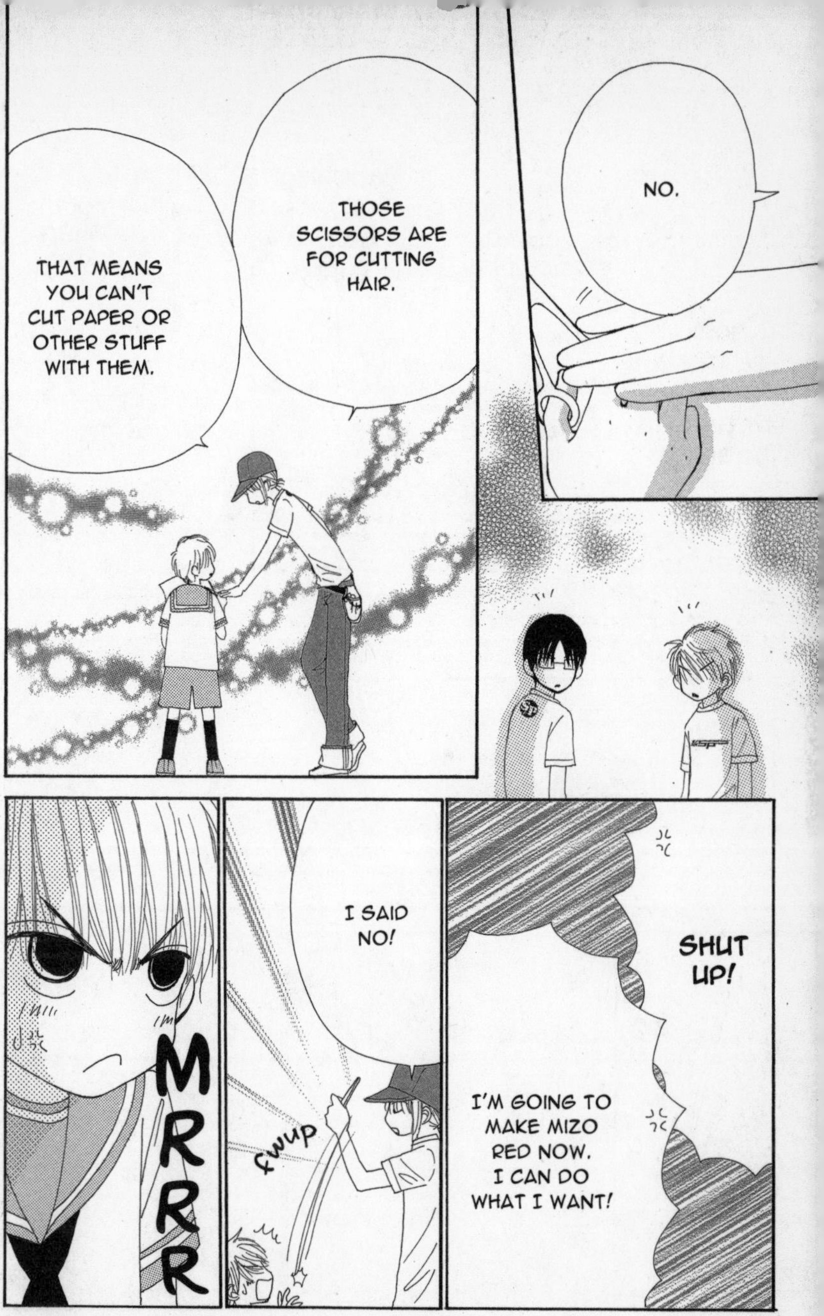
NO.
THOSE SCISSORS ARE FOR CUTTING HAIR.
THAT MEANS YOU CAN'T CUT PAPER OR OTHER STUFF WITH THEM.
SHUT UP!
I'M GOING TO MAKE MIZO RED NOW. I CAN DO WHAT I WANT!
I SAID NO!
FWUP
MRRR

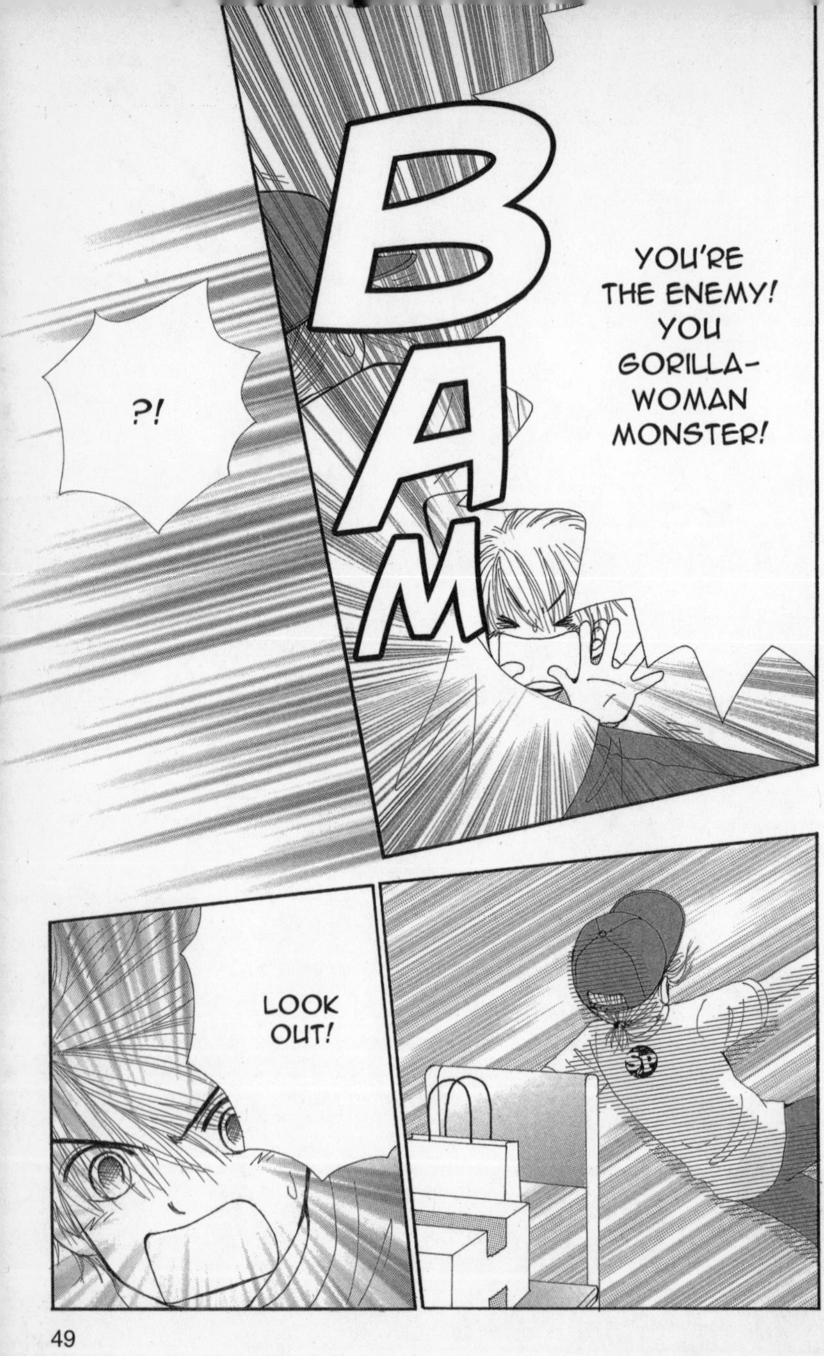
BAM
YOU'RE THE ENEMY! YOU GORILLA-WOMAN MONSTER!
?!
LOOK OUT!

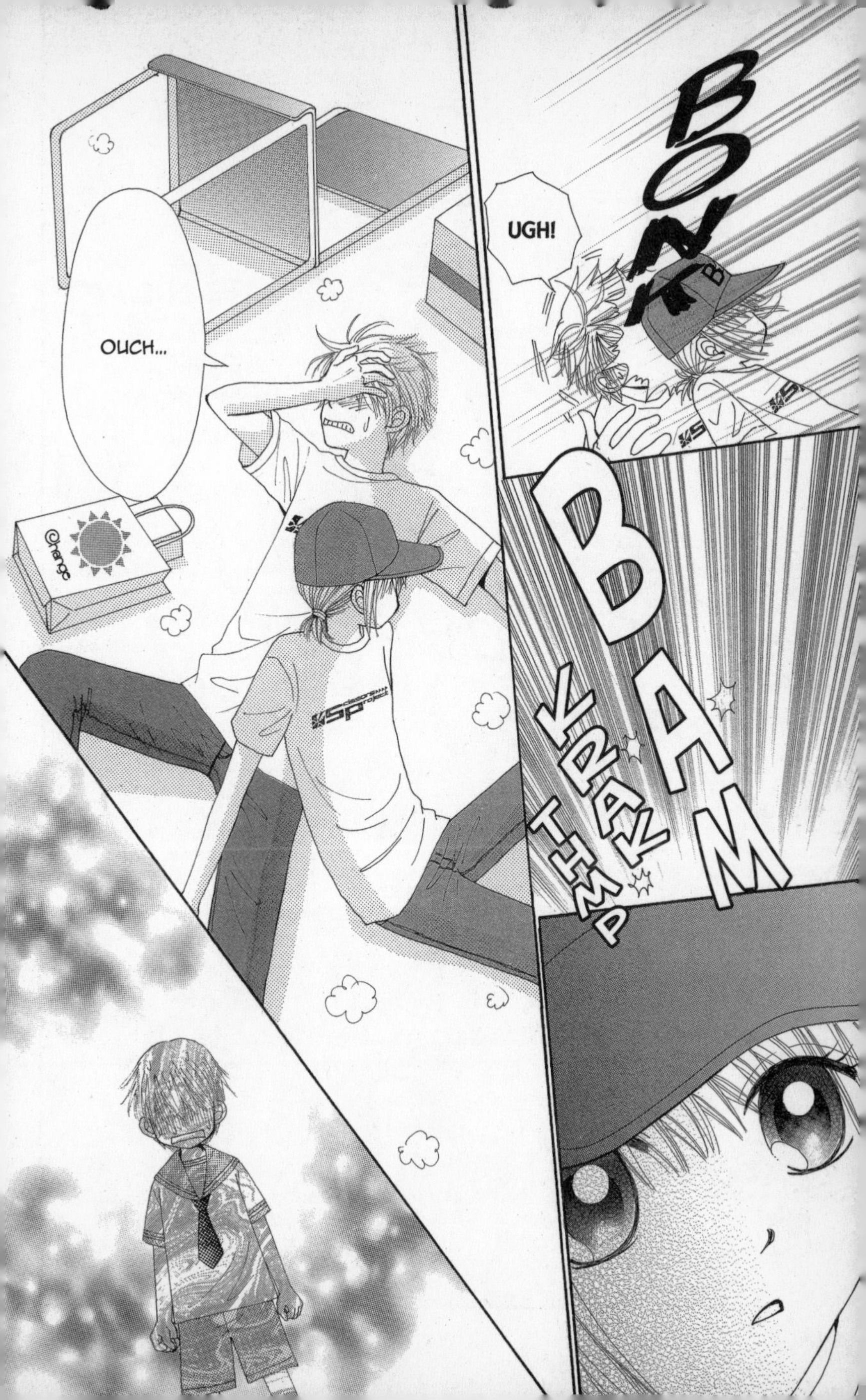
BONK
UGH!
BAM
KRAK
THMP
OUCH...

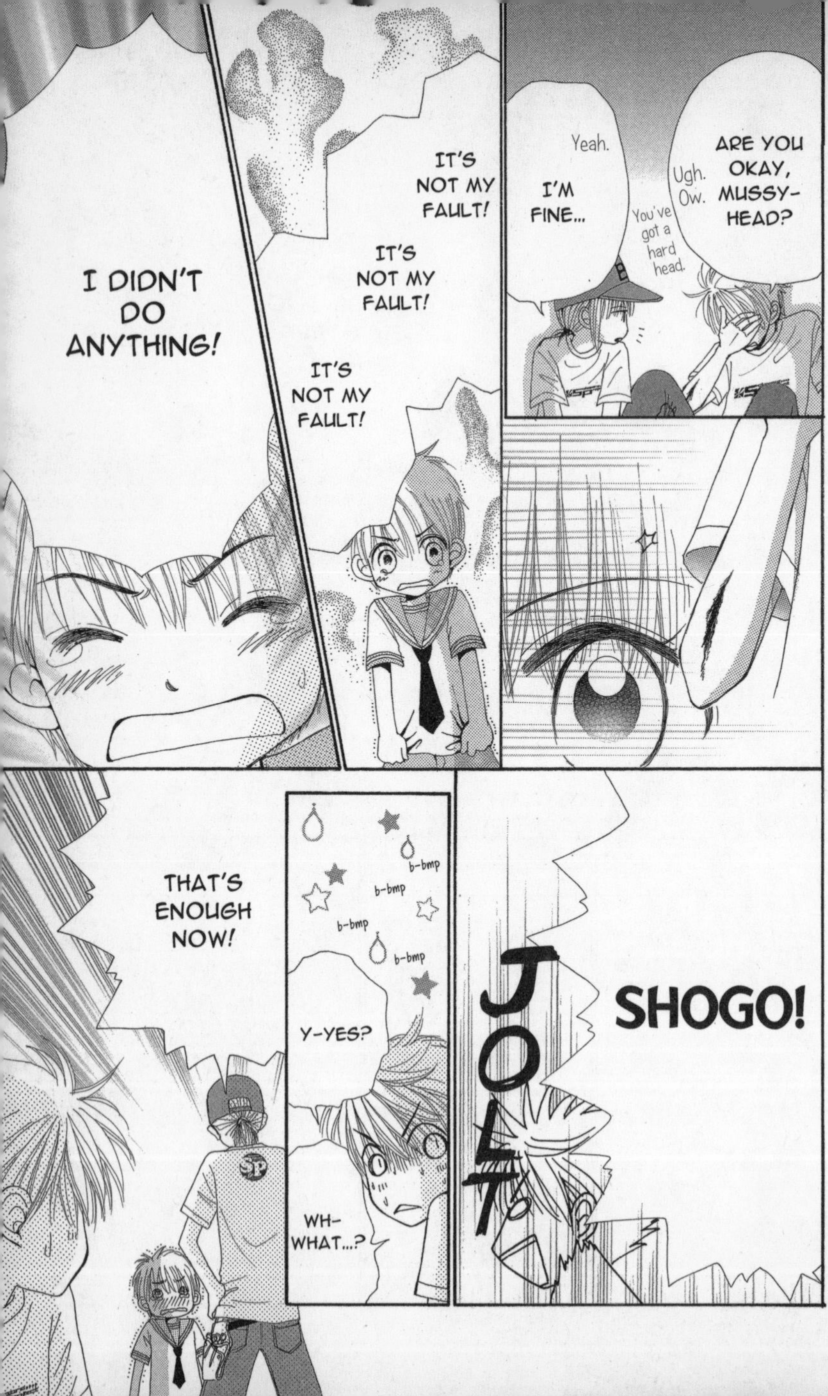
ARE YOU OKAY, MUSSY-HEAD?
Ugh. Ow.
You've got a hard head.
Yeah.
I'M FINE...
IT'S NOT MY FAULT!
IT'S NOT MY FAULT!
IT'S NOT MY FAULT!
I DIDN'T DO ANYTHING!
SHOGO!
JOLT
b-bmp
b-bmp
b-bmp
b-bmp
Y-YES?
WH-WHAT...?
THAT'S ENOUGH NOW!

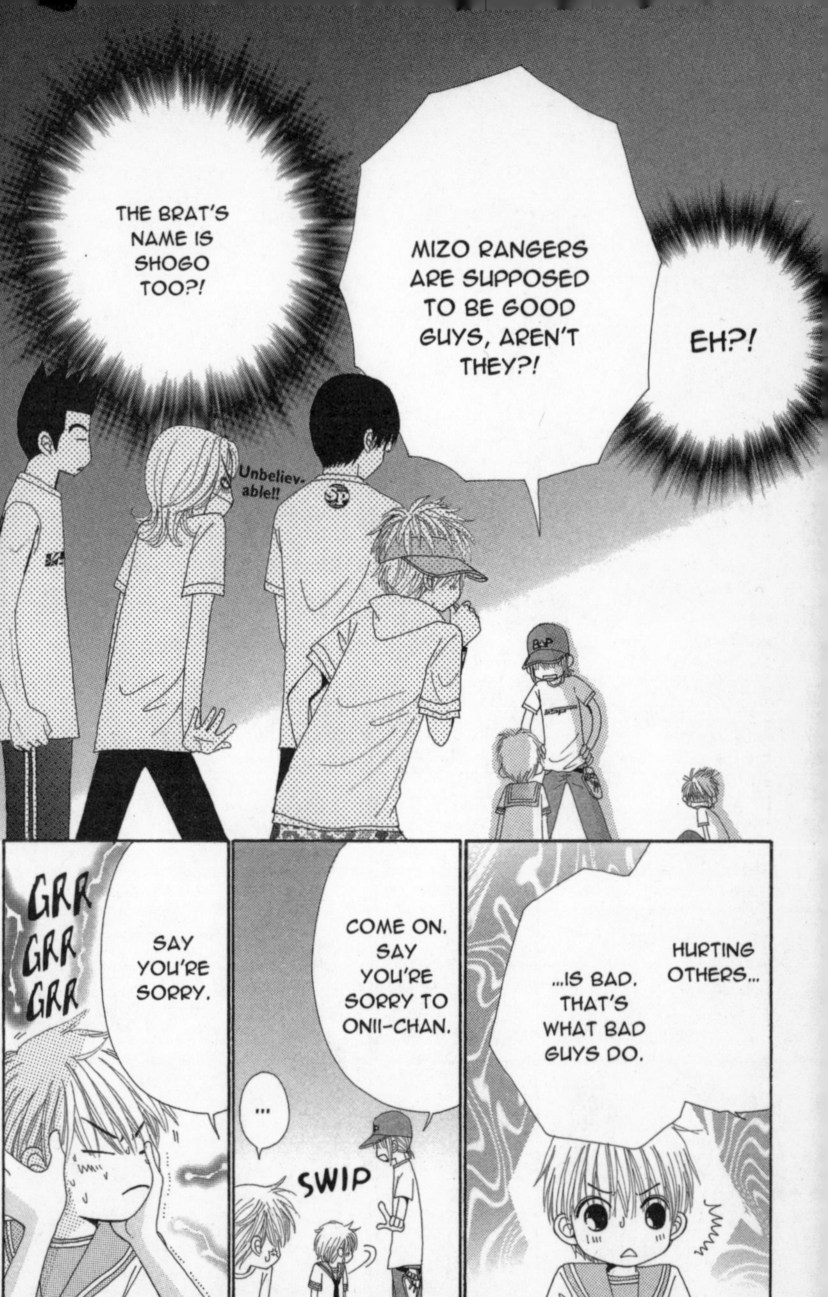
EH?!
MIZO RANGERS ARE SUPPOSED TO BE GOOD GUYS, AREN'T THEY?!
THE BRAT'S NAME IS SHOGO TOO?!
Unbeliev-able!!
HURTING OTHERS...
...IS BAD. THAT'S WHAT BAD GUYS DO.
COME ON. SAY YOU'RE SORRY TO ONII-CHAN.
...
SWIP
SAY YOU'RE SORRY.
GRR GRR GRR

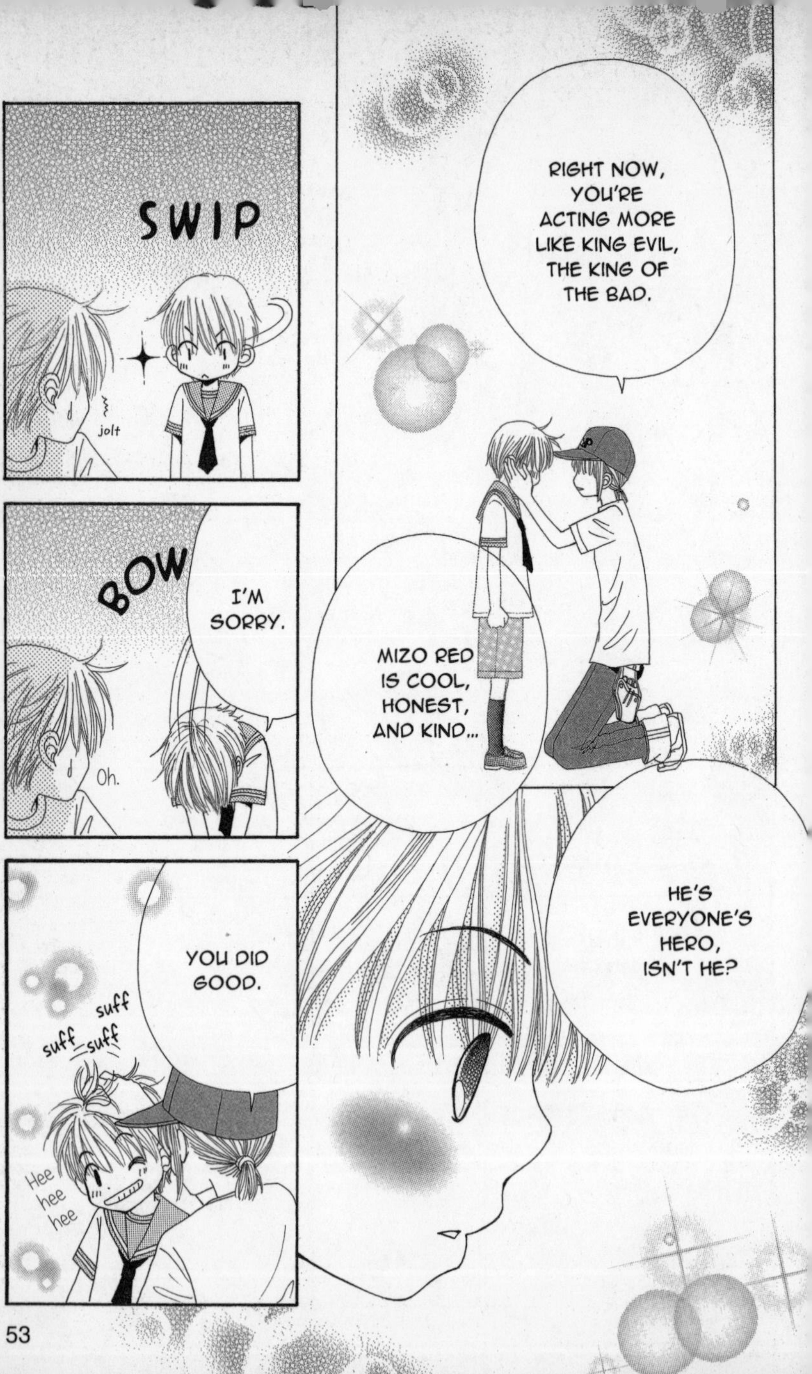
RIGHT NOW, YOU'RE ACTING MORE LIKE KING EVIL, THE KING OF THE BAD.
MIZO RED IS COOL, HONEST, AND KIND...
HE'S EVERYONE'S HERO, ISN'T HE?
SWIP
jolt
BOW
I'M SORRY.
Oh.
YOU DID GOOD.
suff suff suff
Hee hee hee

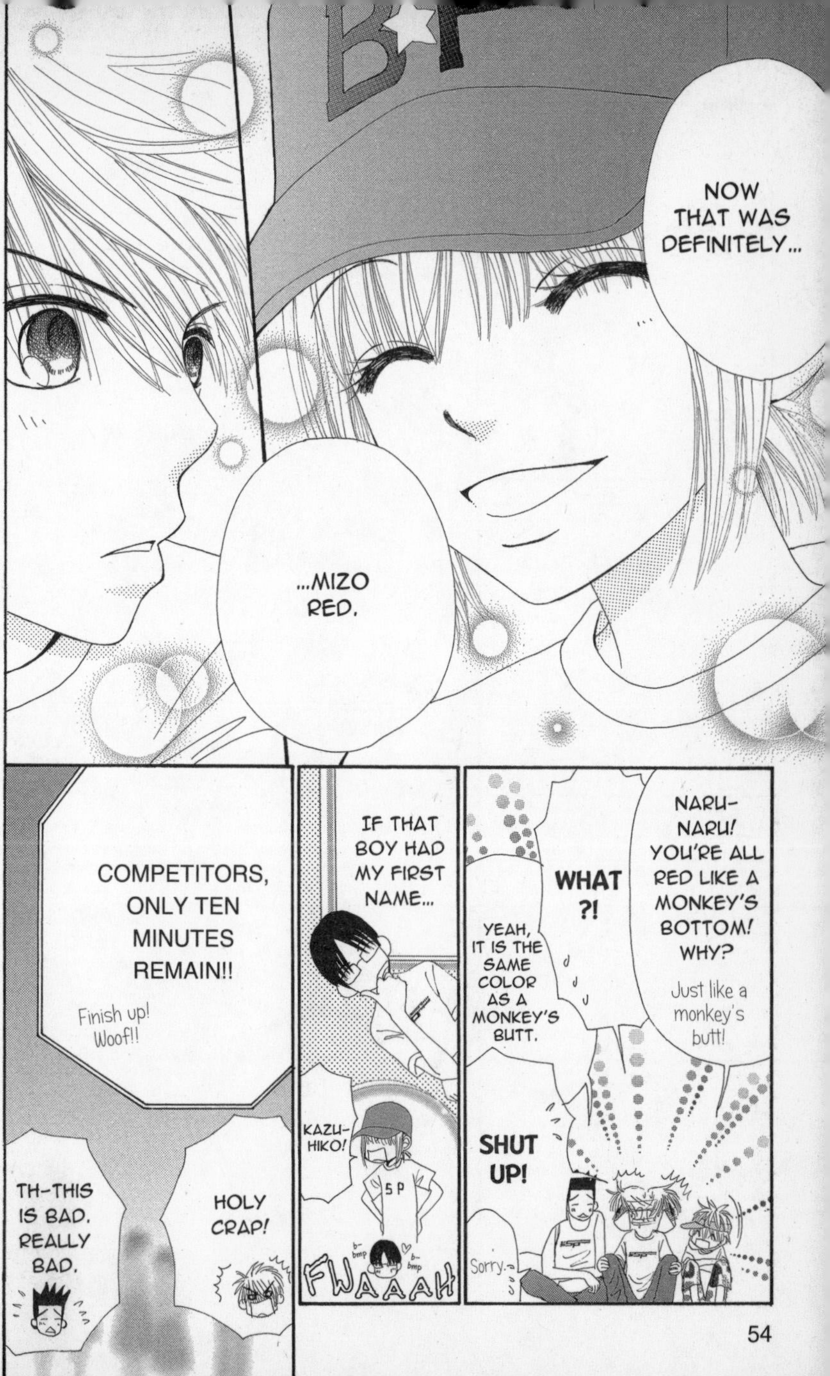
NOW THAT WAS DEFINITELY...
...MIZO RED.
NARU-NARU! YOU'RE ALL RED LIKE A MONKEY'S BOTTOM! WHY?
Just like a monkey's butt!
WHAT?!
YEAH, IT IS THE SAME COLOR AS A MONKEY'S BUTT.
SHUT UP!
Sorry.
IF THAT BOY HAD MY FIRST NAME...
KAZU-HIKO!
b-bmp
b-bmp
FWAAAH
COMPETITORS, ONLY TEN MINUTES REMAIN!!
Finish up! Woof!!
HOLY CRAP!
TH-THIS IS BAD. REALLY BAD.

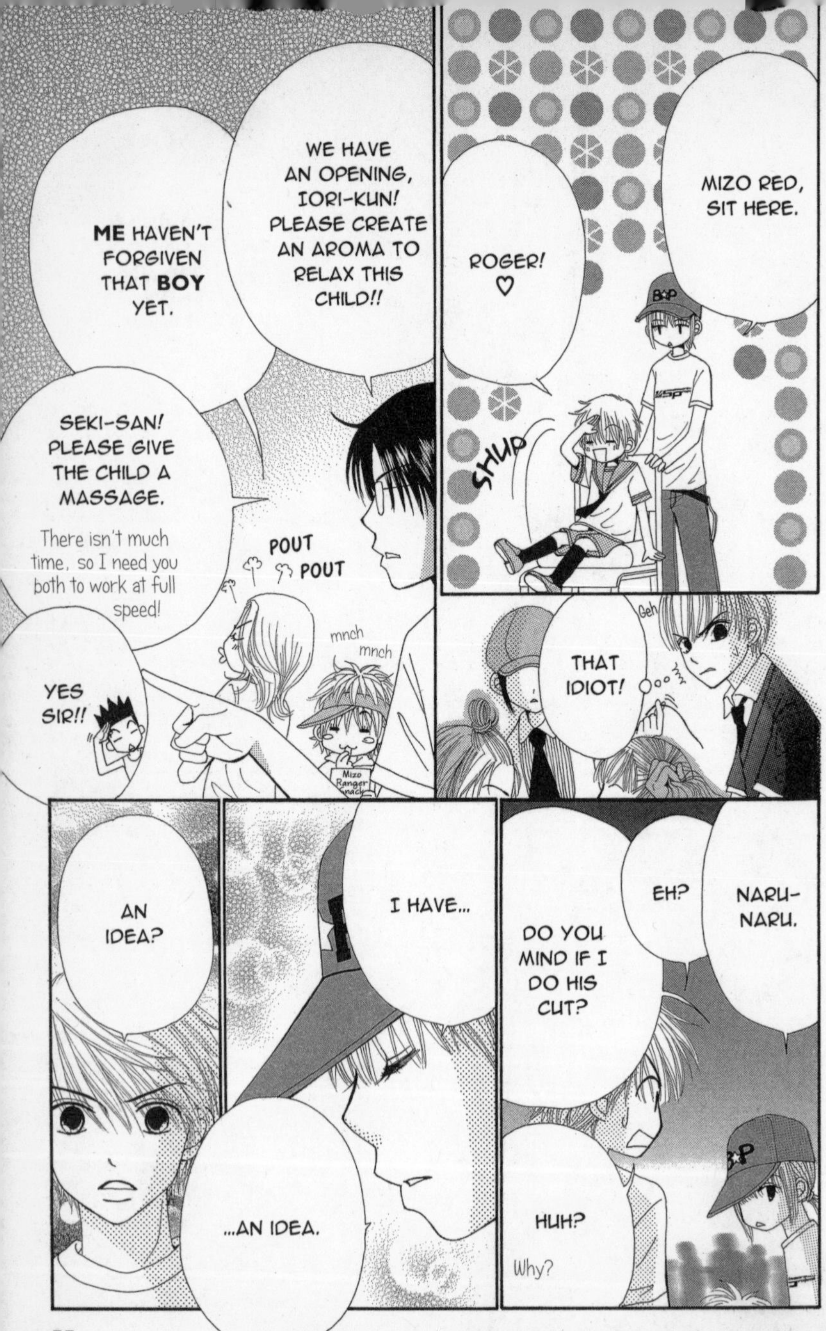
MIZO RED, SIT HERE.
ROGER! ♡
SHUP
Geh
THAT IDIOT!
WE HAVE AN OPENING, IORI-KUN! PLEASE CREATE AN AROMA TO RELAX THIS CHILD!!
ME HAVEN'T FORGIVEN THAT BOY YET.
SEKI-SAN! PLEASE GIVE THE CHILD A MASSAGE.
There isn't much time, so I need you both to work at full speed!
POUT
POUT
mnch
mnch
YES SIR!!
NARU-NARU.
EH?
DO YOU MIND IF I DO HIS CUT?
HUH?
Why?
I HAVE...
...AN IDEA.
AN IDEA?

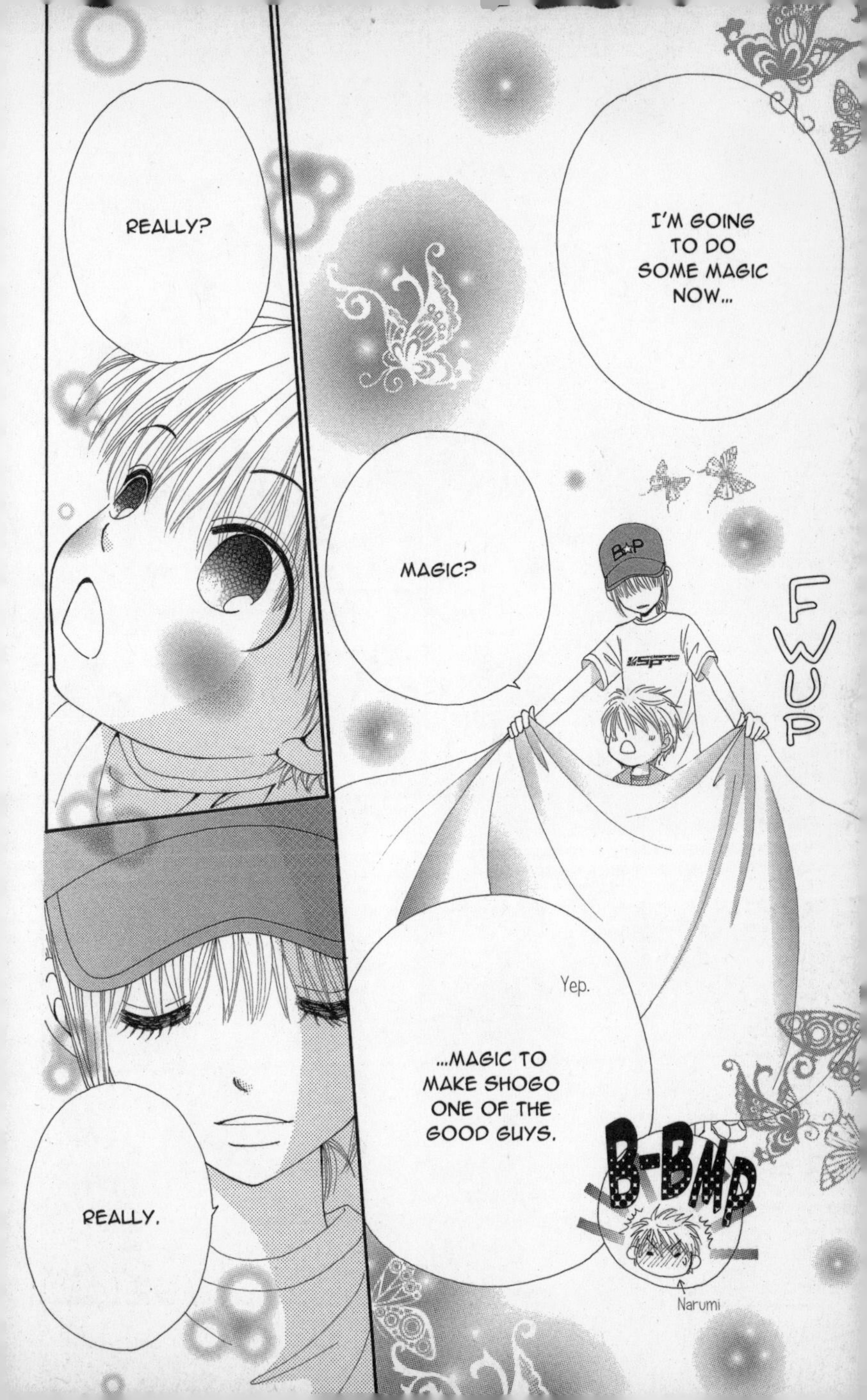
I'M GOING TO DO SOME MAGIC NOW...
MAGIC?
FWUP
Yep.
...MAGIC TO MAKE SHOGO ONE OF THE GOOD GUYS.
B-BMP
Narumi
REALLY?
REALLY.

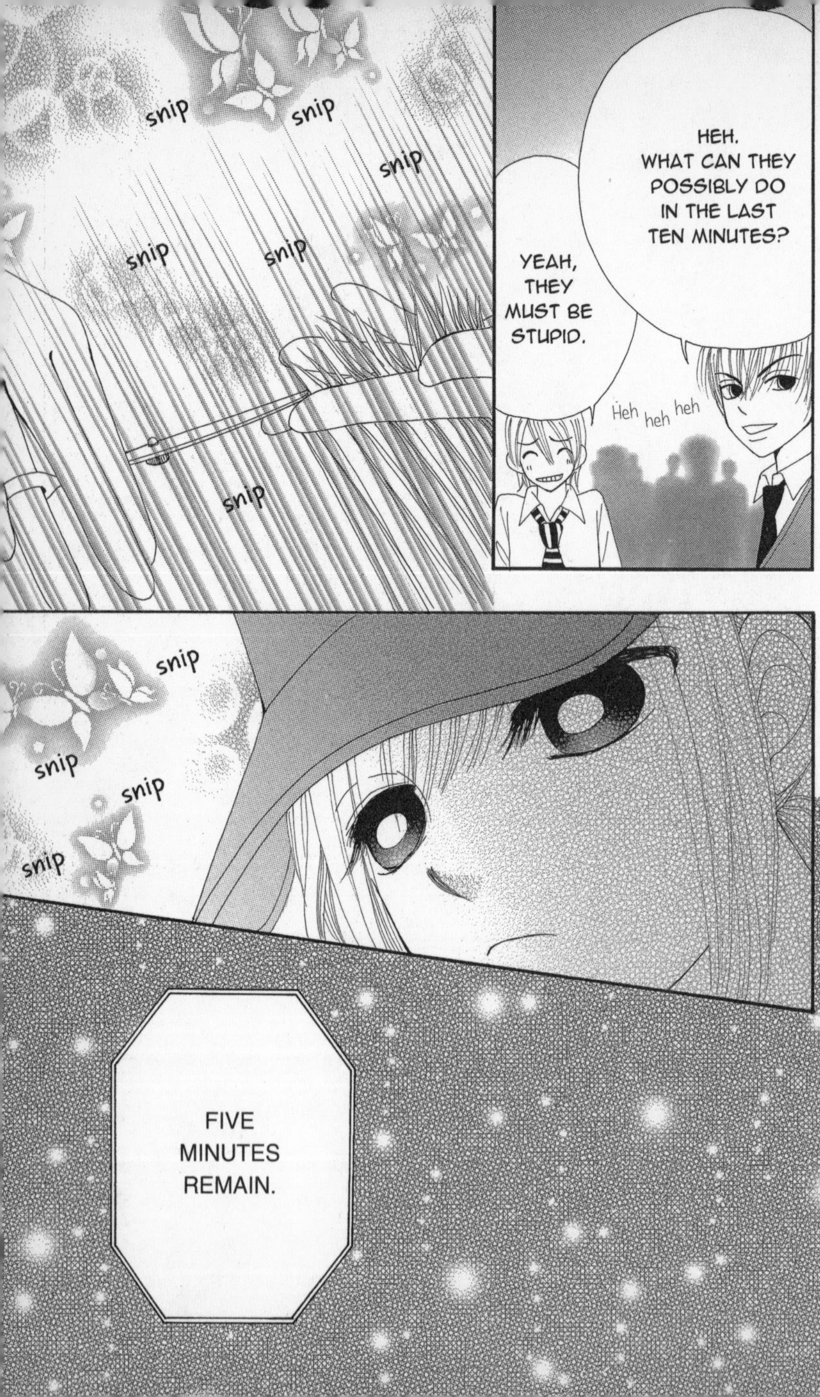
HEH. WHAT CAN THEY POSSIBLY DO IN THE LAST TEN MINUTES?
YEAH, THEY MUST BE STUPID.
Heh heh heh
snip
snip
snip
snip
snip
snip
snip
snip
snip
snip
FIVE MINUTES REMAIN.

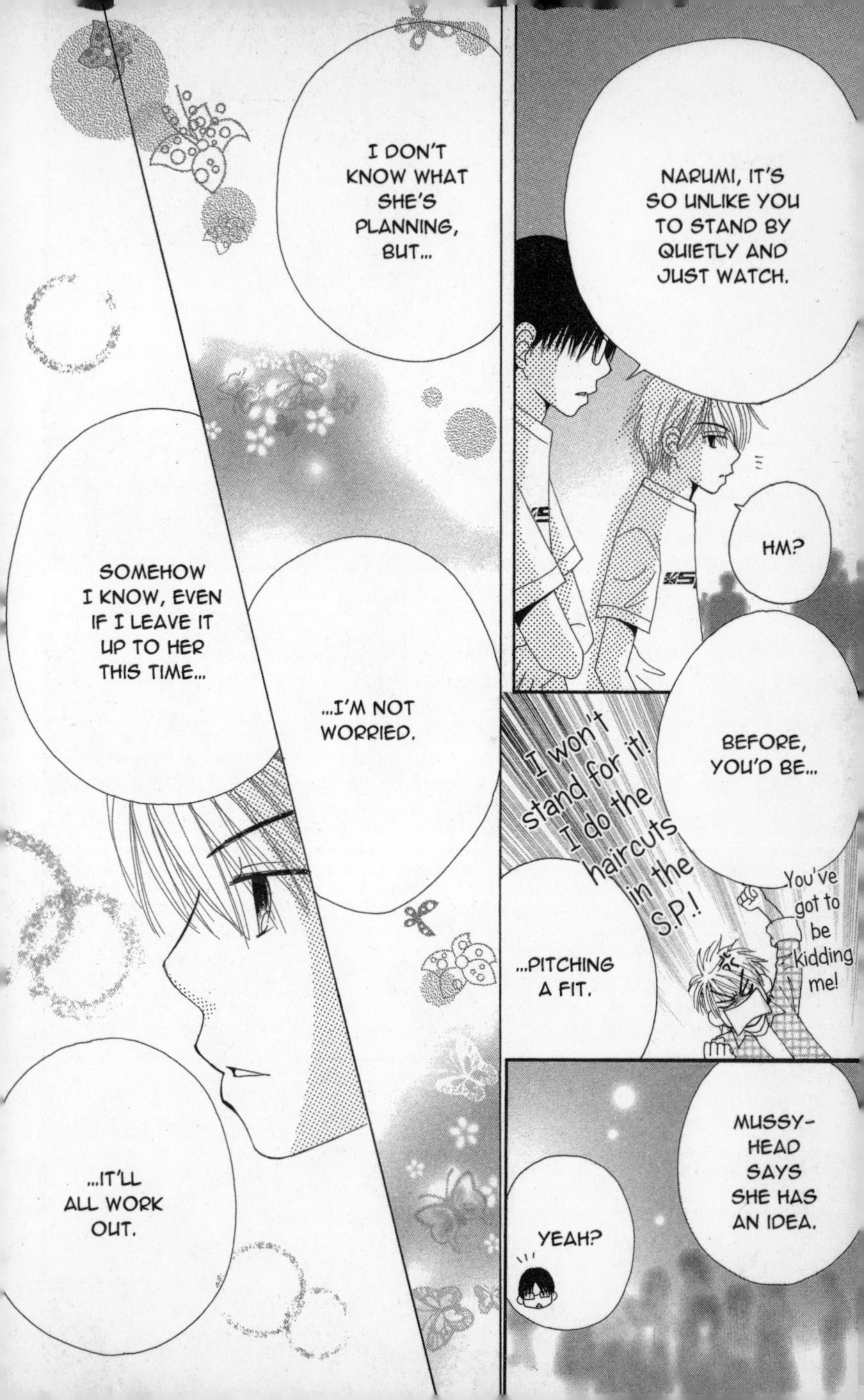
NARUMI, IT'S SO UNLIKE YOU TO STAND BY QUIETLY AND JUST WATCH.
HM?
BEFORE, YOU'D BE...
You've got to be kidding me!
I won't stand for it! I do the haircuts in the S.P.!
...PITCHING A FIT.
MUSSY-HEAD SAYS SHE HAS AN IDEA.
YEAH?
I DON'T KNOW WHAT SHE'S PLANNING, BUT...
SOMEHOW I KNOW, EVEN IF I LEAVE IT UP TO HER THIS TIME...
...I'M NOT WORRIED.
...IT'LL ALL WORK OUT.

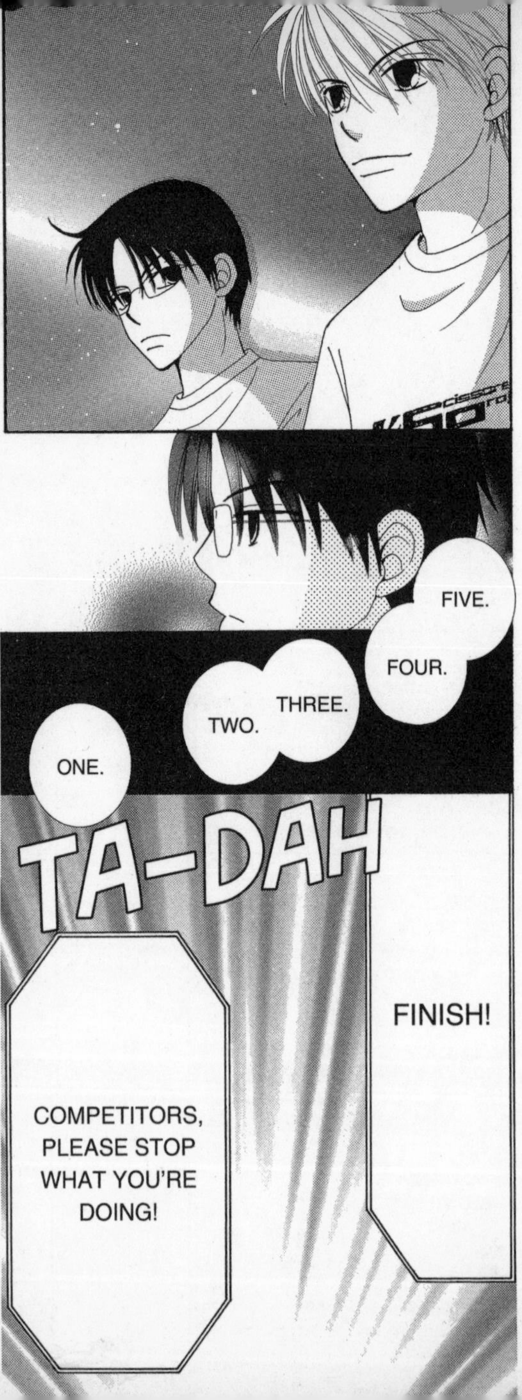
FIVE.
FOUR.
THREE.
TWO.
ONE.
TA-DAH
FINISH!
COMPETITORS, PLEASE STOP WHAT YOU'RE DOING!

K's Club Talk

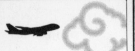

If we're talking about the original setup, Narumi was actually different too. ♪
I wanted him to be the kind of guy who always has girls around him and doesn't reject anyone--going out with several girls at a time. He was meant to be a budding genius beautician who could turn girls on with his words and then would transform them into beautiful creatures.
This Narumi would blow his father's money but then act like a perfect son in front of the father he despises. Even though he had many girlfriends, he would never get serious with any of them. He would never trust them. Then this Narumi would meet Kiri, who is different from the girls he knows, and though she initially infuriates him, he'd eventually fall for her...or something like that. In all honesty, I wanted to see and draw a Narumi like that, but the current Narumi is definitely cuter and I really like him. ♡ Because even though he gets mad easily, he's a straightforward and honest guy. But now, the idea that he's supposed to be popular with girls--but has absolutely no experience with them by his third year of high school--makes Mommy sad.

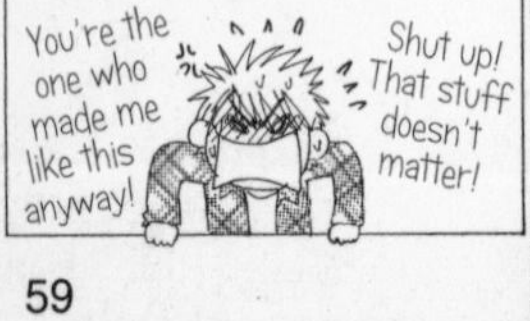
Shut up! That stuff doesn't matter!
You're the one who made me like this anyway!

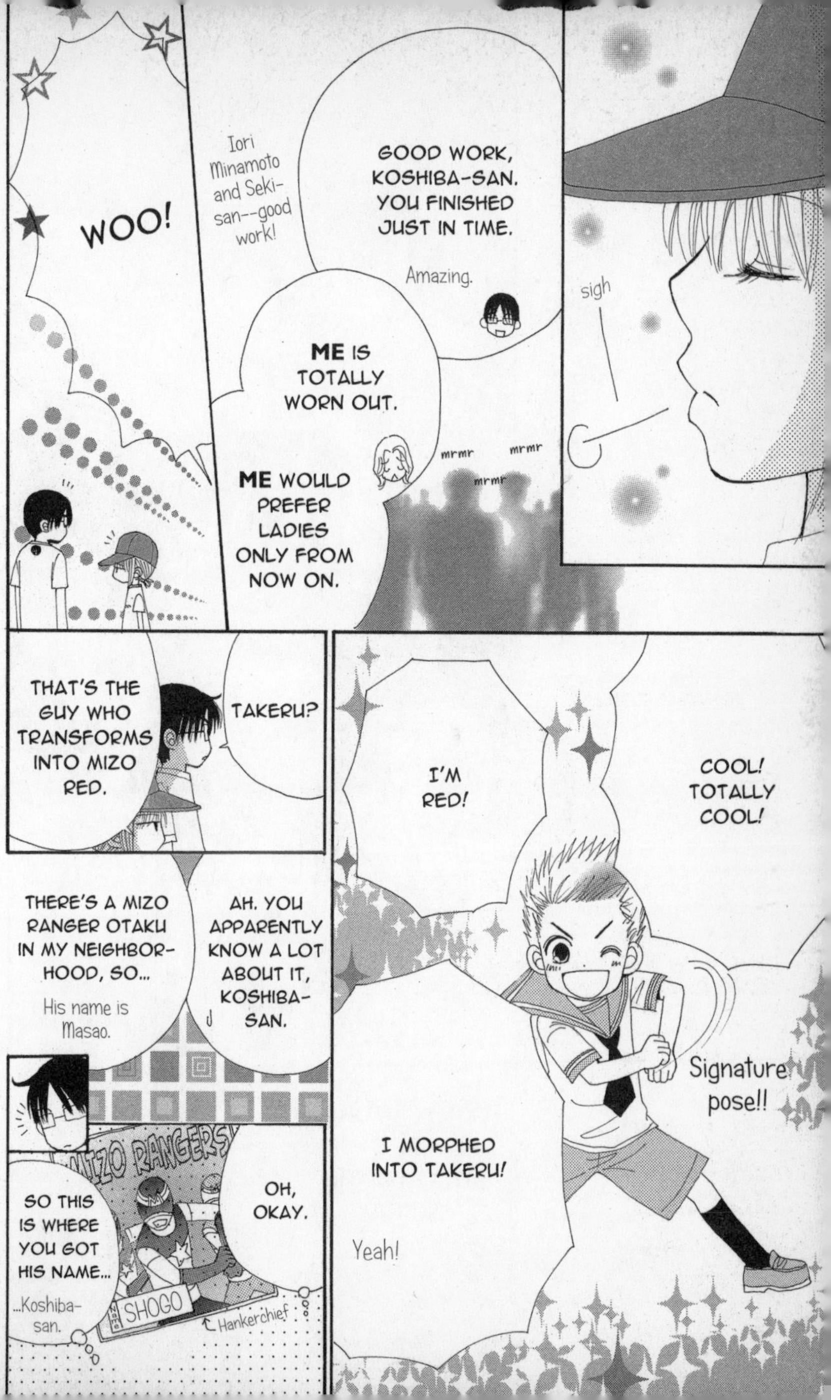
sigh
GOOD WORK, KOSHIBA-SAN. YOU FINISHED JUST IN TIME.
Amazing.
ME IS TOTALLY WORN OUT.
ME WOULD PREFER LADIES ONLY FROM NOW ON.
mrmr
mrmr
mrmr
Iori Minamoto and Seki-san--good work!
WOO!
COOL! TOTALLY COOL!
I'M RED!
Signature pose!!
I MORPHED INTO TAKERU!
Yeah!
TAKERU?
THAT'S THE GUY WHO TRANSFORMS INTO MIZO RED.
AH. YOU APPARENTLY KNOW A LOT ABOUT IT, KOSHIBA-SAN.
THERE'S A MIZO RANGER OTAKU IN MY NEIGHBOR-HOOD, SO...
His name is Masao.
OH, OKAY.
SO THIS IS WHERE YOU GOT HIS NAME...
...Koshiba-san.
MIZO RANGERS
Name SHOGO
Hankerchief

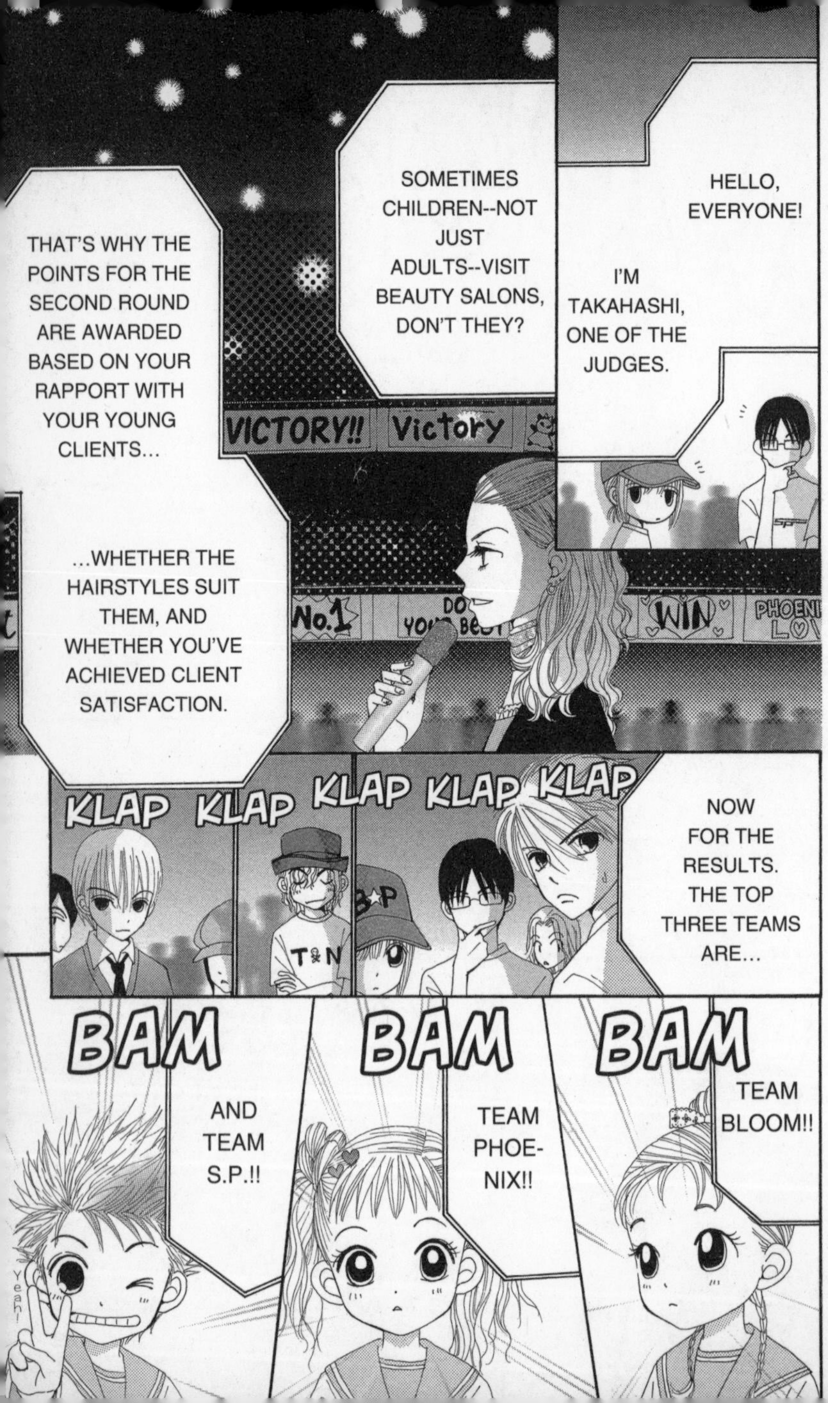
HELLO, EVERYONE!
I'M TAKAHASHI, ONE OF THE JUDGES.
SOMETIMES CHILDREN--NOT JUST ADULTS--VISIT BEAUTY SALONS, DON'T THEY?
VICTORY!!
Victory
THAT'S WHY THE POINTS FOR THE SECOND ROUND ARE AWARDED BASED ON YOUR RAPPORT WITH YOUR YOUNG CLIENTS...
...WHETHER THE HAIRSTYLES SUIT THEM, AND WHETHER YOU'VE ACHIEVED CLIENT SATISFACTION.
No.1
WIN
NOW FOR THE RESULTS. THE TOP THREE TEAMS ARE...
KLAP KLAP KLAP KLAP KLAP
BAM
TEAM BLOOM!!
BAM
TEAM PHOE-NIX!!
BAM
AND TEAM S.P.!!
Yeah!

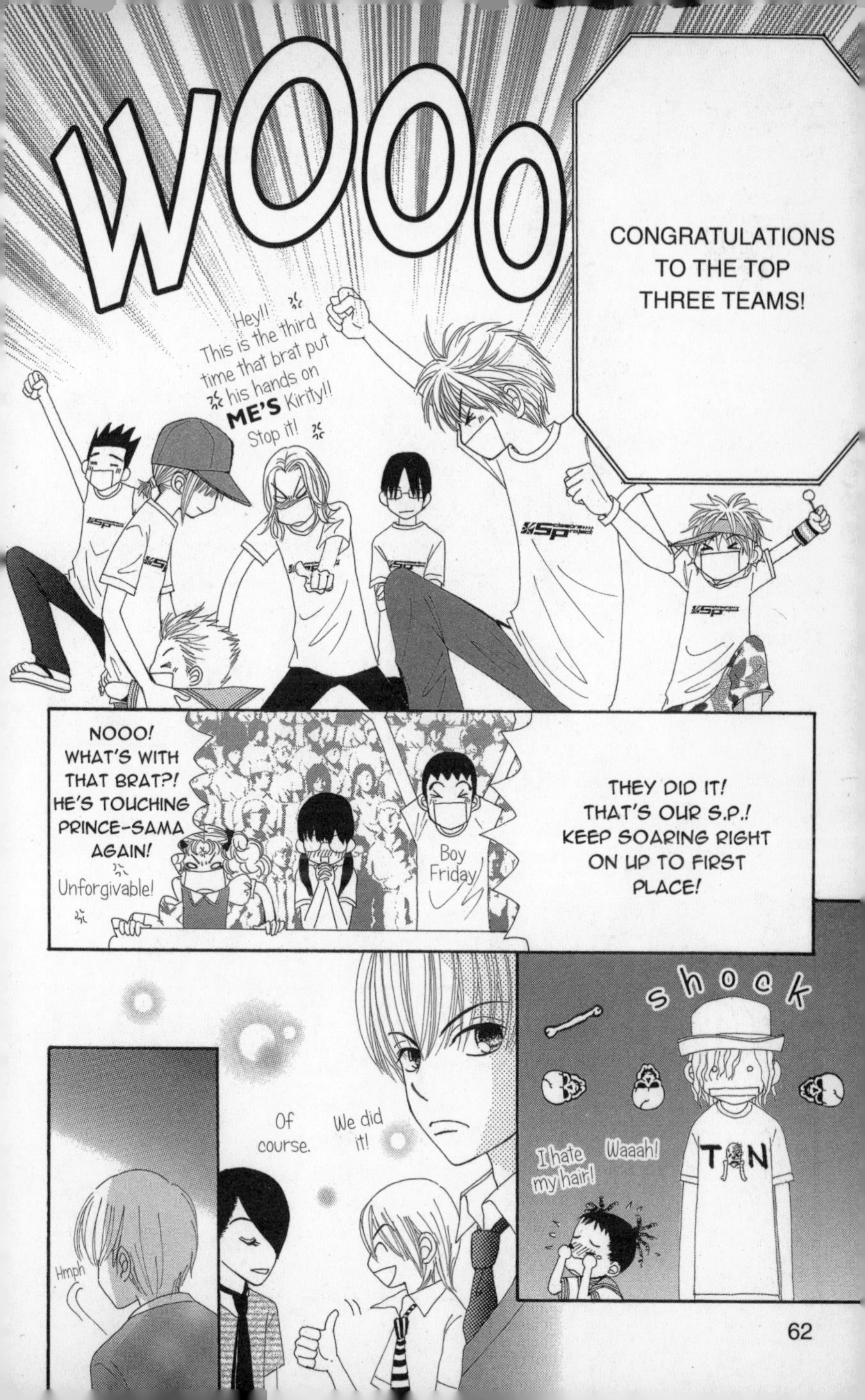
CONGRATULATIONS TO THE TOP THREE TEAMS!
WOOO
Hey!! This is the third time that brat put his hands on ME'S Kirity!! Stop it!
THEY DID IT! THAT'S OUR S.P.! KEEP SOARING RIGHT ON UP TO FIRST PLACE!
Boy Friday
NOOO! WHAT'S WITH THAT BRAT?! HE'S TOUCHING PRINCE-SAMA AGAIN!
Unforgivable!
shock
TN
Waaah!
I hate my hair!
We did it!
Of course.
Hmph

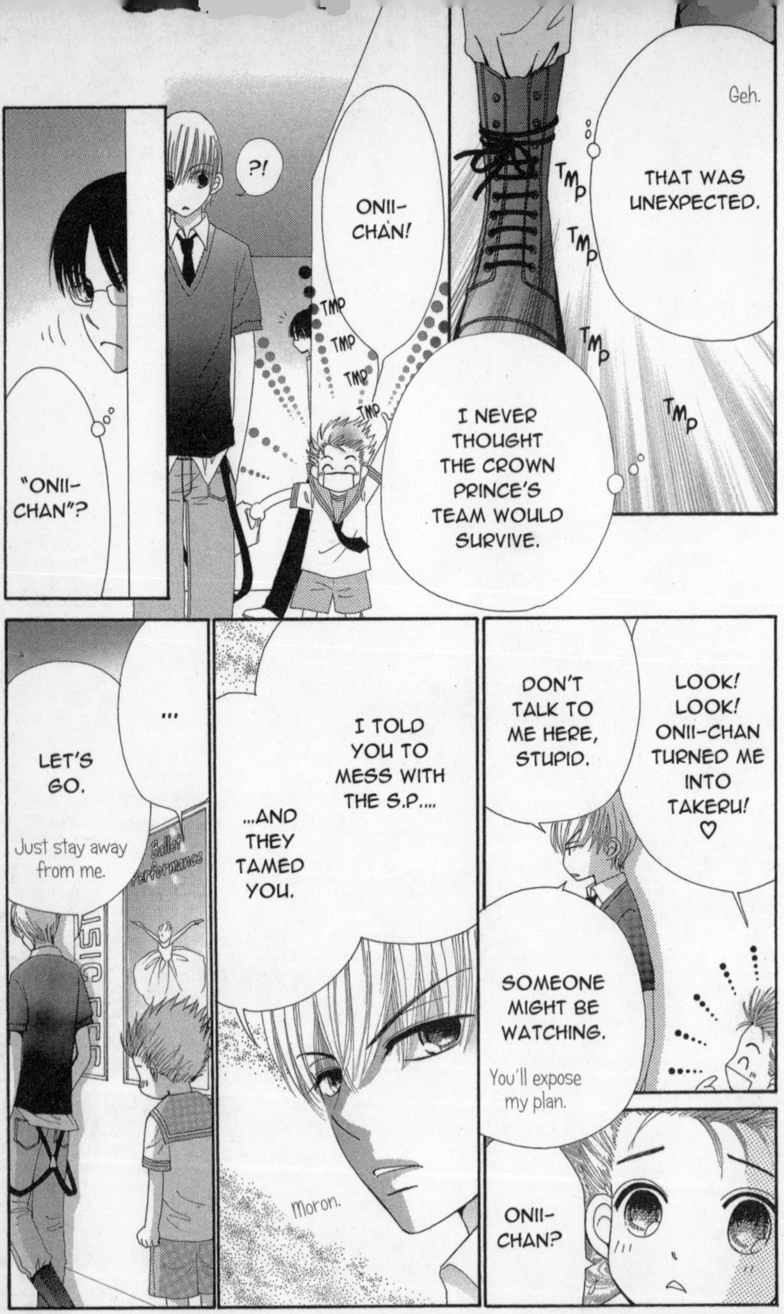
Geh.
THAT WAS UNEXPECTED.
TMP
TMP
TMP
TMP
I NEVER THOUGHT THE CROWN PRINCE'S TEAM WOULD SURVIVE.
ONII-CHAN!
TMP
TMP
TMP
TMP
?!
"ONII-CHAN"?
LOOK! LOOK! ONII-CHAN TURNED ME INTO TAKERU! ♡
DON'T TALK TO ME HERE, STUPID.
SOMEONE MIGHT BE WATCHING.
You'll expose my plan.
ONII-CHAN?
I TOLD YOU TO MESS WITH THE S.P....
...AND THEY TAMED YOU.
Moron.
...
LET'S GO.
Just stay away from me.
Ballet Performance

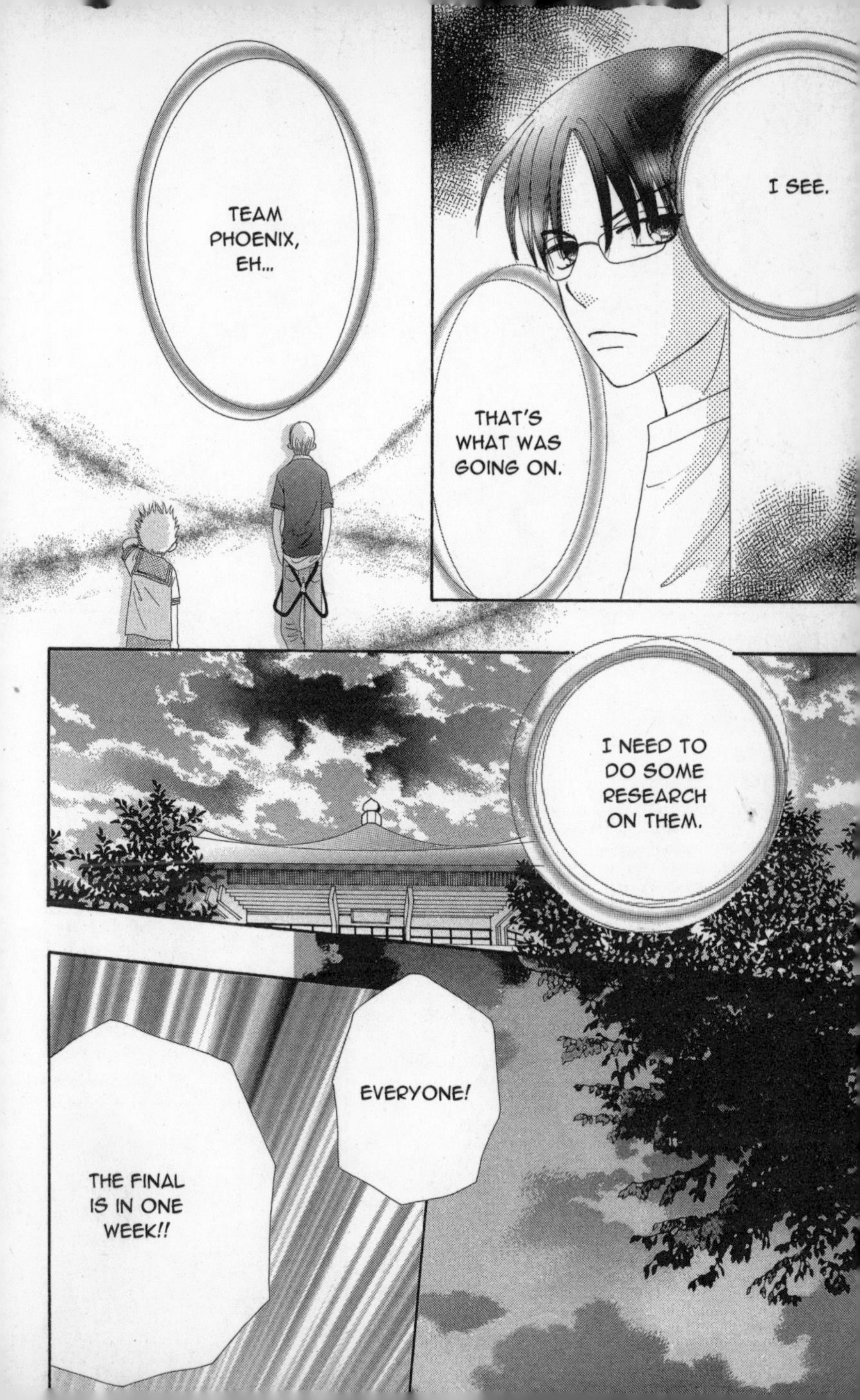
I SEE.
THAT'S WHAT WAS GOING ON.
TEAM PHOENIX, EH...
I NEED TO DO SOME RESEARCH ON THEM.
EVERYONE!
THE FINAL IS IN ONE WEEK!!

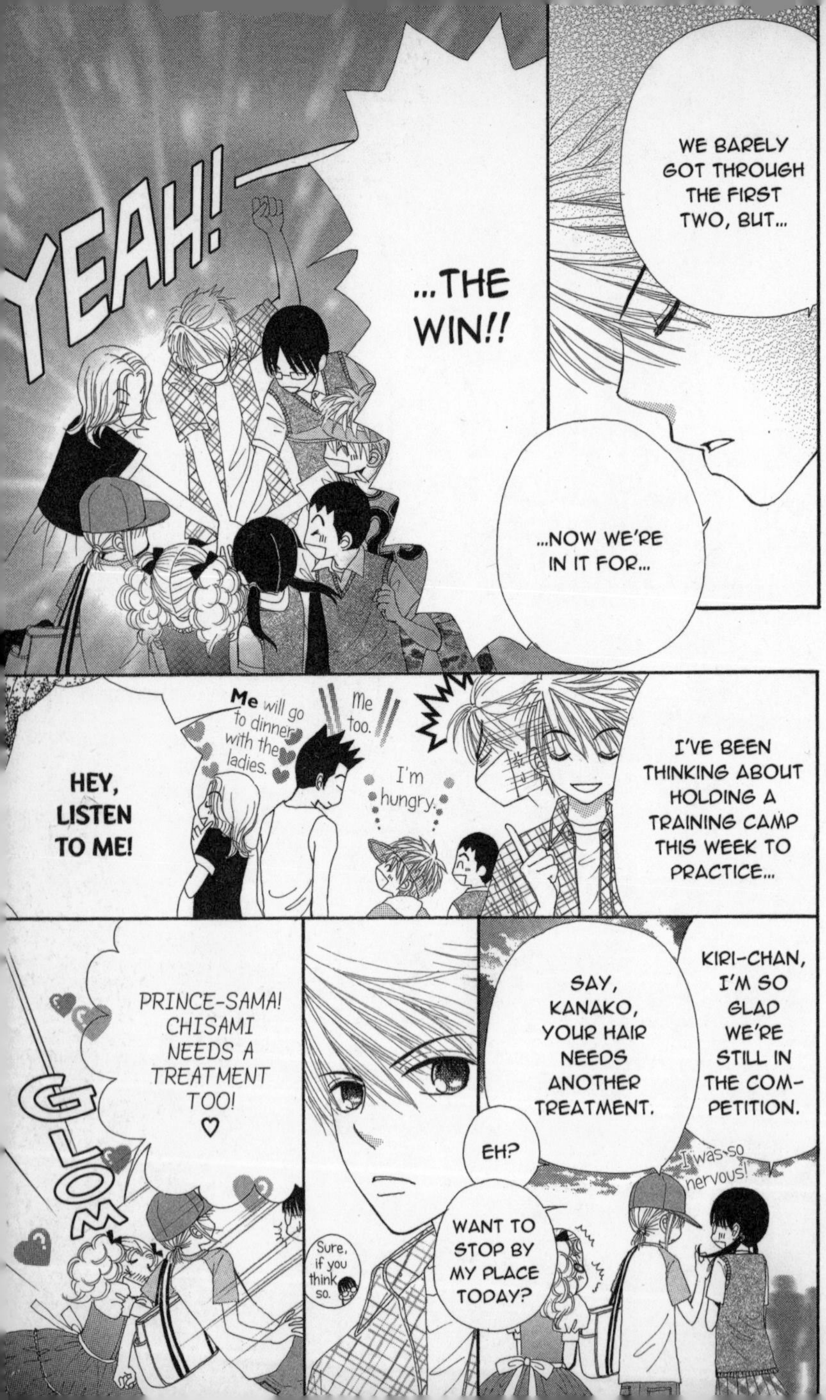
WE BARELY GOT THROUGH THE FIRST TWO, BUT...
...NOW WE'RE IN IT FOR...
...THE WIN!!
YEAH!
I'VE BEEN THINKING ABOUT HOLDING A TRAINING CAMP THIS WEEK TO PRACTICE...
Me too.
I'm hungry.
Me will go to dinner with the ladies.
HEY, LISTEN TO ME!
KIRI-CHAN, I'M SO GLAD WE'RE STILL IN THE COMPETITION.
I was so nervous!
SAY, KANAKO, YOUR HAIR NEEDS ANOTHER TREATMENT.
EH?
WANT TO STOP BY MY PLACE TODAY?
Sure, if you think so.
PRINCE-SAMA! CHISAMI NEEDS A TREATMENT TOO! ♡
GLOM

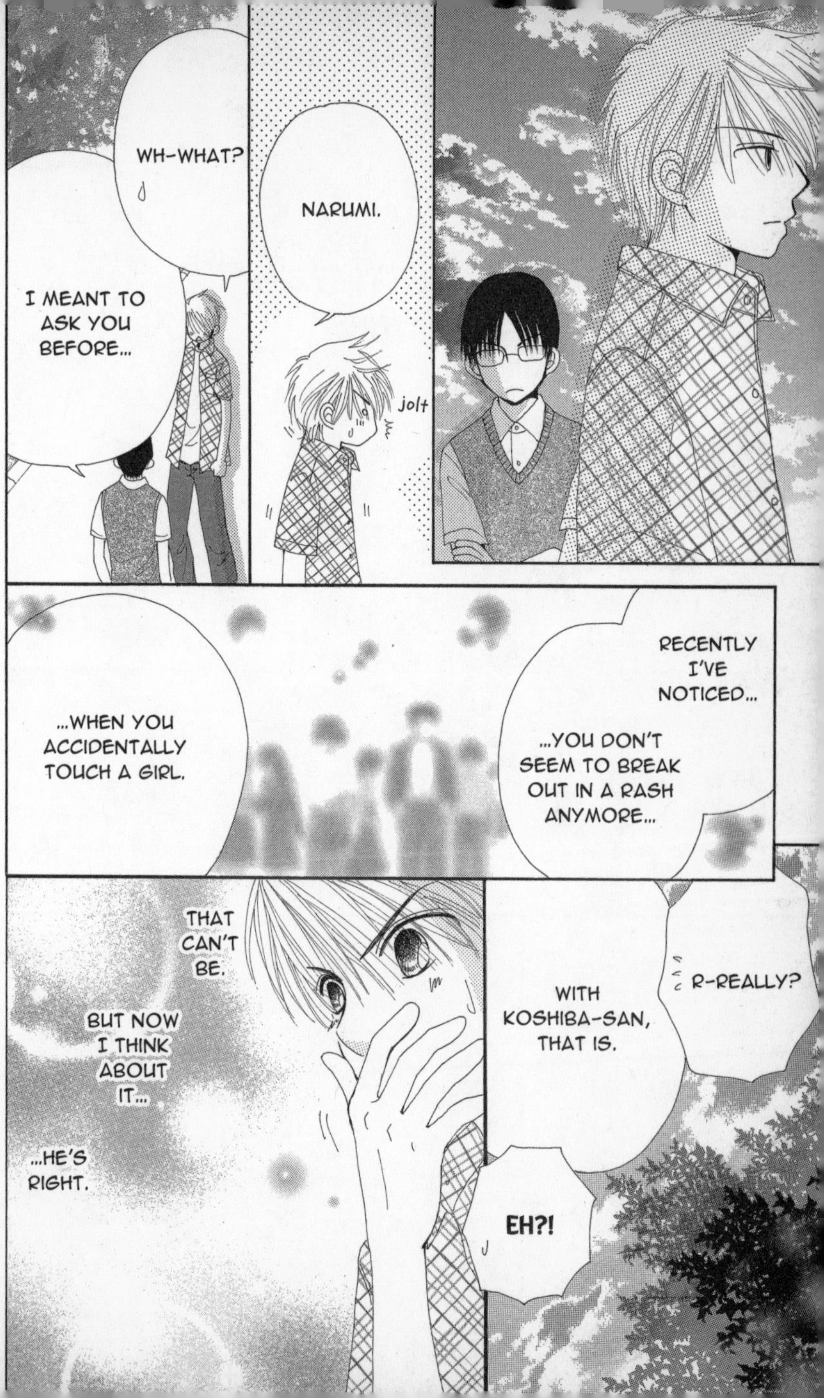
NARUMI.
jolt
WH-WHAT?
I MEANT TO ASK YOU BEFORE...
RECENTLY I'VE NOTICED...
...YOU DON'T SEEM TO BREAK OUT IN A RASH ANYMORE...
...WHEN YOU ACCIDENTALLY TOUCH A GIRL.
R-REALLY?
WITH KOSHIBA-SAN, THAT IS.
EH?!
THAT CAN'T BE.
BUT NOW I THINK ABOUT IT...
...HE'S RIGHT.

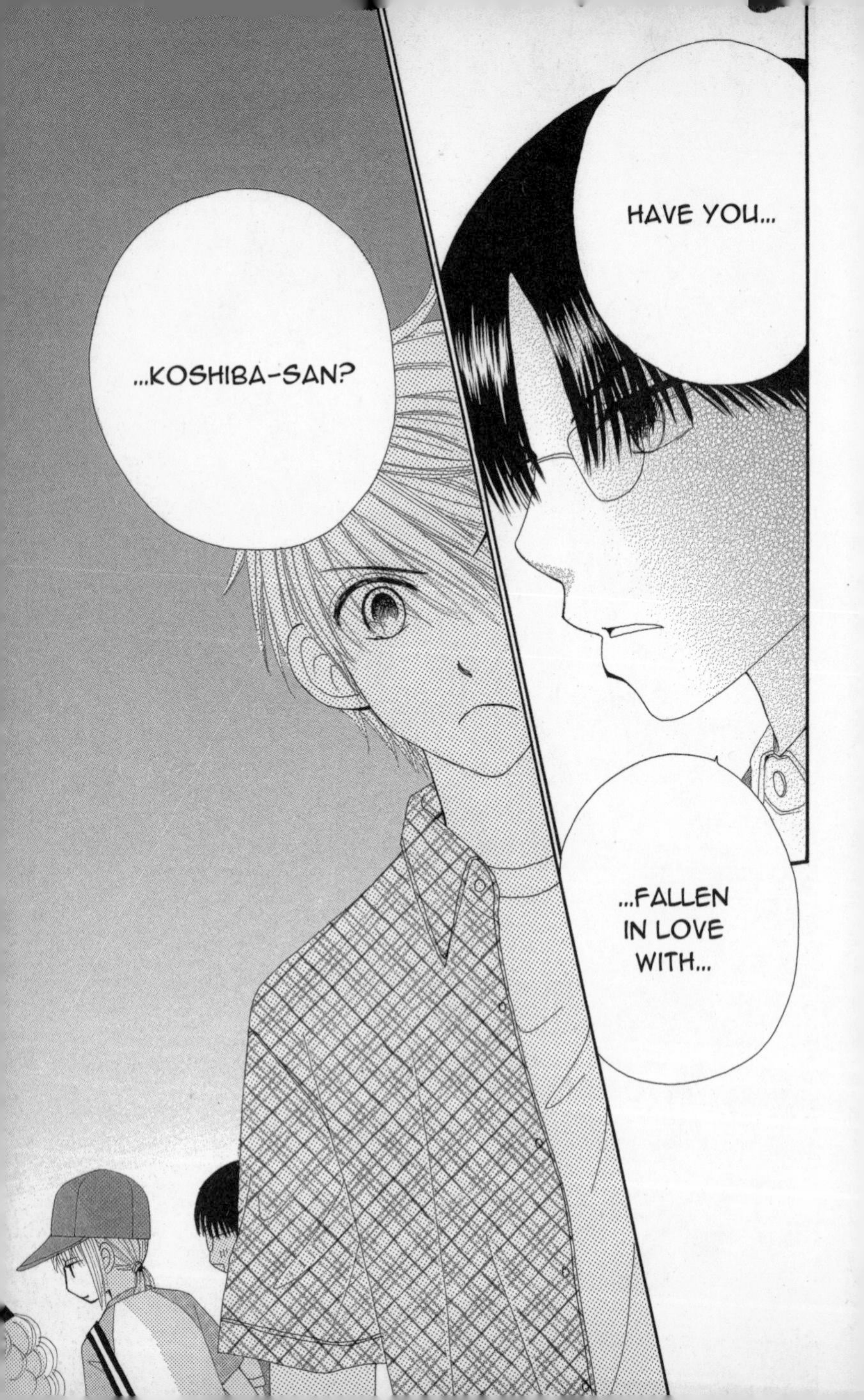
HAVE YOU...
...FALLEN IN LOVE WITH...
...KOSHIBA-SAN?

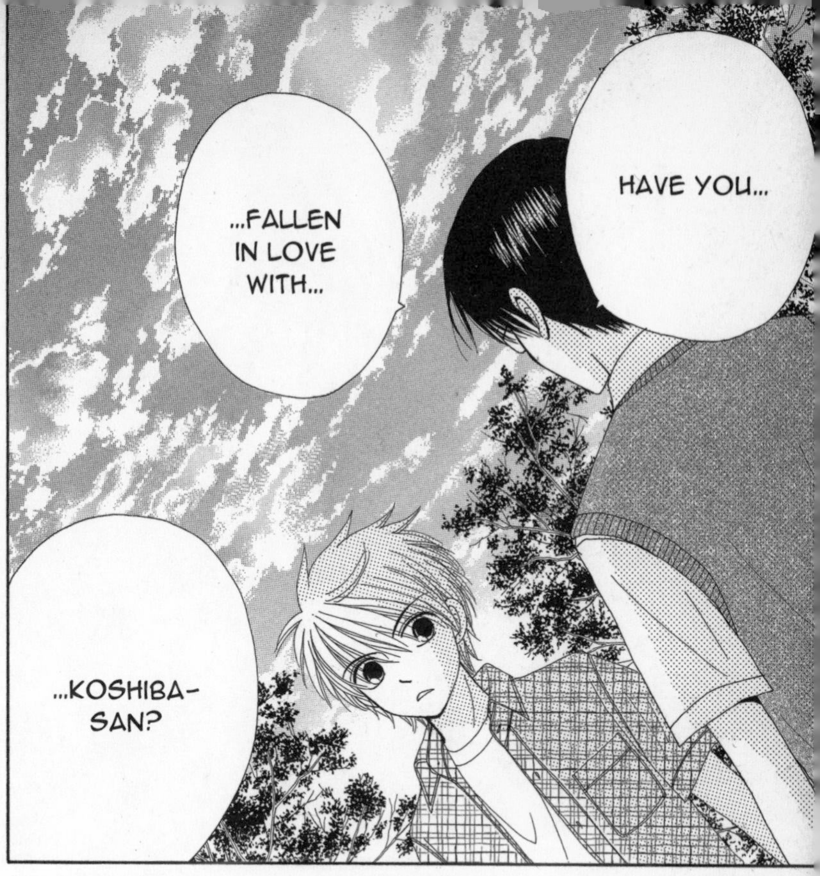
HAVE YOU...
...FALLEN IN LOVE WITH...
...KOSHIBA-SAN?

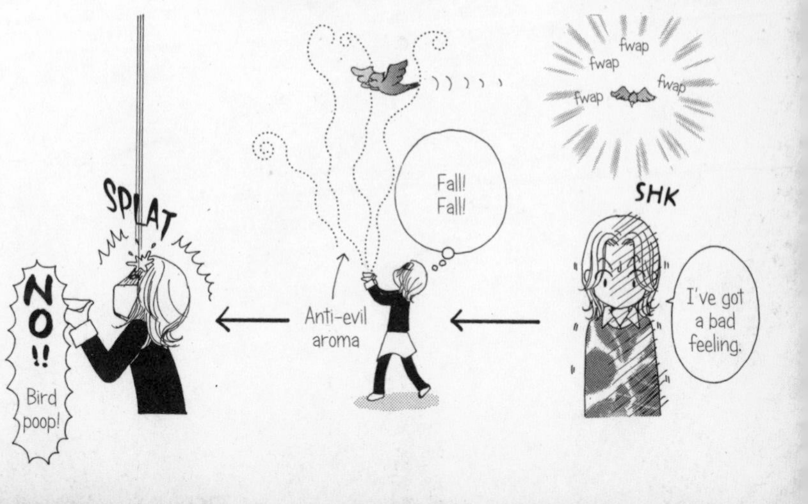
fwap fwap fwap fwap
SHK
I've got a bad feeling.
Fall! Fall!
Anti-evil aroma
SPLAT
NO!!
Bird poop!

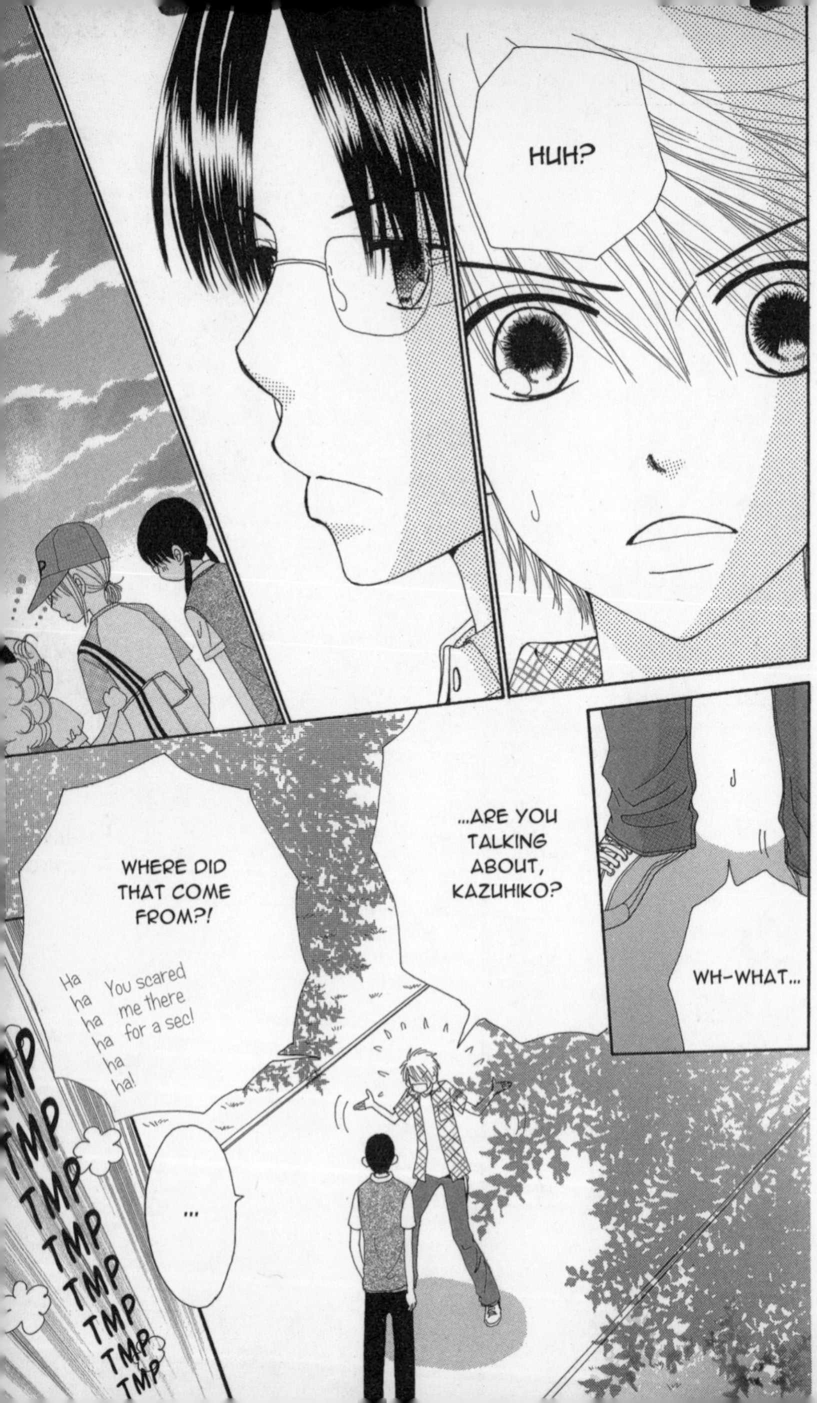
HUH?
WH-WHAT...
...ARE YOU TALKING ABOUT, KAZUHIKO?
WHERE DID THAT COME FROM?!
Ha ha ha ha ha ha! You scared me there for a sec!
...
TMP TMP TMP TMP TMP TMP TMP TMP TMP TMP

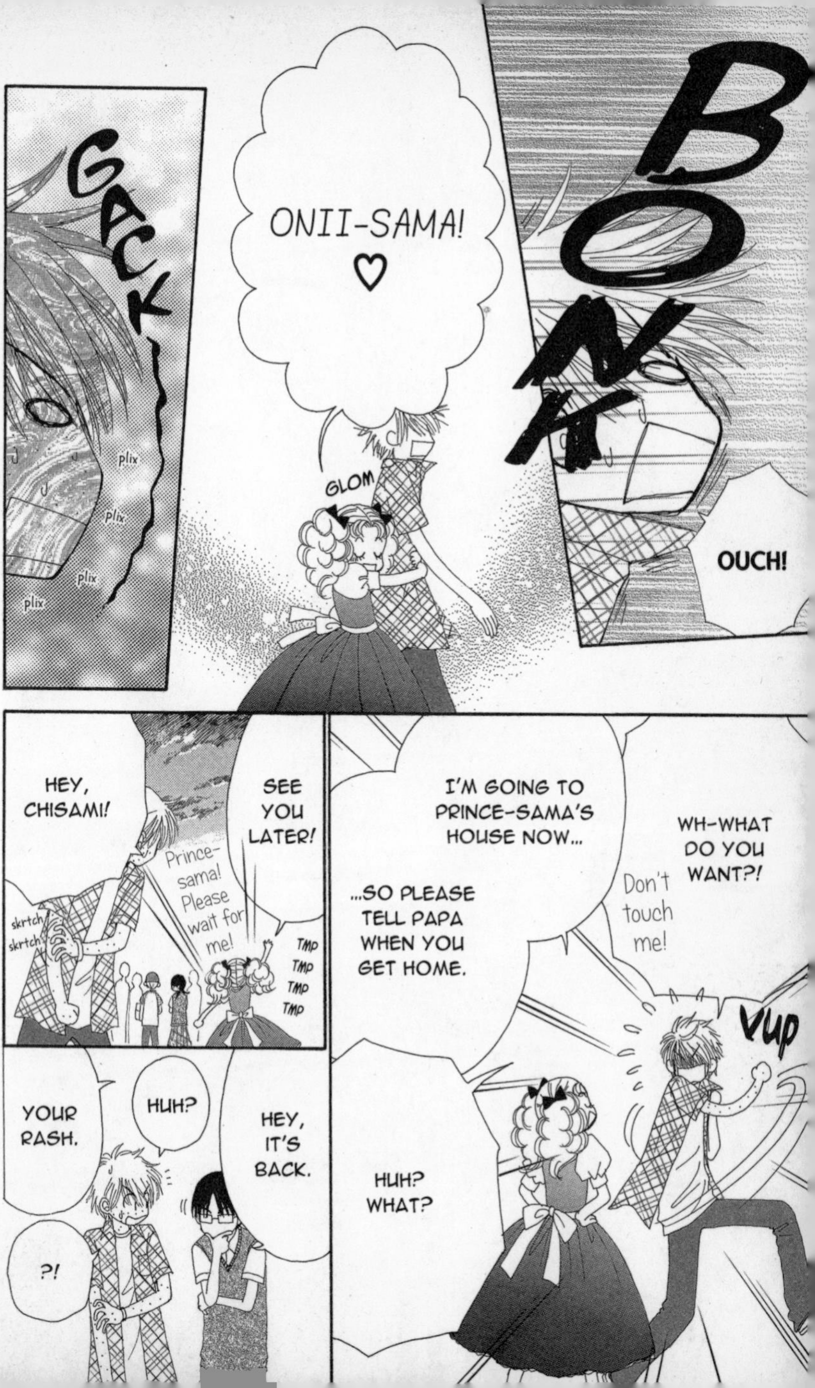
BONK
OUCH!
ONII-SAMA! ♥
GLOM
GACK
plix
plix
plix
plix
WH-WHAT DO YOU WANT?!
Don't touch me!
VUP
I'M GOING TO PRINCE-SAMA'S HOUSE NOW...
...SO PLEASE TELL PAPA WHEN YOU GET HOME.
HUH? WHAT?
SEE YOU LATER!
Prince-sama! Please wait for me!
TMP TMP TMP TMP
HEY, CHISAMI!
skrtch skrtch
HEY, IT'S BACK.
HUH?
YOUR RASH.
?!

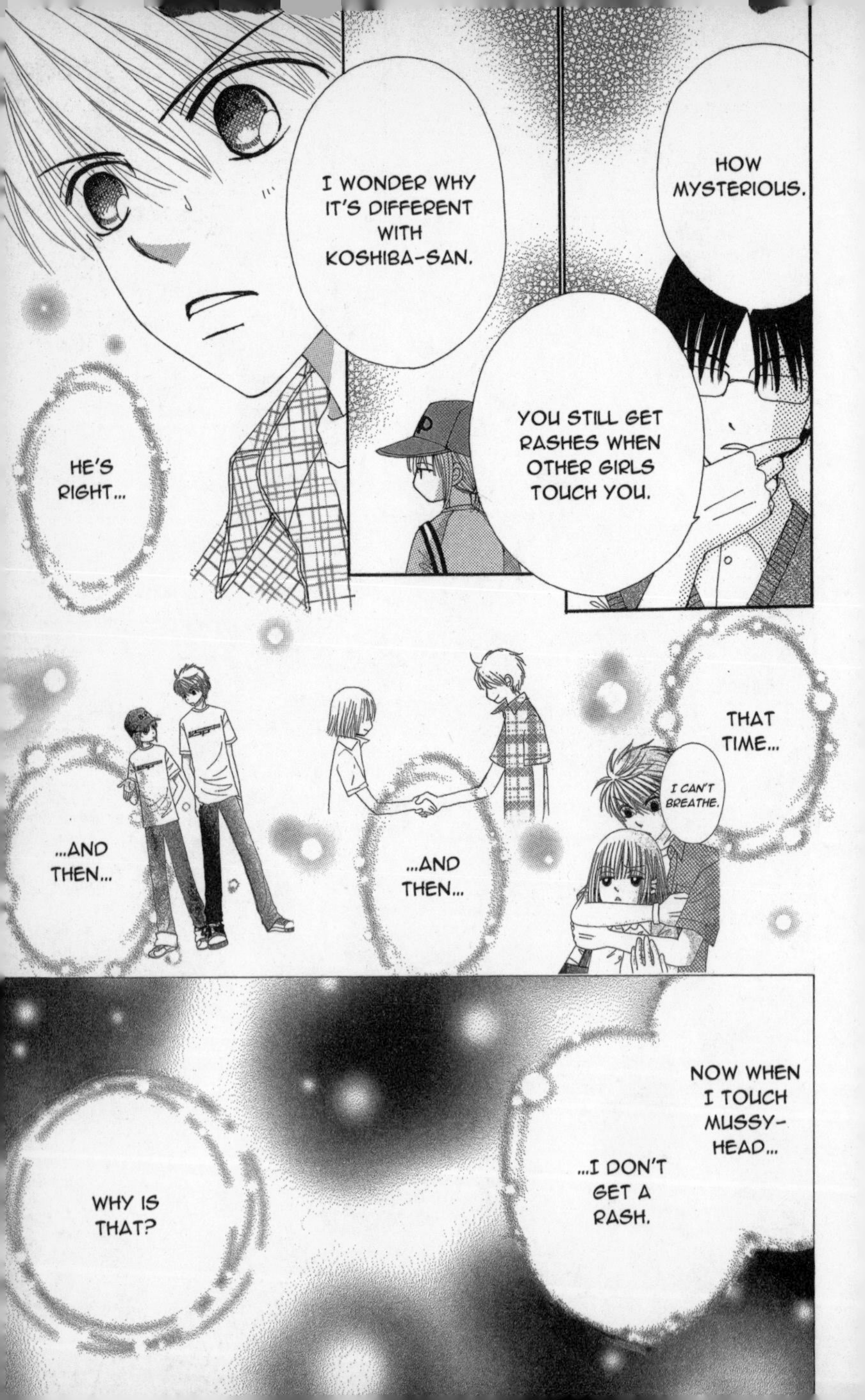
HOW MYSTERIOUS.
YOU STILL GET RASHES WHEN OTHER GIRLS TOUCH YOU.
I WONDER WHY IT'S DIFFERENT WITH KOSHIBA-SAN.
HE'S RIGHT...
THAT TIME...
I CAN'T BREATHE.
...AND THEN...
...AND THEN...
NOW WHEN I TOUCH MUSSY-HEAD...
...I DON'T GET A RASH.
WHY IS THAT?

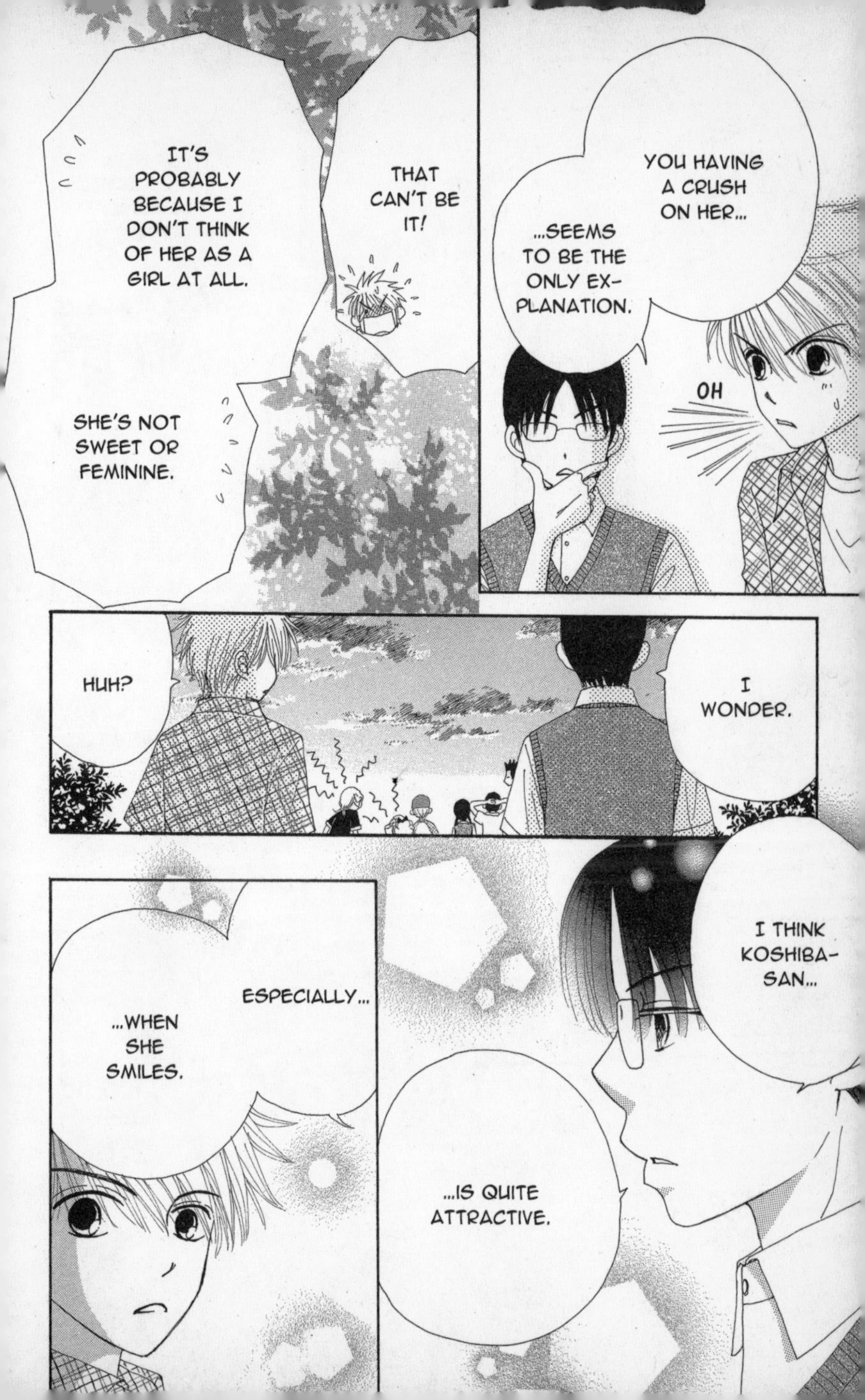
YOU HAVING A CRUSH ON HER...
...SEEMS TO BE THE ONLY EX-PLANATION.
OH
THAT CAN'T BE IT!
IT'S PROBABLY BECAUSE I DON'T THINK OF HER AS A GIRL AT ALL.
SHE'S NOT SWEET OR FEMININE.
I WONDER.
HUH?
I THINK KOSHIBA-SAN...
...IS QUITE ATTRACTIVE.
ESPECIALLY...
...WHEN SHE SMILES.

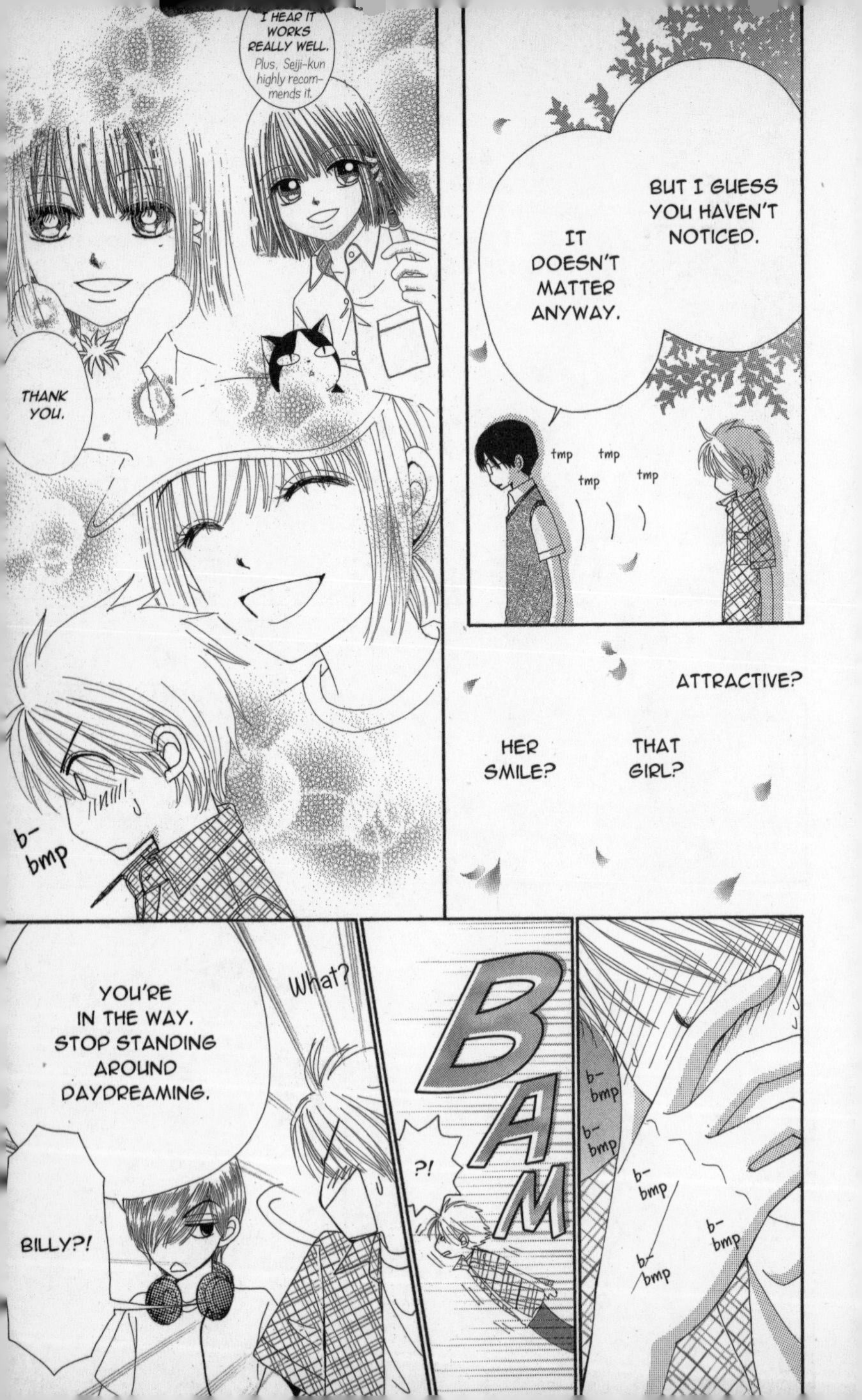
BUT I GUESS YOU HAVEN'T NOTICED.
IT DOESN'T MATTER ANYWAY.
tmp tmp
tmp tmp
ATTRACTIVE?
THAT GIRL?
HER SMILE?
I HEAR IT WORKS REALLY WELL. Plus, Seiji-kun highly recommends it.
THANK YOU.
b-bmp
b-bmp
b-bmp
b-bmp
b-bmp
b-bmp
BAM
?!
What?
YOU'RE IN THE WAY. STOP STANDING AROUND DAYDREAMING.
BILLY?!

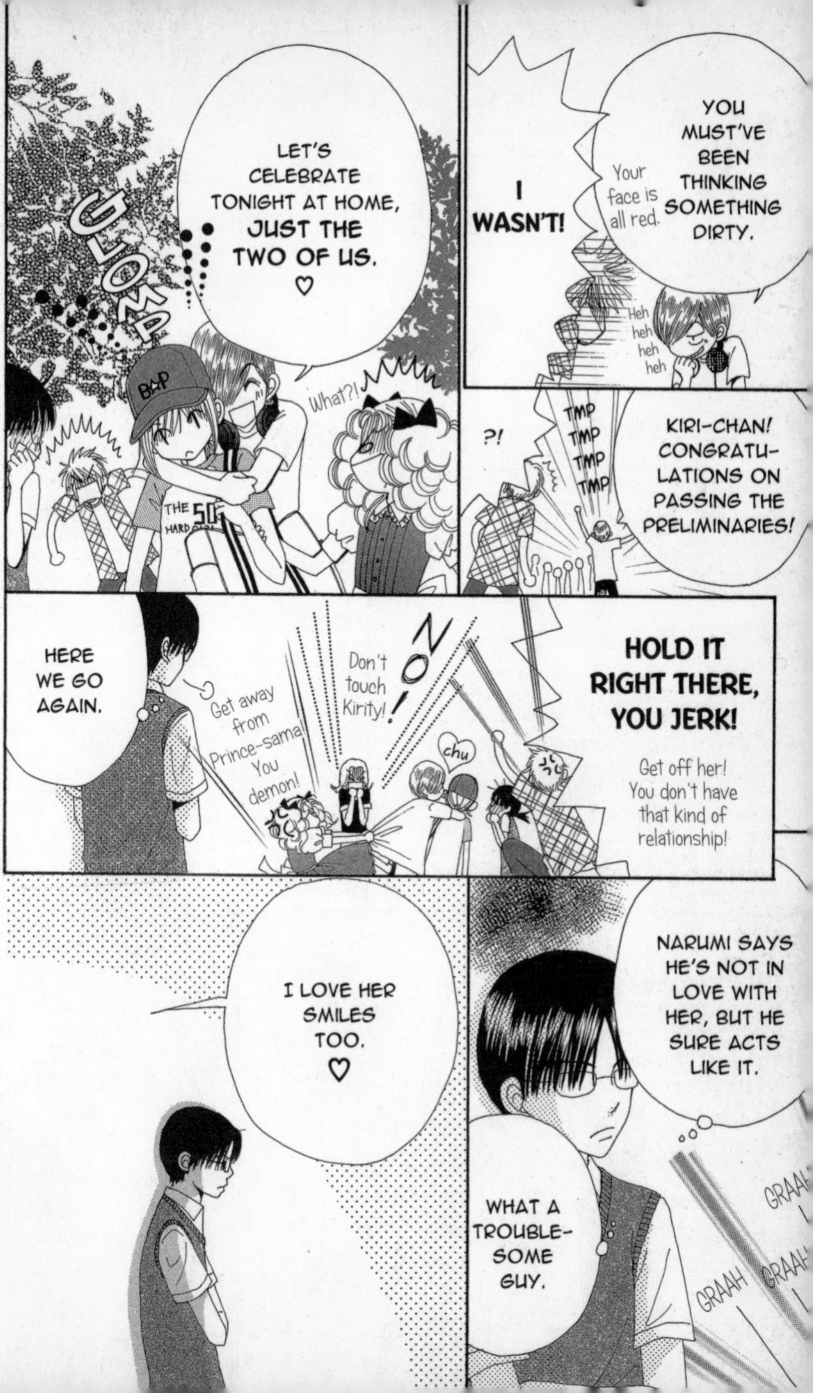
YOU MUST'VE BEEN THINKING SOMETHING DIRTY.
Your face is all red.
I WASN'T!
Heh heh heh heh
KIRI-CHAN! CONGRATU-LATIONS ON PASSING THE PRELIMINARIES!
TMP TMP TMP TMP
?!
LET'S CELEBRATE TONIGHT AT HOME, JUST THE TWO OF US. ♡
GLOMP
What?!
HOLD IT RIGHT THERE, YOU JERK!
Get off her! You don't have that kind of relationship!
chu
NO!
Don't touch Kirity!
Get away from Prince-sama! You demon!
HERE WE GO AGAIN.
NARUMI SAYS HE'S NOT IN LOVE WITH HER, BUT HE SURE ACTS LIKE IT.
WHAT A TROUBLE-SOME GUY.
GRAAH GRAAH GRAAH
I LOVE HER SMILES TOO. ♡

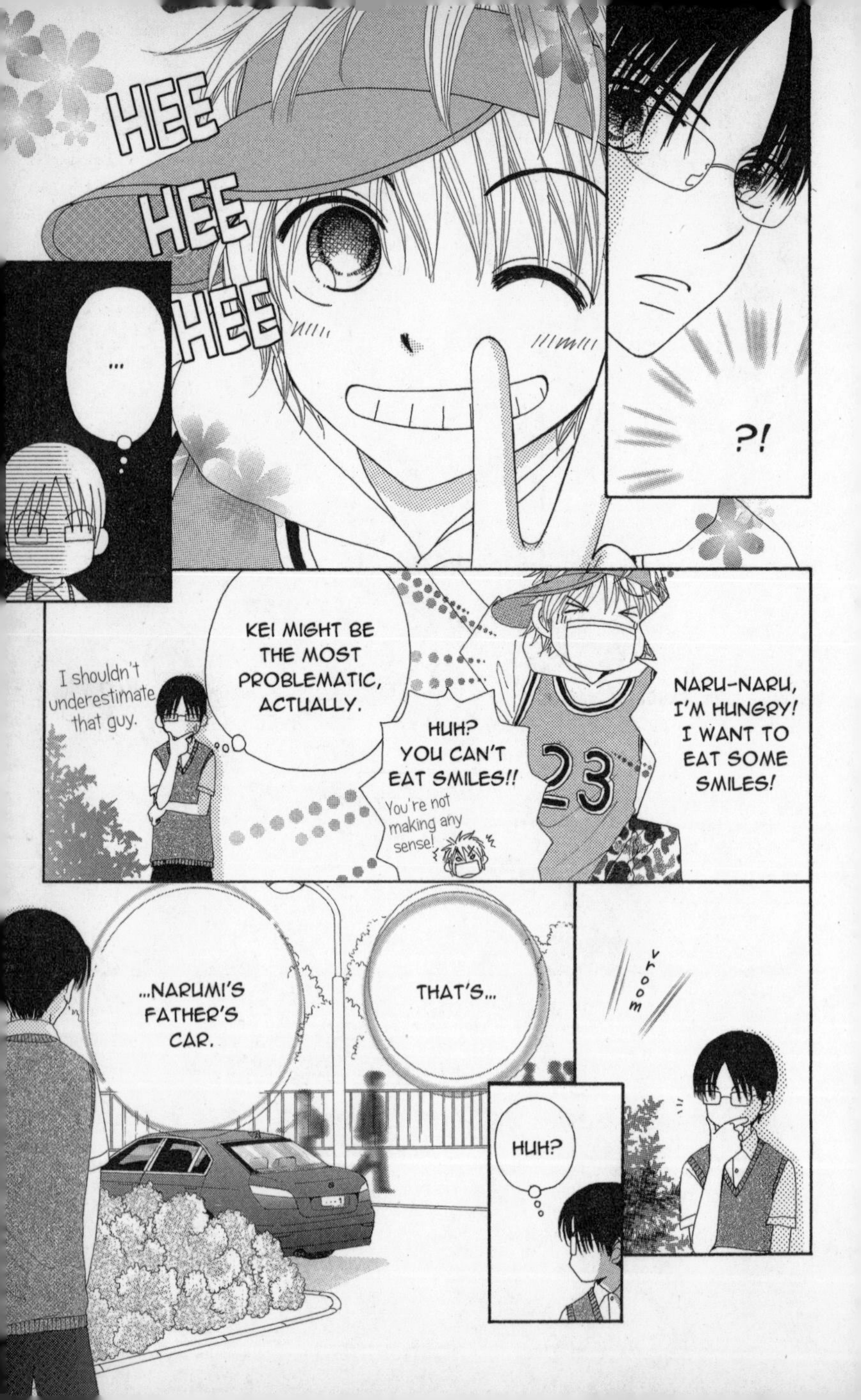
?!
HEE HEE HEE
...
NARU-NARU, I'M HUNGRY! I WANT TO EAT SOME SMILES!
HUH? YOU CAN'T EAT SMILES!!
You're not making any sense!
KEI MIGHT BE THE MOST PROBLEMATIC, ACTUALLY.
I shouldn't underestimate that guy.
vroom
HUH?
THAT'S...
...NARUMI'S FATHER'S CAR.

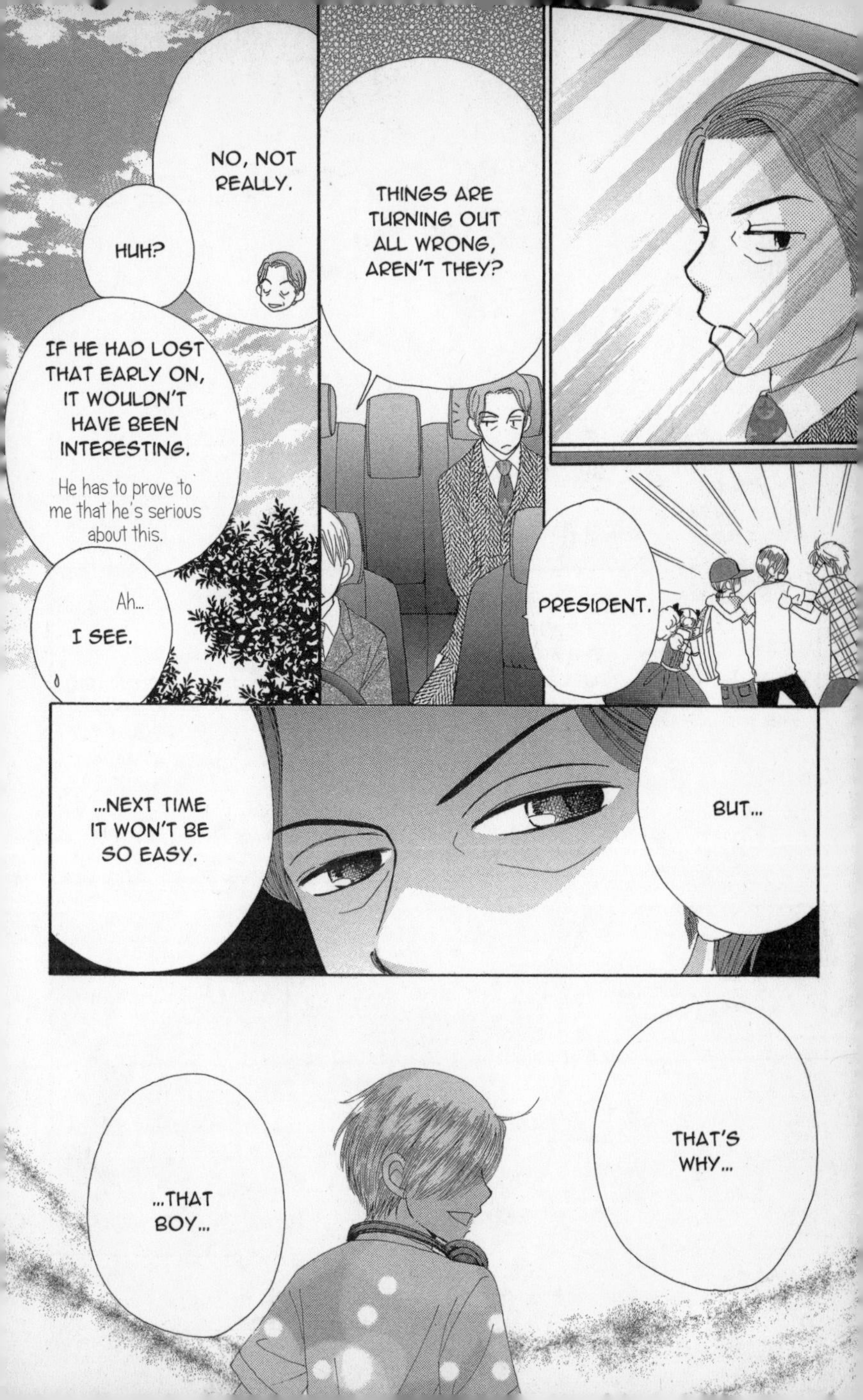
PRESIDENT.
THINGS ARE TURNING OUT ALL WRONG, AREN'T THEY?
NO, NOT REALLY.
HUH?
IF HE HAD LOST THAT EARLY ON, IT WOULDN'T HAVE BEEN INTERESTING.
He has to prove to me that he's serious about this.
Ah... I SEE.
BUT...
...NEXT TIME IT WON'T BE SO EASY.
THAT'S WHY...
...THAT BOY...

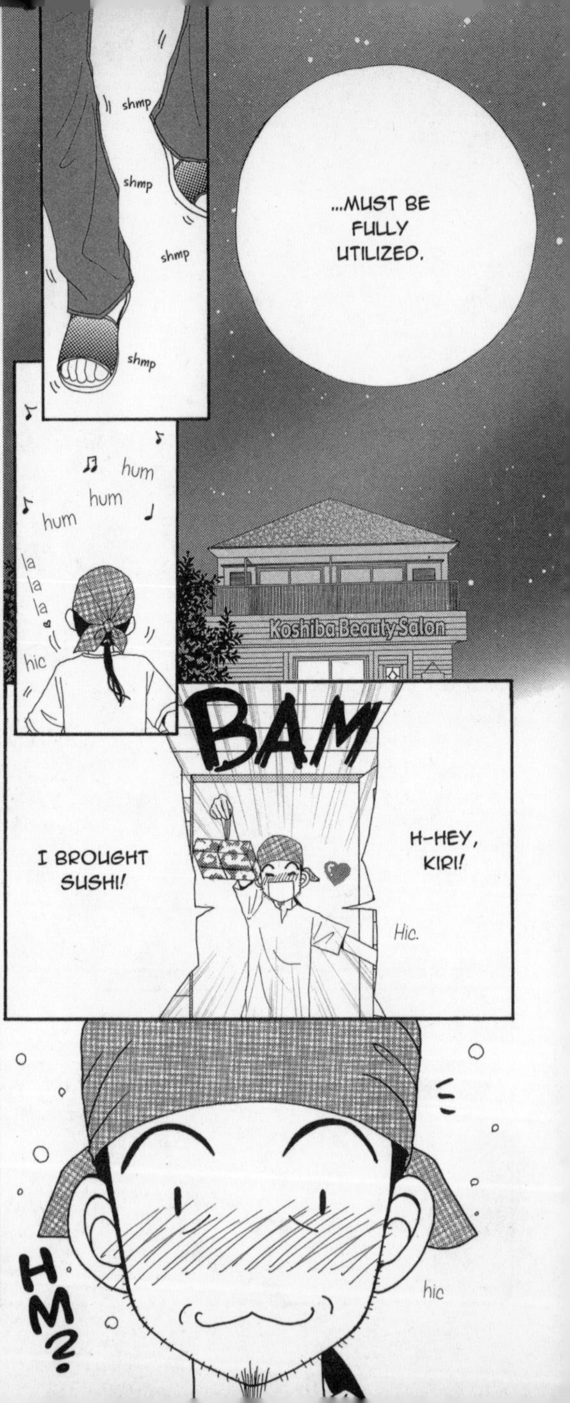
...MUST BE FULLY UTILIZED.
shmp
shmp
shmp
shmp
hum
hum
hum
la
la
la
hic
BAM
H-HEY, KIRI!
I BROUGHT SUSHI!
Hic.
hic
HM?

K's Club Talk

The night before a deadline, as the morning approaches, sleepiness begins to attack. (I should just sleep, but you know, the deadline situation is usually pretty bad, so...) At times like this, we keep ourselves awake by telling scary stories. Everyone gets wrapped up in talking about things that have happened to them, and we are instantly revived. But afterwards, we're too scared to go to the bathroom alone...

One time, the talk turned to the old studio we used before we moved to our current location. Then, at the exact same time, two of my assistants said, "Somehow my eyes would always go to a certain spot in that creepy room!" Thinking about it now, my assistants got sick all the time back then. And we often had to replace assistants too...

Their eyes were always drawn to this spot in the room, but what was there?!

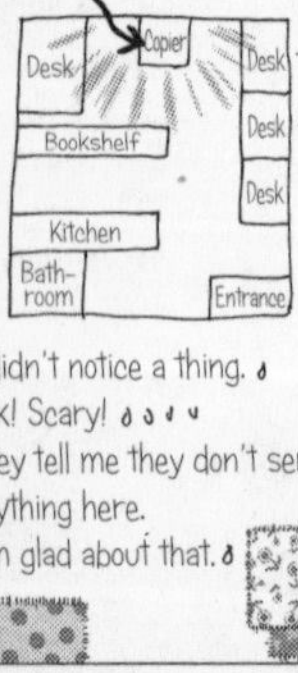
Copier
Desk
Desk
Desk
Desk
Bookshelf
Kitchen
Bath-room
Entrance

Eek!

I didn't notice a thing.
Eek! Scary!
They tell me they don't sense anything here.
I'm glad about that.

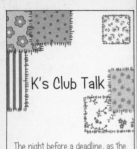

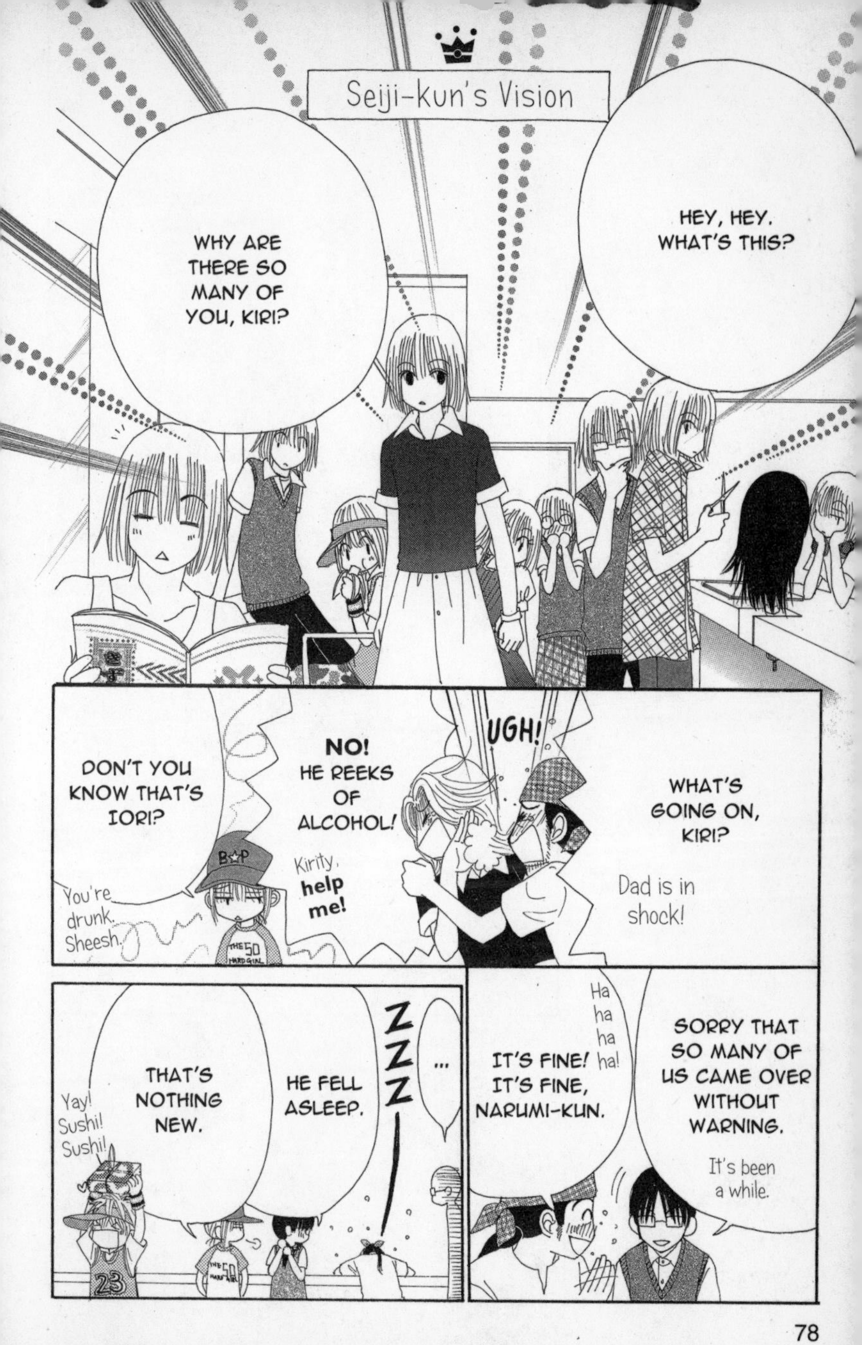

Seiji-kun's Vision
HEY, HEY. WHAT'S THIS?
WHY ARE THERE SO MANY OF YOU, KIRI?
WHAT'S GOING ON, KIRI?
Dad is in shock!
UGH!
NO! HE REEKS OF ALCOHOL!
Kirity, help me!
DON'T YOU KNOW THAT'S IORI?
You're drunk. Sheesh.
SORRY THAT SO MANY OF US CAME OVER WITHOUT WARNING.
It's been a while.
IT'S FINE! IT'S FINE, NARUMI-KUN.
Ha ha ha ha!
...
ZZZ
HE FELL ASLEEP.
THAT'S NOTHING NEW.
Yay! Sushi! Sushi!

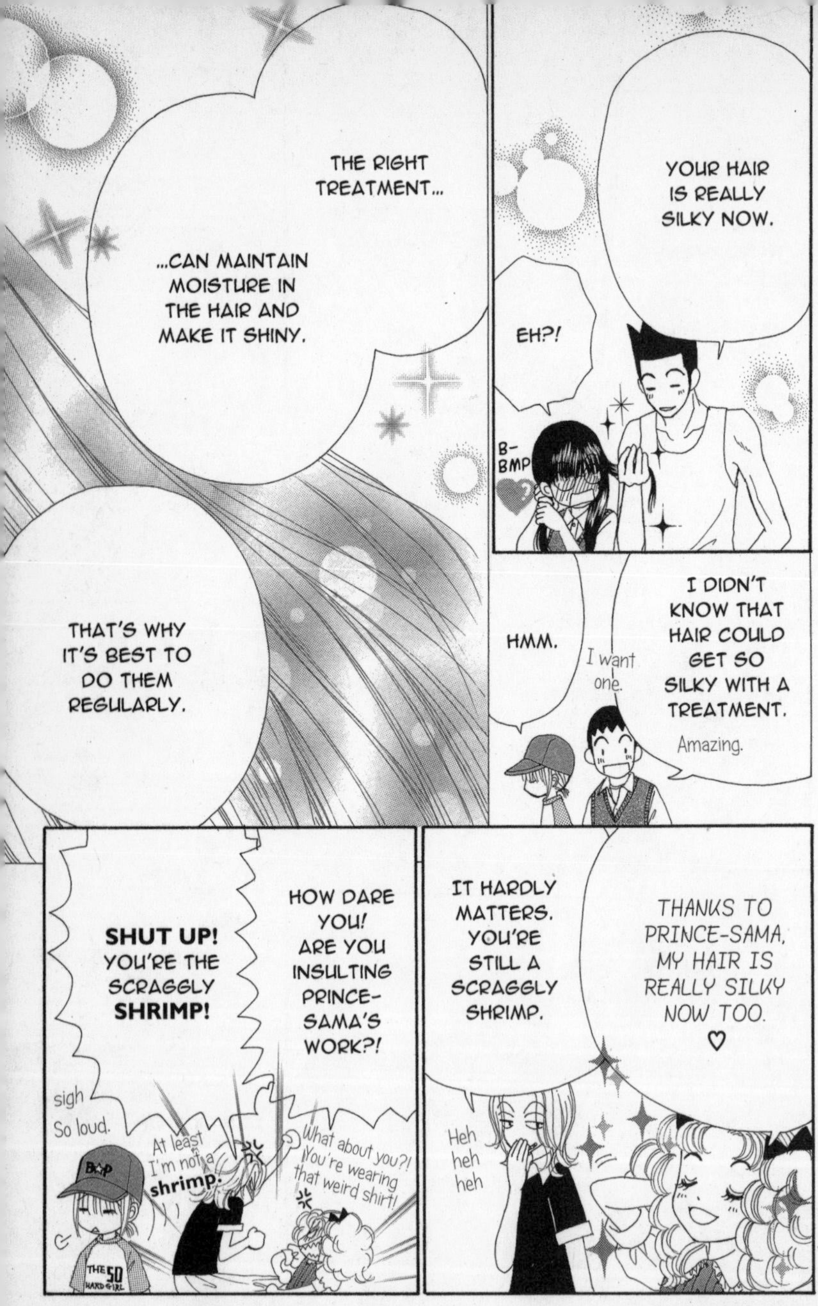
YOUR HAIR IS REALLY SILKY NOW.
EH?!
B-BMP
I DIDN'T KNOW THAT HAIR COULD GET SO SILKY WITH A TREATMENT.
Amazing.
HMM.
I want one.
THE RIGHT TREATMENT...
...CAN MAINTAIN MOISTURE IN THE HAIR AND MAKE IT SHINY.
THAT'S WHY IT'S BEST TO DO THEM REGULARLY.
THANKS TO PRINCE-SAMA, MY HAIR IS REALLY SILKY NOW TOO. ♡
IT HARDLY MATTERS. YOU'RE STILL A SCRAGGLY SHRIMP.
Heh heh heh
HOW DARE YOU! ARE YOU INSULTING PRINCE-SAMA'S WORK?!
SHUT UP! YOU'RE THE SCRAGGLY **SHRIMP!**
What about you?! You're wearing that weird shirt!
At least I'm not a **shrimp**.
sigh
So loud.

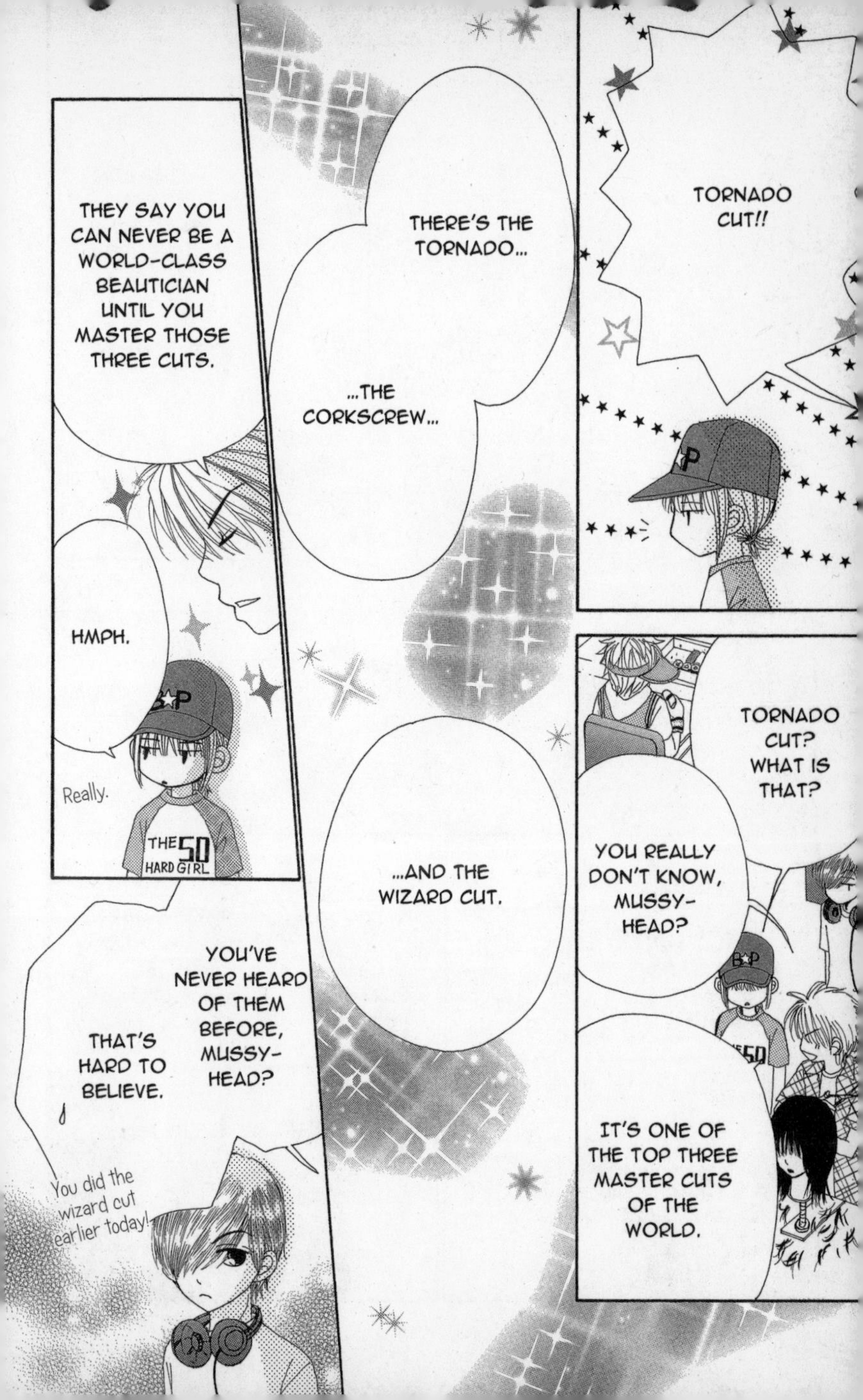
TORNADO CUT!!
TORNADO CUT? WHAT IS THAT?
YOU REALLY DON'T KNOW, MUSSY-HEAD?
IT'S ONE OF THE TOP THREE MASTER CUTS OF THE WORLD.
THERE'S THE TORNADO...
...THE CORKSCREW...
...AND THE WIZARD CUT.
THEY SAY YOU CAN NEVER BE A WORLD-CLASS BEAUTICIAN UNTIL YOU MASTER THOSE THREE CUTS.
HMPH.
Really.
THE 50 HARD GIRL
YOU'VE NEVER HEARD OF THEM BEFORE, MUSSY-HEAD?
THAT'S HARD TO BELIEVE.
You did the wizard cut earlier today!

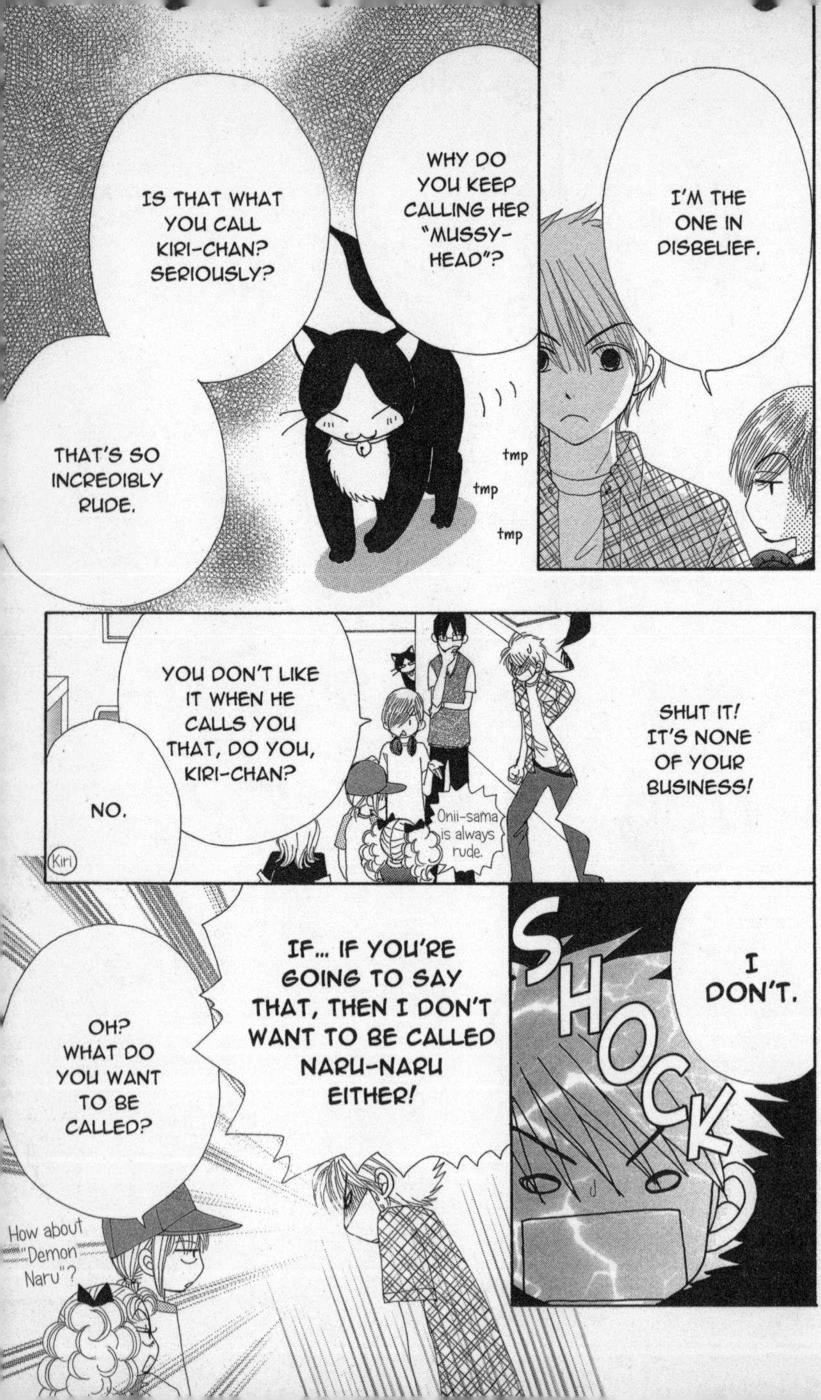
I'M THE ONE IN DISBELIEF.
WHY DO YOU KEEP CALLING HER "MUSSY-HEAD"?
IS THAT WHAT YOU CALL KIRI-CHAN? SERIOUSLY?
tmp
tmp
tmp
THAT'S SO INCREDIBLY RUDE.
SHUT IT! IT'S NONE OF YOUR BUSINESS!
Onii-sama is always rude.
YOU DON'T LIKE IT WHEN HE CALLS YOU THAT, DO YOU, KIRI-CHAN?
NO.
Kiri
I DON'T.
SHOCK
IF... IF YOU'RE GOING TO SAY THAT, THEN I DON'T WANT TO BE CALLED NARU-NARU EITHER!
OH? WHAT DO YOU WANT TO BE CALLED?
How about "Demon Naru"?

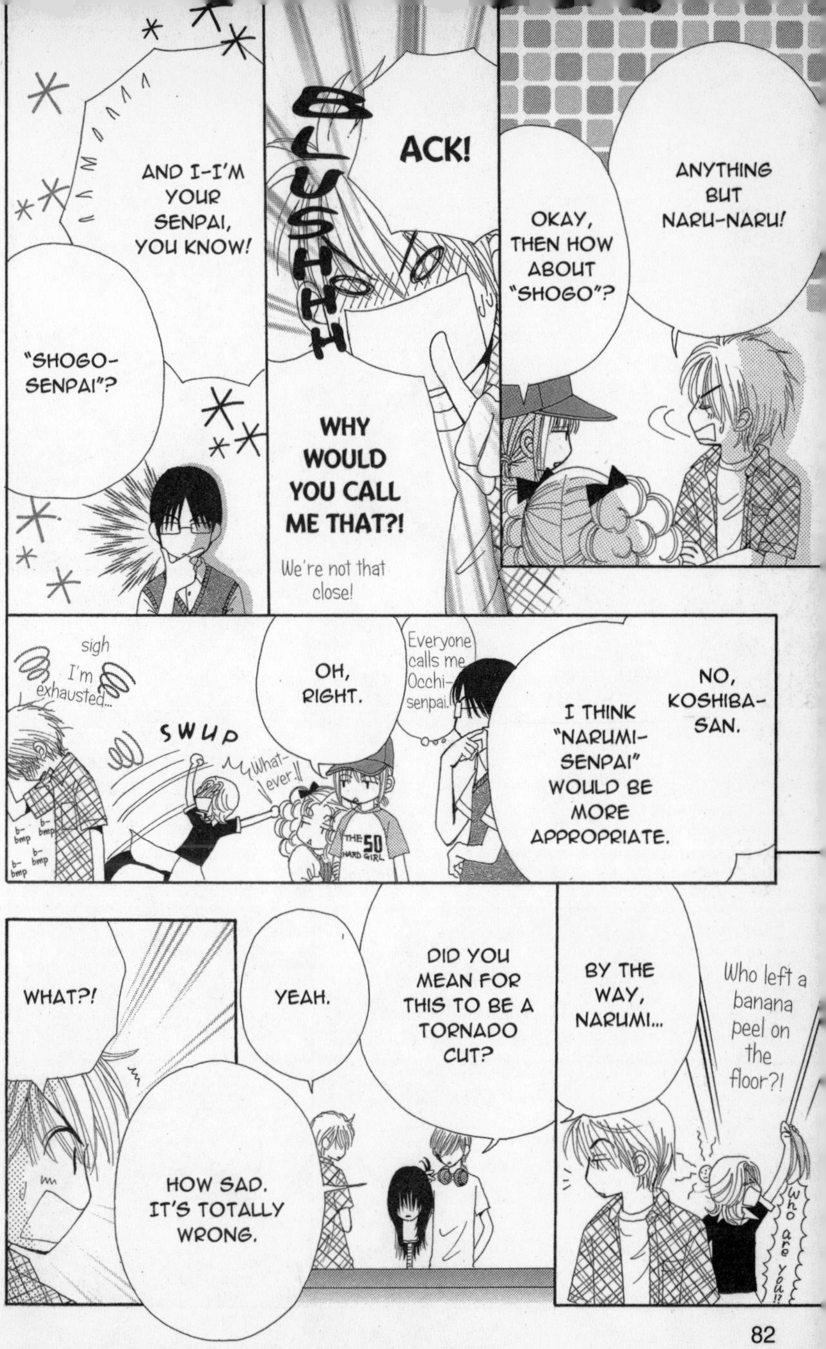
ANYTHING BUT NARU-NARU!
OKAY, THEN HOW ABOUT "SHOGO"?
BLUSHHH
ACK!
WHY WOULD YOU CALL ME THAT?!
We're not that close!
AND I-I'M YOUR SENPAI, YOU KNOW!
"SHOGO-SENPAI"?
NO, KOSHIBA-SAN.
I THINK "NARUMI-SENPAI" WOULD BE MORE APPROPRIATE.
Everyone calls me Occhi-senpai.
OH, RIGHT.
Whatever!!
SWUP
sigh
I'm exhausted...
b-bmp b-bmp
b-bmp b-bmp
Who left a banana peel on the floor?!
Who are you!?
BY THE WAY, NARUMI...
DID YOU MEAN FOR THIS TO BE A TORNADO CUT?
YEAH.
HOW SAD. IT'S TOTALLY WRONG.
WHAT?!

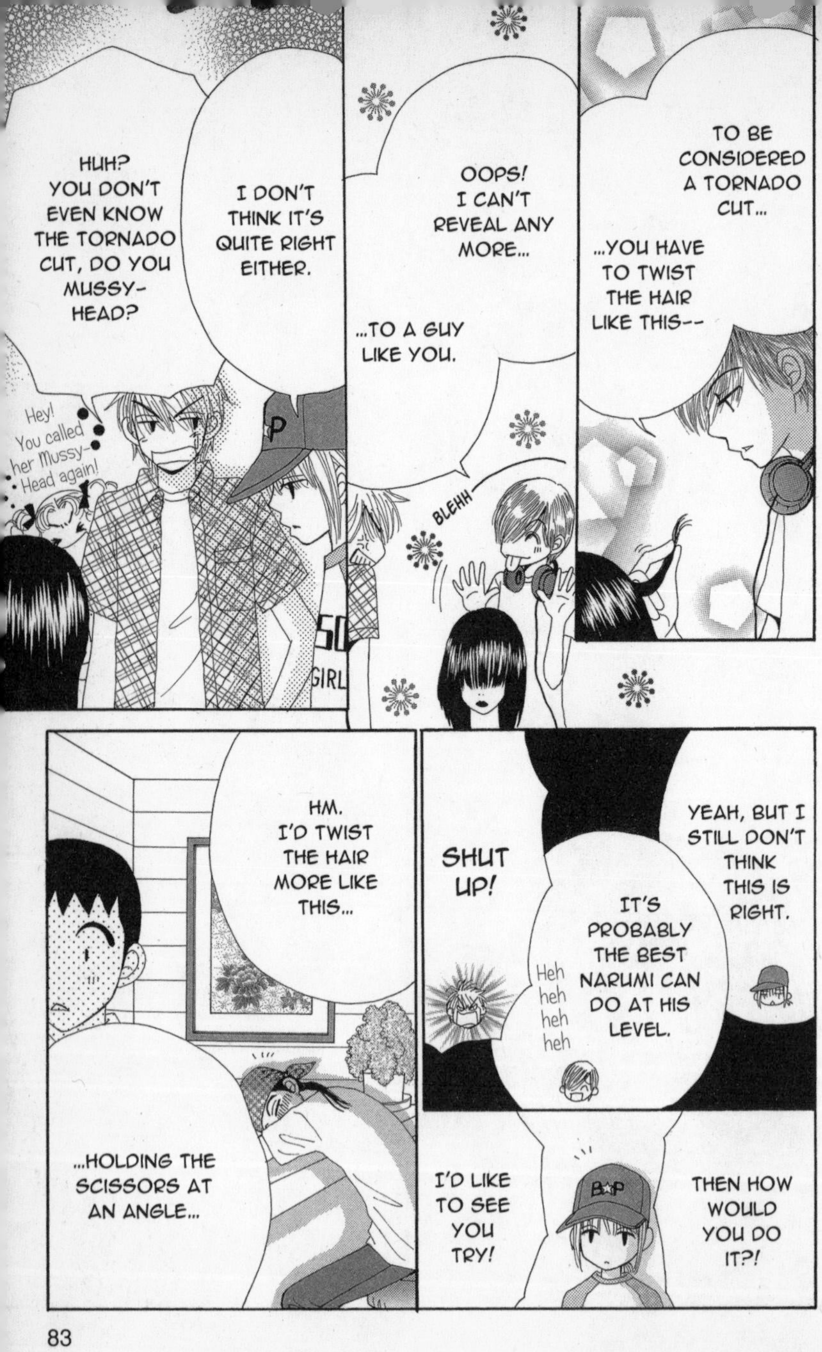
TO BE CONSIDERED A TORNADO CUT...
...YOU HAVE TO TWIST THE HAIR LIKE THIS--
OOPS! I CAN'T REVEAL ANY MORE...
...TO A GUY LIKE YOU.
BLEHH
I DON'T THINK IT'S QUITE RIGHT EITHER.
HUH? YOU DON'T EVEN KNOW THE TORNADO CUT, DO YOU MUSSY-HEAD?
Hey! You called her Mussy-Head again!
YEAH, BUT I STILL DON'T THINK THIS IS RIGHT.
IT'S PROBABLY THE BEST NARUMI CAN DO AT HIS LEVEL.
Heh heh heh heh
SHUT UP!
THEN HOW WOULD YOU DO IT?!
I'D LIKE TO SEE YOU TRY!
HM. I'D TWIST THE HAIR MORE LIKE THIS...
...HOLDING THE SCISSORS AT AN ANGLE...

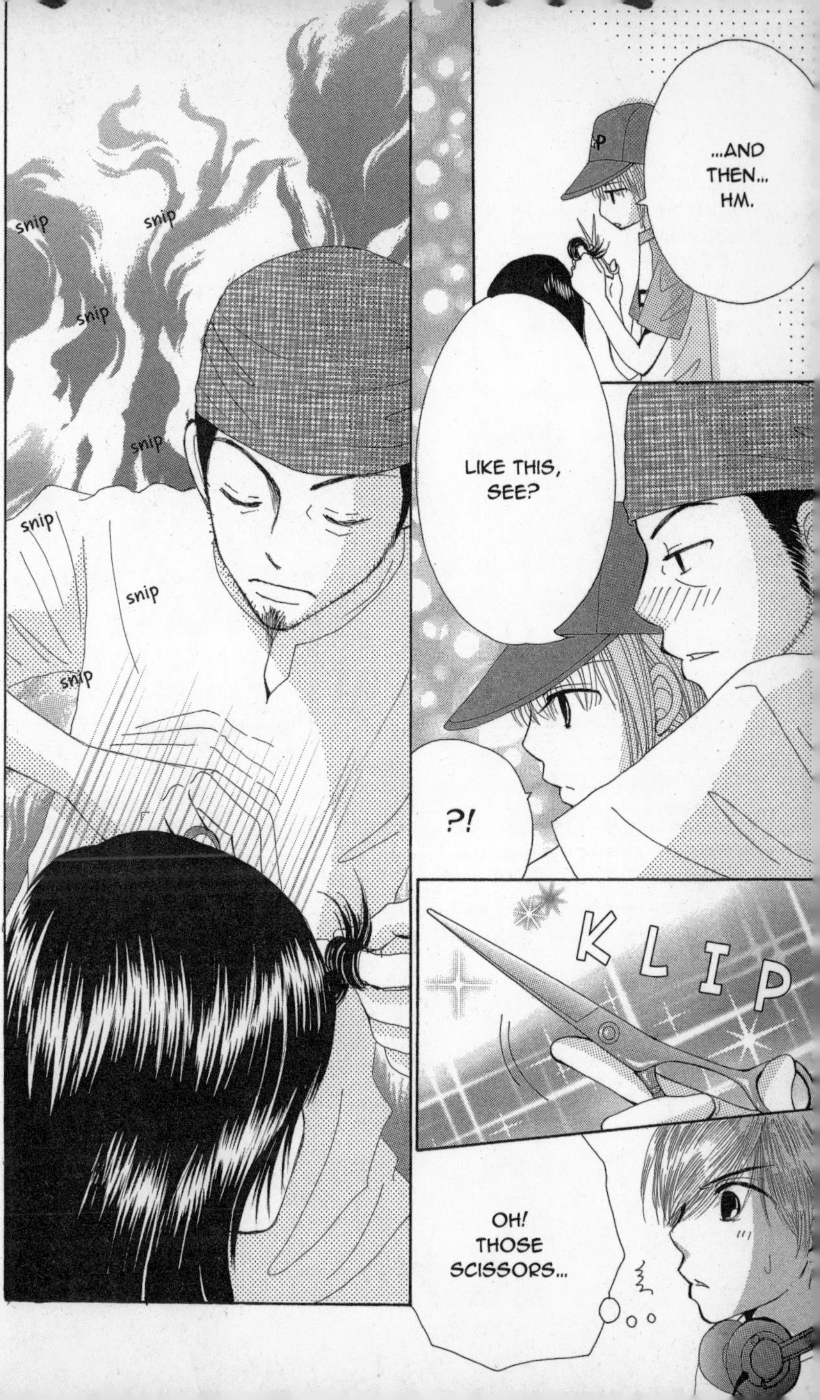
...AND THEN... HM.
LIKE THIS, SEE?
?!
KLIP
OH! THOSE SCISSORS...
snip
snip
snip
snip
snip
snip
snip

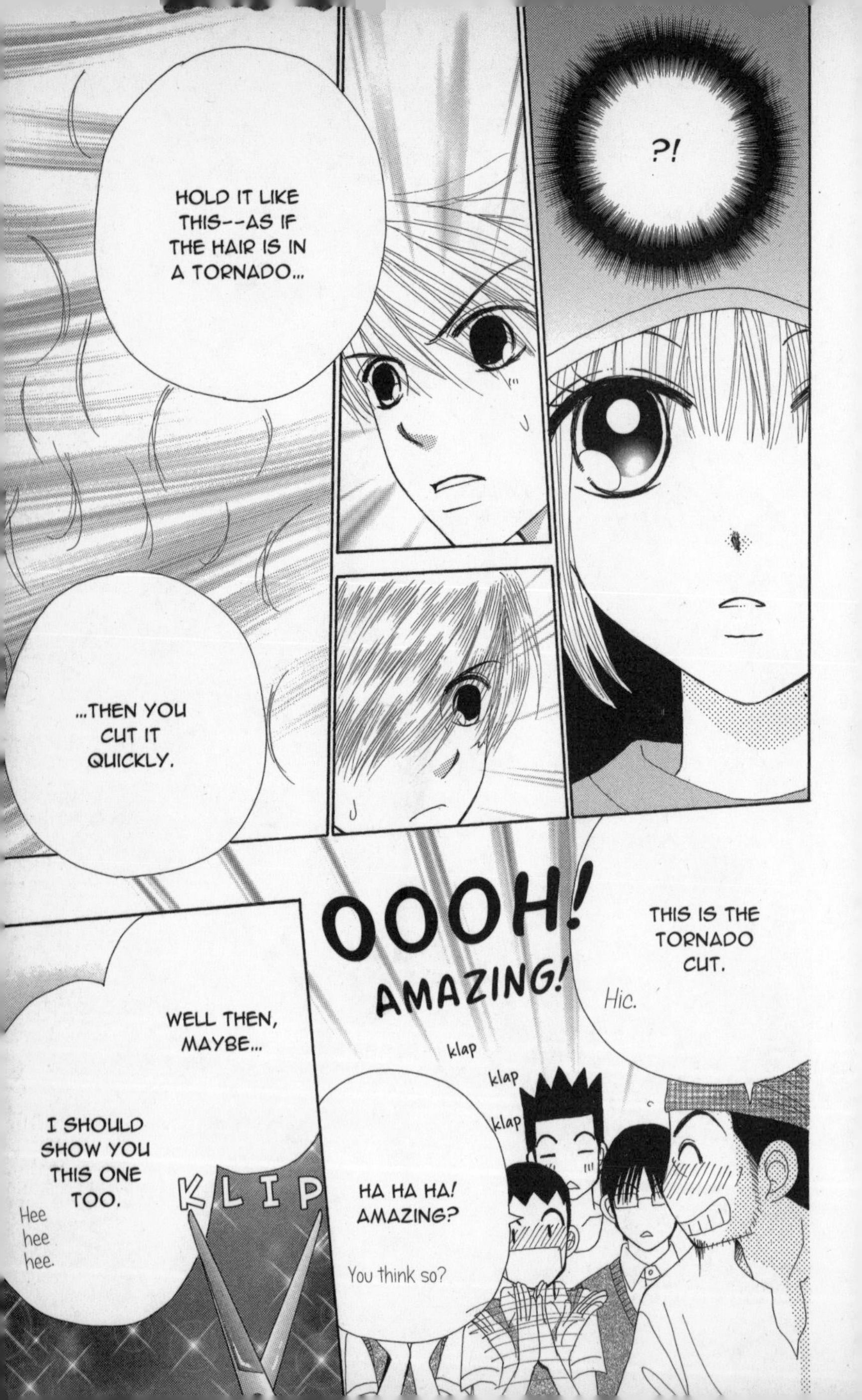
?!
HOLD IT LIKE THIS--AS IF THE HAIR IS IN A TORNADO...
...THEN YOU CUT IT QUICKLY.
THIS IS THE TORNADO CUT.
Hic.
OOOH!
AMAZING!
klap
klap
klap
HA HA HA! AMAZING?
You think so?
WELL THEN, MAYBE...
I SHOULD SHOW YOU THIS ONE TOO.
Hee hee hee.
KLIP

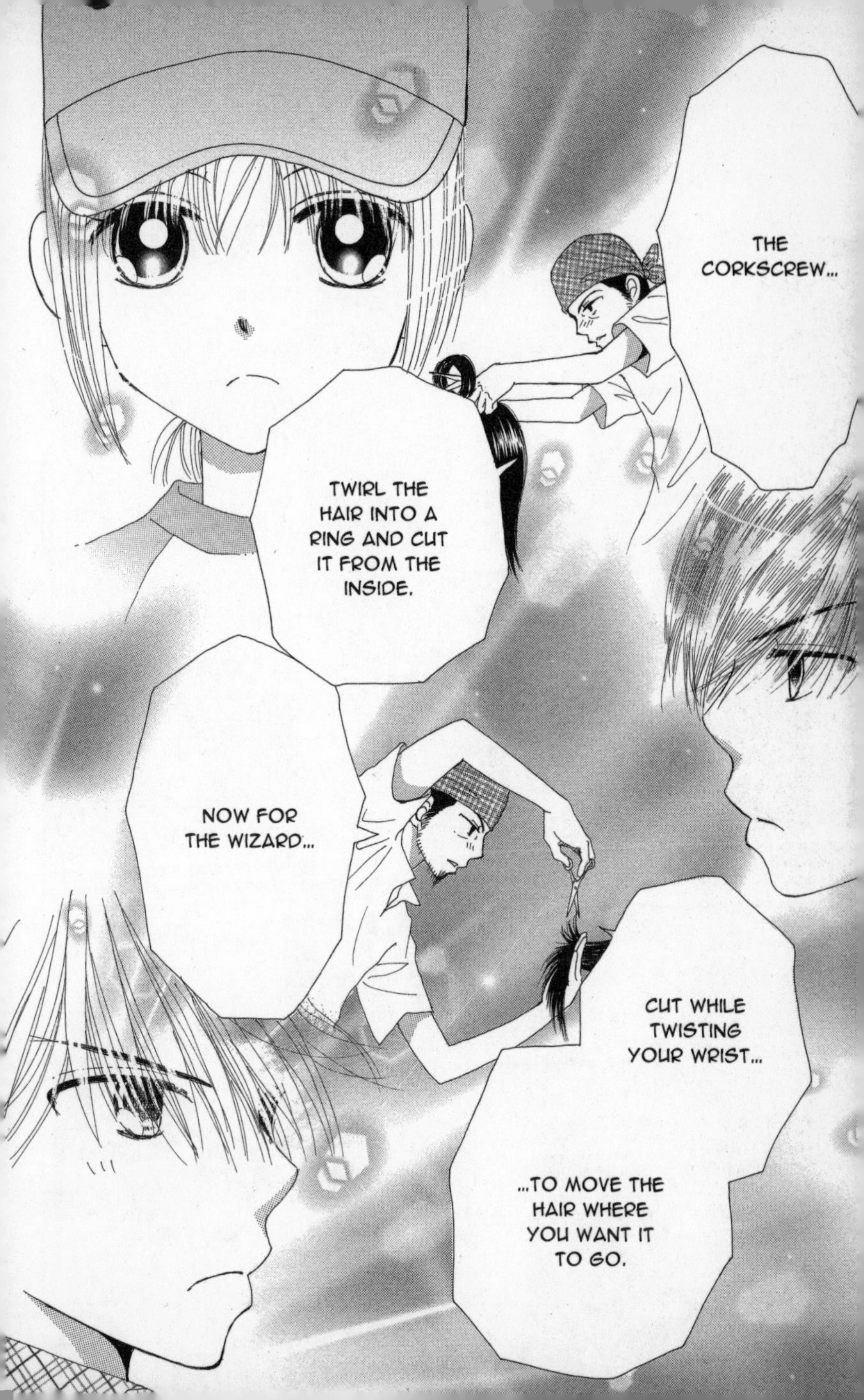
THE CORKSCREW...
TWIRL THE HAIR INTO A RING AND CUT IT FROM THE INSIDE.
NOW FOR THE WIZARD...
CUT WHILE TWISTING YOUR WRIST...
...TO MOVE THE HAIR WHERE YOU WANT IT TO GO.

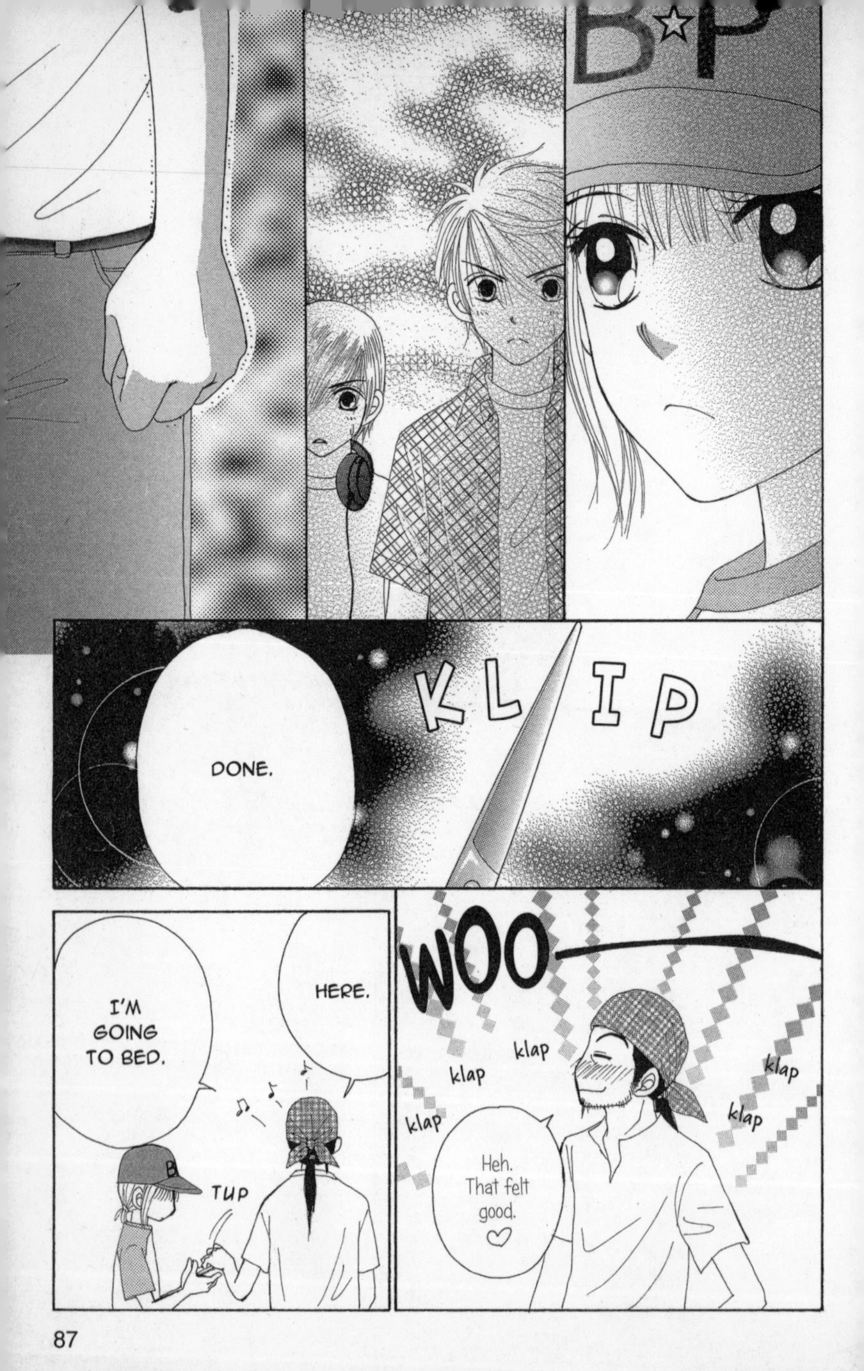
KL IP
DONE.
WOO
klap
klap
klap
klap
klap
Heh. That felt good. ♡
HERE.
I'M GOING TO BED.
TUP

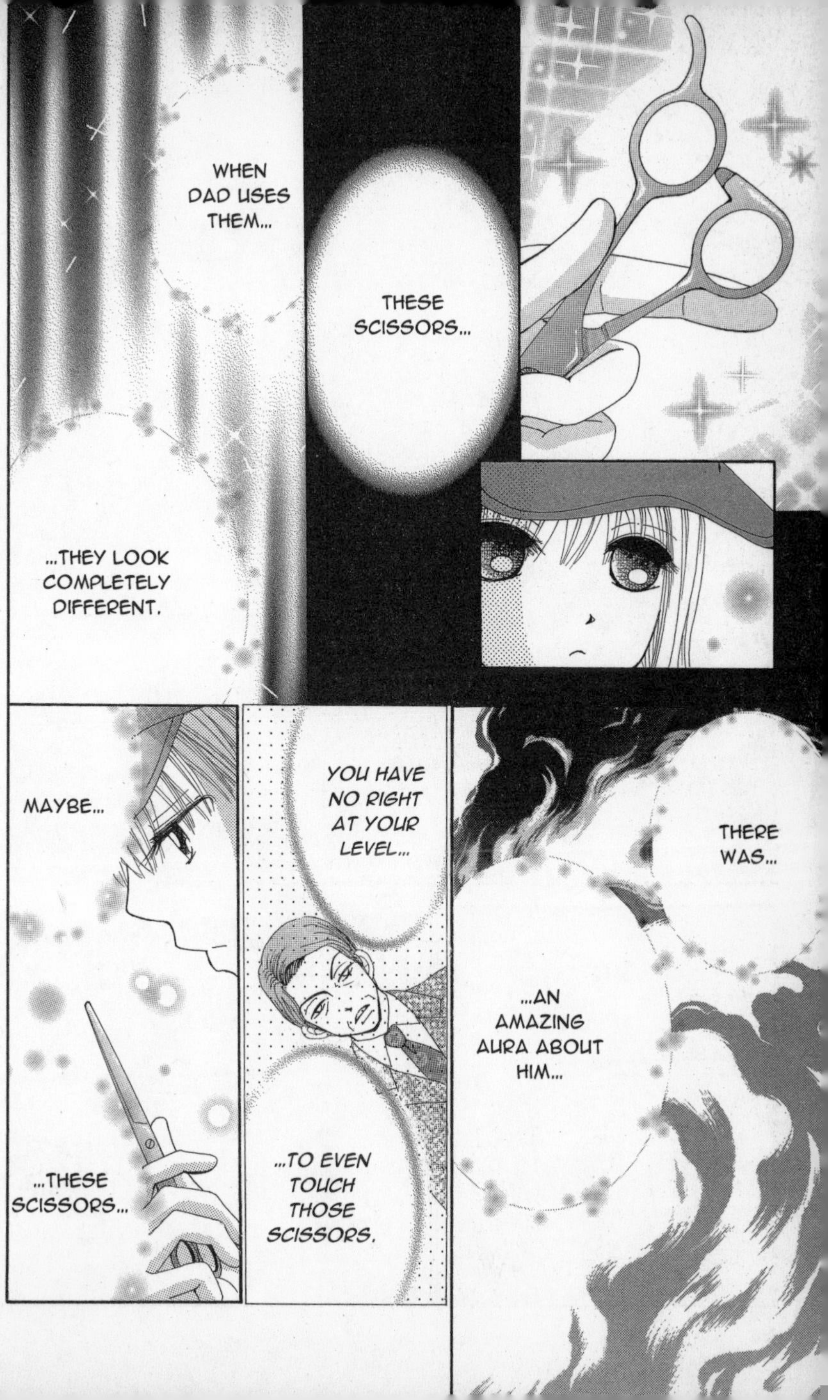
THESE SCISSORS...
WHEN DAD USES THEM...
...THEY LOOK COMPLETELY DIFFERENT.
THERE WAS...
...AN AMAZING AURA ABOUT HIM...
YOU HAVE NO RIGHT AT YOUR LEVEL...
...TO EVEN TOUCH THOSE SCISSORS.
MAYBE...
...THESE SCISSORS...

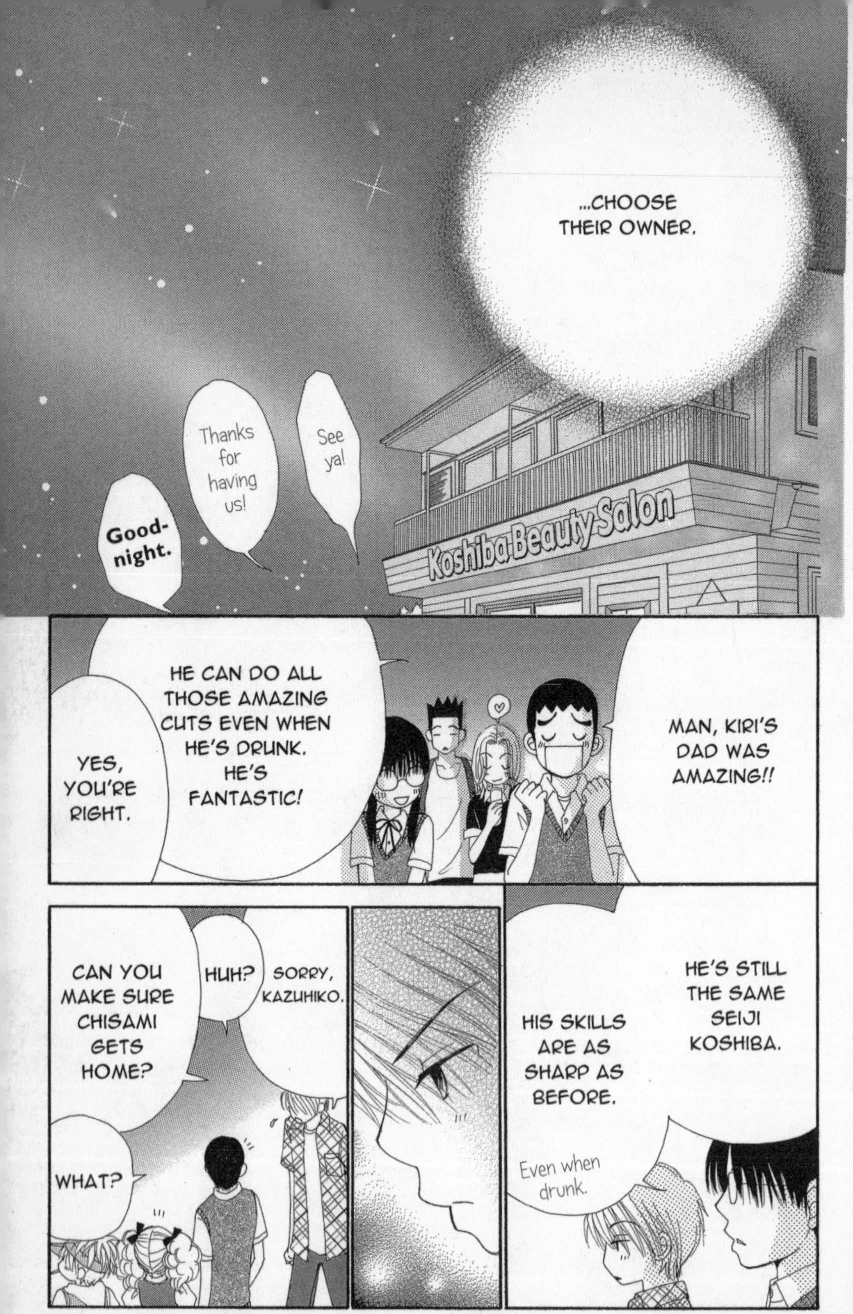
...CHOOSE THEIR OWNER.
See ya!
Thanks for having us!
Good-night.
Koshiba Beauty Salon
MAN, KIRI'S DAD WAS AMAZING!!
HE CAN DO ALL THOSE AMAZING CUTS EVEN WHEN HE'S DRUNK. HE'S FANTASTIC!
YES, YOU'RE RIGHT.
HE'S STILL THE SAME SEIJI KOSHIBA.
HIS SKILLS ARE AS SHARP AS BEFORE.
Even when drunk.
SORRY, KAZUHIKO.
HUH?
CAN YOU MAKE SURE CHISAMI GETS HOME?
WHAT?

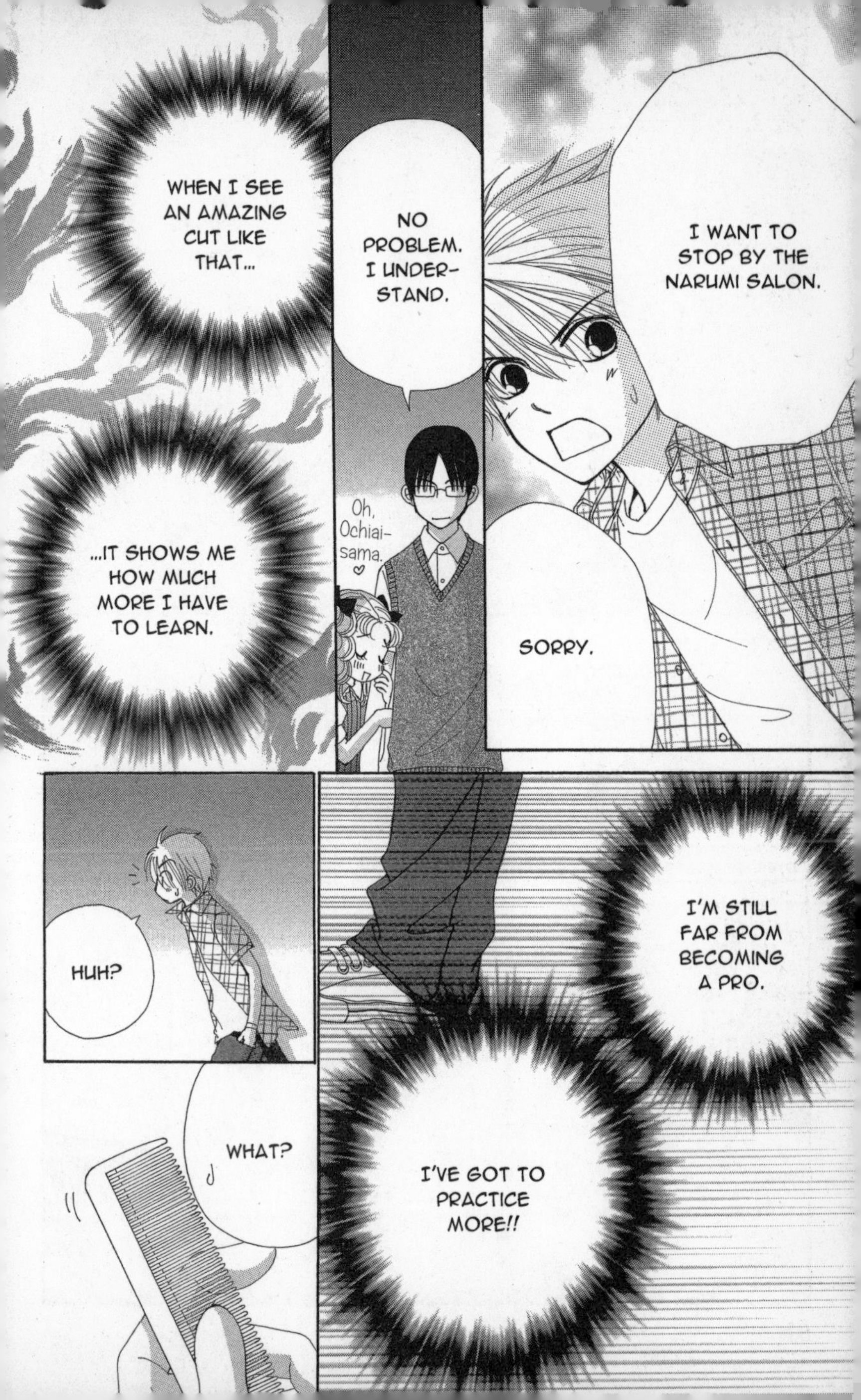
I WANT TO STOP BY THE NARUMI SALON.
SORRY.
NO PROBLEM. I UNDER-STAND.
Oh, Ochiai-sama. ♥
WHEN I SEE AN AMAZING CUT LIKE THAT...
...IT SHOWS ME HOW MUCH MORE I HAVE TO LEARN.
I'M STILL FAR FROM BECOMING A PRO.
I'VE GOT TO PRACTICE MORE!!
HUH?
WHAT?

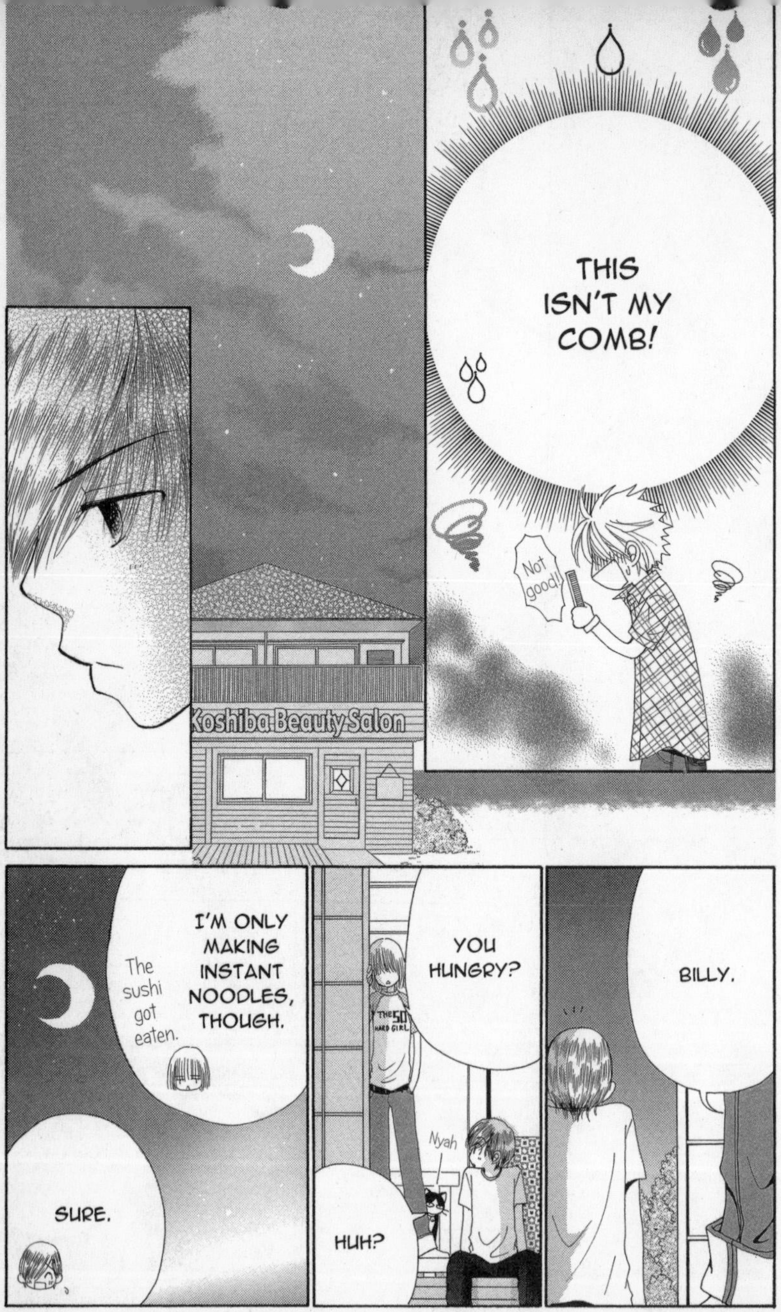
THIS ISN'T MY COMB!
Not good!
Koshiba Beauty Salon
BILLY.
YOU HUNGRY?
Nyah
HUH?
I'M ONLY MAKING INSTANT NOODLES, THOUGH.
The sushi got eaten.
SURE.

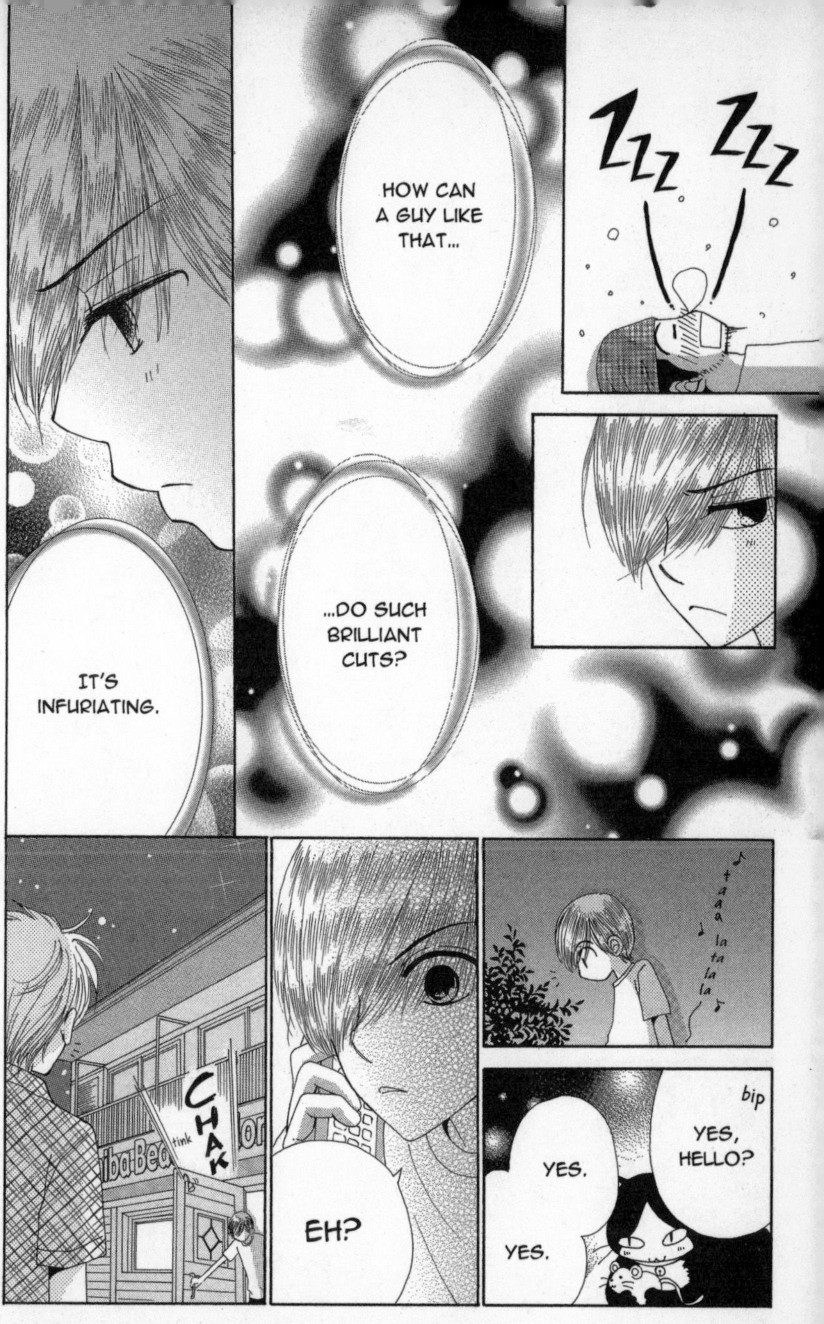
ZZZ ZZZ
HOW CAN A GUY LIKE THAT...
...DO SUCH BRILLIANT CUTS?
IT'S INFURIATING.
taaa la ta la la
bip
YES, HELLO?
YES.
YES.
EH?
CHAK
tink

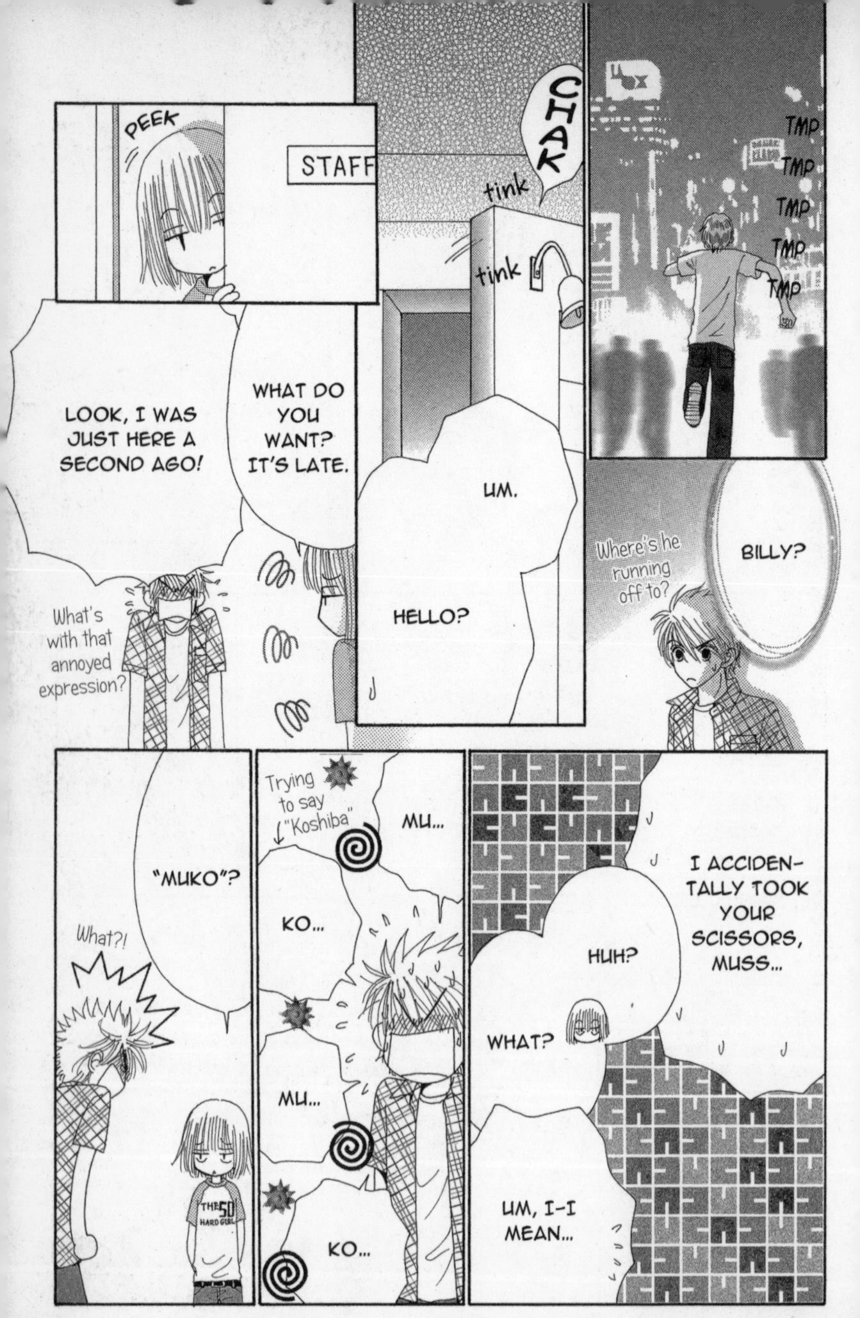
TMP
TMP
TMP
TMP
TMP
Where's he running off to?
BILLY?
CHAK
tink
tink
UM.
HELLO?
PEEK
STAFF
WHAT DO YOU WANT? IT'S LATE.
LOOK, I WAS JUST HERE A SECOND AGO!
What's with that annoyed expression?
I ACCIDEN-TALLY TOOK YOUR SCISSORS, MUSS...
HUH?
WHAT?
UM, I-I MEAN...
MU...
KO...
Trying to say "Koshiba"
MU...
KO...
"MUKO"?
What?!
THE 50 HARD GIRL

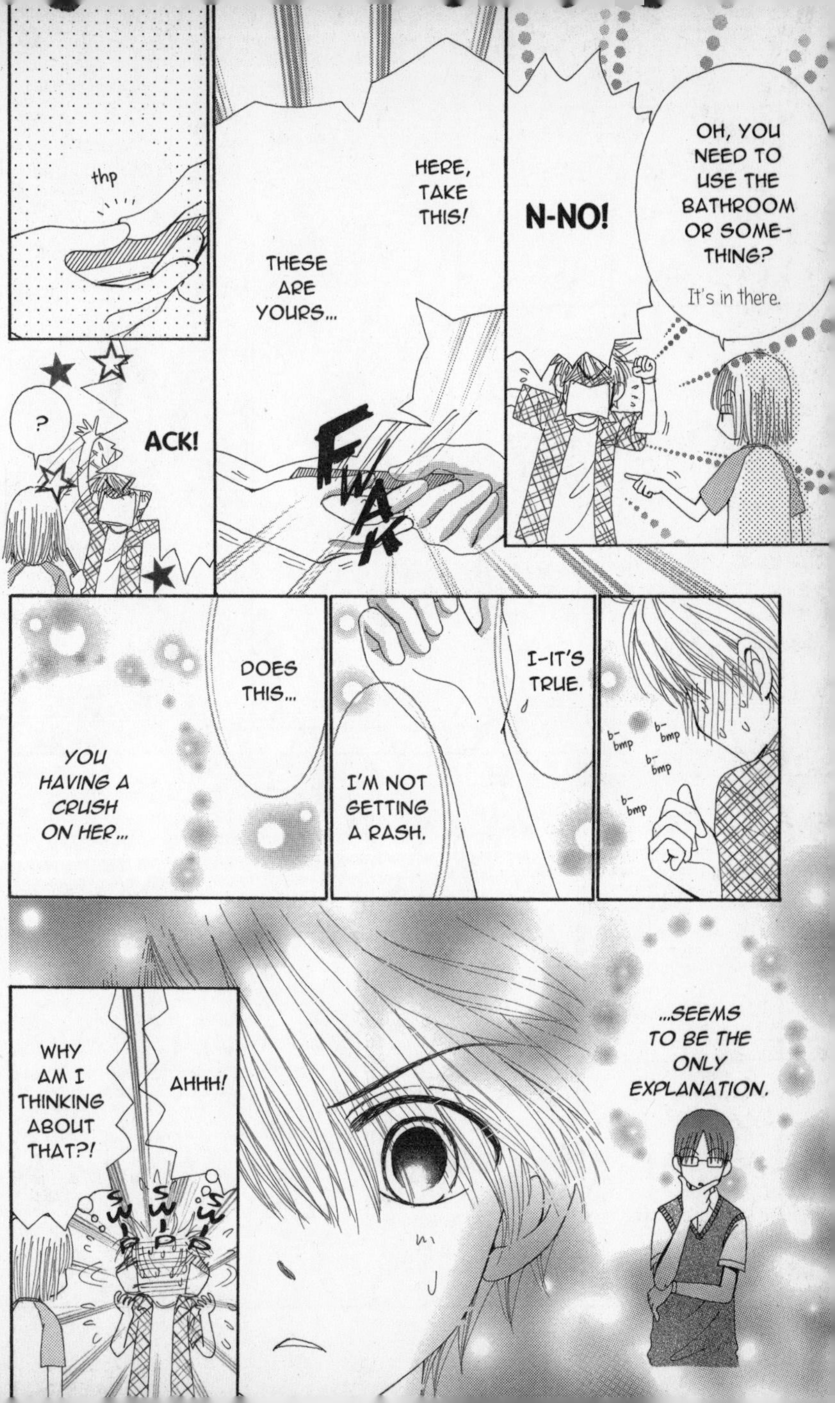
OH, YOU NEED TO USE THE BATHROOM OR SOME-THING?
It's in there.
N-NO!
HERE, TAKE THIS!
THESE ARE YOURS...
FWAK
thp
ACK!
?
b-bmp
b-bmp
b-bmp
b-bmp
I-IT'S TRUE.
I'M NOT GETTING A RASH.
DOES THIS...
YOU HAVING A CRUSH ON HER...
...SEEMS TO BE THE ONLY EXPLANATION.
AHHH!
WHY AM I THINKING ABOUT THAT?!
SWIP
SWIP
SWIP

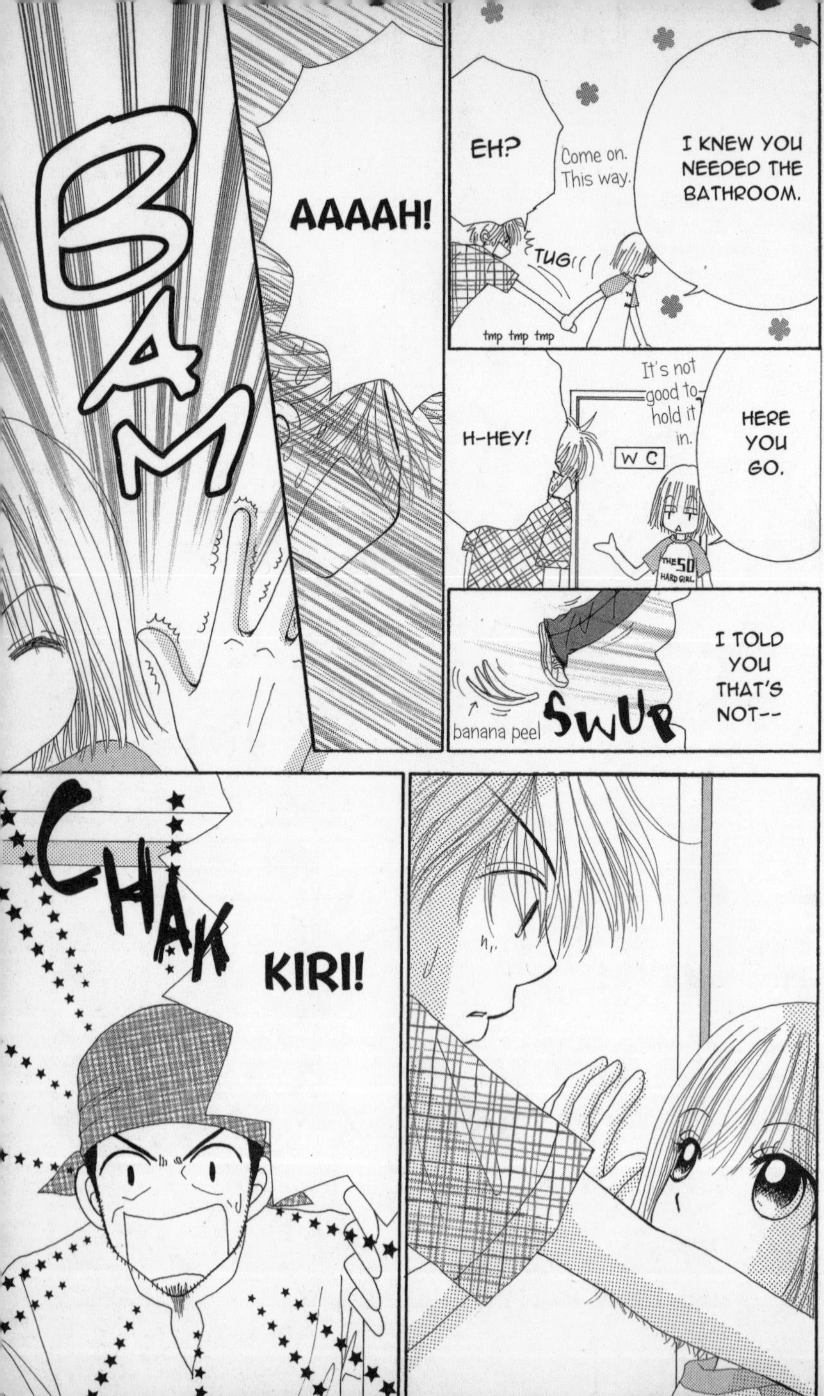
I KNEW YOU NEEDED THE BATHROOM.
Come on. This way.
EH?
TUG
tmp tmp tmp
HERE YOU GO.
It's not good to hold it in.
H-HEY!
W C
I TOLD YOU THAT'S NOT--
SWUP
banana peel
AAAAH!
BAM
CHAK
KIRI!

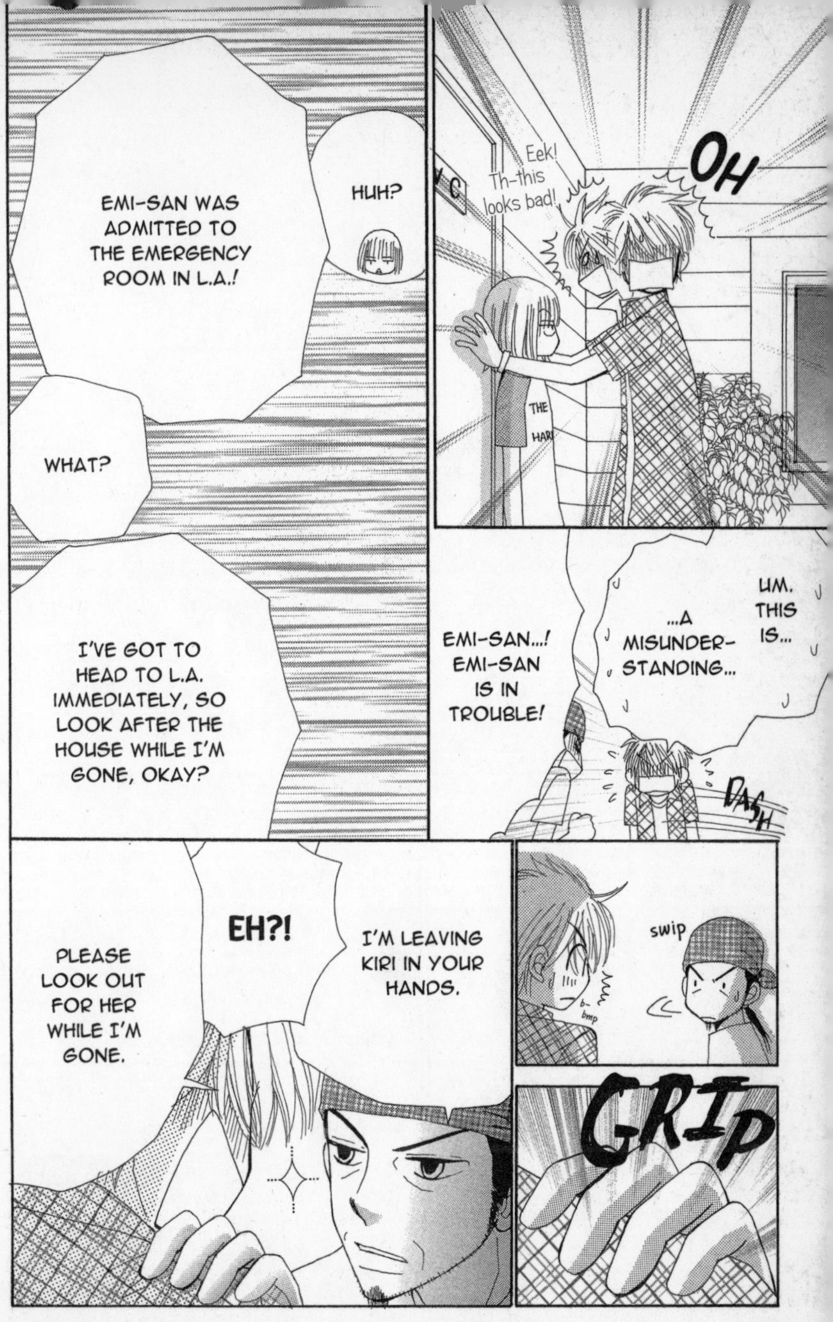
OH
Eek! Th-this looks bad!
UM. THIS IS...
...A MISUNDER-STANDING...
EMI-SAN...! EMI-SAN IS IN TROUBLE!
DASH
HUH?
EMI-SAN WAS ADMITTED TO THE EMERGENCY ROOM IN L.A.!
WHAT?
I'VE GOT TO HEAD TO L.A. IMMEDIATELY, SO LOOK AFTER THE HOUSE WHILE I'M GONE, OKAY?
swip
b-bmp
GRIP
I'M LEAVING KIRI IN YOUR HANDS.
EH?!
PLEASE LOOK OUT FOR HER WHILE I'M GONE.

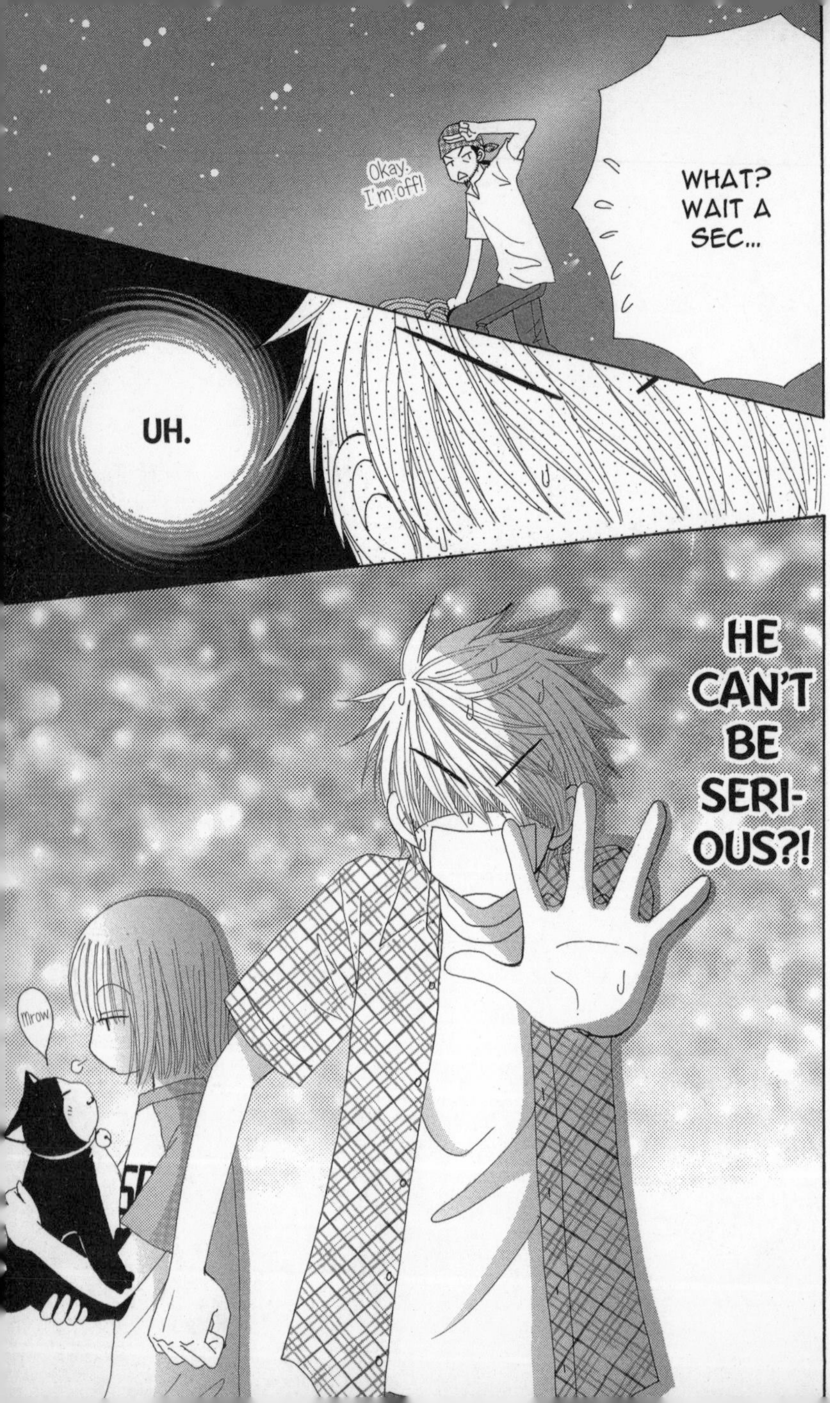
WHAT? WAIT A SEC...
Okay. I'm off!
UH.
HE CAN'T BE SERI-OUS?!
Mrow

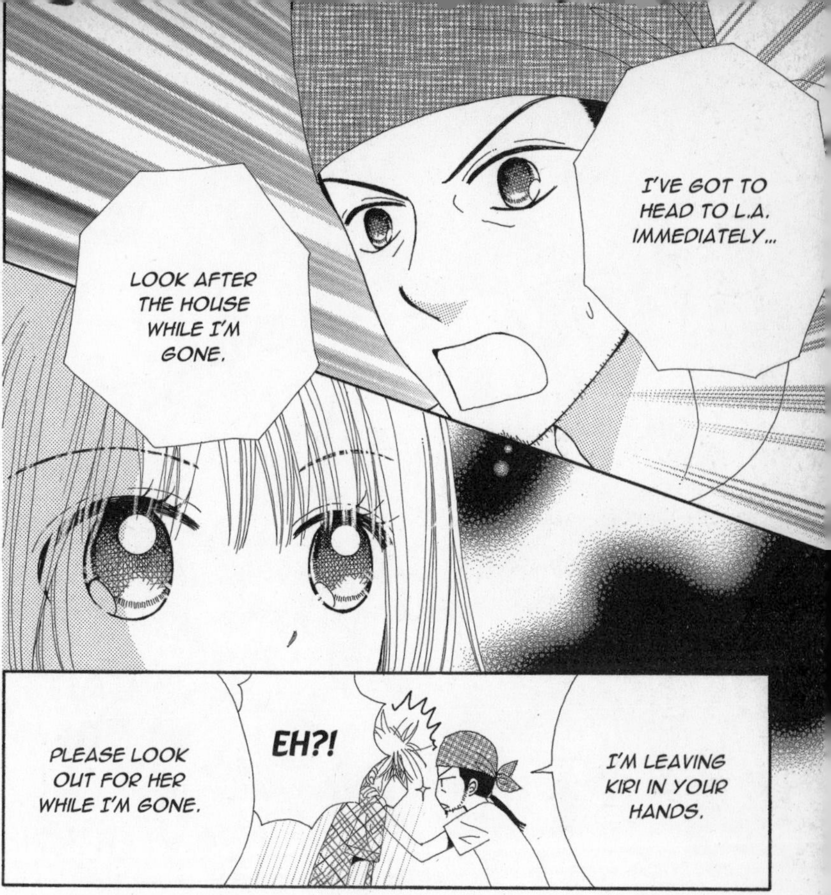
I'VE GOT TO HEAD TO L.A. IMMEDIATELY...
LOOK AFTER THE HOUSE WHILE I'M GONE.
I'M LEAVING KIRI IN YOUR HANDS.
EH?!
PLEASE LOOK OUT FOR HER WHILE I'M GONE.
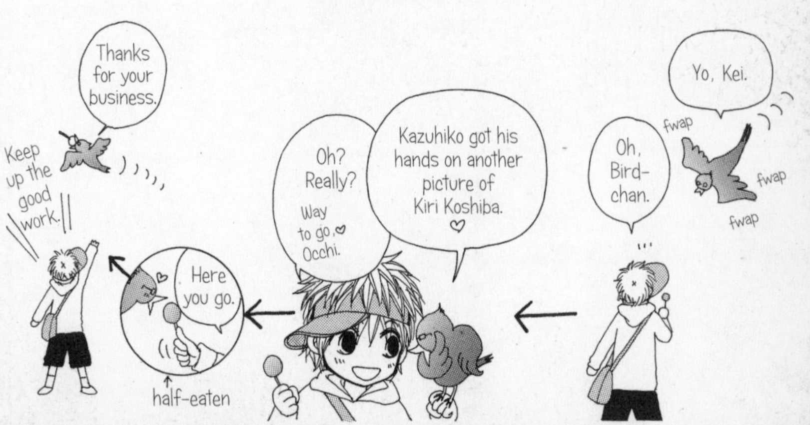
Yo, Kei.
fwap
fwap
fwap
Oh, Bird-chan.
Kazuhiko got his hands on another picture of Kiri Koshiba.
Oh? Really?
Way to go, Occhi.
Here you go.
half-eaten
Thanks for your business.
Keep up the good work.

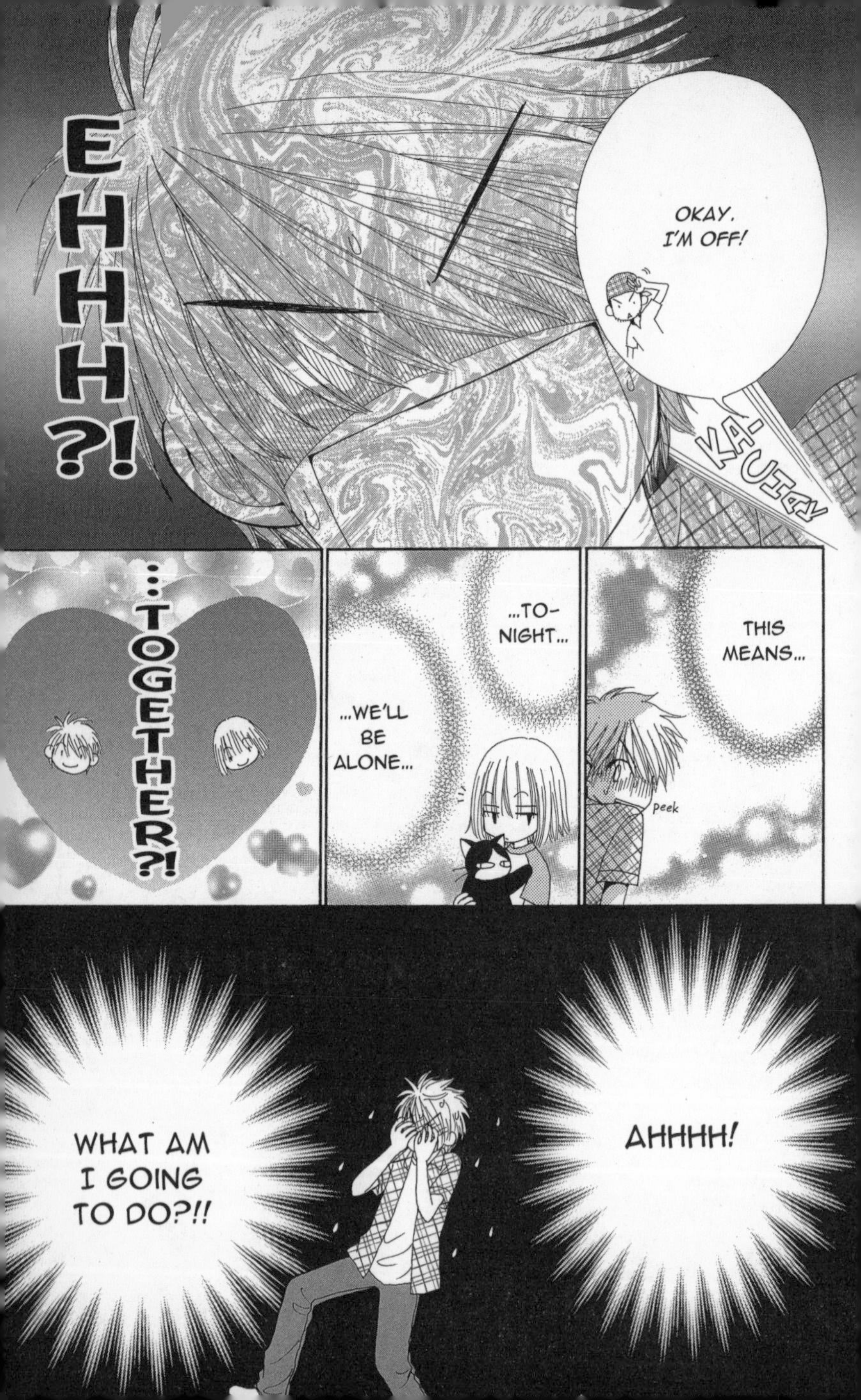
OKAY. I'M OFF!
KA-CHUNK
EHHHH?!
THIS MEANS...
peek
...TO-NIGHT...
...WE'LL BE ALONE...
...TOGETHER?!
AHHHH!
WHAT AM I GOING TO DO?!!

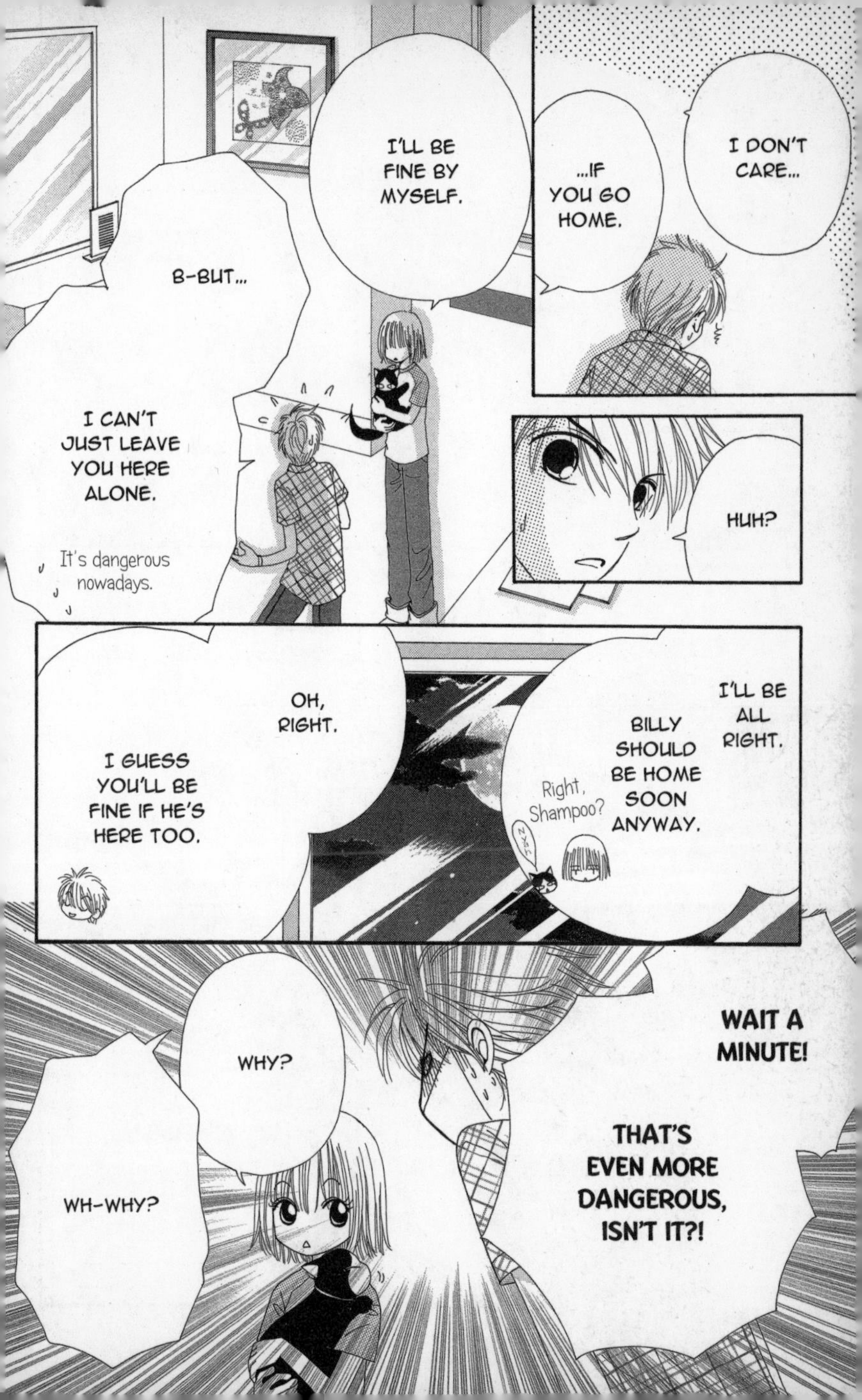
I DON'T CARE...
...IF YOU GO HOME.
HUH?
I'LL BE FINE BY MYSELF.
B-BUT...
I CAN'T JUST LEAVE YOU HERE ALONE.
It's dangerous nowadays.
I'LL BE ALL RIGHT.
BILLY SHOULD BE HOME SOON ANYWAY.
Right, Shampoo?
OH, RIGHT.
I GUESS YOU'LL BE FINE IF HE'S HERE TOO.
WAIT A MINUTE!
THAT'S EVEN MORE DANGEROUS, ISN'T IT?!
WHY?
WH-WHY?

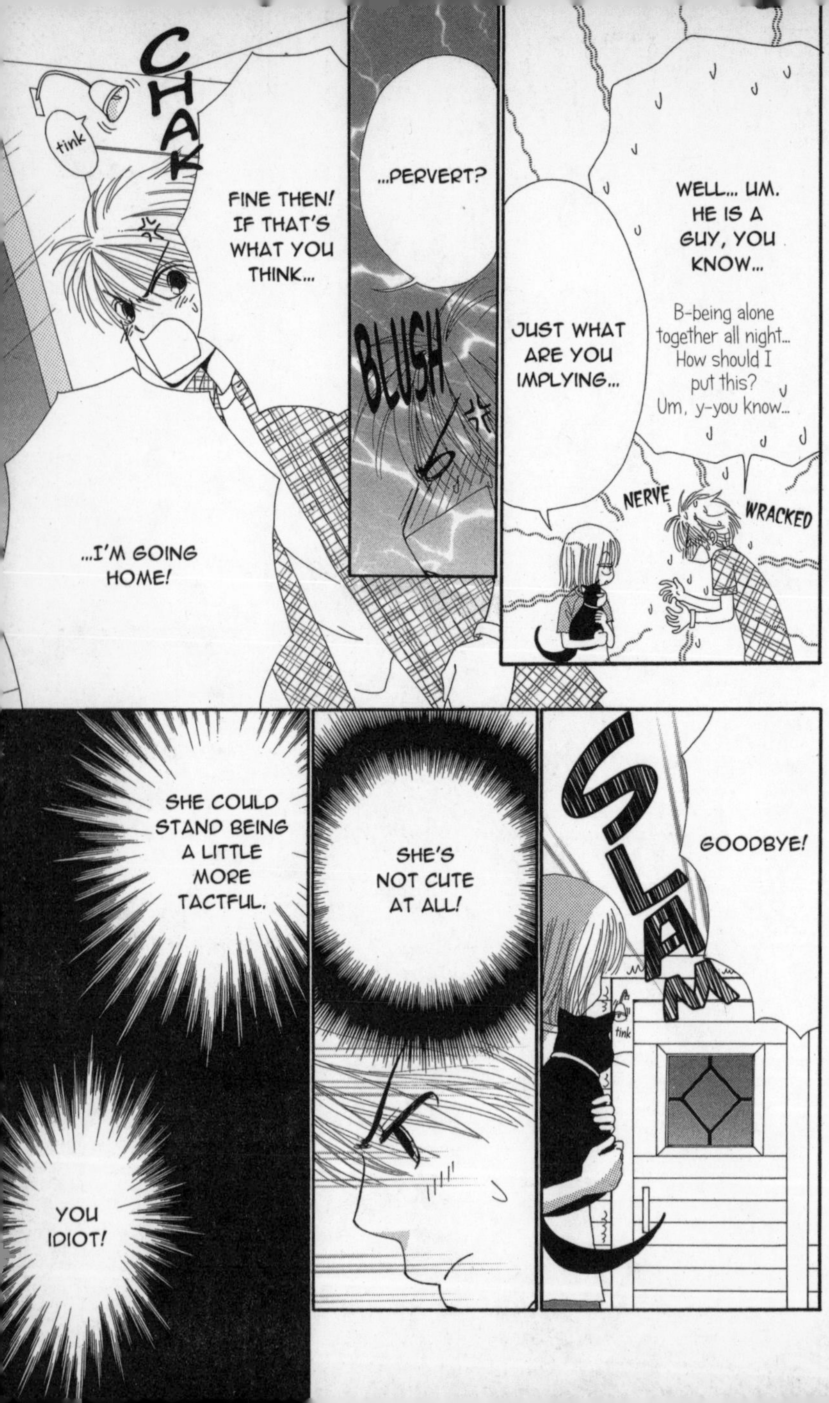
WELL... UM. HE IS A GUY, YOU KNOW...
B-being alone together all night... How should I put this? Um, y-you know...
JUST WHAT ARE YOU IMPLYING...
NERVE WRACKED
...PERVERT?
BLUSH
CHAK
tink
FINE THEN! IF THAT'S WHAT YOU THINK...
...I'M GOING HOME!
GOODBYE!
SLAM
tink
SHE'S NOT CUTE AT ALL!
SHE COULD STAND BEING A LITTLE MORE TACTFUL.
YOU IDIOT!

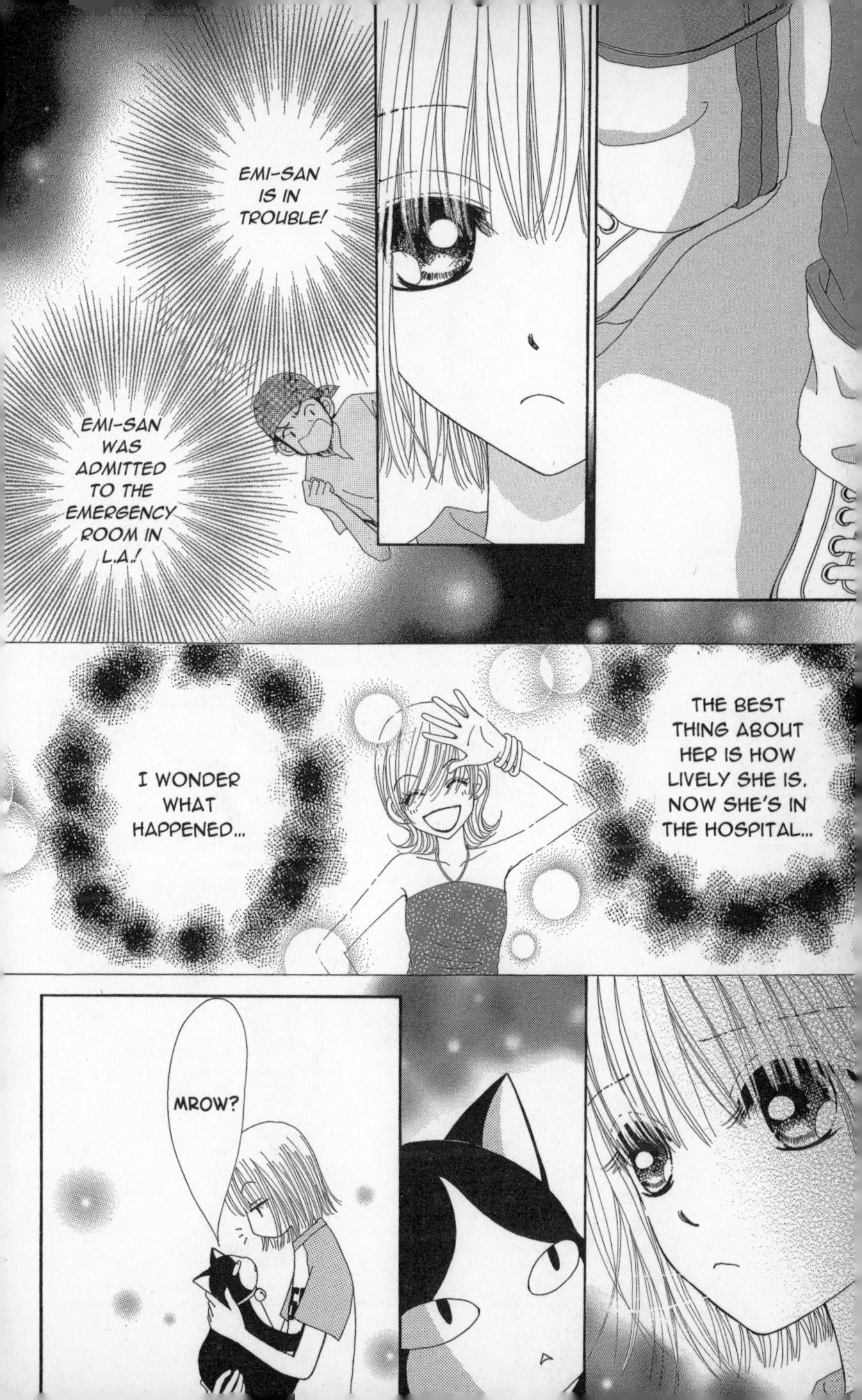
EMI-SAN IS IN TROUBLE!
EMI-SAN WAS ADMITTED TO THE EMERGENCY ROOM IN L.A.!
THE BEST THING ABOUT HER IS HOW LIVELY SHE IS. NOW SHE'S IN THE HOSPITAL...
I WONDER WHAT HAPPENED...
MROW?

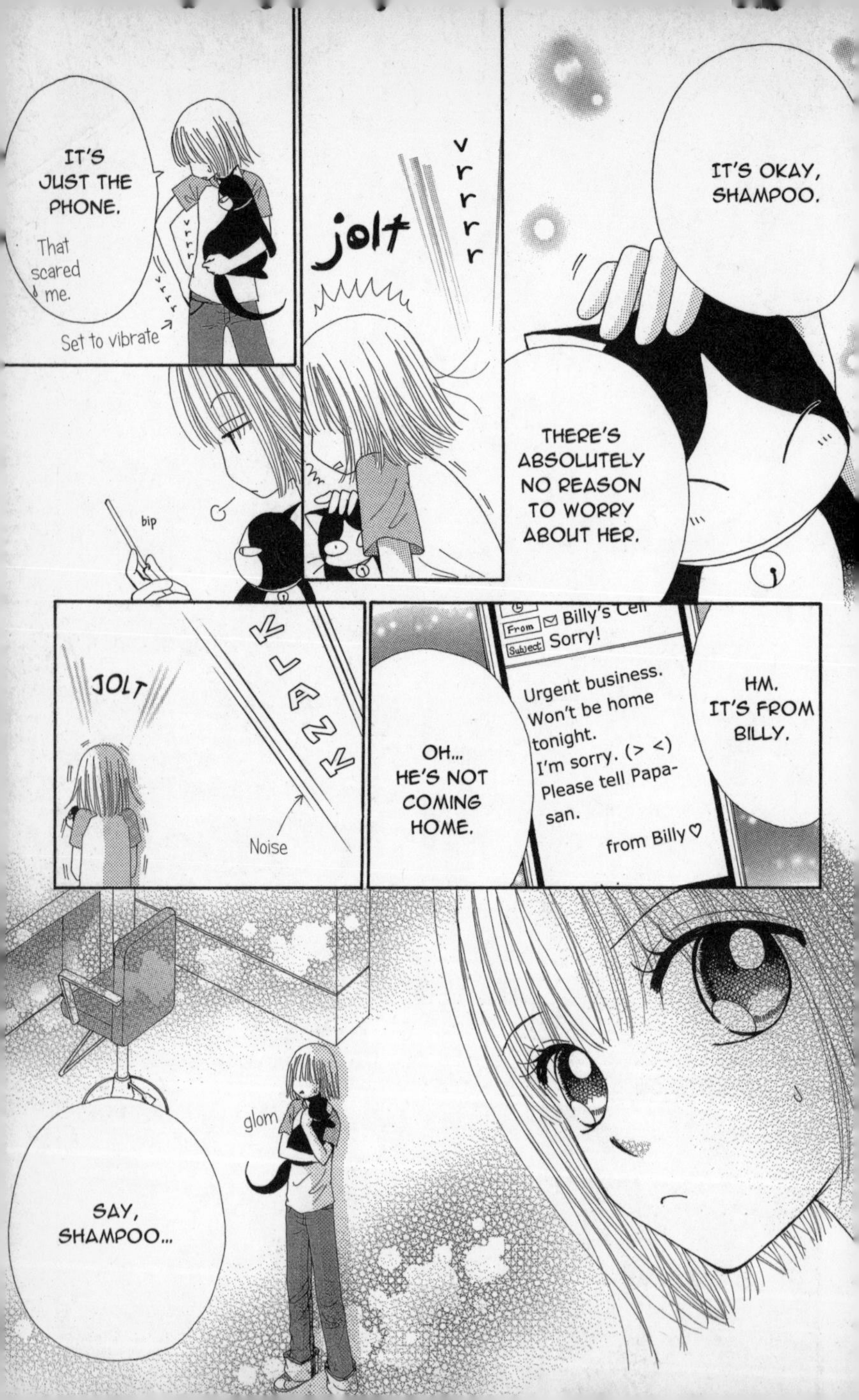
IT'S OKAY, SHAMPOO.
THERE'S ABSOLUTELY NO REASON TO WORRY ABOUT HER.
vrrrr
jolt
IT'S JUST THE PHONE.
That scared me.
vrrr
vrrr
Set to vibrate
bip
HM. IT'S FROM BILLY.
From Billy's Cell
Subject Sorry!
Urgent business. Won't be home tonight. I'm sorry. (> <) Please tell Papa-san.
from Billy ♡
OH... HE'S NOT COMING HOME.
KLANK
JOLT
Noise
glom
SAY, SHAMPOO...

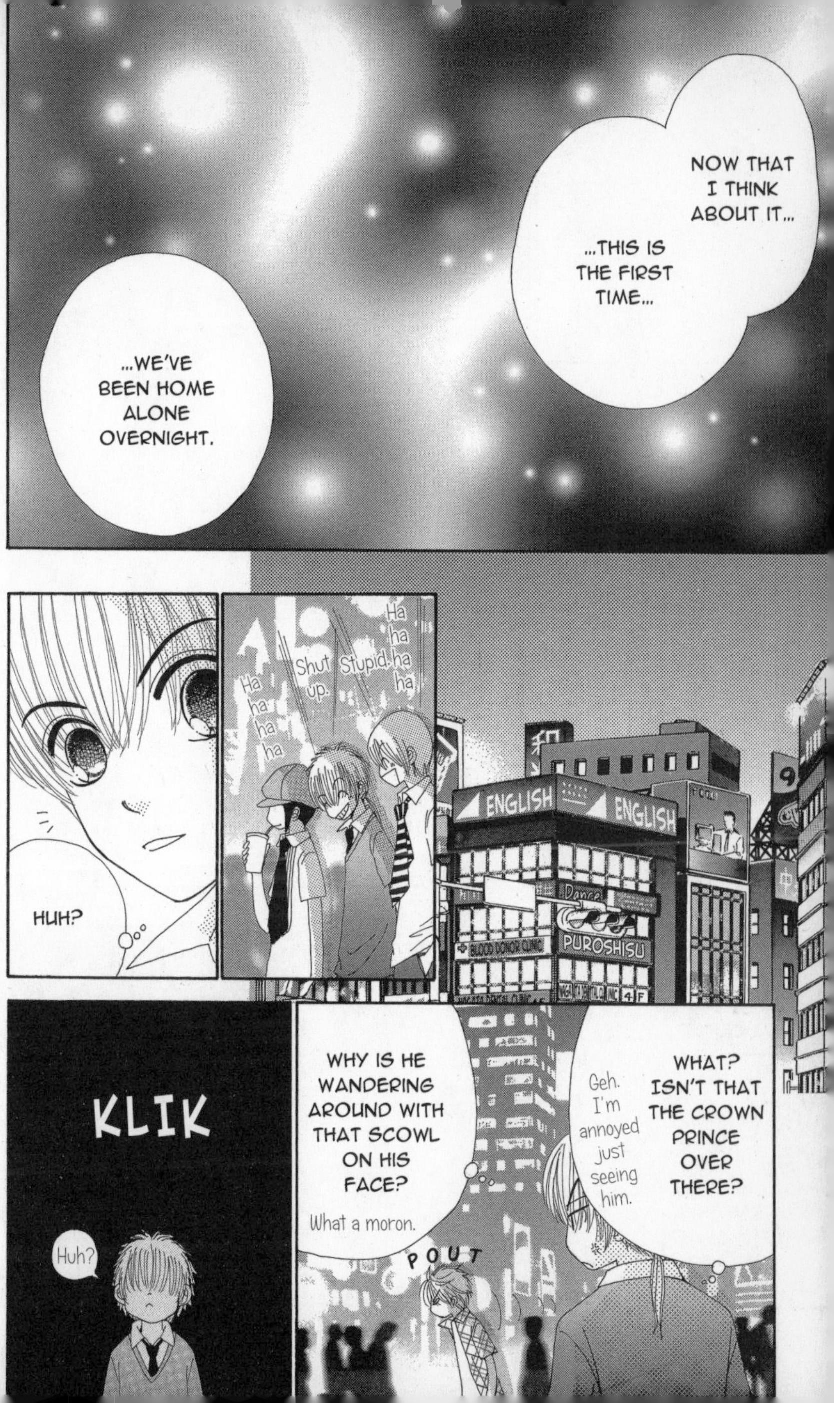
NOW THAT I THINK ABOUT IT...
...THIS IS THE FIRST TIME...
...WE'VE BEEN HOME ALONE OVERNIGHT.
ENGLISH
ENGLISH
Dance
PUROSHISU
BLOOD DONOR CLINIC
Ha ha ha ha
Stupid.
Shut up.
Ha ha ha ha
HUH?
WHAT? ISN'T THAT THE CROWN PRINCE OVER THERE?
Geh. I'm annoyed just seeing him.
WHY IS HE WANDERING AROUND WITH THAT SCOWL ON HIS FACE?
What a moron.
POUT
KLIK
Huh?

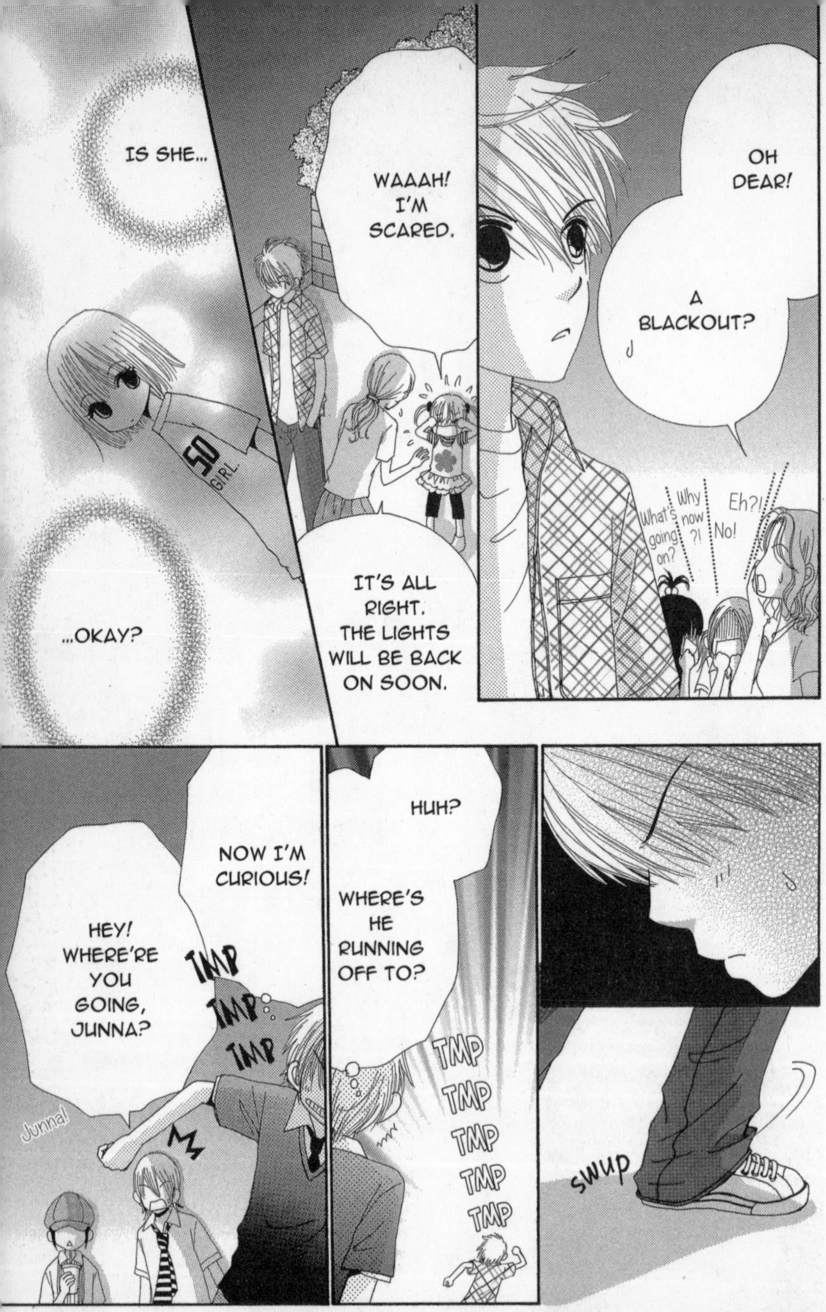
OH DEAR!
A BLACKOUT?
Eh?!
No!
Why now?!
What's going on?
WAAAH! I'M SCARED.
IT'S ALL RIGHT. THE LIGHTS WILL BE BACK ON SOON.
IS SHE...
...OKAY?
SWUP
HUH?
WHERE'S HE RUNNING OFF TO?
TMP
TMP
TMP
TMP
TMP
NOW I'M CURIOUS!
HEY! WHERE'RE YOU GOING, JUNNA?
TMP
TMP
TMP
Junna!

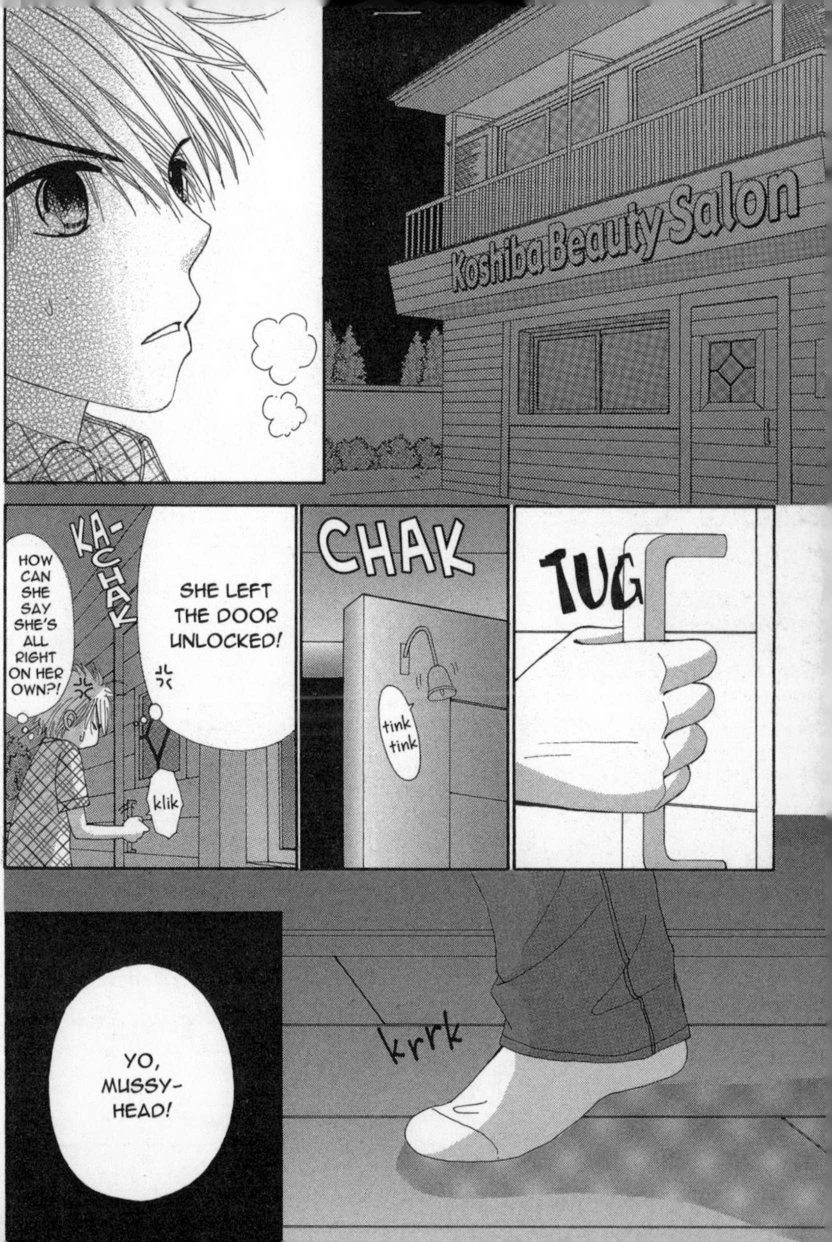
Koshiba Beauty Salon
TUG
CHAK
tink tink
SHE LEFT THE DOOR UNLOCKED!
KA-CHAK
HOW CAN SHE SAY SHE'S ALL RIGHT ON HER OWN?!
klik
krrk
YO, MUSSY-HEAD!

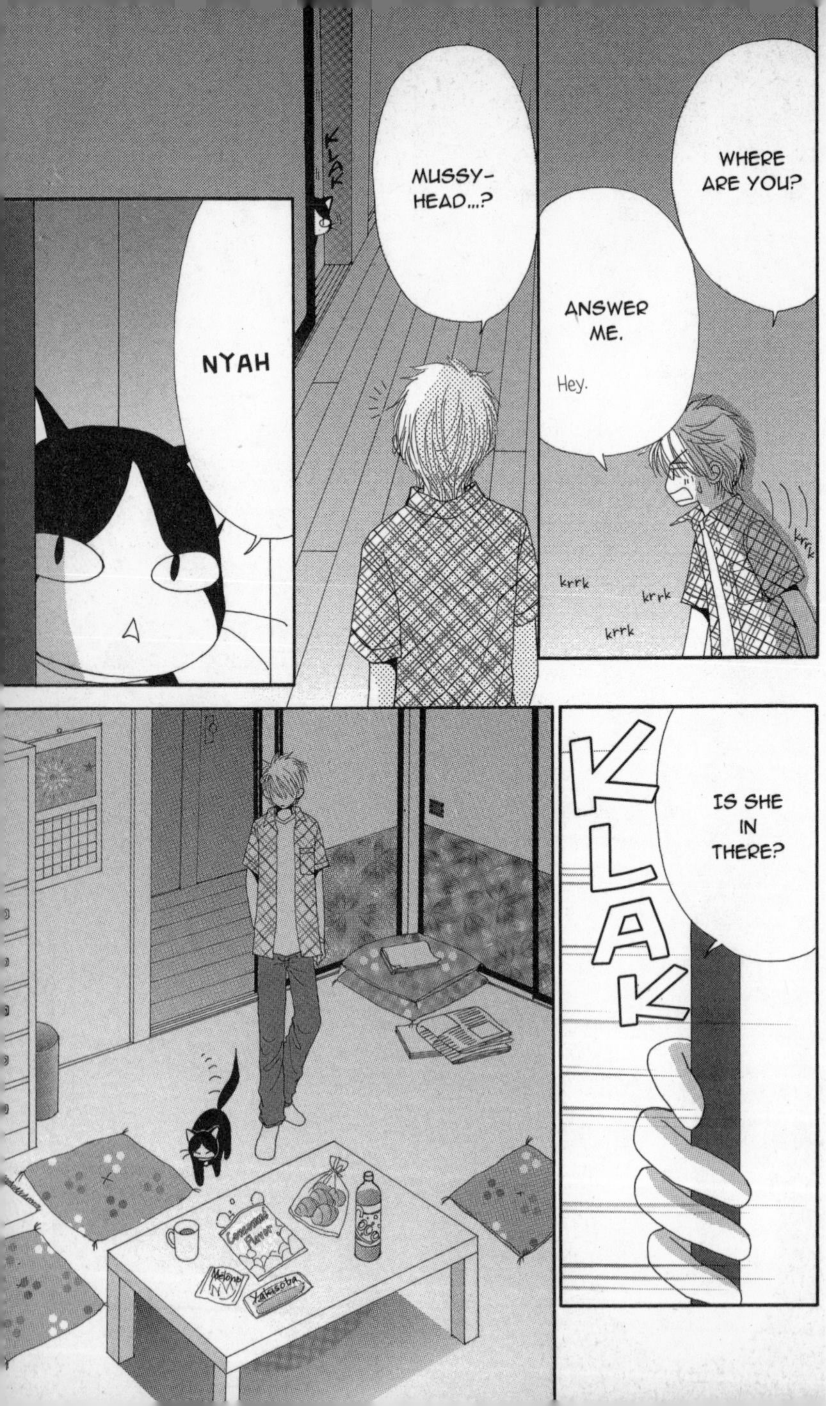
WHERE ARE YOU?
ANSWER ME.
Hey.
krrk
krrk
krrk
krrk
MUSSY-HEAD...?
KLAK
NYAH
KLAK
IS SHE IN THERE?
Consommé Flavor
Melon
Yakisoba

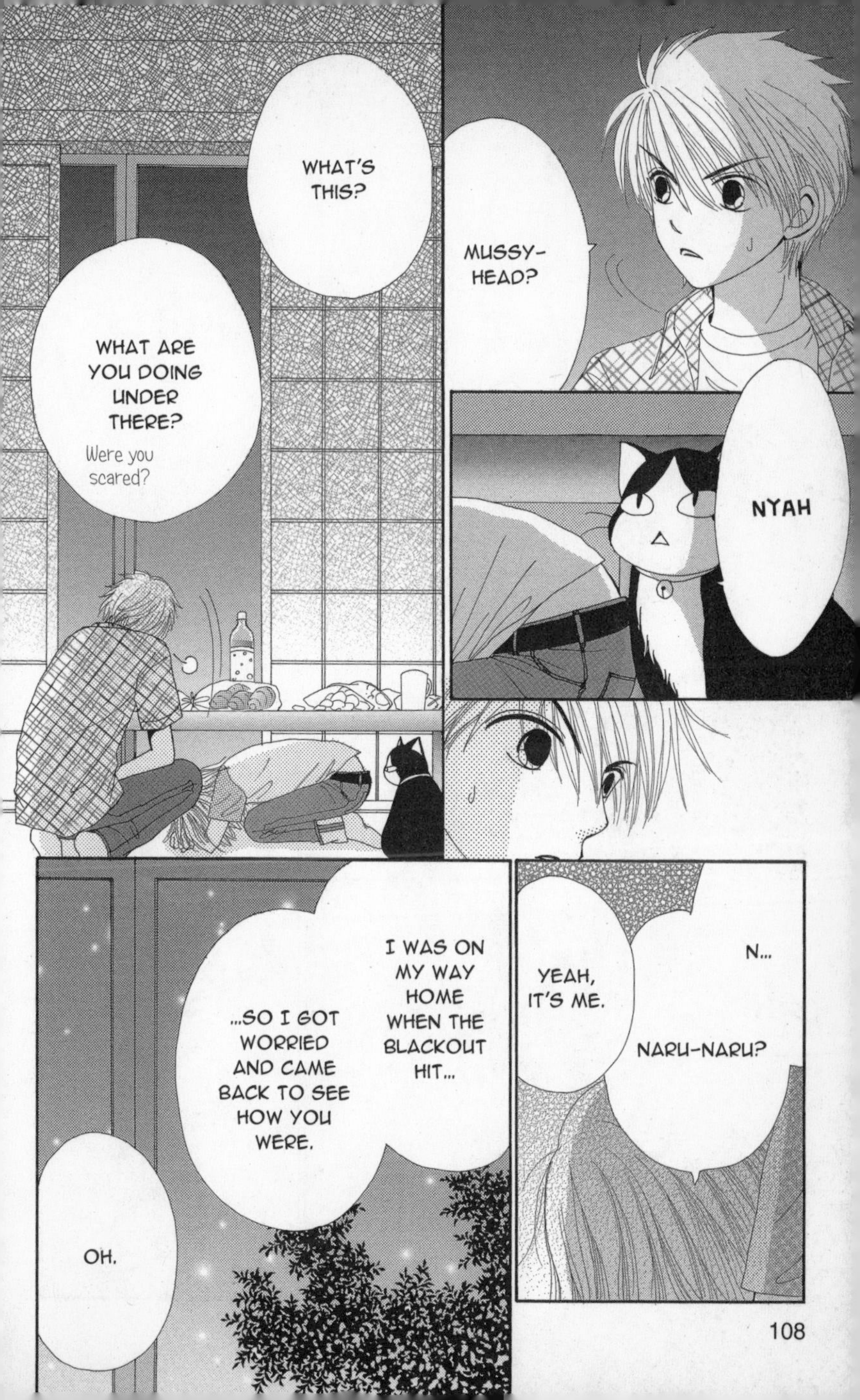
MUSSY-HEAD?
NYAH
WHAT'S THIS?
WHAT ARE YOU DOING UNDER THERE?
Were you scared?
N...
NARU-NARU?
YEAH, IT'S ME.
I WAS ON MY WAY HOME WHEN THE BLACKOUT HIT...
...SO I GOT WORRIED AND CAME BACK TO SEE HOW YOU WERE.
OH.

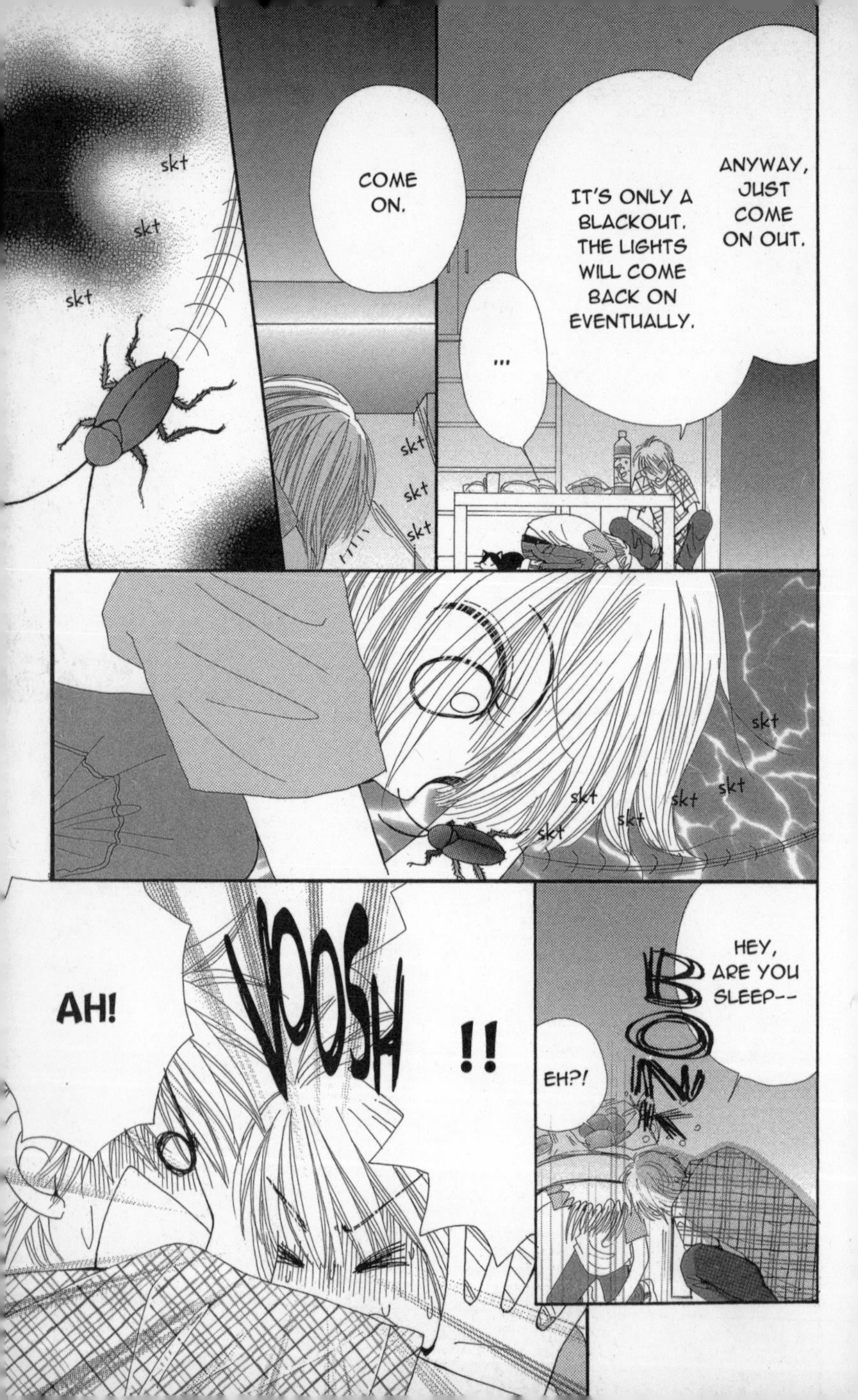
ANYWAY, JUST COME ON OUT.
IT'S ONLY A BLACKOUT. THE LIGHTS WILL COME BACK ON EVENTUALLY.
...
COME ON.
skt
skt
skt
skt
skt
skt
skt
skt
skt
skt
skt
skt
HEY, ARE YOU SLEEP--
BONK
EH?!
!!
VOOSH
AH!

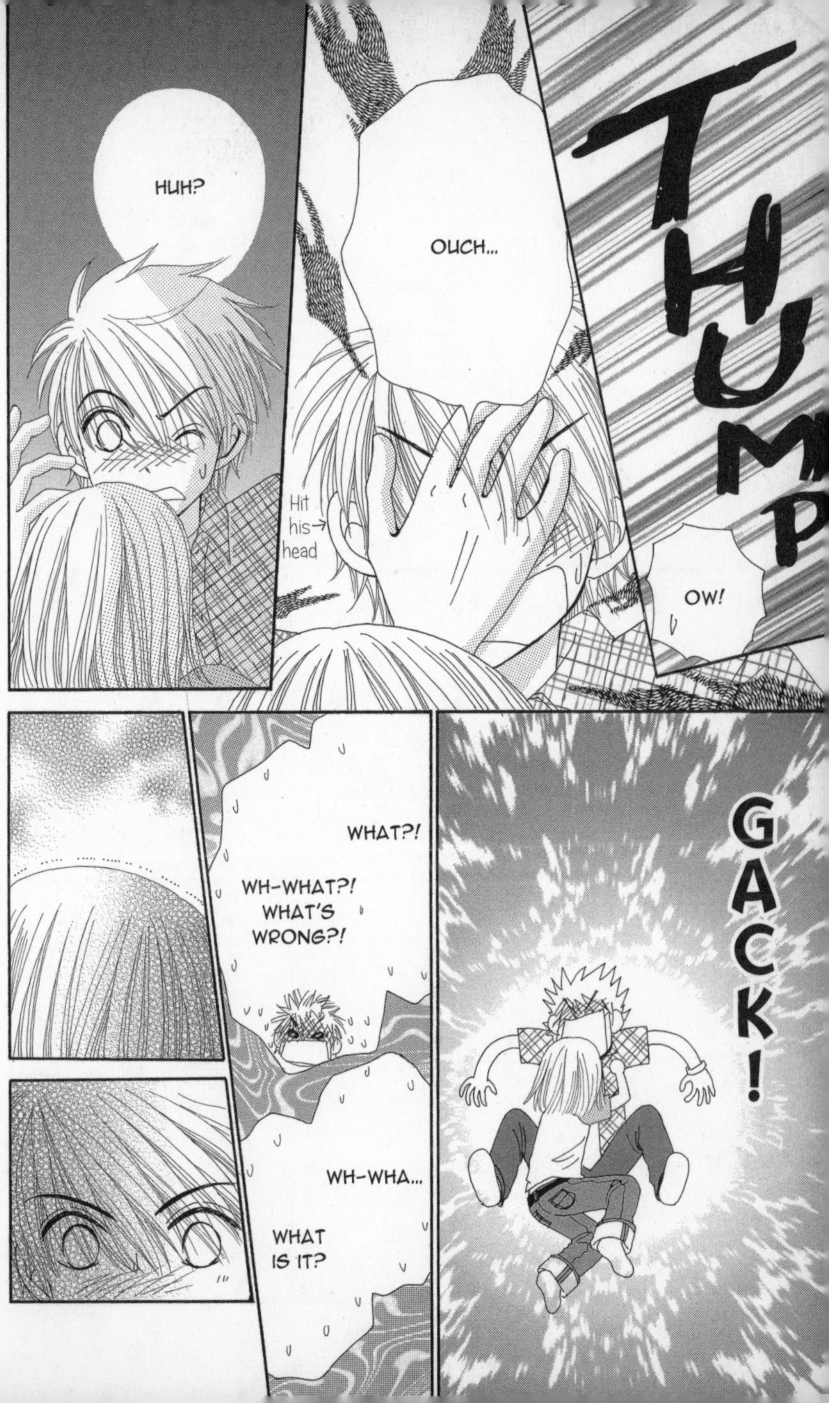
THUMP
OW!
OUCH...
Hit his head
HUH?
GACK!
WHAT?!
WH-WHAT?! WHAT'S WRONG?!
WH-WHA...
WHAT IS IT?

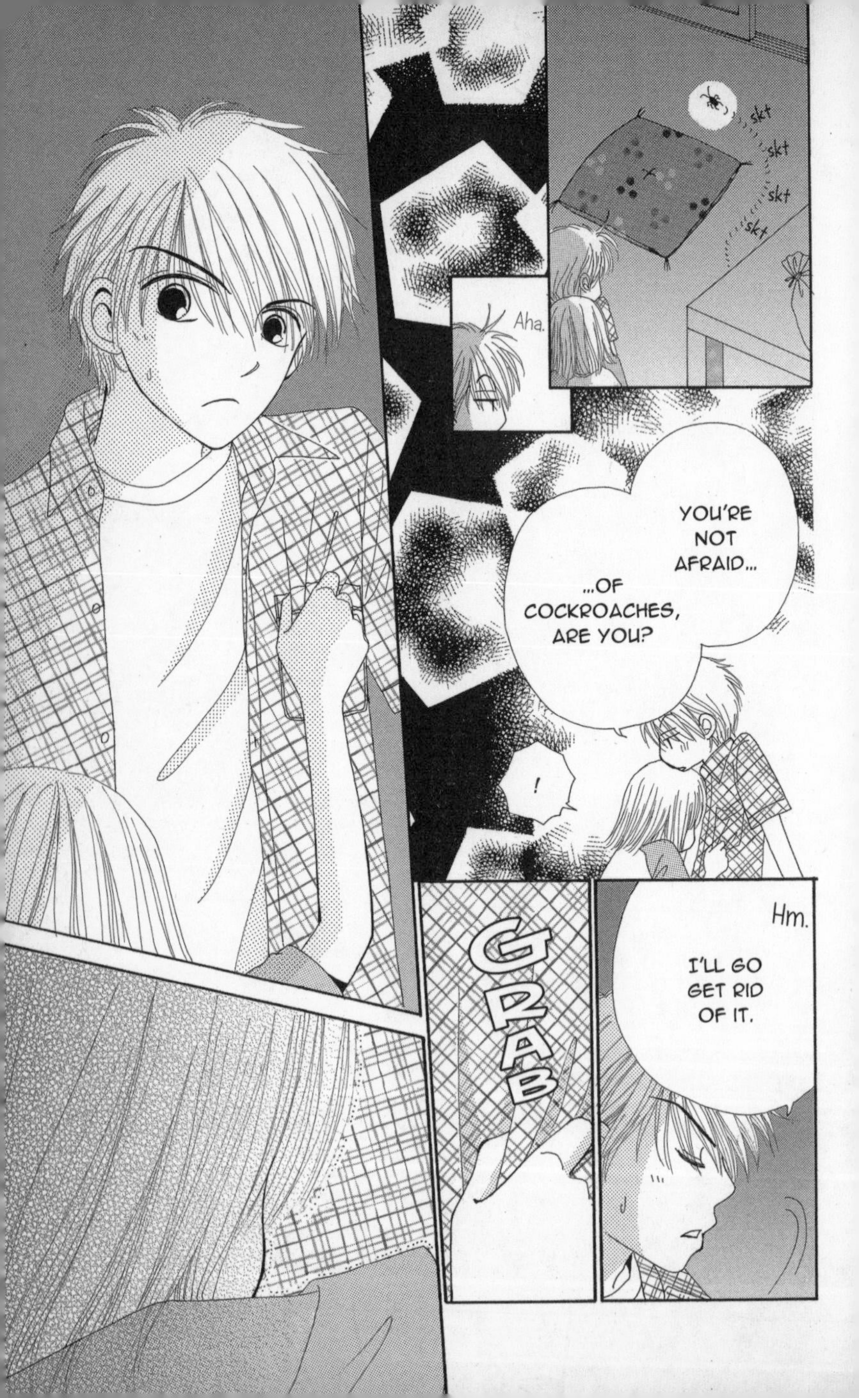
skt
skt
skt
skt
Aha.
YOU'RE NOT AFRAID...
...OF COCKROACHES, ARE YOU?
!
Hm.
I'LL GO GET RID OF IT.
GRAB

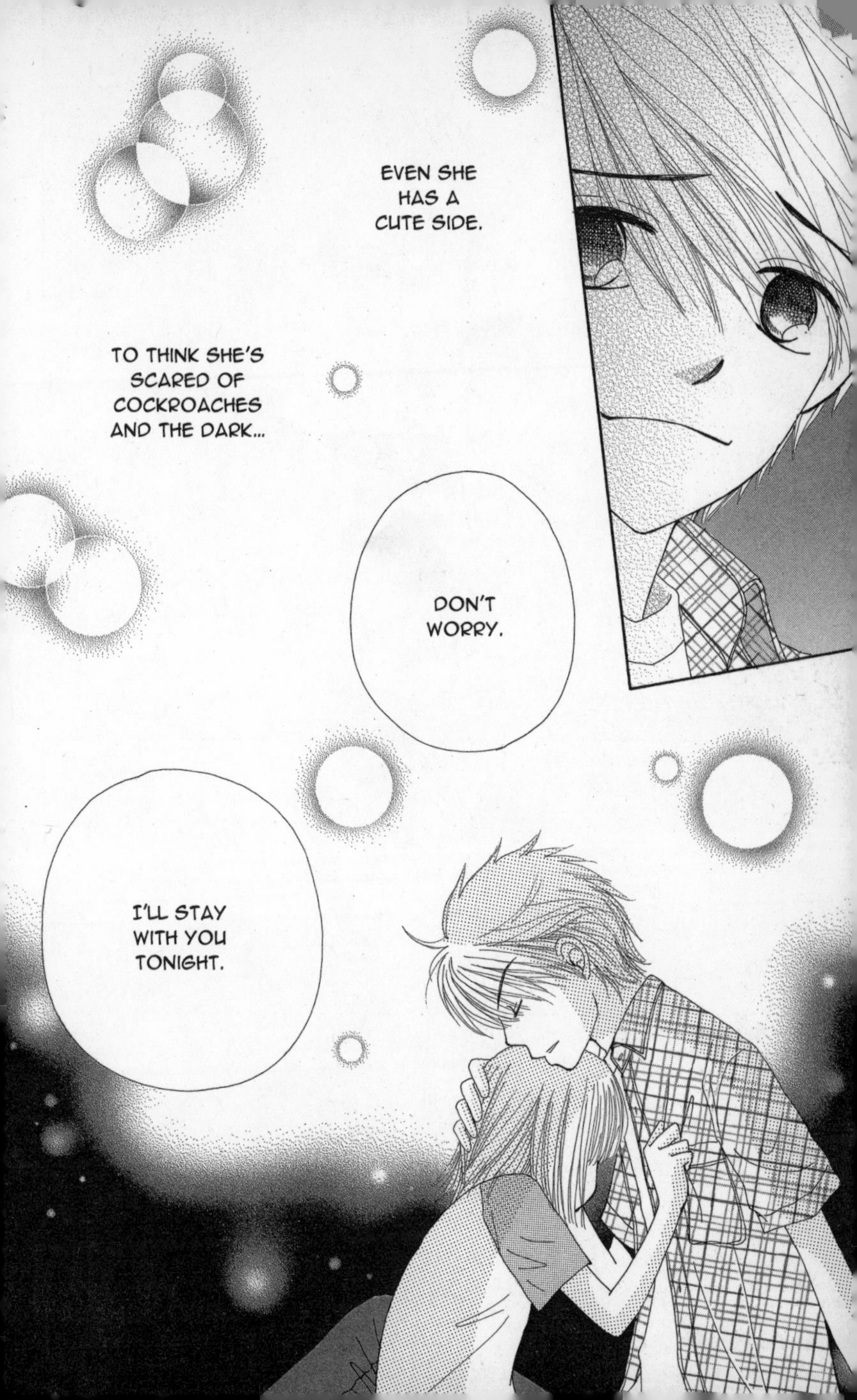
EVEN SHE HAS A CUTE SIDE.
TO THINK SHE'S SCARED OF COCKROACHES AND THE DARK...
DON'T WORRY.
I'LL STAY WITH YOU TONIGHT.

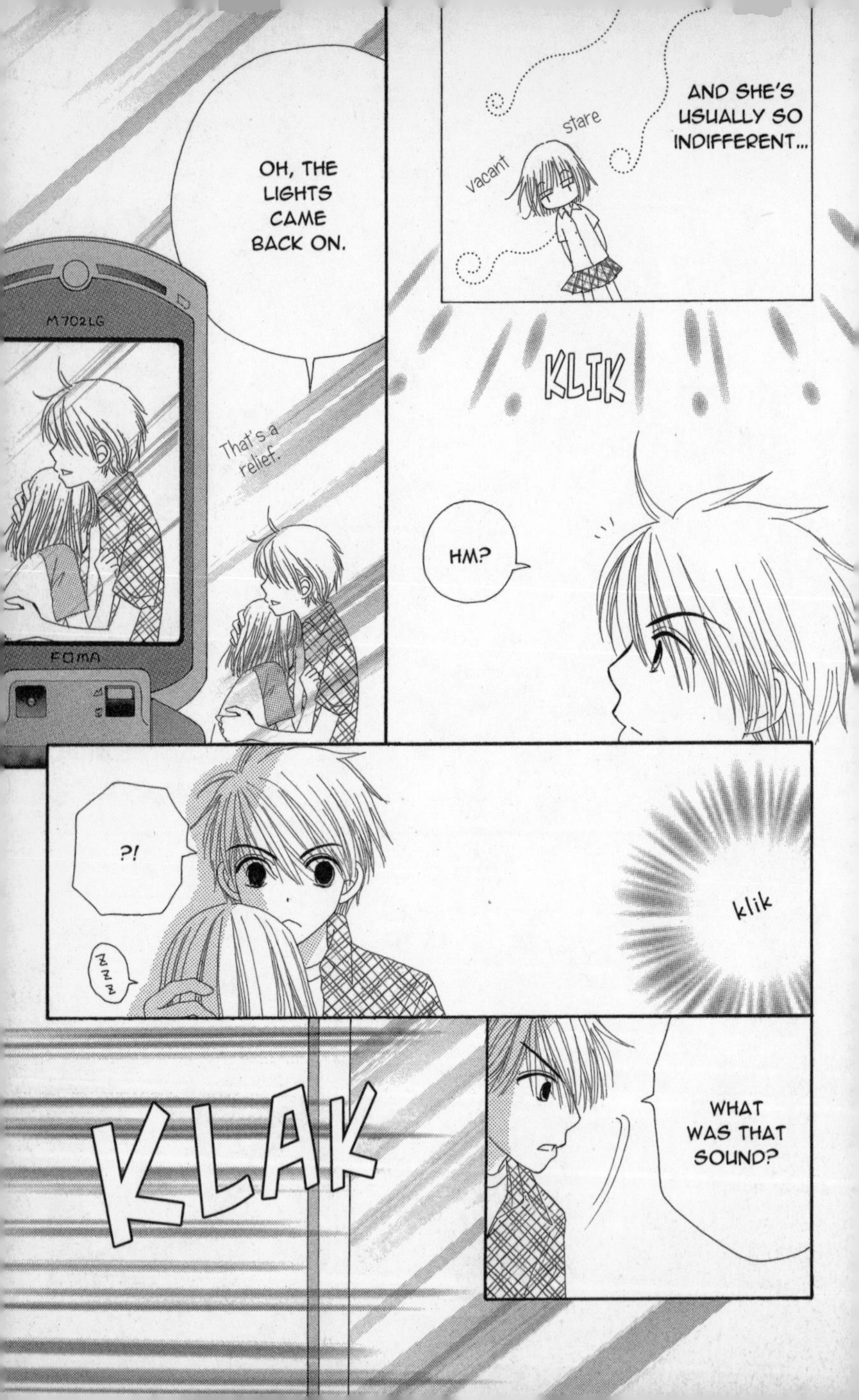
AND SHE'S USUALLY SO INDIFFERENT...
stare
Vacant
KLIK
HM?
OH, THE LIGHTS CAME BACK ON.
That's a relief.
M702LG
FOMA
klik
?!
ZZZ
WHAT WAS THAT SOUND?
KLAK

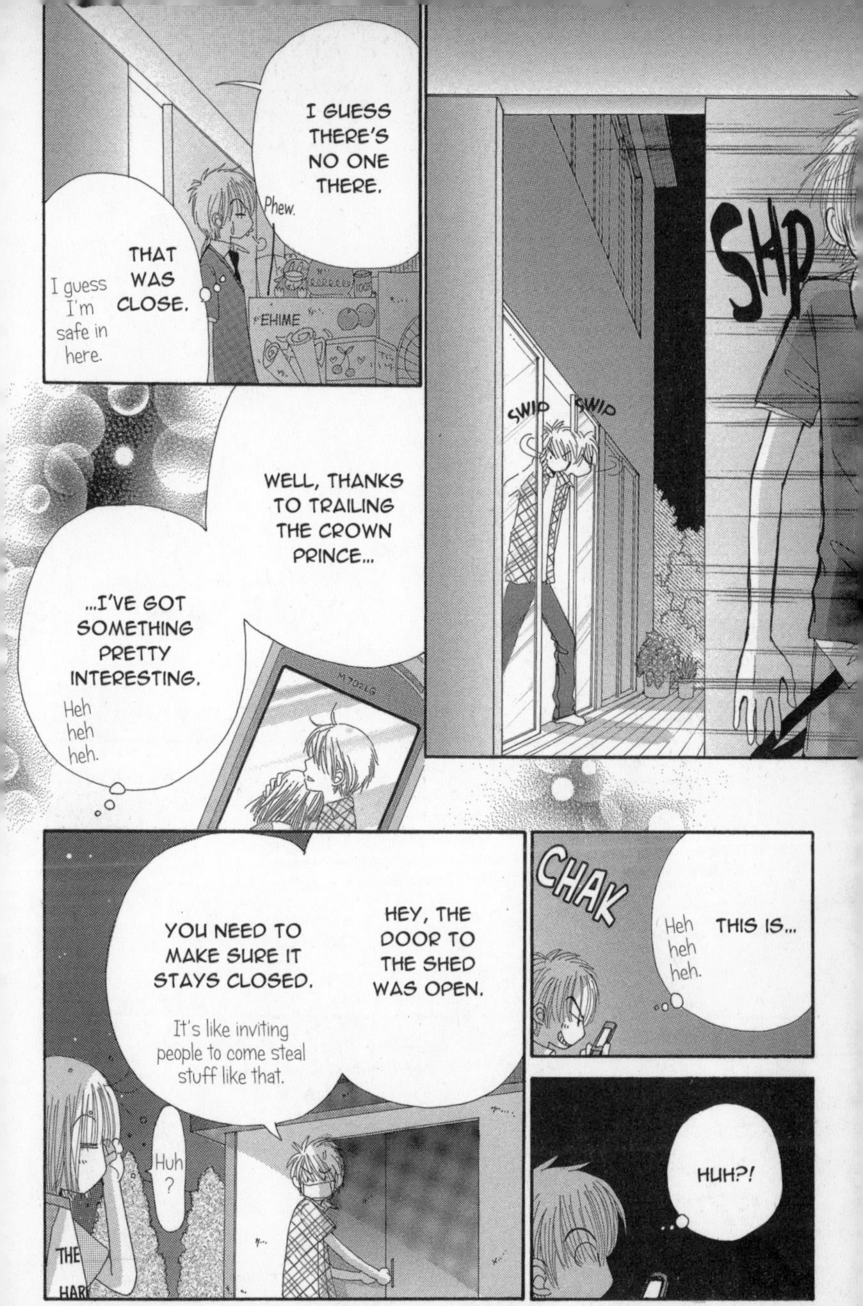
SHP
SWIP SWIP
I GUESS THERE'S NO ONE THERE.
Phew.
THAT WAS CLOSE.
I guess I'm safe in here.
WELL, THANKS TO TRAILING THE CROWN PRINCE...
...I'VE GOT SOMETHING PRETTY INTERESTING.
Heh heh heh.
CHAK
THIS IS...
Heh heh heh.
HUH?!
HEY, THE DOOR TO THE SHED WAS OPEN.
YOU NEED TO MAKE SURE IT STAYS CLOSED.
It's like inviting people to come steal stuff like that.
Huh?
THE

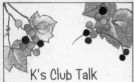

K's Club Talk

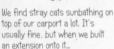

We find stray cats sunbathing on top of our carport a lot. It's usually fine, but when we built an extension onto it...

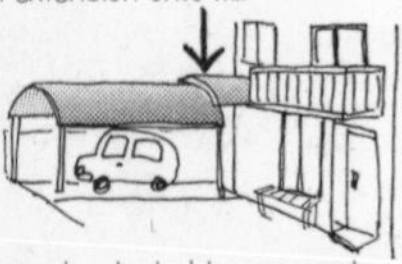

...the cats started to come onto our balcony!! Stray cats are usually infested with fleas, so we had to buy stuff to keep them out. We were worried that we wouldn't be able to hang our washing and air out the futon out there.

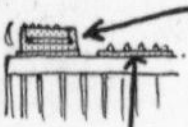

Thing that scares stray cats by rocking on top of the handrail of the balcony
Thing with plastic thorns so stray cats can't walk on them

Thanks to these things, the stray cats haven't come onto the balcony, but one day after a typhoon passed, when I was hanging my laundry out to dry...

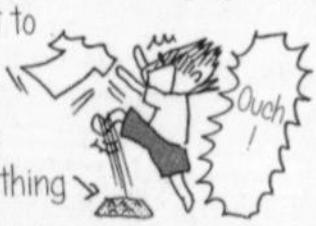

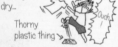

Ouch!
Thorny plastic thing

The thorny plastic thing had blown off the handrail and was lying on the balcony floor...
It seriously hurt! (The cats' revenge?!)
Ever since then, they've been sunbathing like normal.

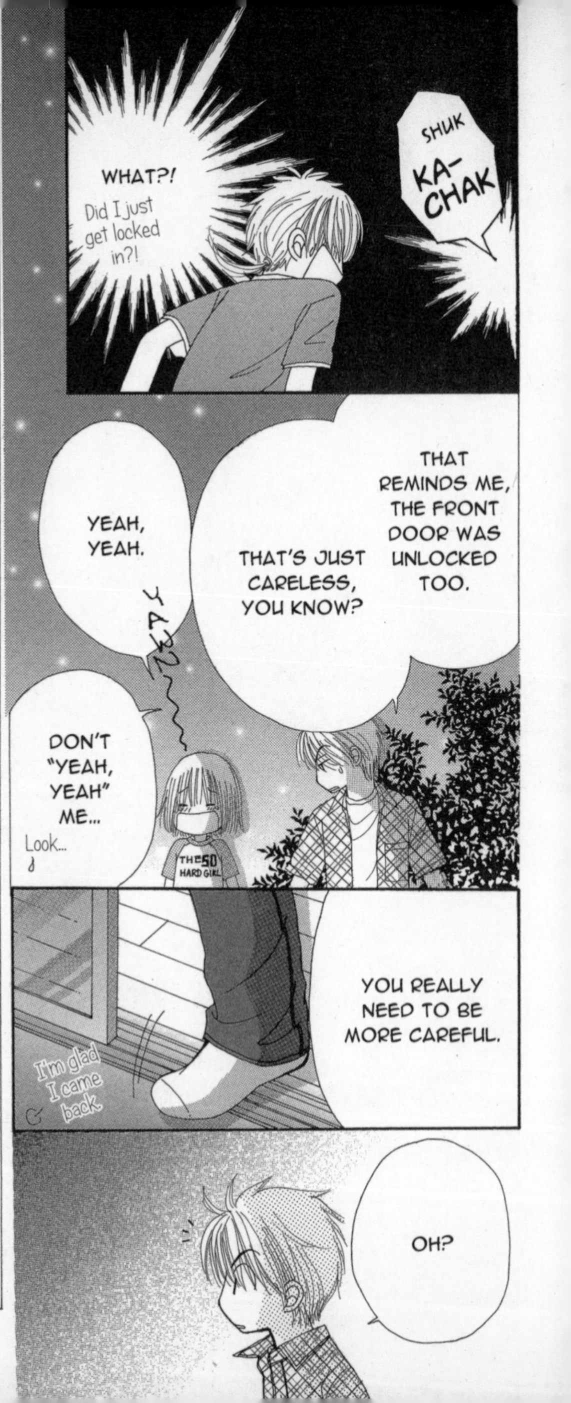

SHUK
KA-CHAK
WHAT?!
Did I just get locked in?!
THAT REMINDS ME, THE FRONT DOOR WAS UNLOCKED TOO.
THAT'S JUST CARELESS, YOU KNOW?
YEAH, YEAH.
DON'T "YEAH, YEAH" ME...
Look...
THE 50 HARD GIRL
YOU REALLY NEED TO BE MORE CAREFUL.
I'm glad I came back
OH?

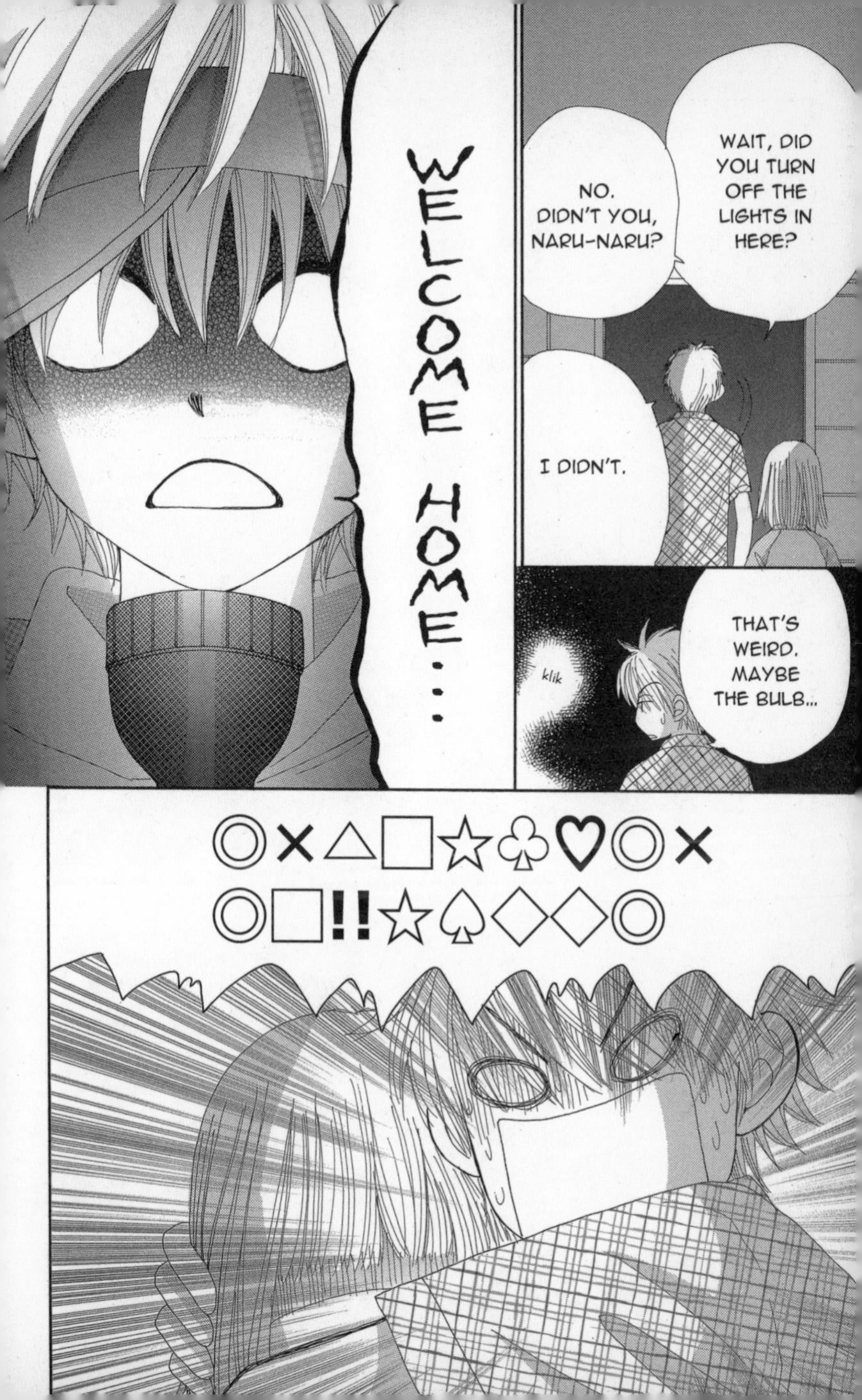
WAIT, DID YOU TURN OFF THE LIGHTS IN HERE?
NO. DIDN'T YOU, NARU-NARU?
I DIDN'T.
THAT'S WEIRD. MAYBE THE BULB...
klik
WELCOME HOME...
◎×△□☆♧♡◎×
◎□!!☆♤◇◇◎

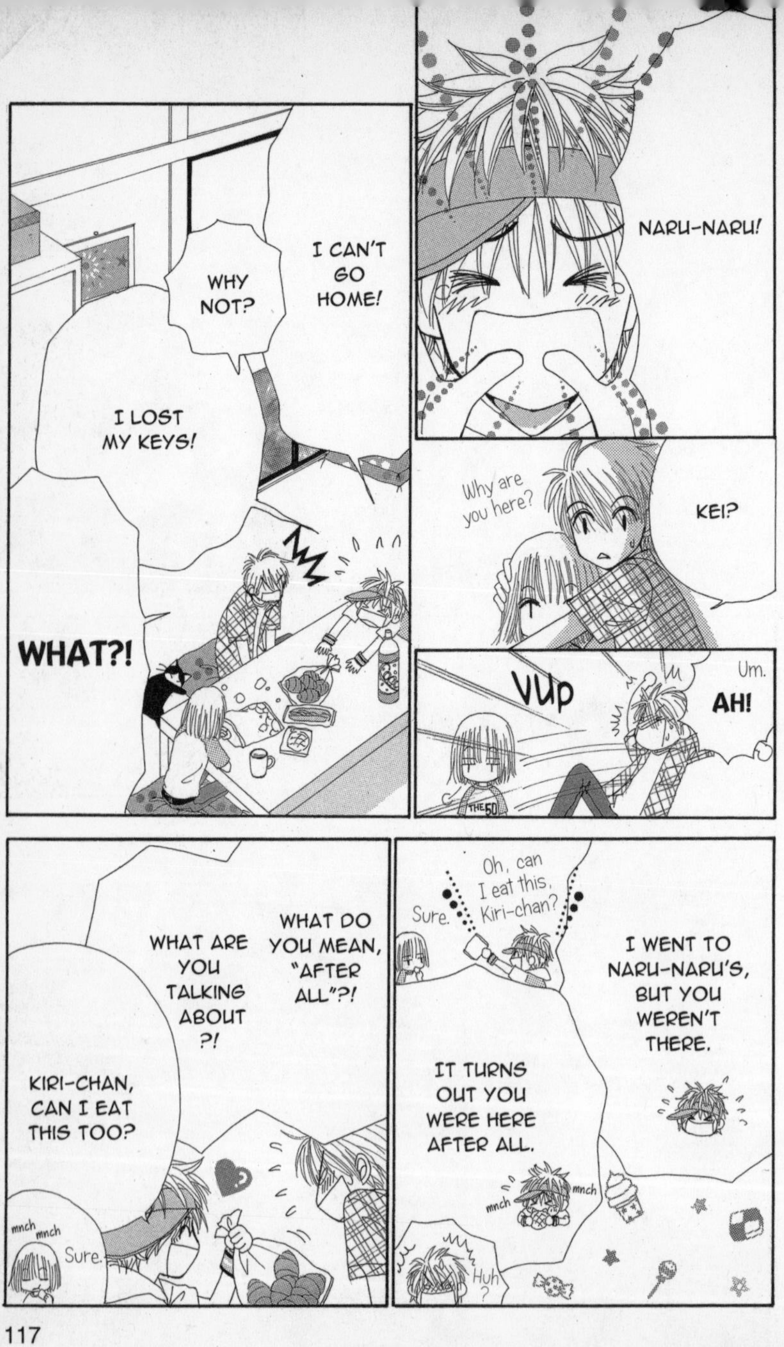
NARU-NARU!
KEI?
Why are you here?
Um.
AH!
VUp
I CAN'T GO HOME!
WHY NOT?
I LOST MY KEYS!
WHAT?!
Oh, can I eat this, Kiri-chan?
Sure.
I WENT TO NARU-NARU'S, BUT YOU WEREN'T THERE.
IT TURNS OUT YOU WERE HERE AFTER ALL.
mnch
mnch
Huh?
WHAT DO YOU MEAN, "AFTER ALL"?!
WHAT ARE YOU TALKING ABOUT?!
KIRI-CHAN, CAN I EAT THIS TOO?
Sure.
mnch mnch

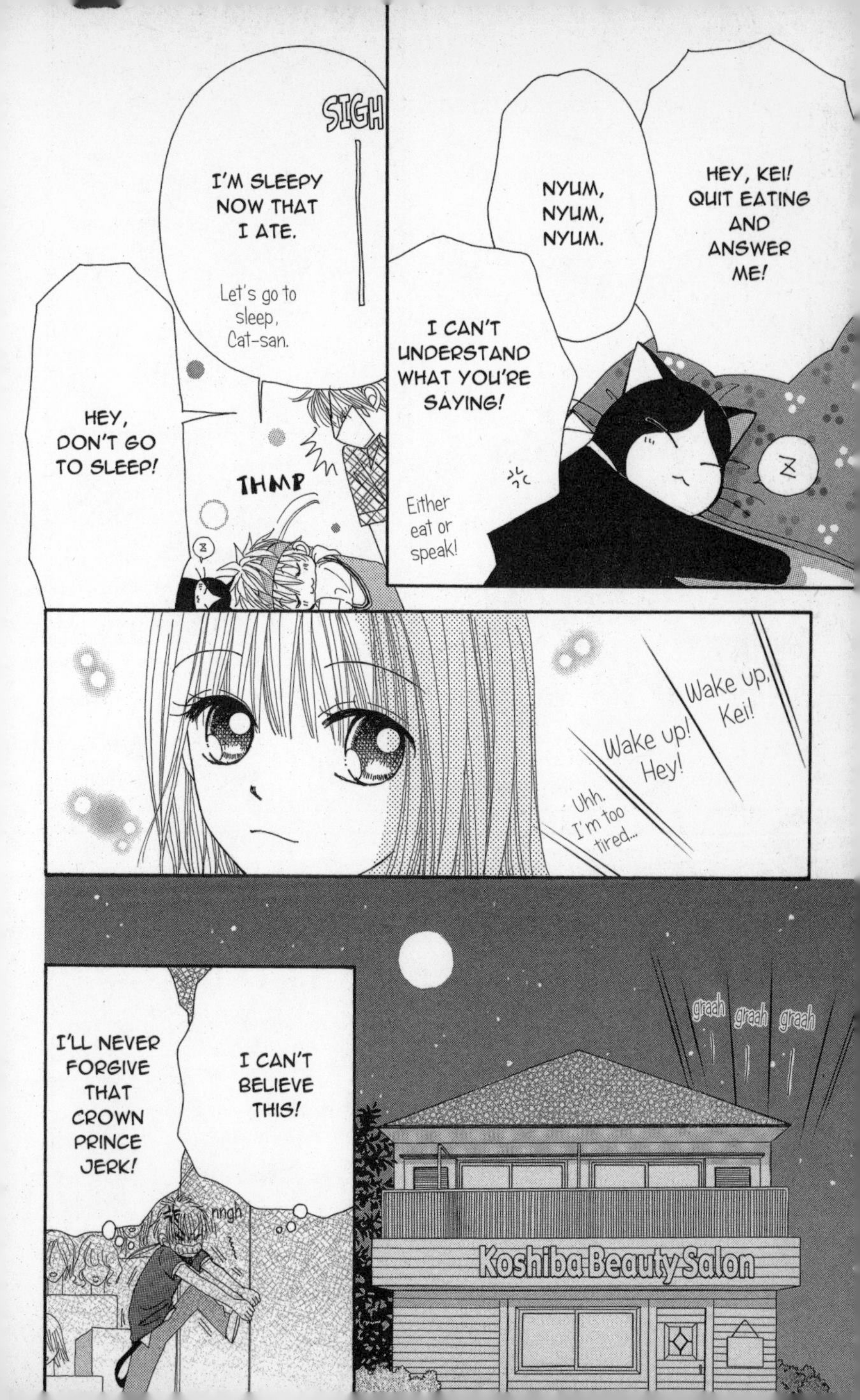
HEY, KEI! QUIT EATING AND ANSWER ME!
NYUM, NYUM, NYUM.
I CAN'T UNDERSTAND WHAT YOU'RE SAYING!
Either eat or speak!
SIGH
I'M SLEEPY NOW THAT I ATE.
Let's go to sleep, Cat-san.
HEY, DON'T GO TO SLEEP!
THMP
Wake up, Kei!
Wake up! Hey!
Uhh. I'm too tired...
graah graah graah
Koshiba Beauty Salon
I CAN'T BELIEVE THIS!
I'LL NEVER FORGIVE THAT CROWN PRINCE JERK!
nngh

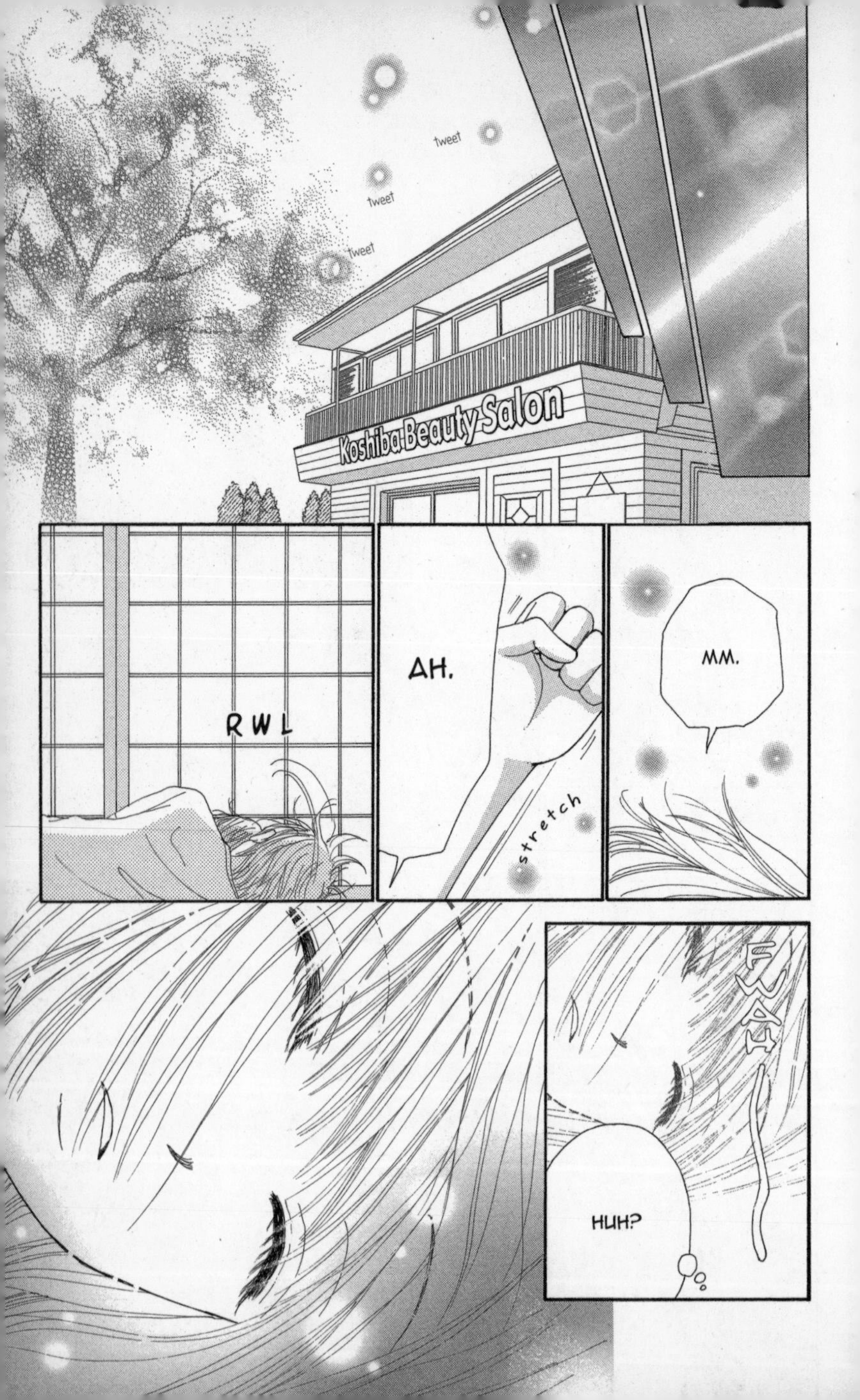
tweet
tweet
tweet
Koshiba Beauty Salon
MM.
AH.
stretch
RWL
FWAH
HUH?

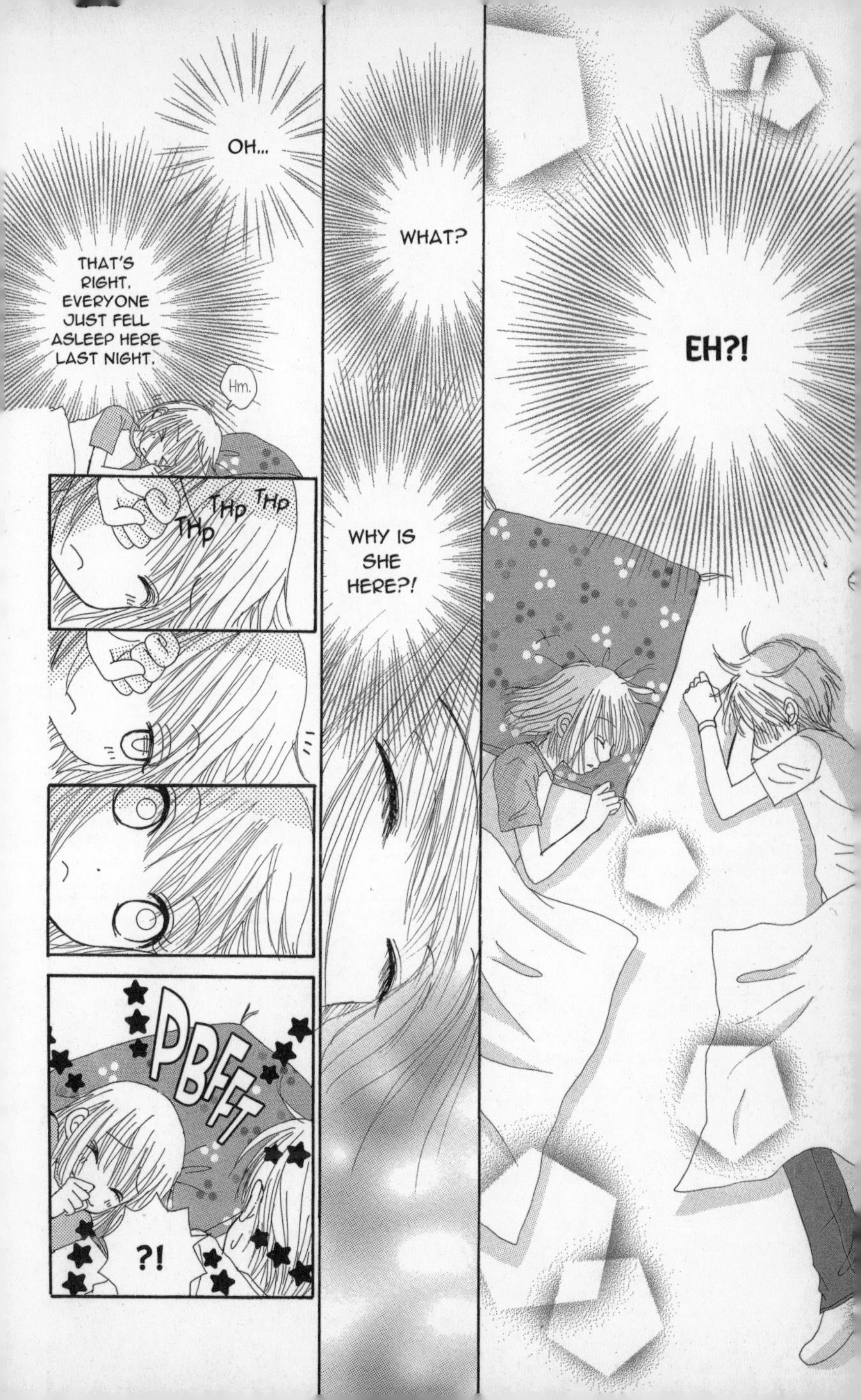
EH?!
WHAT?
WHY IS SHE HERE?!
OH...
THAT'S RIGHT. EVERYONE JUST FELL ASLEEP HERE LAST NIGHT.
Hm.
THp THp THp
PBFFT
?!

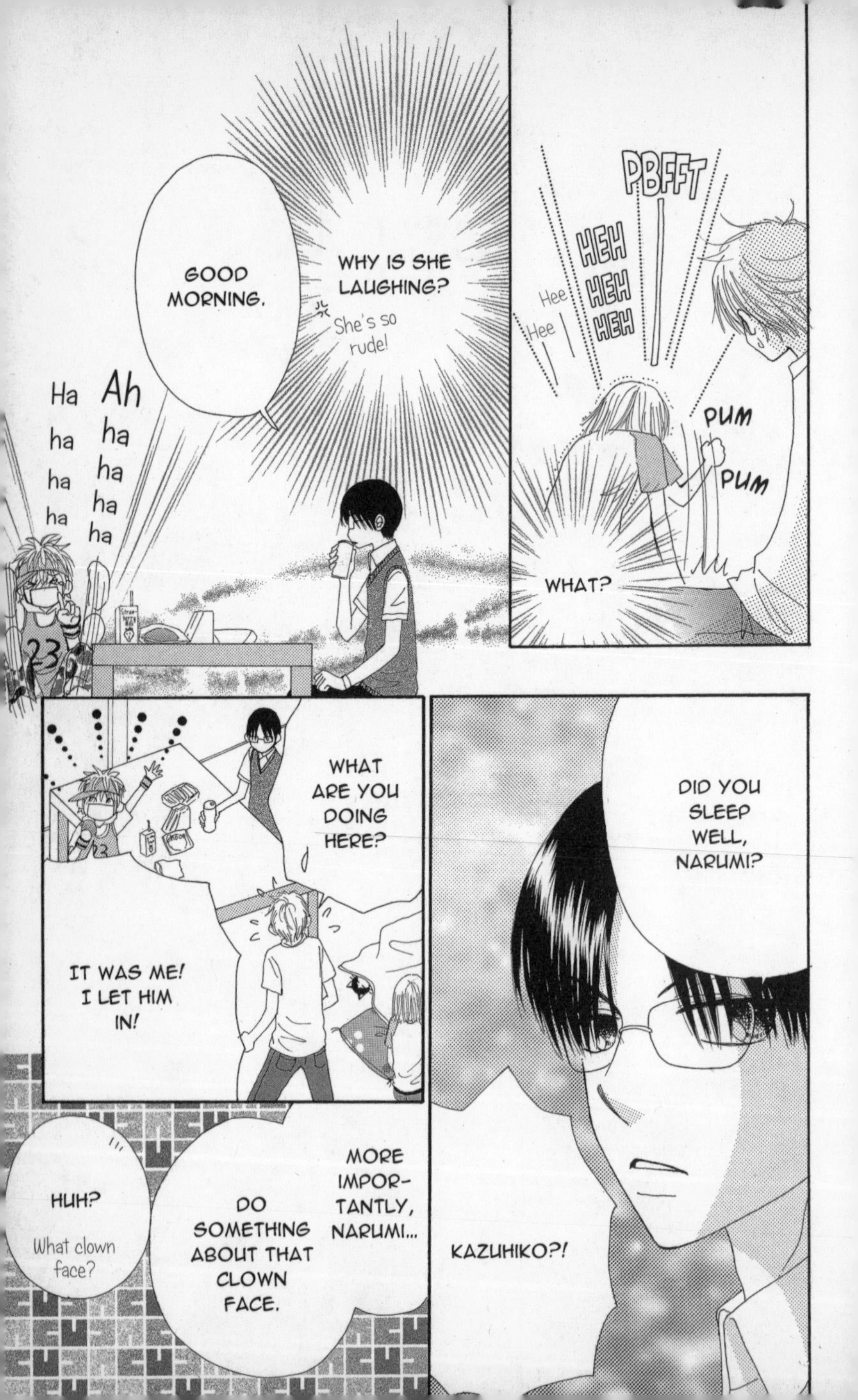
PBFFT
HEH HEH HEH
Hee Hee
PUM PUM
WHAT?
WHY IS SHE LAUGHING?
She's so rude!
GOOD MORNING.
Ah ha ha ha ha
Ha ha ha ha
DID YOU SLEEP WELL, NARUMI?
KAZUHIKO?!
WHAT ARE YOU DOING HERE?
IT WAS ME! I LET HIM IN!
MORE IMPOR-TANTLY, NARUMI...
DO SOMETHING ABOUT THAT CLOWN FACE.
HUH?
What clown face?

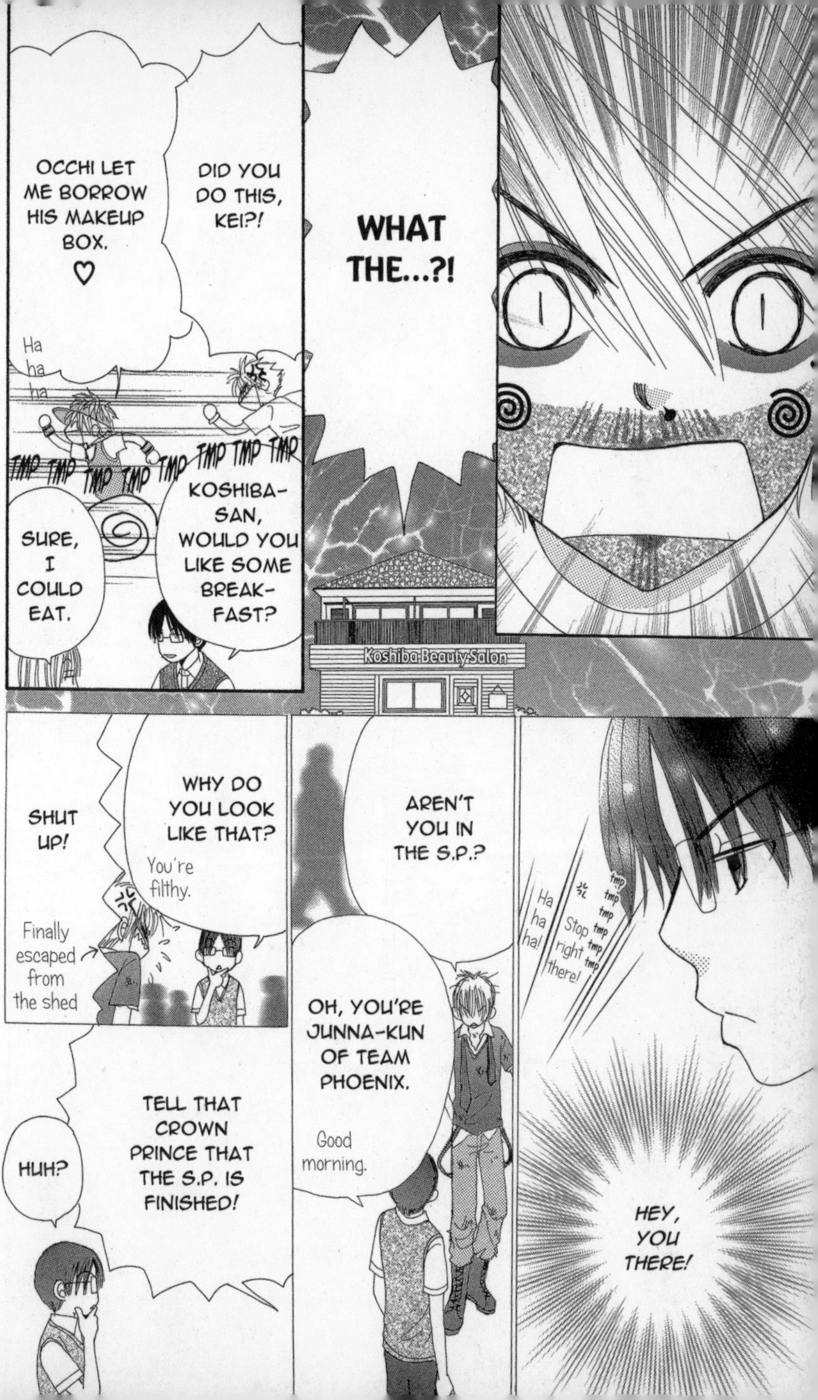
WHAT THE...?!
Koshiba Beauty Salon
DID YOU DO THIS, KEI?!
OCCHI LET ME BORROW HIS MAKEUP BOX. ♡
Ha ha ha
TMP TMP TMP TMP TMP TMP TMP TMP TMP
KOSHIBA-SAN, WOULD YOU LIKE SOME BREAKFAST?
SURE, I COULD EAT.
Ha ha ha!
tmp tmp tmp tmp tmp tmp
Stop right there!
HEY, YOU THERE!
AREN'T YOU IN THE S.P.?
OH, YOU'RE JUNNA-KUN OF TEAM PHOENIX.
Good morning.
WHY DO YOU LOOK LIKE THAT?
You're filthy.
SHUT UP!
Finally escaped from the shed
TELL THAT CROWN PRINCE THAT THE S.P. IS FINISHED!
HUH?

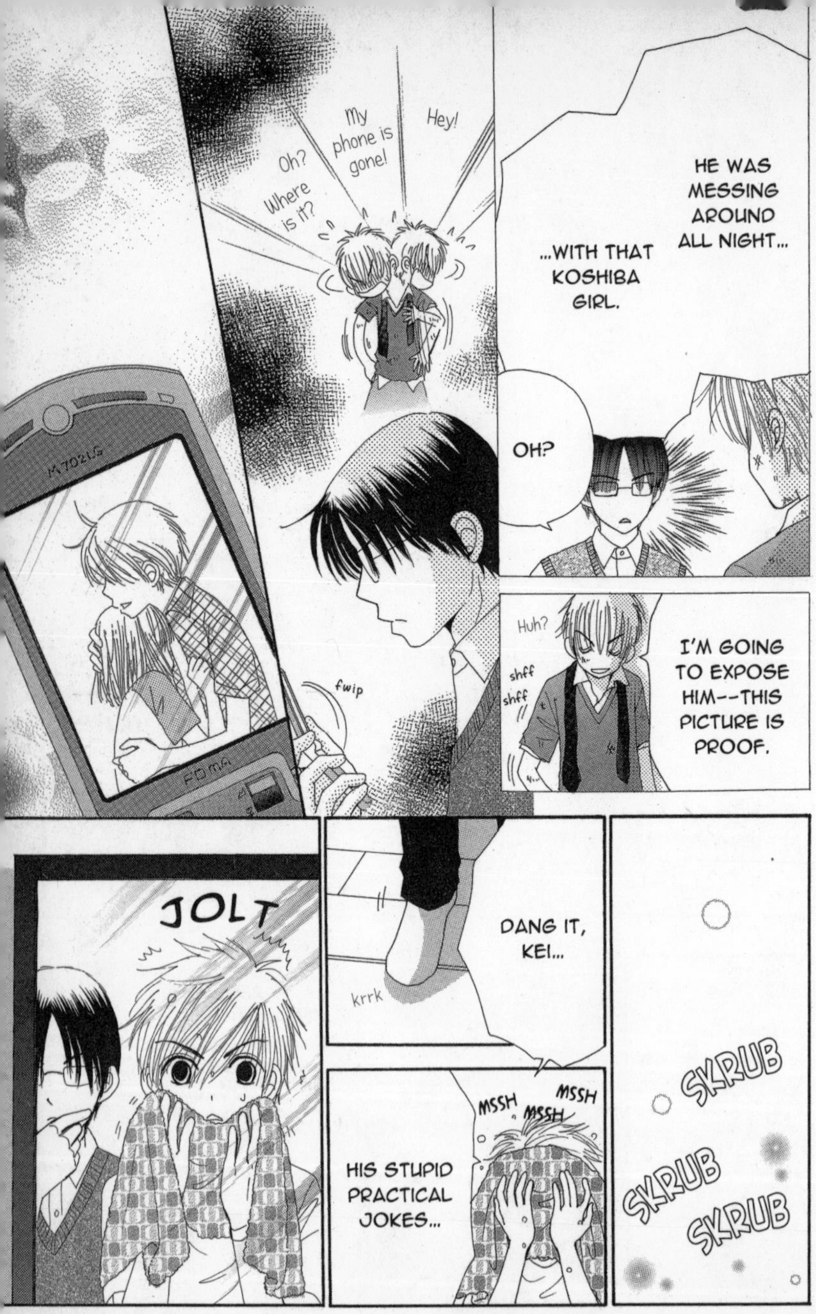
HE WAS MESSING AROUND ALL NIGHT...
...WITH THAT KOSHIBA GIRL.
OH?
I'M GOING TO EXPOSE HIM--THIS PICTURE IS PROOF.
Huh?
shff
shff
Hey!
My phone is gone!
Oh? Where is it?
fwip
SKRUB
SKRUB
SKRUB
DANG IT, KEI...
krrk
HIS STUPID PRACTICAL JOKES...
MSSH
MSSH
MSSH
JOLT

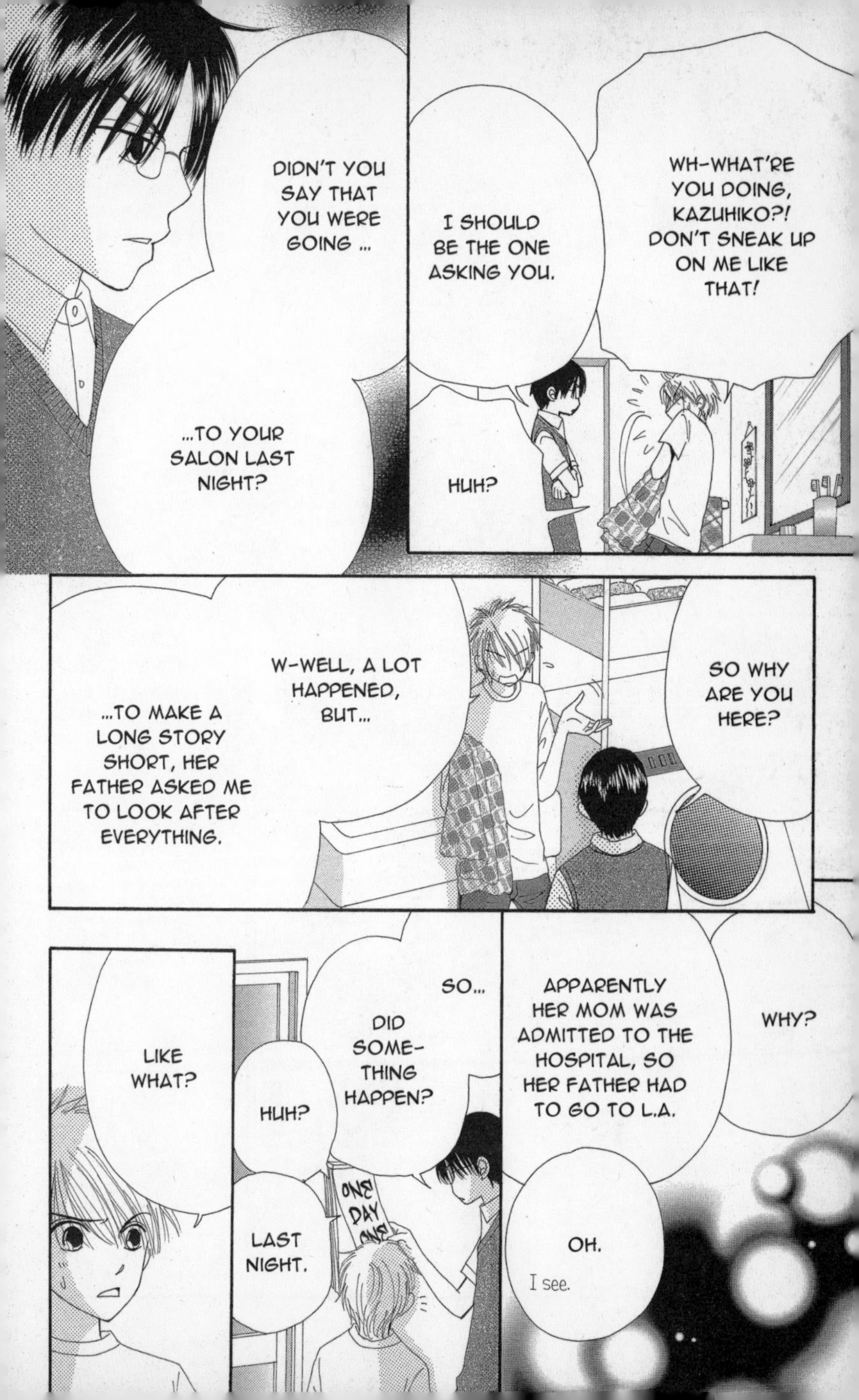
WH-WHAT'RE YOU DOING, KAZUHIKO?! DON'T SNEAK UP ON ME LIKE THAT!
I SHOULD BE THE ONE ASKING YOU.
HUH?
DIDN'T YOU SAY THAT YOU WERE GOING ...
...TO YOUR SALON LAST NIGHT?
SO WHY ARE YOU HERE?
W-WELL, A LOT HAPPENED, BUT...
...TO MAKE A LONG STORY SHORT, HER FATHER ASKED ME TO LOOK AFTER EVERYTHING.
WHY?
APPARENTLY HER MOM WAS ADMITTED TO THE HOSPITAL, SO HER FATHER HAD TO GO TO L.A.
OH.
I see.
SO...
DID SOMETHING HAPPEN?
HUH?
LAST NIGHT.
LIKE WHAT?

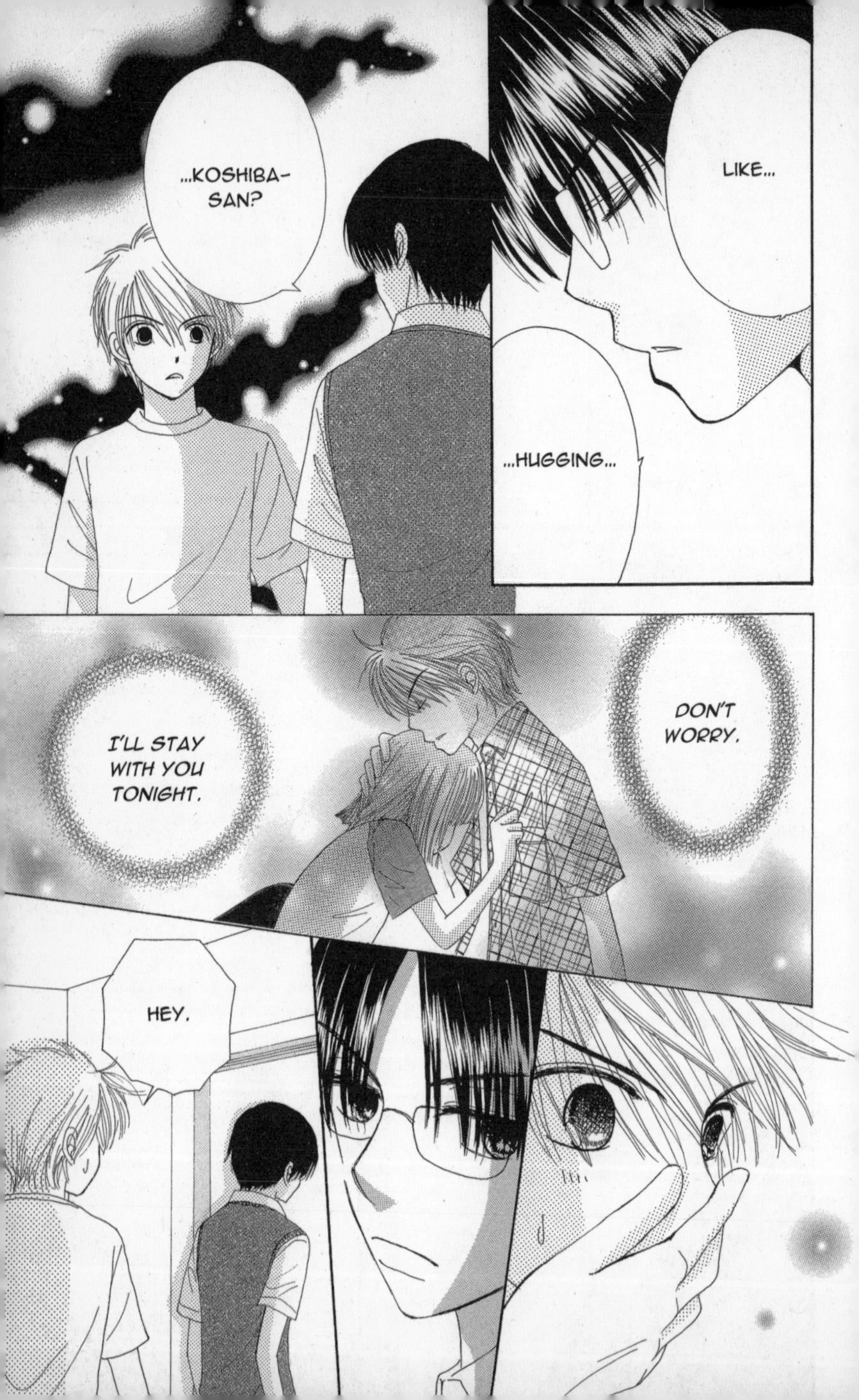
LIKE...
...HUGGING...
...KOSHIBA-SAN?
DON'T WORRY.
I'LL STAY WITH YOU TONIGHT.
HEY.

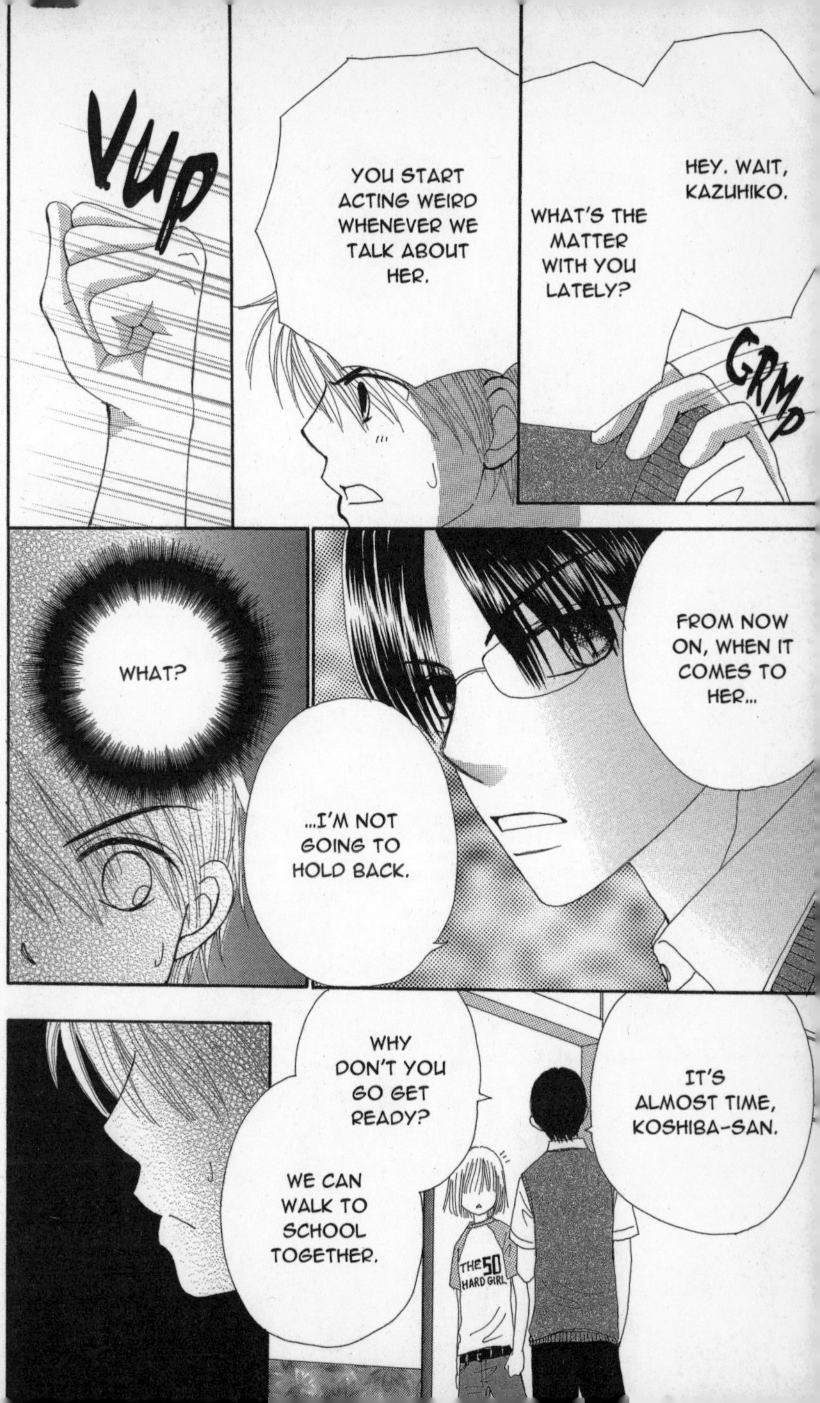
HEY. WAIT, KAZUHIKO.
WHAT'S THE MATTER WITH YOU LATELY?
GRMP
YOU START ACTING WEIRD WHENEVER WE TALK ABOUT HER.
VUP
FROM NOW ON, WHEN IT COMES TO HER...
...I'M NOT GOING TO HOLD BACK.
WHAT?
IT'S ALMOST TIME, KOSHIBA-SAN.
WHY DON'T YOU GO GET READY?
WE CAN WALK TO SCHOOL TOGETHER.
THE 50 HARD GIRL

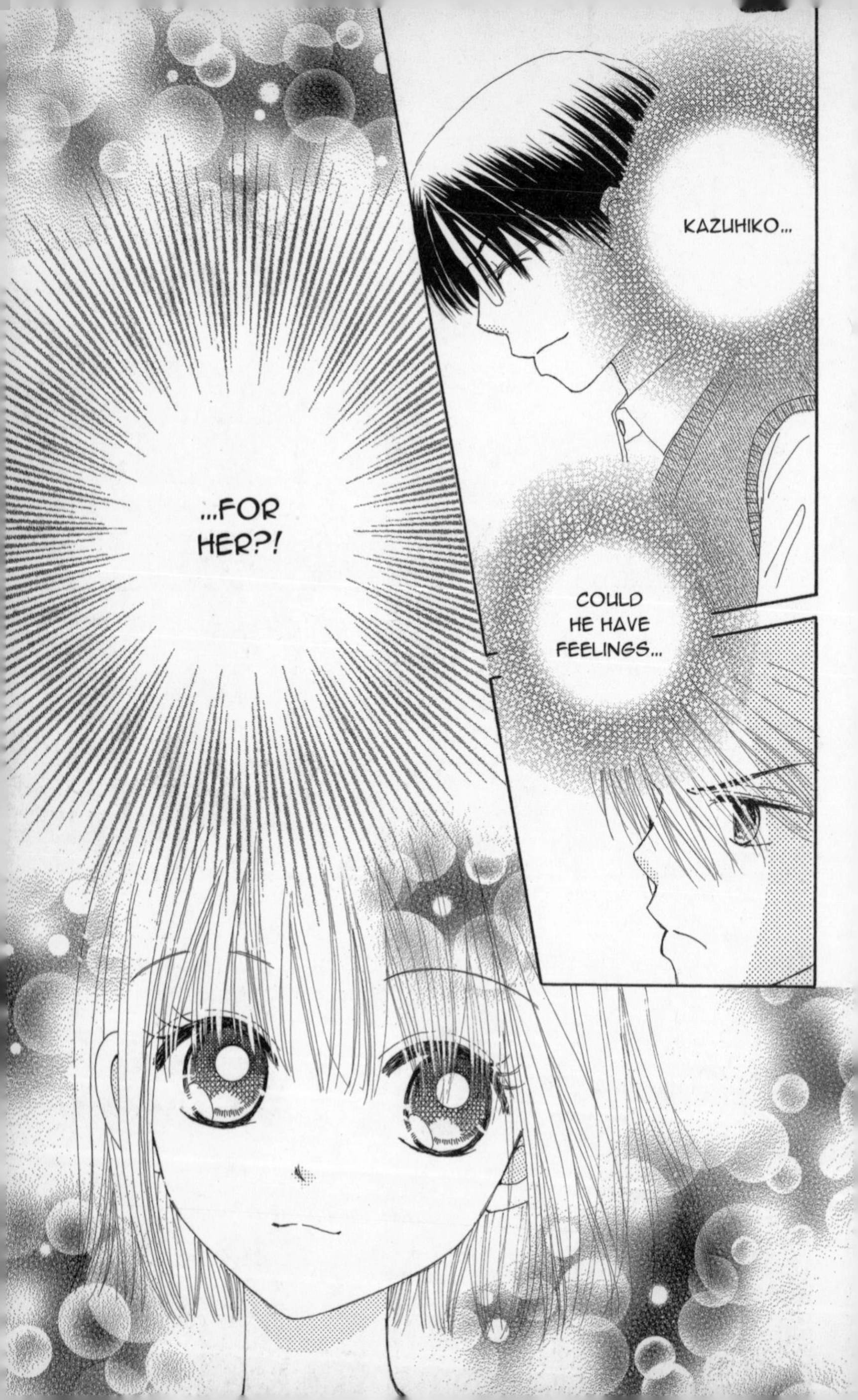
KAZUHIKO...
COULD HE HAVE FEELINGS...
...FOR HER?!

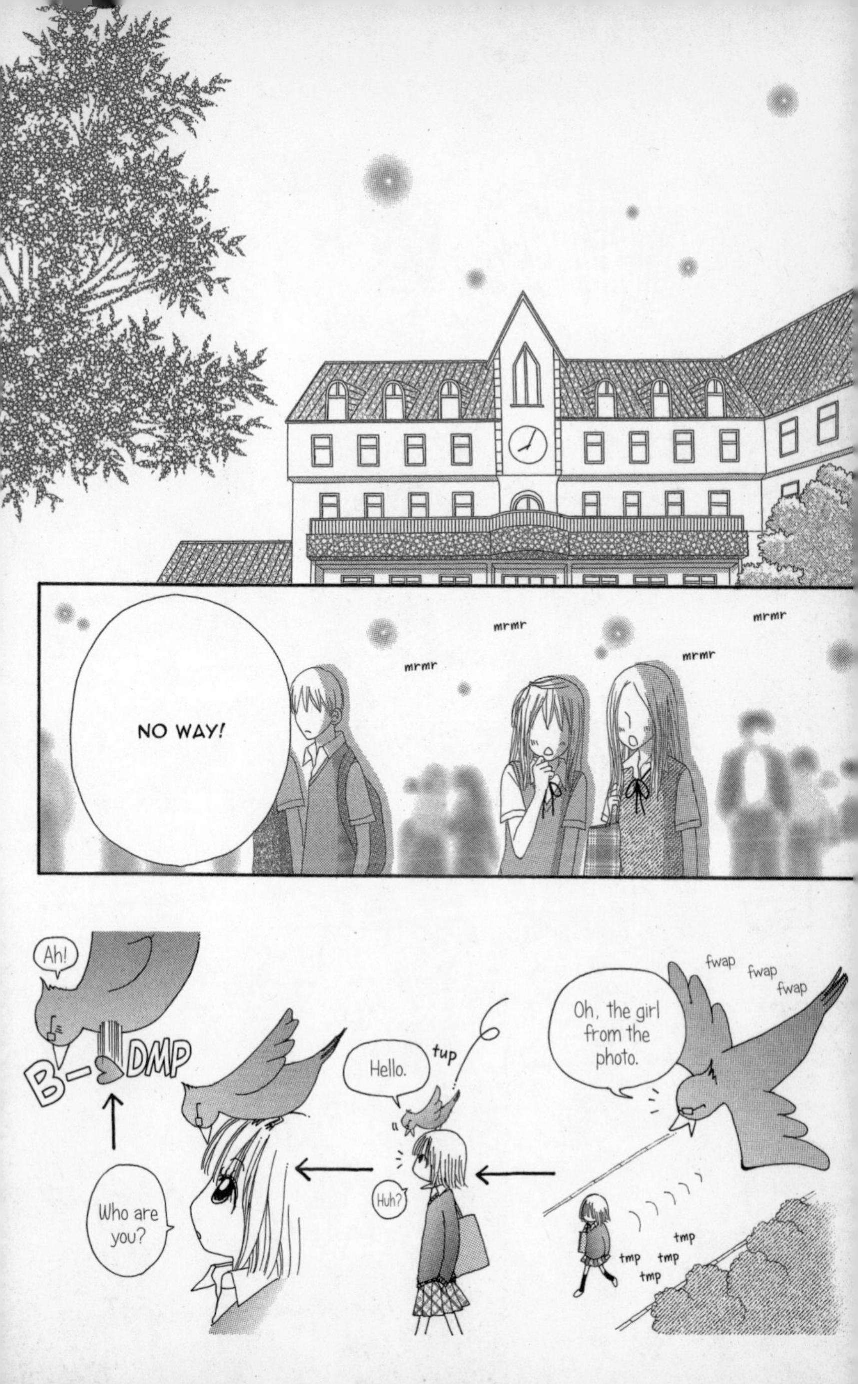
mrmr
mrmr
mrmr
mrmr
NO WAY!
fwap
fwap
fwap
Oh, the girl from the photo.
tmp
tmp
tmp
tmp
tup
Hello.
Huh?
Who are you?
Ah!
B-DMP

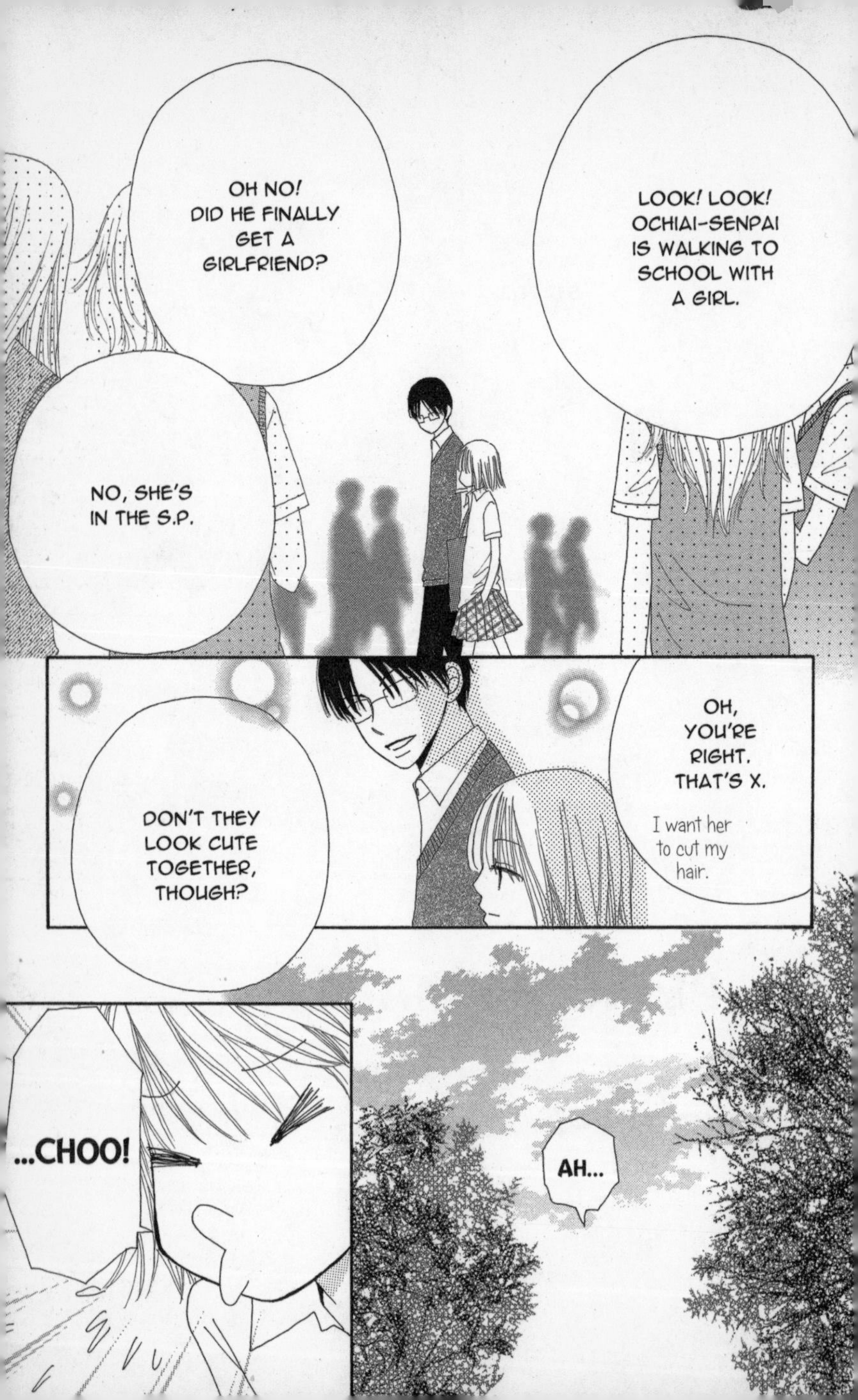
LOOK! LOOK! OCHIAI-SENPAI IS WALKING TO SCHOOL WITH A GIRL.
OH NO! DID HE FINALLY GET A GIRLFRIEND?
NO, SHE'S IN THE S.P.
OH, YOU'RE RIGHT. THAT'S X.
I want her to cut my hair.
DON'T THEY LOOK CUTE TOGETHER, THOUGH?
AH...
...CHOO!

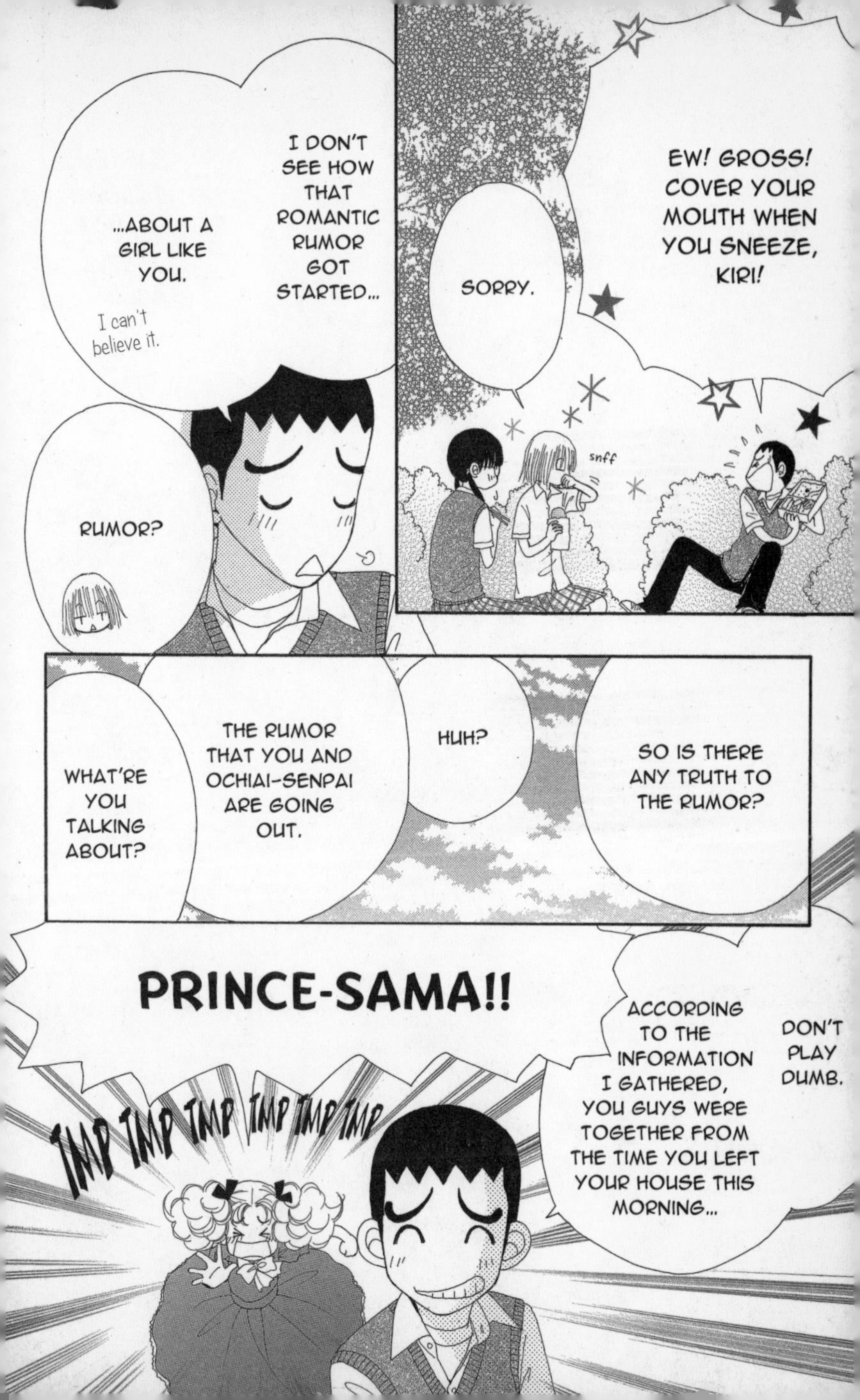
EW! GROSS! COVER YOUR MOUTH WHEN YOU SNEEZE, KIRI!
SORRY.
snff
I DON'T SEE HOW THAT ROMANTIC RUMOR GOT STARTED...
...ABOUT A GIRL LIKE YOU.
I can't believe it.
RUMOR?
SO IS THERE ANY TRUTH TO THE RUMOR?
HUH?
THE RUMOR THAT YOU AND OCHIAI-SENPAI ARE GOING OUT.
WHAT'RE YOU TALKING ABOUT?
DON'T PLAY DUMB.
ACCORDING TO THE INFORMATION I GATHERED, YOU GUYS WERE TOGETHER FROM THE TIME YOU LEFT YOUR HOUSE THIS MORNING...
PRINCE-SAMA!!
TMP TMP TMP TMP TMP TMP

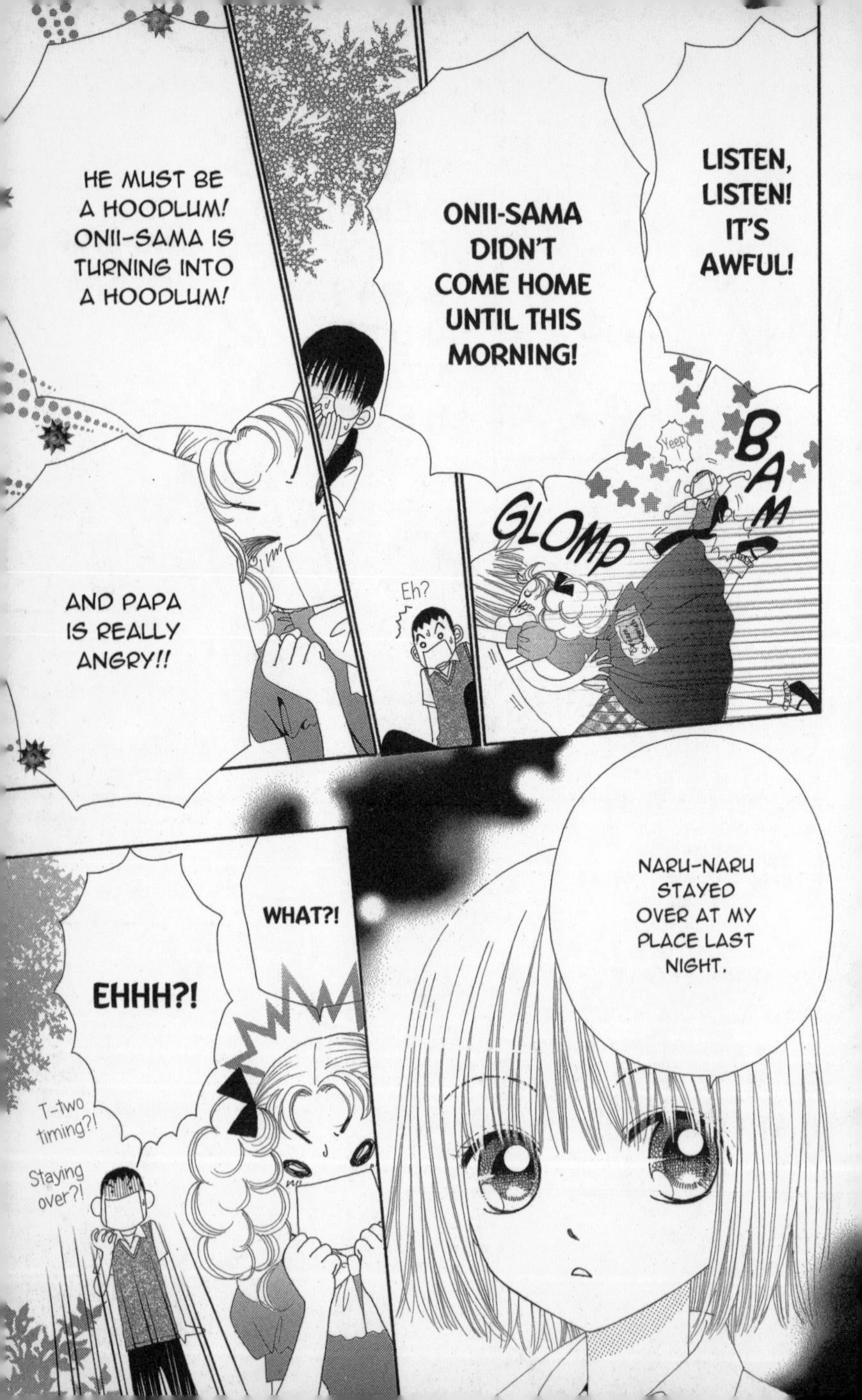
LISTEN, LISTEN! IT'S AWFUL!
Yeep!
BAM
GLOMP
ONII-SAMA DIDN'T COME HOME UNTIL THIS MORNING!
Eh?
HE MUST BE A HOODLUM! ONII-SAMA IS TURNING INTO A HOODLUM!
AND PAPA IS REALLY ANGRY!!
NARU-NARU STAYED OVER AT MY PLACE LAST NIGHT.
WHAT?!
EHHH?!
T-two timing?!
Staying over?!

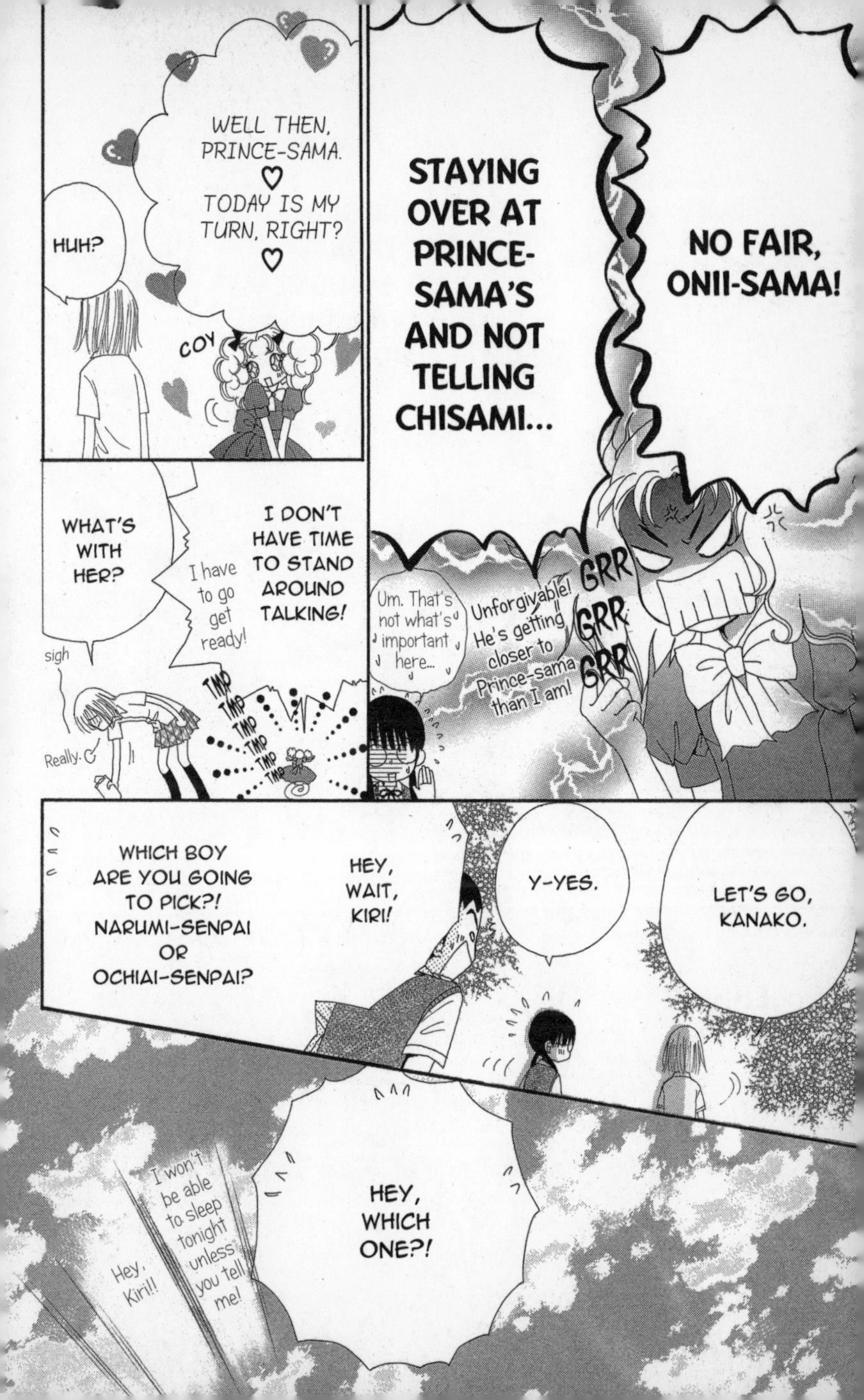
NO FAIR, ONII-SAMA!
STAYING OVER AT PRINCE-SAMA'S AND NOT TELLING CHISAMI...
GRR GRR GRR
Unforgivable! He's getting closer to Prince-sama than I am!
Um. That's not what's important here...
WELL THEN, PRINCE-SAMA. ♡ TODAY IS MY TURN, RIGHT? ♡
HUH?
COY
I DON'T HAVE TIME TO STAND AROUND TALKING!
I have to go get ready!
TMP TMP TMP TMP TMP TMP
WHAT'S WITH HER?
sigh
Really.
LET'S GO, KANAKO.
Y-YES.
HEY, WAIT, KIRI!
WHICH BOY ARE YOU GOING TO PICK?! NARUMI-SENPAI OR OCHIAI-SENPAI?
HEY, WHICH ONE?!
I won't be able to sleep tonight unless you tell me!
Hey, Kiri!!

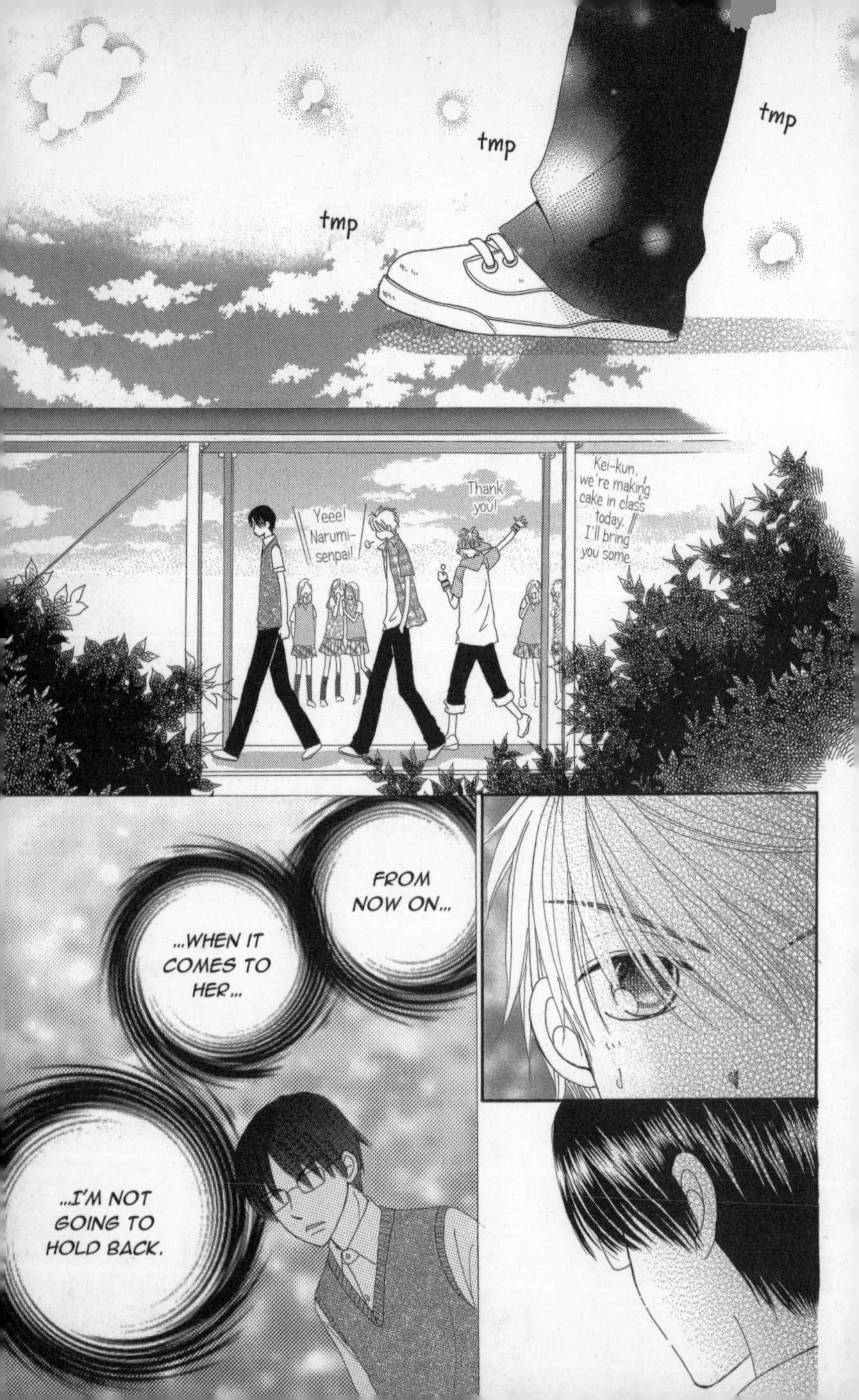
tmp
tmp
tmp
Kei-kun, we're making cake in class today. I'll bring you some.
Thank you!
Yeee! Narumi-senpai!
FROM NOW ON...
...WHEN IT COMES TO HER...
...I'M NOT GOING TO HOLD BACK.

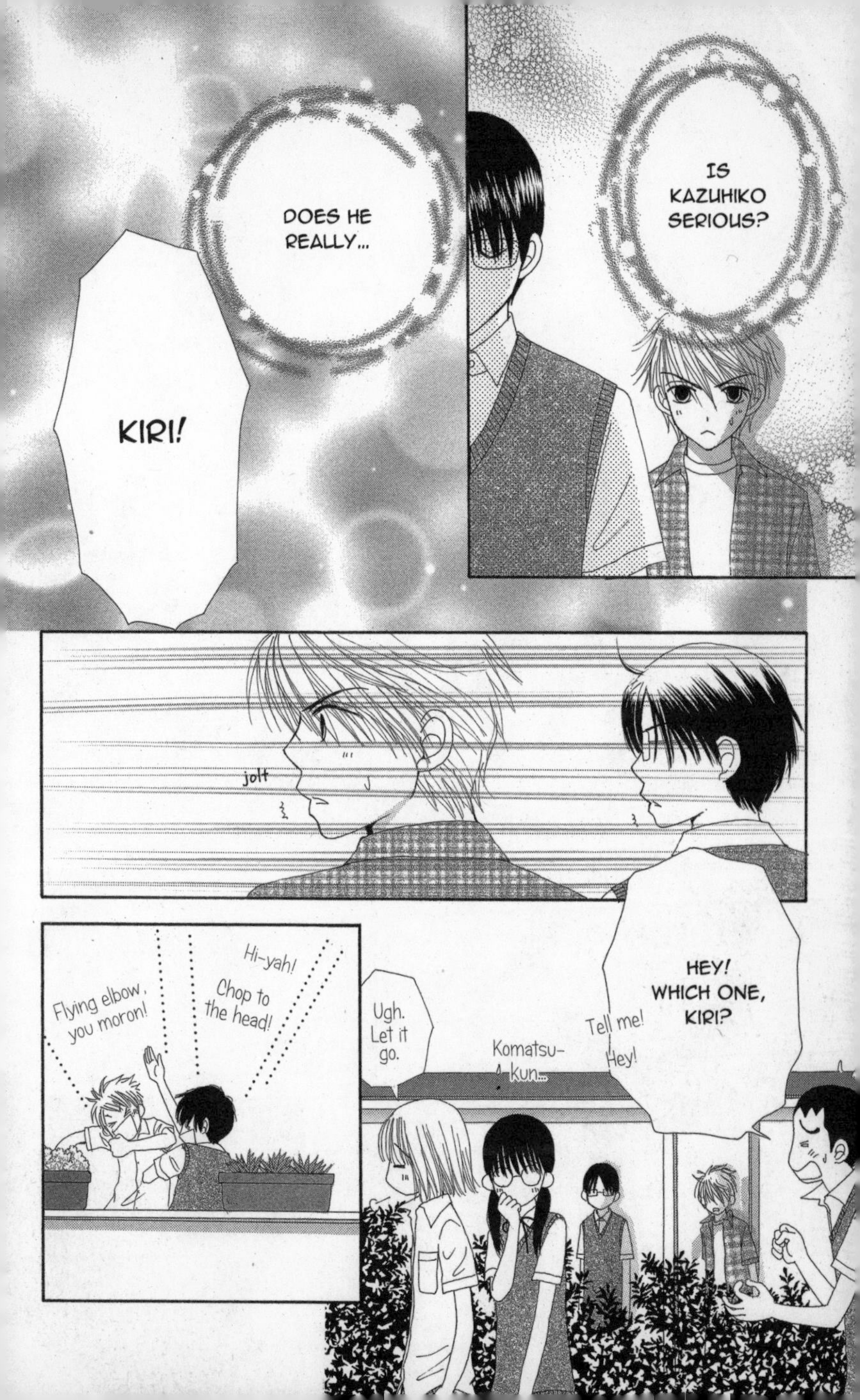
IS KAZUHIKO SERIOUS?
DOES HE REALLY...
KIRI!
jolt
HEY! WHICH ONE, KIRI?
Tell me!
Hey!
Komatsu-kun...
Ugh. Let it go.
Hi-yah!
Chop to the head!
Flying elbow, you moron!

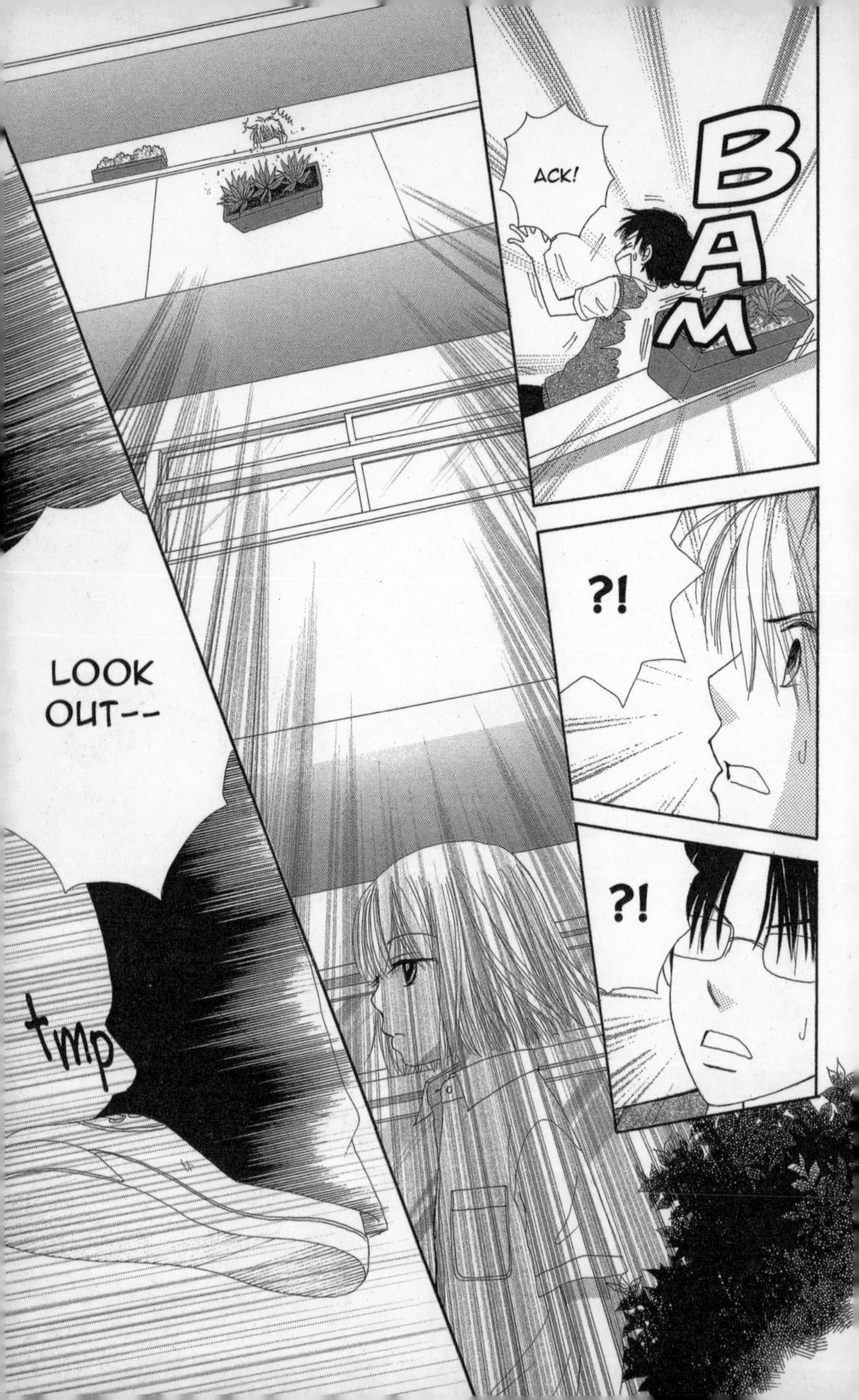
ACK!
BAM
?!
?!
LOOK OUT--
tmp

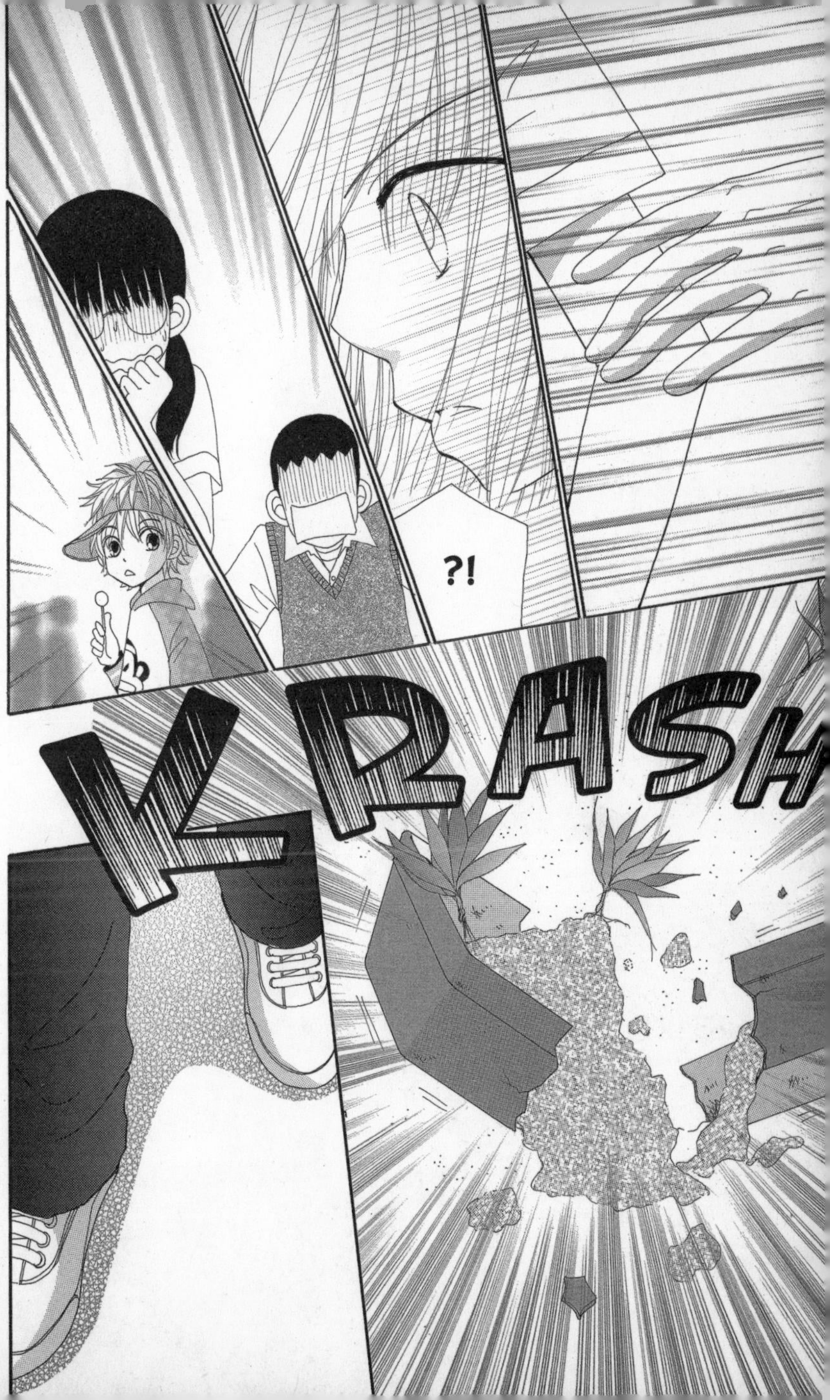
?!
KRASH

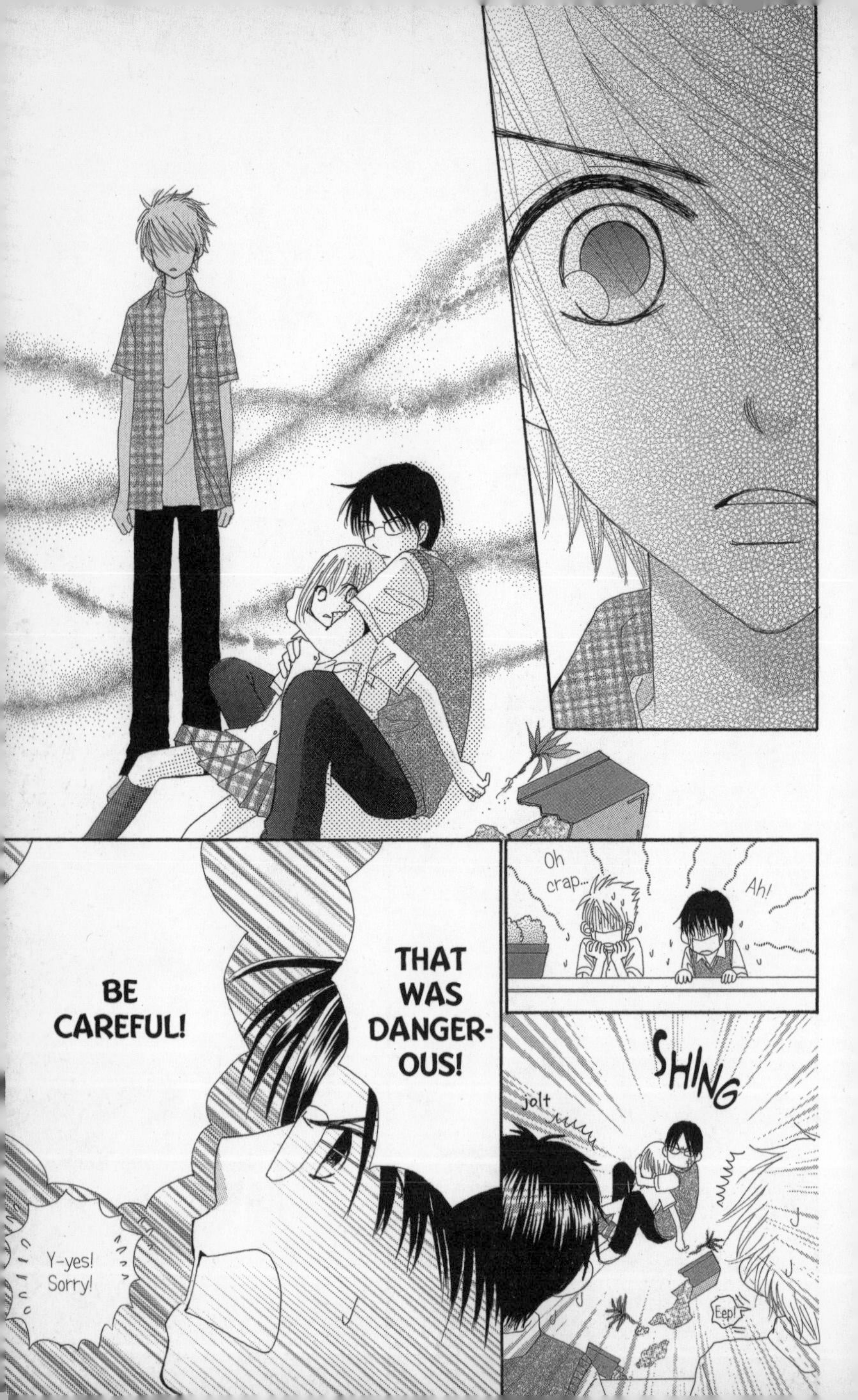
Ah!
Oh crap...
SHING
jolt
Eep!
THAT WAS DANGER-OUS!
BE CAREFUL!
Y-yes! Sorry!

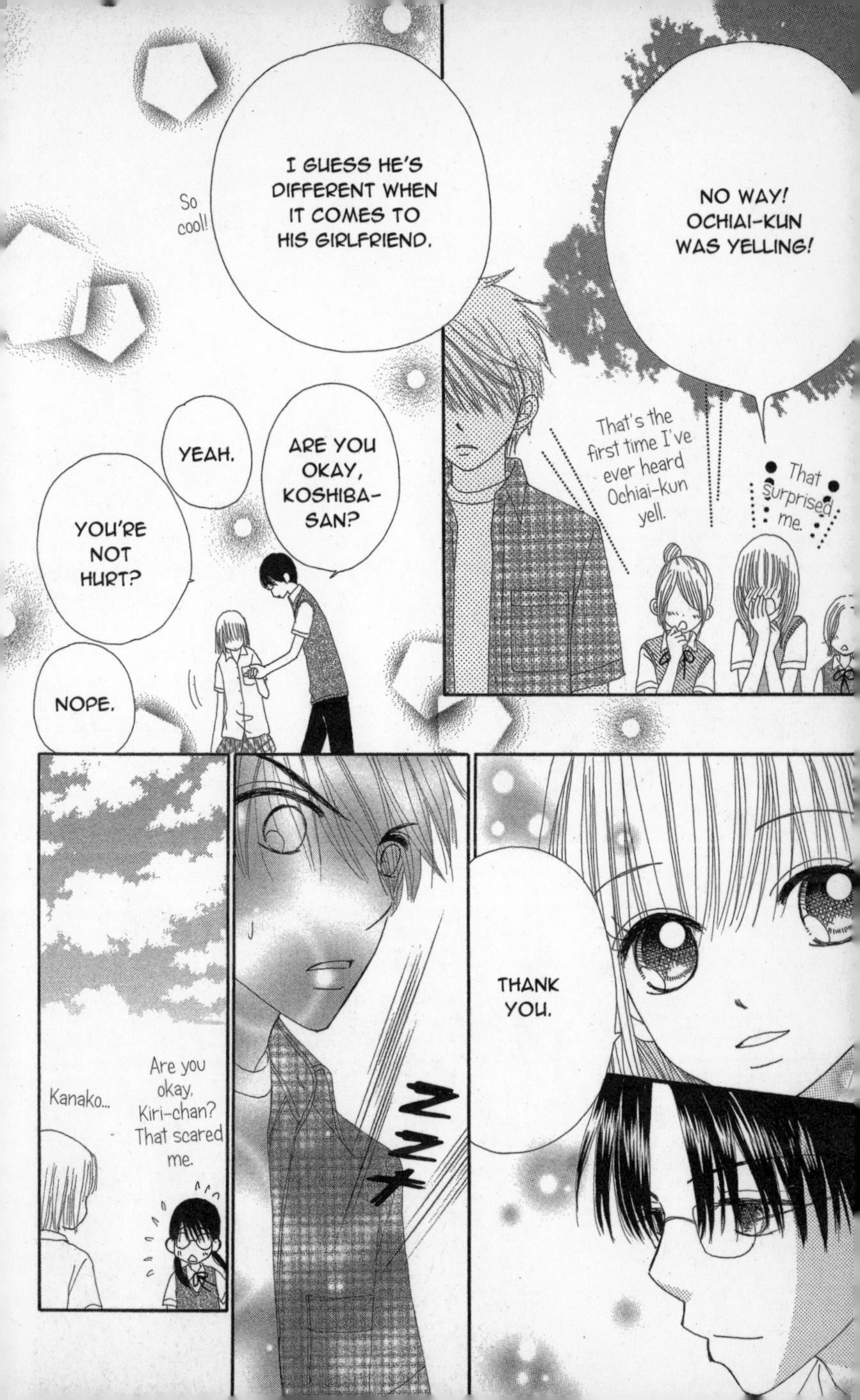
NO WAY! OCHIAI-KUN WAS YELLING!
That surprised me.
That's the first time I've ever heard Ochiai-kun yell.
I GUESS HE'S DIFFERENT WHEN IT COMES TO HIS GIRLFRIEND.
So cool!
ARE YOU OKAY, KOSHIBA-SAN?
YEAH.
YOU'RE NOT HURT?
NOPE.
THANK YOU.
Are you okay, Kiri-chan? That scared me.
Kanako...

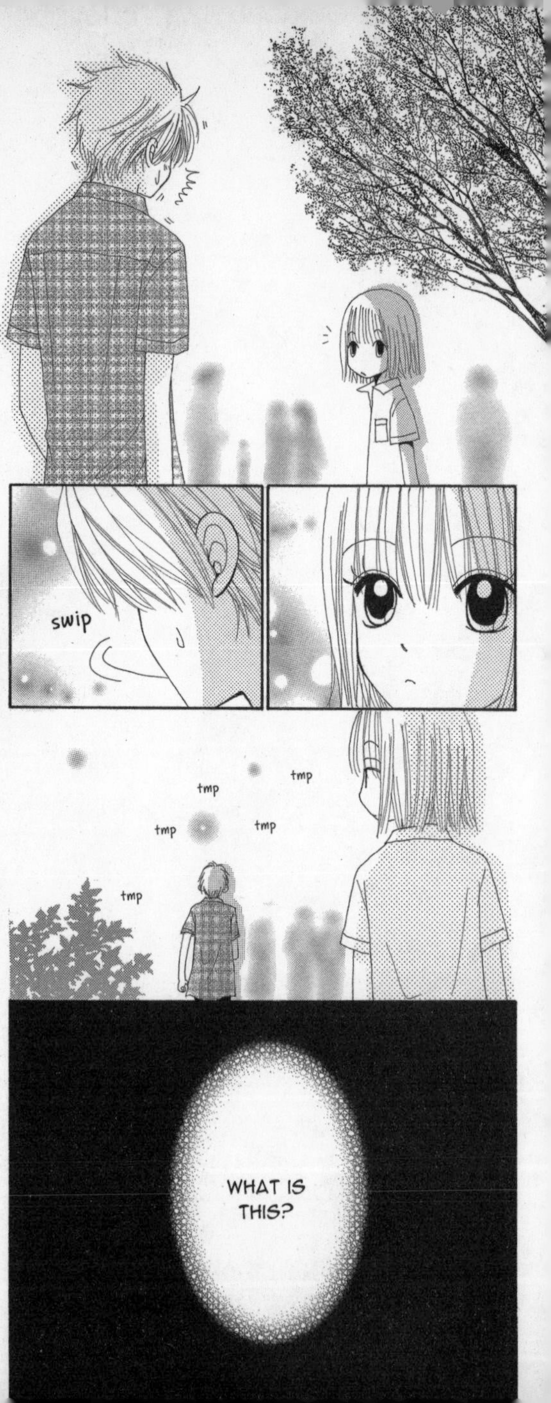
swip
tmp
tmp
tmp
tmp
tmp
WHAT IS THIS?

K's Club Talk

I put Ochiai's mynah bird in the story because a long time ago I wanted a mynah so much! When I was in elementary school, I would ring my friend's intercom and...

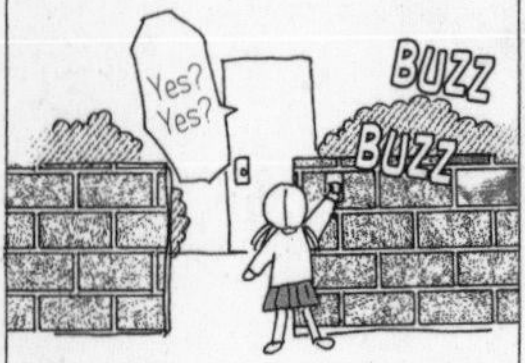
Yes? Yes?
BUZZ
BUZZ

...that's the answer I got, but no one came out. When I rang the intercom again...

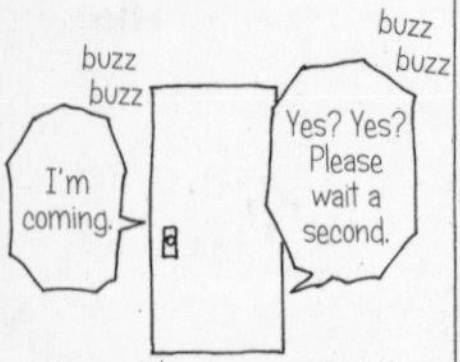
buzz buzz
buzz buzz
Yes? Yes? Please wait a second.
I'm coming.

...the voice just kept answering... Once I gave up and I decided to go home, and my friend came running back from her piano lesson. Finding out where the voice was coming from really gave me a bang!

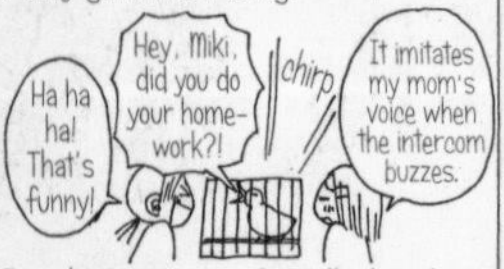
It imitates my mom's voice when the intercom buzzes.
chirp
Hey, Miki, did you do your home-work?!
Ha ha ha! That's funny!

I couldn't get one after all, though.
I did get to have a parakeet, though...

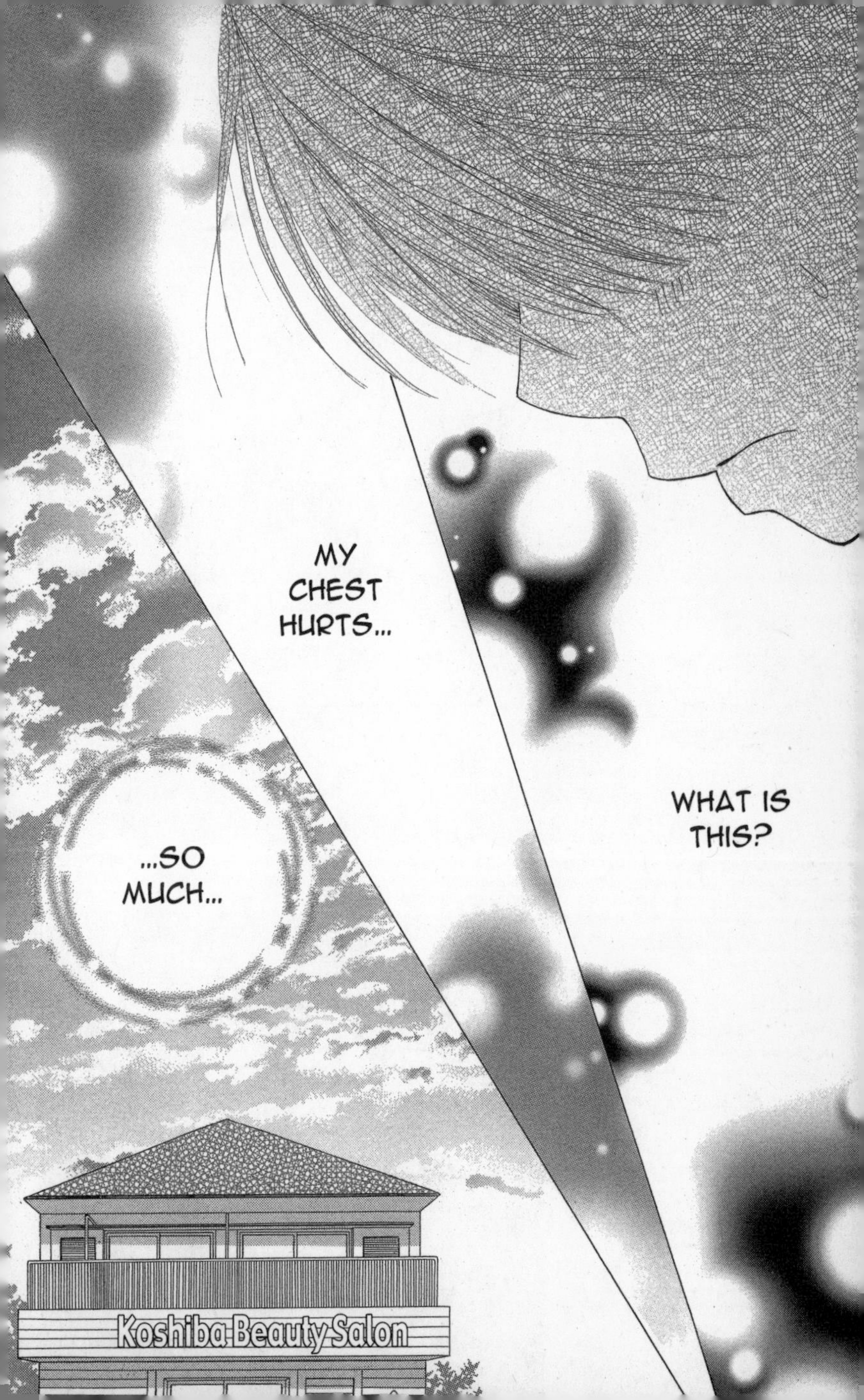
WHAT IS THIS?
MY CHEST HURTS...
...SO MUCH...
Koshiba Beauty Salon

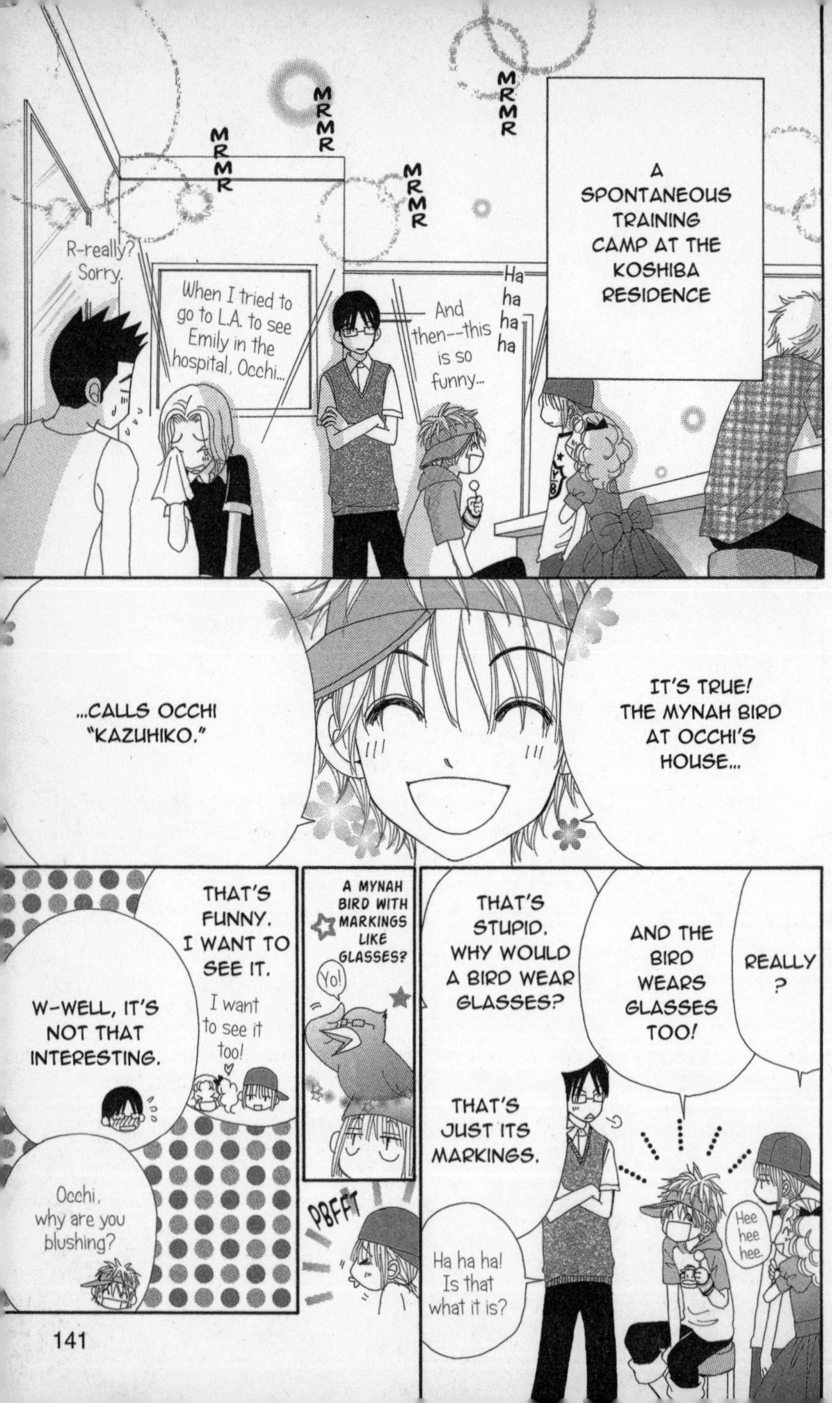
A SPONTANEOUS TRAINING CAMP AT THE KOSHIBA RESIDENCE
MRMR
MRMR
MRMR
MRMR
Ha ha ha ha
And then--this is so funny...
When I tried to go to L.A. to see Emily in the hospital, Occhi...
R-really? Sorry.
IT'S TRUE! THE MYNAH BIRD AT OCCHI'S HOUSE...
...CALLS OCCHI "KAZUHIKO."
REALLY?
AND THE BIRD WEARS GLASSES TOO!
THAT'S STUPID. WHY WOULD A BIRD WEAR GLASSES?
THAT'S JUST ITS MARKINGS.
Hee hee hee.
Ha ha ha! Is that what it is?
PBFFT
A MYNAH BIRD WITH MARKINGS LIKE GLASSES?
Yo!
THAT'S FUNNY. I WANT TO SEE IT.
I want to see it too!
W-WELL, IT'S NOT THAT INTERESTING.
Occhi, why are you blushing?

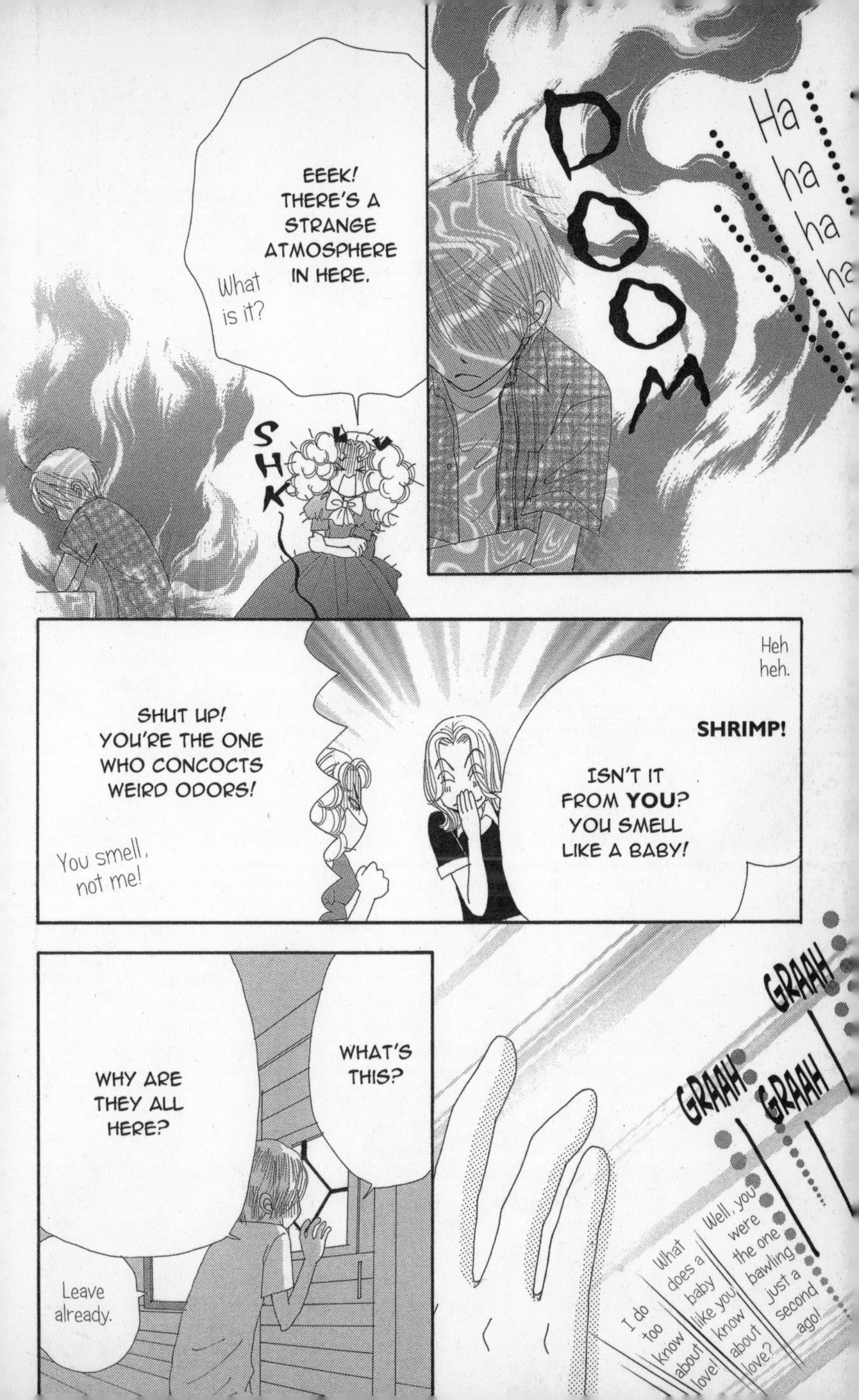
Ha ha ha ha
DOOM
EEEK! THERE'S A STRANGE ATMOSPHERE IN HERE.
What is it?
SHK
Heh heh.
SHRIMP!
ISN'T IT FROM **YOU**? YOU SMELL LIKE A BABY!
SHUT UP! YOU'RE THE ONE WHO CONCOCTS WEIRD ODORS!
You smell, not me!
GRAAH
GRAAH
GRAAH
Well, you were the one bawling just a second ago!
What does a baby like you know about love?
I do too know about love!
WHAT'S THIS?
WHY ARE THEY ALL HERE?
Leave already.

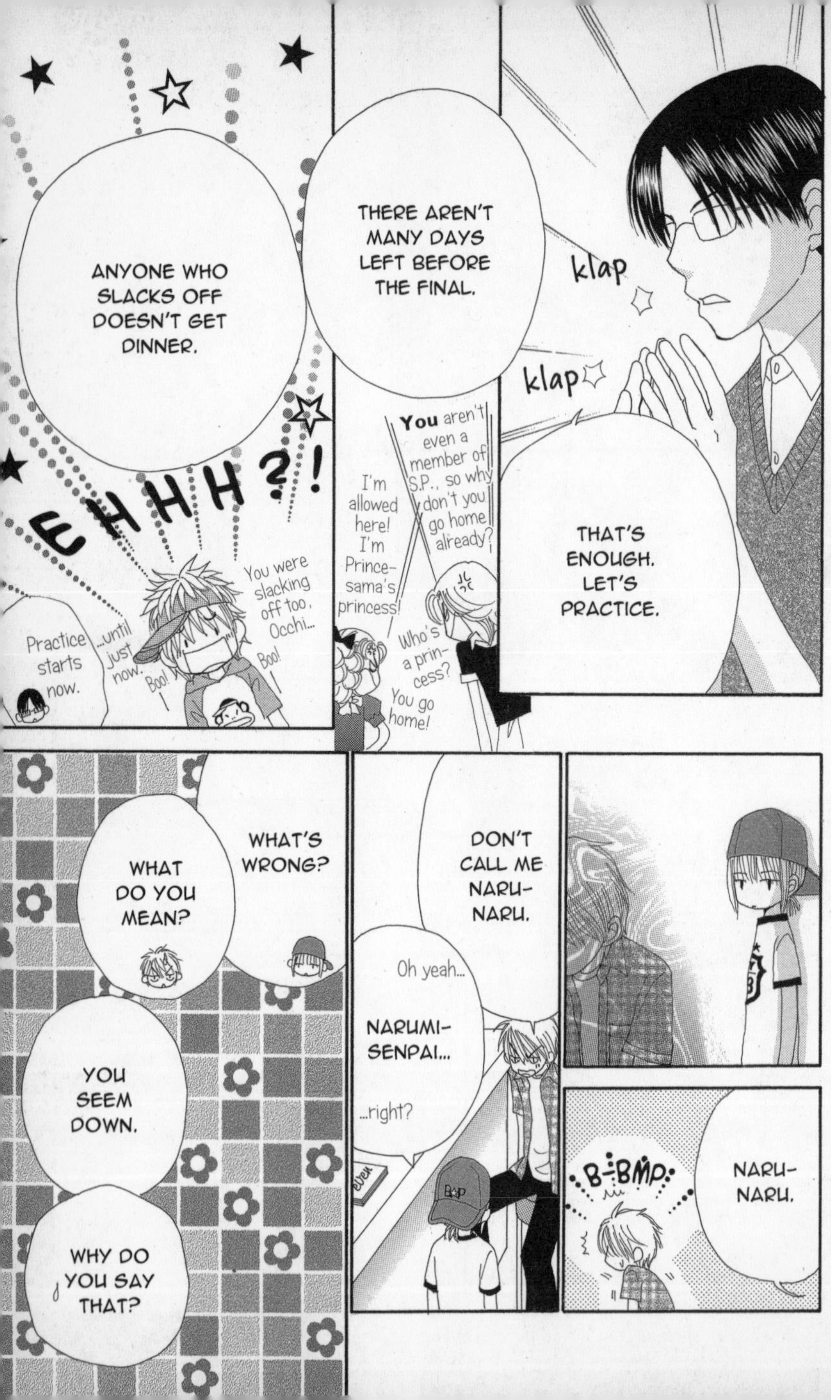
klap
klap
THAT'S ENOUGH. LET'S PRACTICE.
THERE AREN'T MANY DAYS LEFT BEFORE THE FINAL.
You aren't even a member of S.P., so why don't you go home already?
I'm allowed here! I'm Prince-sama's princess!
Who's a princess? You go home!
ANYONE WHO SLACKS OFF DOESN'T GET DINNER.
EHHH?!
You were slacking off too, Occhi...
Boo!
...until just now.
Boo!
Practice starts now.
NARU-NARU.
B-BMP
DON'T CALL ME NARU-NARU.
Oh yeah...
NARUMI-SENPAI...
...right?
WHAT'S WRONG?
WHAT DO YOU MEAN?
YOU SEEM DOWN.
WHY DO YOU SAY THAT?

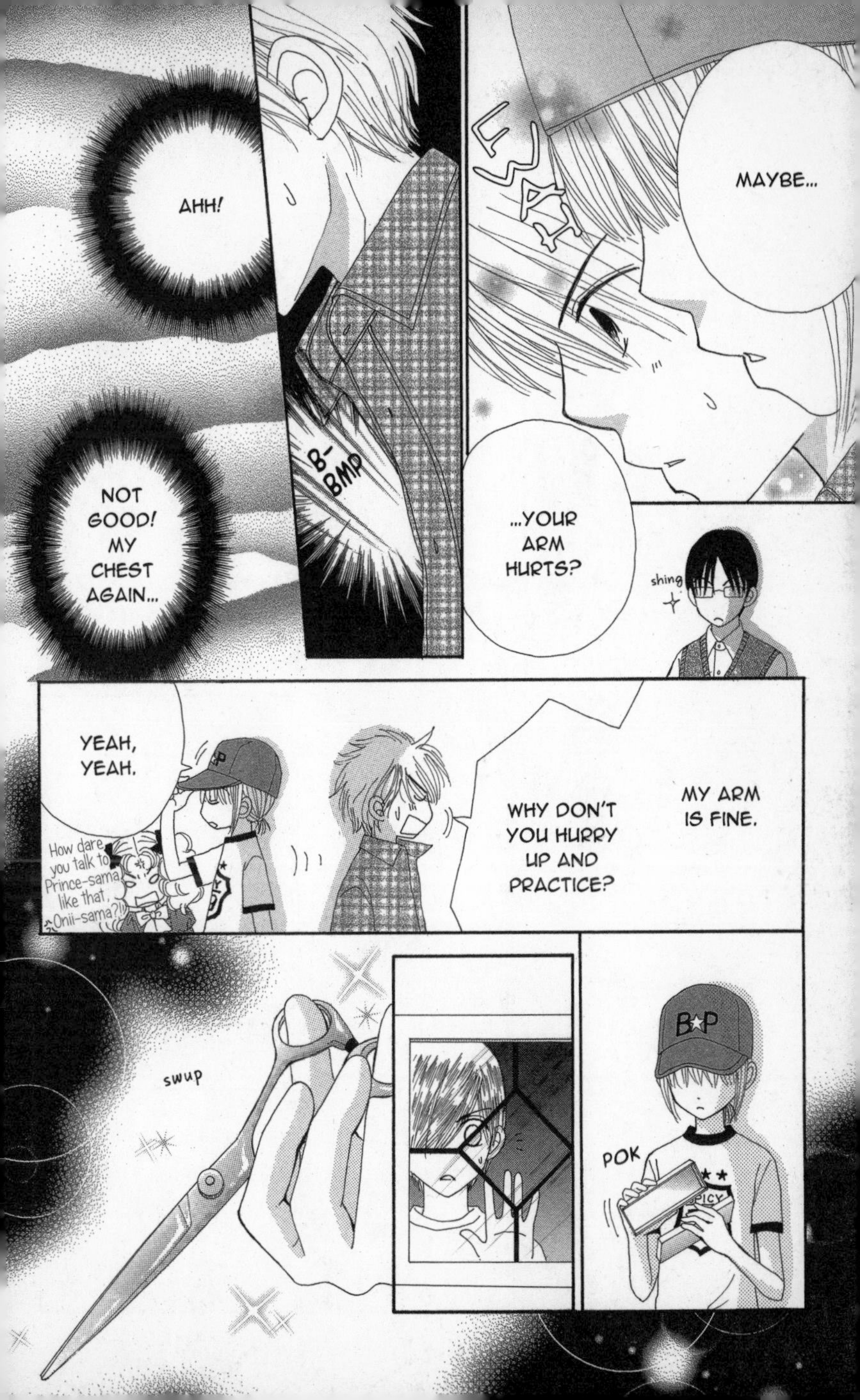
MAYBE...
...YOUR ARM HURTS?
shing
B-BMP
AHH!
NOT GOOD! MY CHEST AGAIN...
MY ARM IS FINE.
WHY DON'T YOU HURRY UP AND PRACTICE?
YEAH, YEAH.
How dare you talk to Prince-sama like that, Onii-sama?!
POK
swup

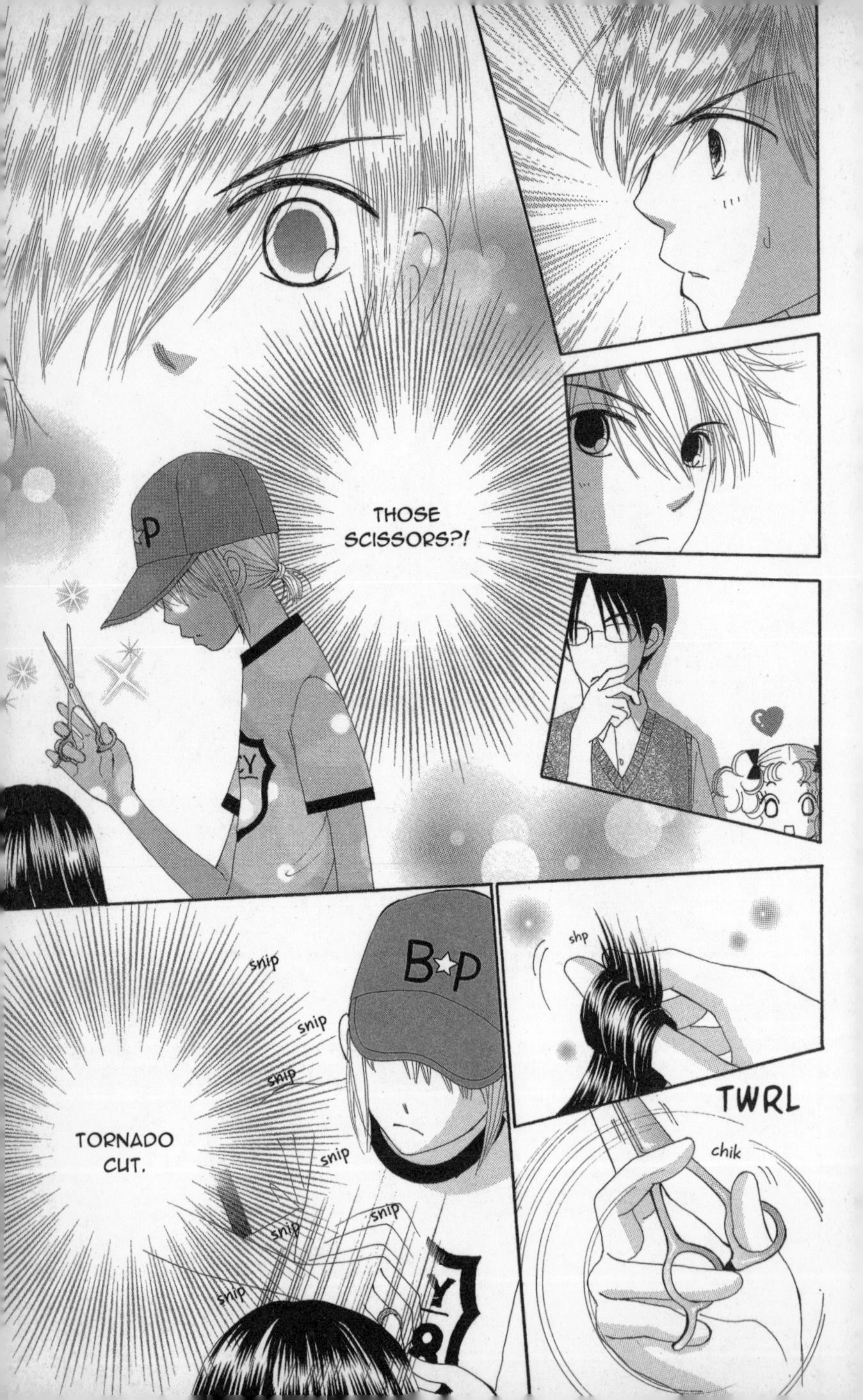
THOSE SCISSORS?!
shp
TWRL
chik
snip
snip
snip
snip
snip
snip
snip
TORNADO CUT.

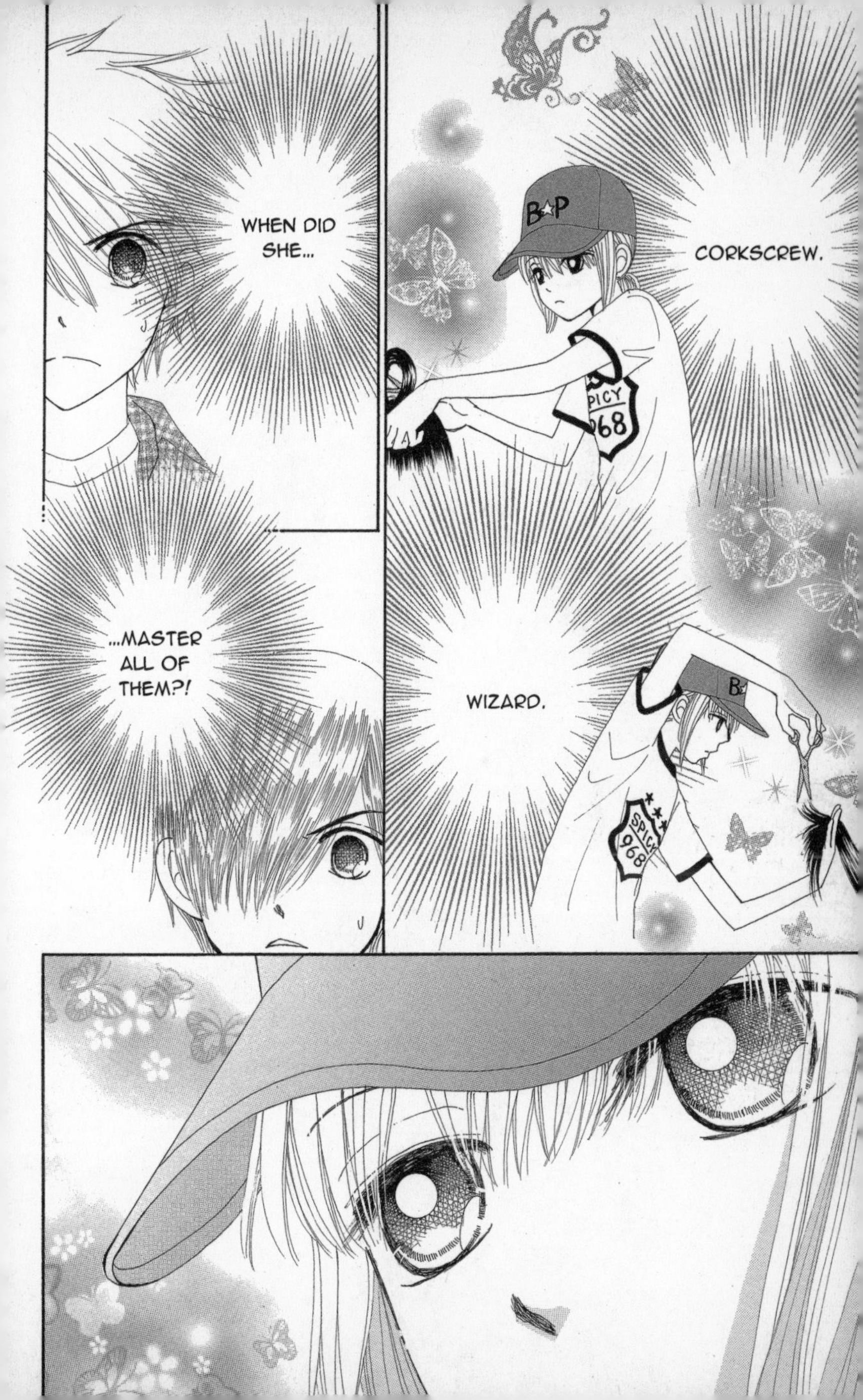
CORKSCREW.
WHEN DID SHE...
WIZARD.
...MASTER ALL OF THEM?!

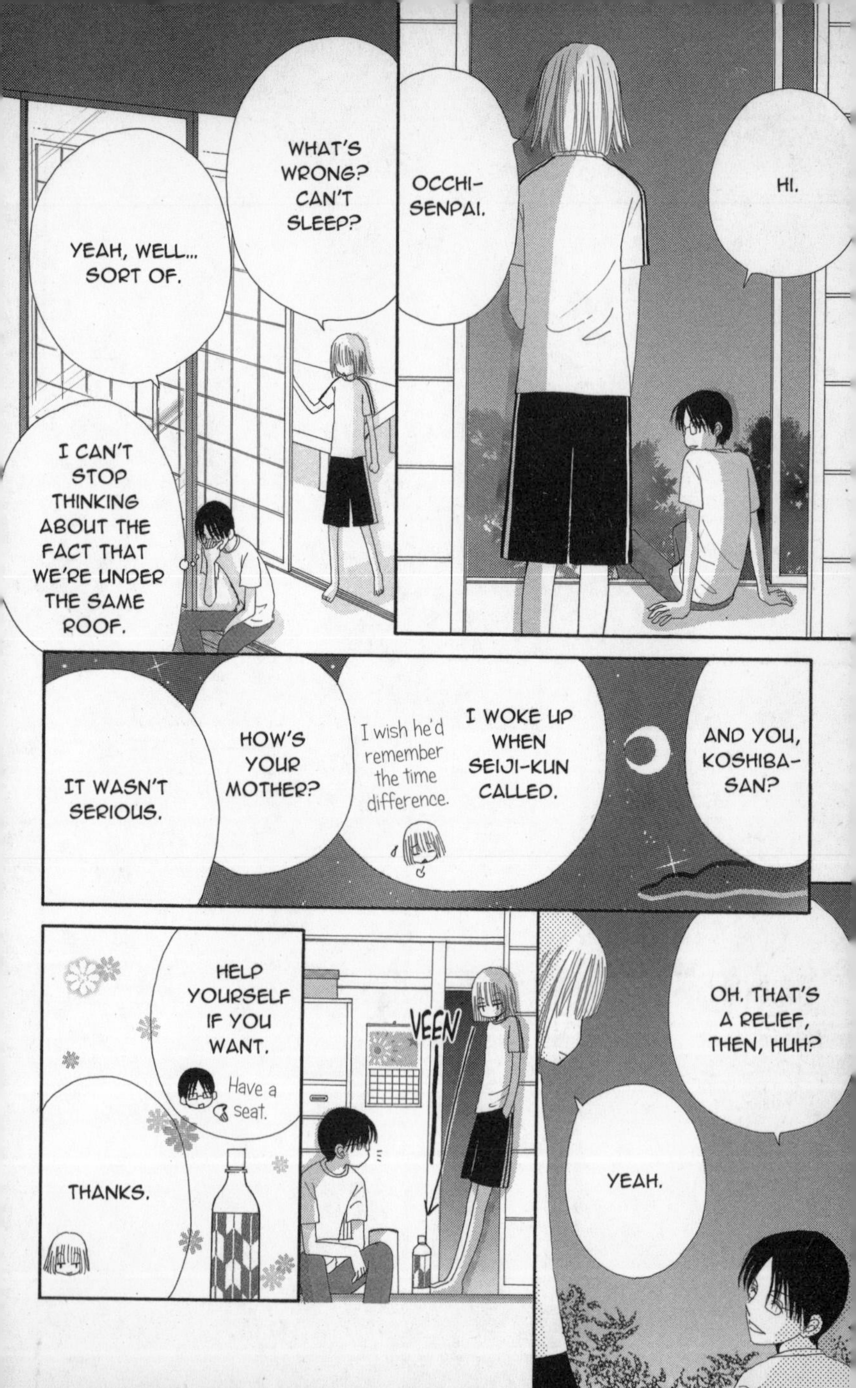
HI.
OCCHI-SENPAI.
WHAT'S WRONG? CAN'T SLEEP?
YEAH, WELL... SORT OF.
I CAN'T STOP THINKING ABOUT THE FACT THAT WE'RE UNDER THE SAME ROOF.
AND YOU, KOSHIBA-SAN?
I WOKE UP WHEN SEIJI-KUN CALLED.
I wish he'd remember the time difference.
HOW'S YOUR MOTHER?
IT WASN'T SERIOUS.
OH. THAT'S A RELIEF, THEN, HUH?
YEAH.
HELP YOURSELF IF YOU WANT.
Have a seat.
VEEN
THANKS.

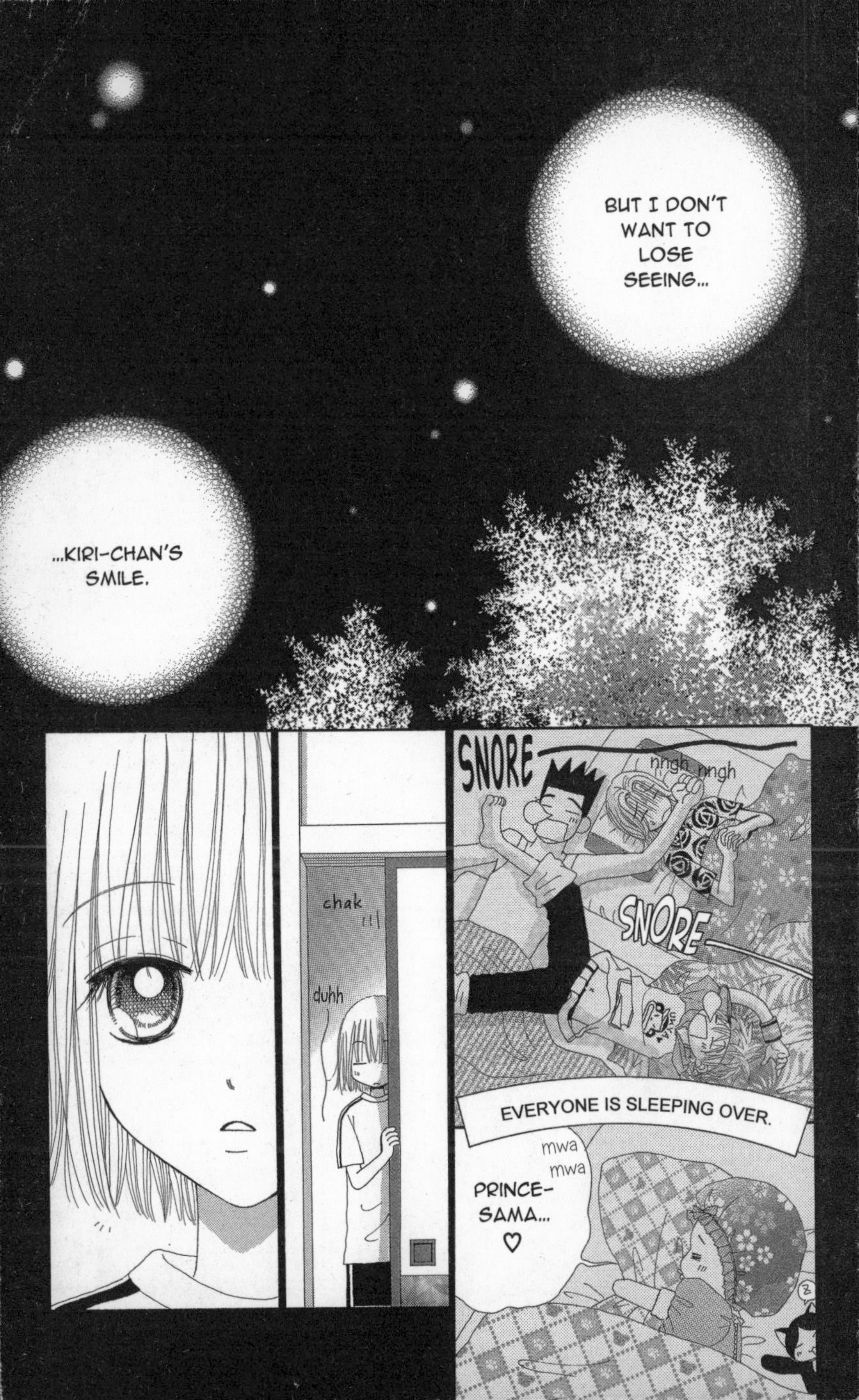
BUT I DON'T WANT TO LOSE SEEING...
...KIRI-CHAN'S SMILE.
nngh nngh
SNORE
SNORE
EVERYONE IS SLEEPING OVER.
mwa mwa
PRINCE-SAMA... ♡
chak
duhh

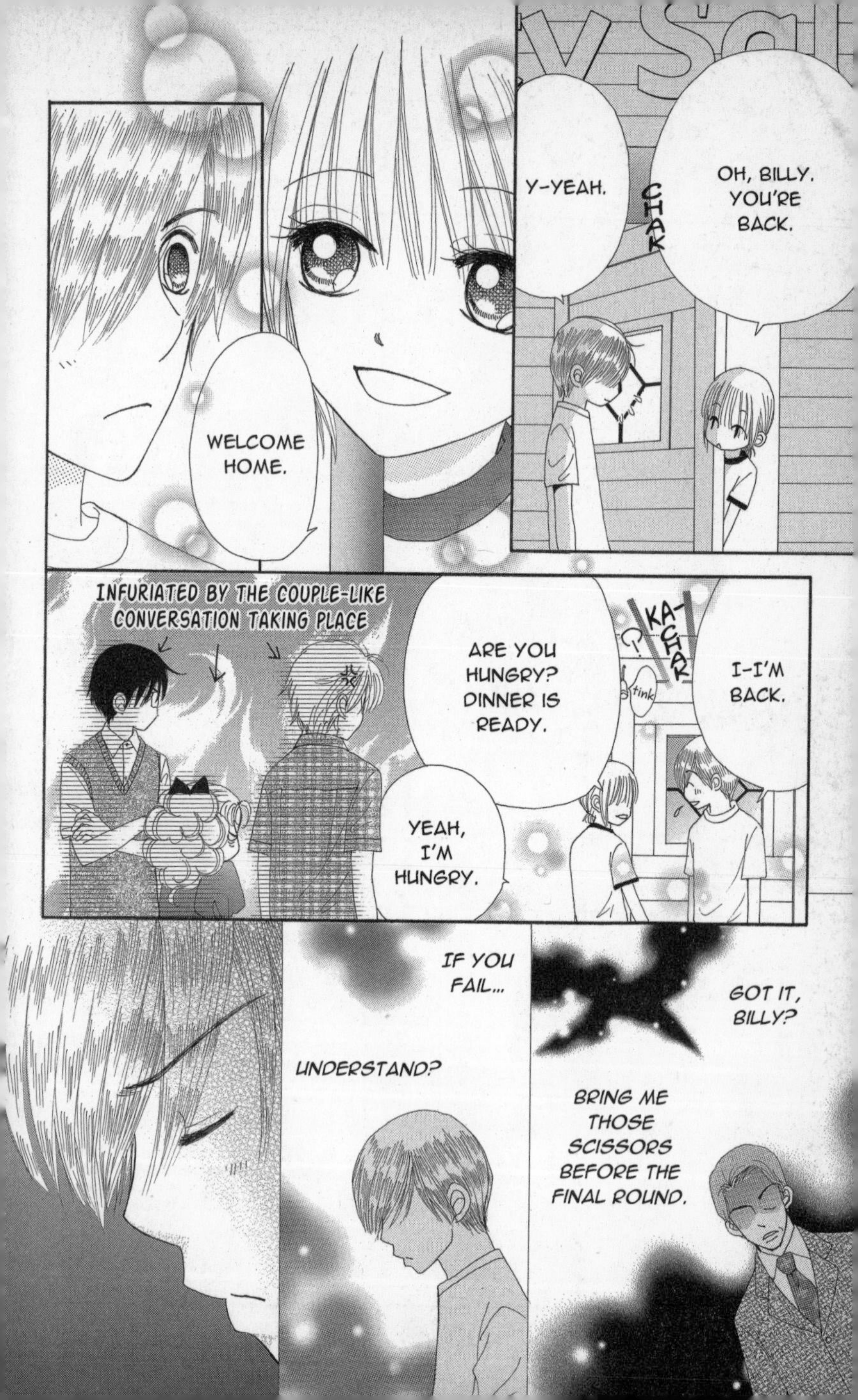
OH, BILLY. YOU'RE BACK.
CHAK
Y-YEAH.
WELCOME HOME.
I-I'M BACK.
KA-CHAK
tink
ARE YOU HUNGRY? DINNER IS READY.
YEAH, I'M HUNGRY.
INFURIATED BY THE COUPLE-LIKE CONVERSATION TAKING PLACE
GOT IT, BILLY?
BRING ME THOSE SCISSORS BEFORE THE FINAL ROUND.
IF YOU FAIL...
UNDERSTAND?

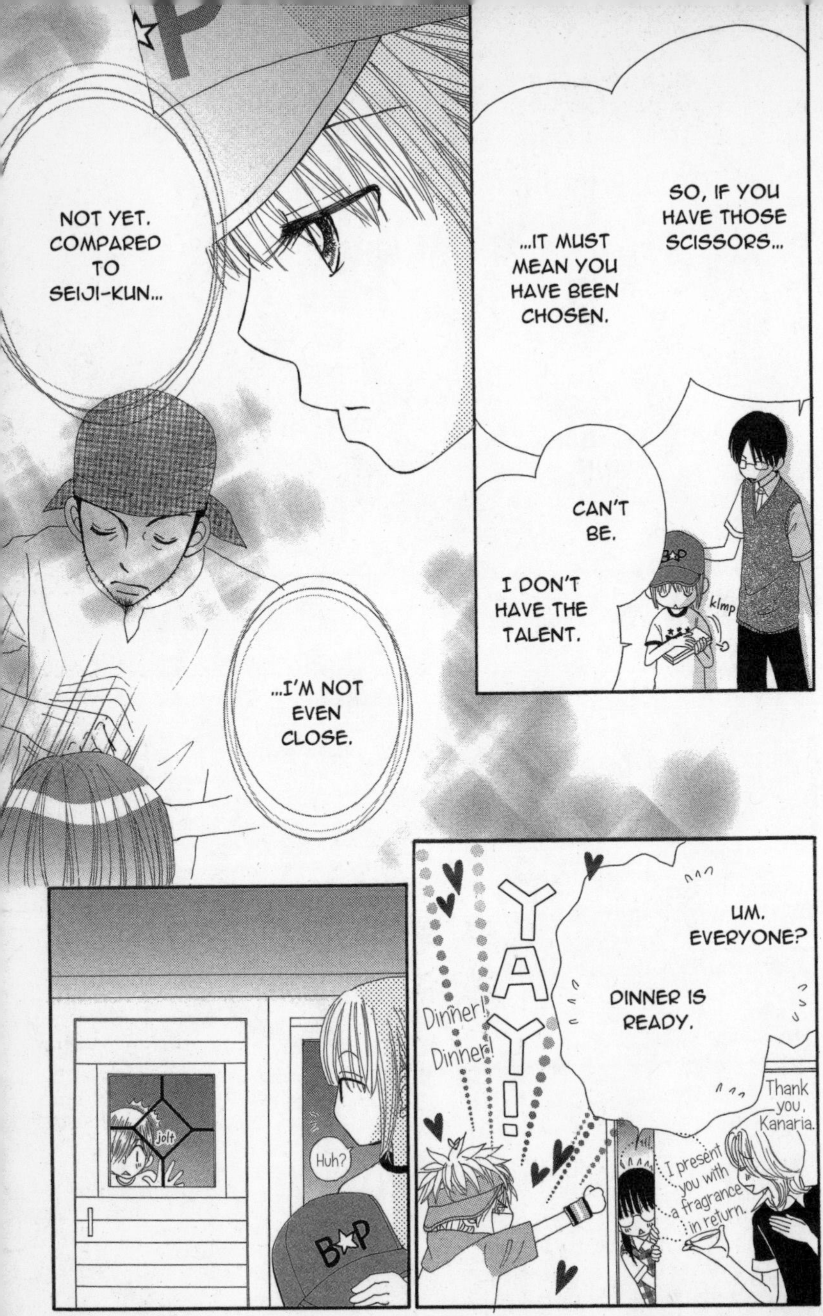
SO, IF YOU HAVE THOSE SCISSORS...
...IT MUST MEAN YOU HAVE BEEN CHOSEN.
CAN'T BE.
I DON'T HAVE THE TALENT.
klmp
NOT YET. COMPARED TO SEIJI-KUN...
...I'M NOT EVEN CLOSE.
UM. EVERYONE?
DINNER IS READY.
YAY!
Dinner! Dinner!
Thank you, Kanaria.
I present you with a fragrance in return.
jolt
!
Huh?

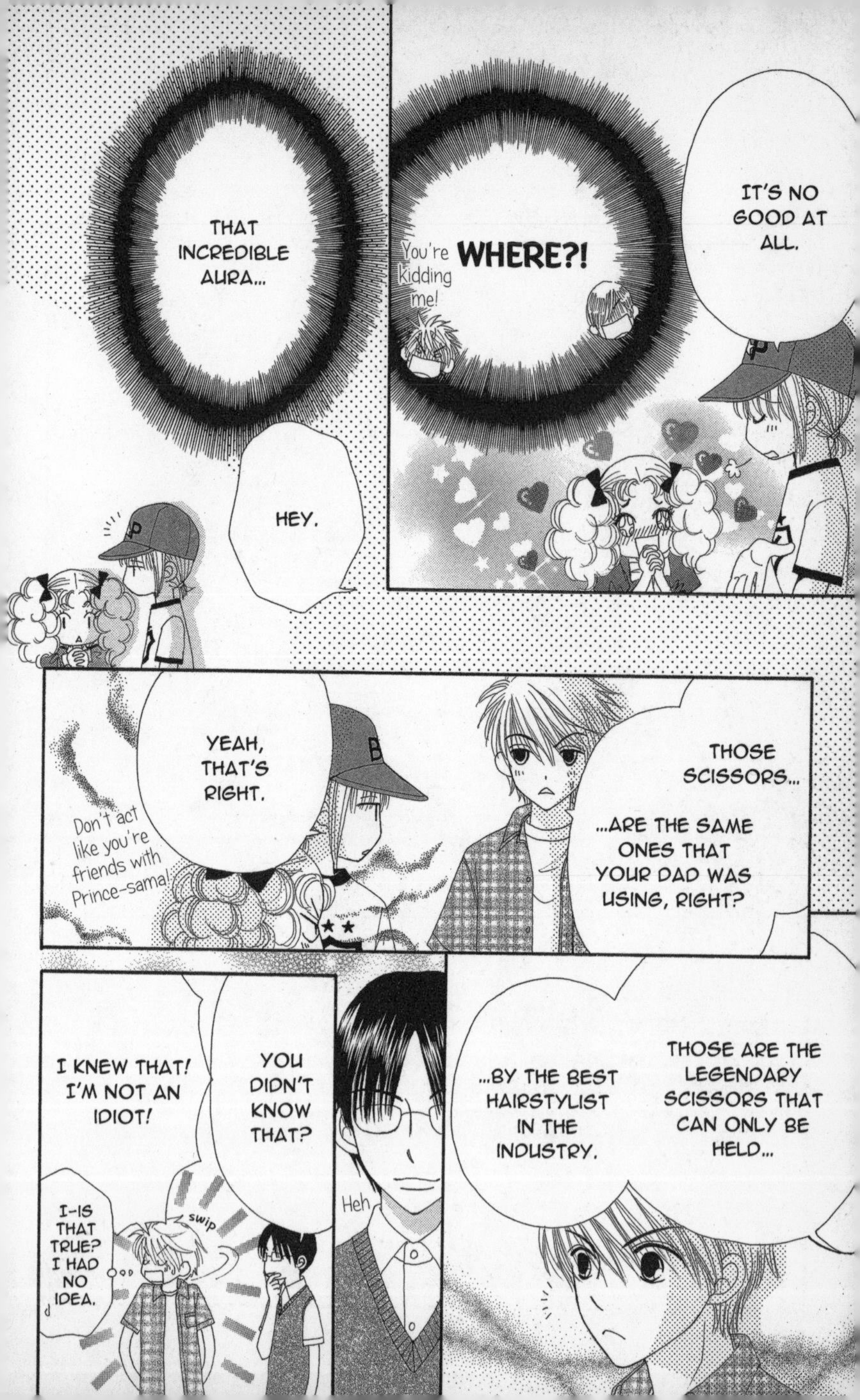
IT'S NO GOOD AT ALL.
WHERE?!
You're kidding me!
THAT INCREDIBLE AURA...
HEY.
THOSE SCISSORS...
...ARE THE SAME ONES THAT YOUR DAD WAS USING, RIGHT?
YEAH, THAT'S RIGHT.
Don't act like you're friends with Prince-sama!
THOSE ARE THE LEGENDARY SCISSORS THAT CAN ONLY BE HELD...
...BY THE BEST HAIRSTYLIST IN THE INDUSTRY.
YOU DIDN'T KNOW THAT?
Heh
I KNEW THAT! I'M NOT AN IDIOT!
swip
I-IS THAT TRUE? I HAD NO IDEA.

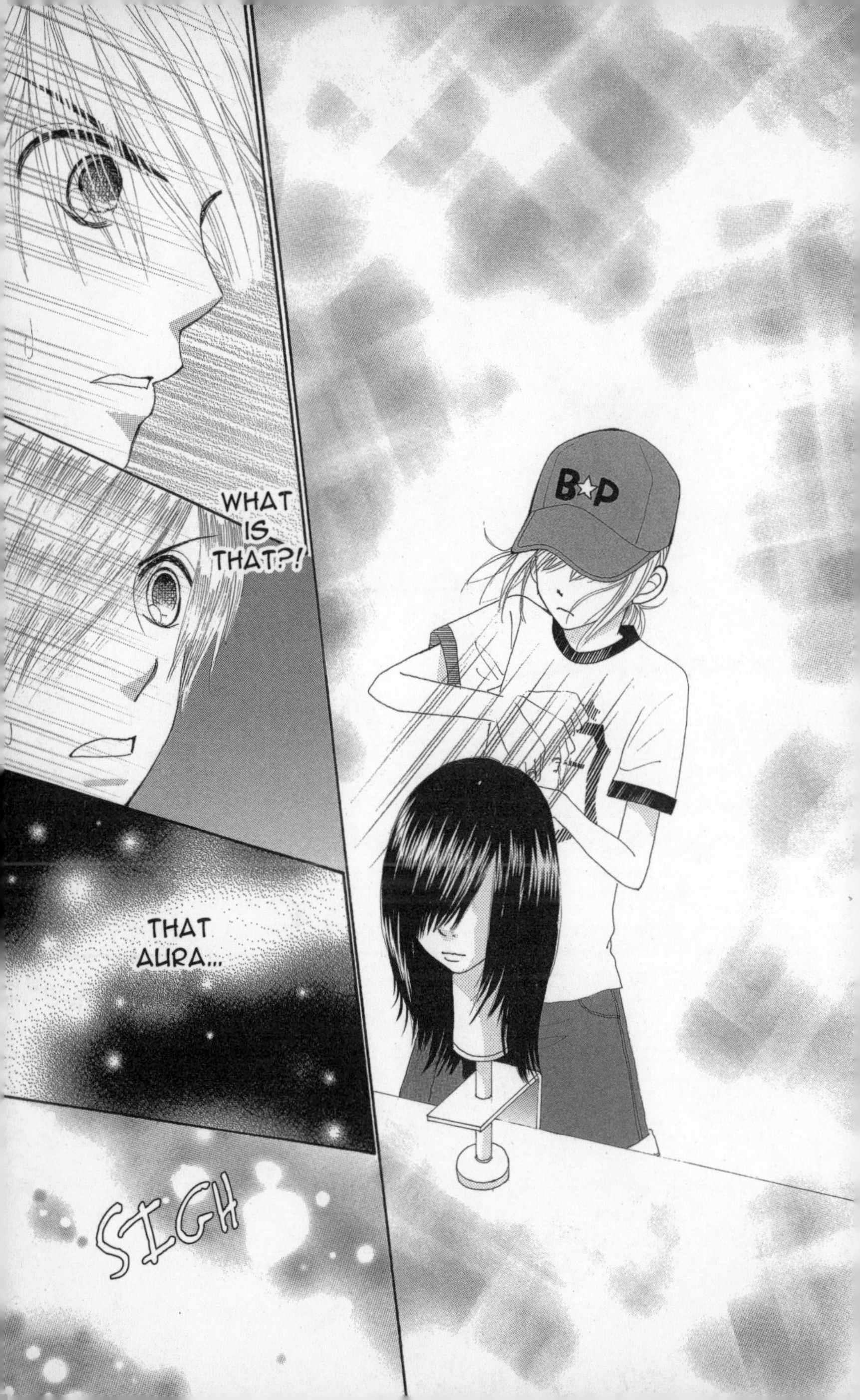
B★P
WHAT IS THAT?!
THAT AURA...
SIGH

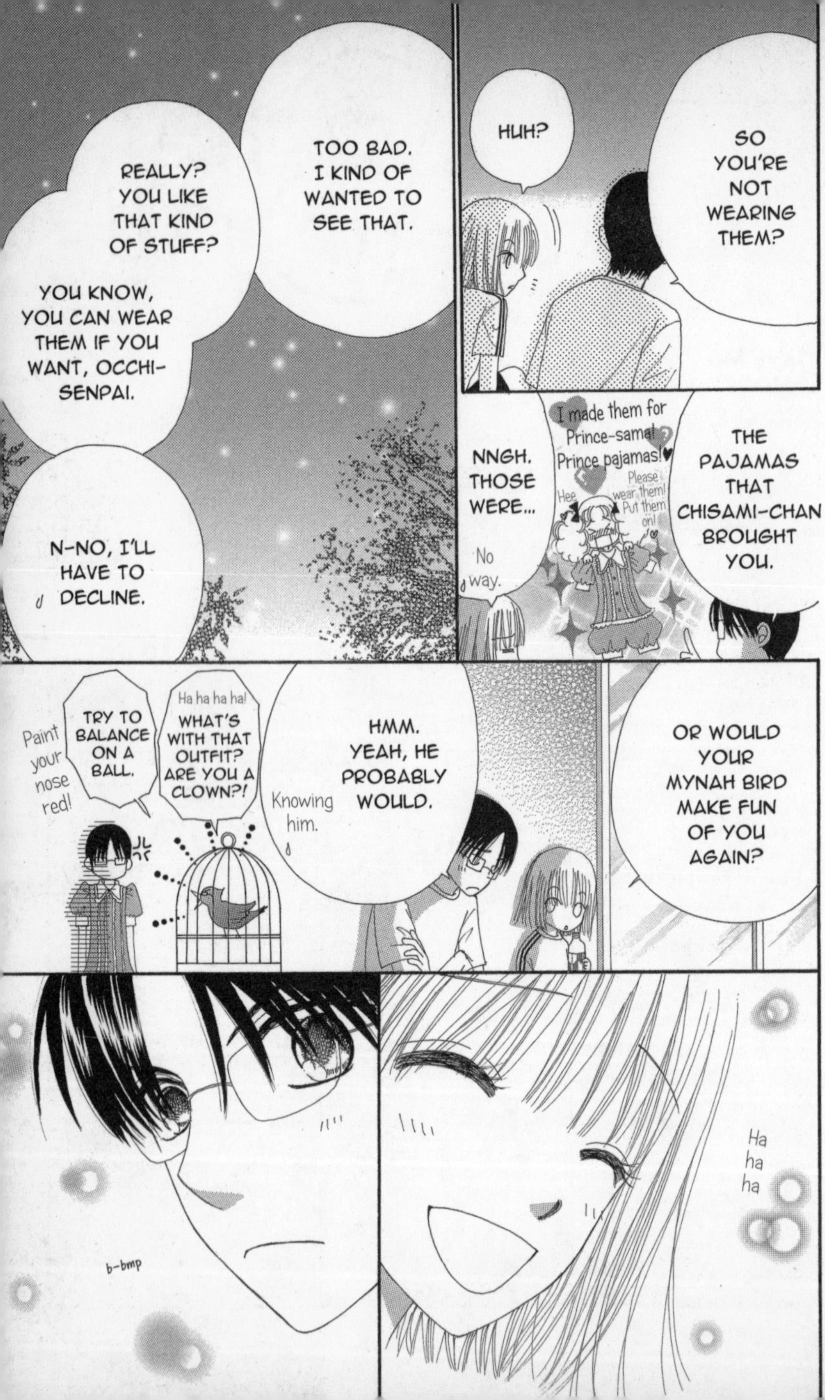

SO YOU'RE NOT WEARING THEM?
HUH?
THE PAJAMAS THAT CHISAMI-CHAN BROUGHT YOU.
I made them for Prince-sama! Prince pajamas!♥
Please wear them! Put them on!
Hee
NNGH. THOSE WERE...
No way.
TOO BAD. I KIND OF WANTED TO SEE THAT.
REALLY? YOU LIKE THAT KIND OF STUFF?
YOU KNOW, YOU CAN WEAR THEM IF YOU WANT, OCCHI-SENPAI.
N-NO, I'LL HAVE TO DECLINE.
OR WOULD YOUR MYNAH BIRD MAKE FUN OF YOU AGAIN?
HMM. YEAH, HE PROBABLY WOULD.
Knowing him.
Ha ha ha ha!
WHAT'S WITH THAT OUTFIT? ARE YOU A CLOWN?!
TRY TO BALANCE ON A BALL.
Paint your nose red!
Ha ha ha
b-bmp

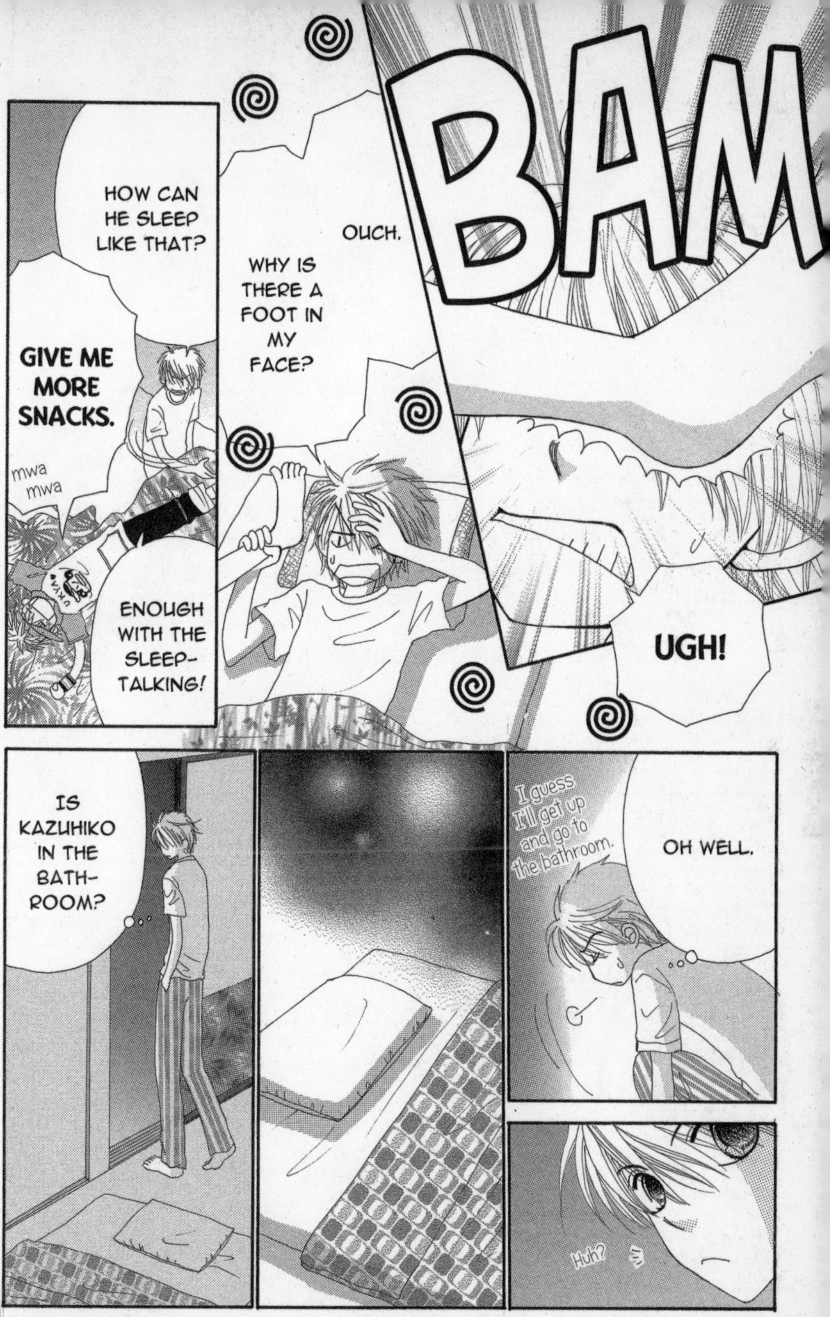
BAM
UGH!
OUCH.
WHY IS THERE A FOOT IN MY FACE?
HOW CAN HE SLEEP LIKE THAT?
GIVE ME MORE SNACKS.
mwa mwa
ENOUGH WITH THE SLEEP-TALKING!
OH WELL.
I guess I'll get up and go to the bathroom.
Huh?
IS KAZUHIKO IN THE BATHROOM?

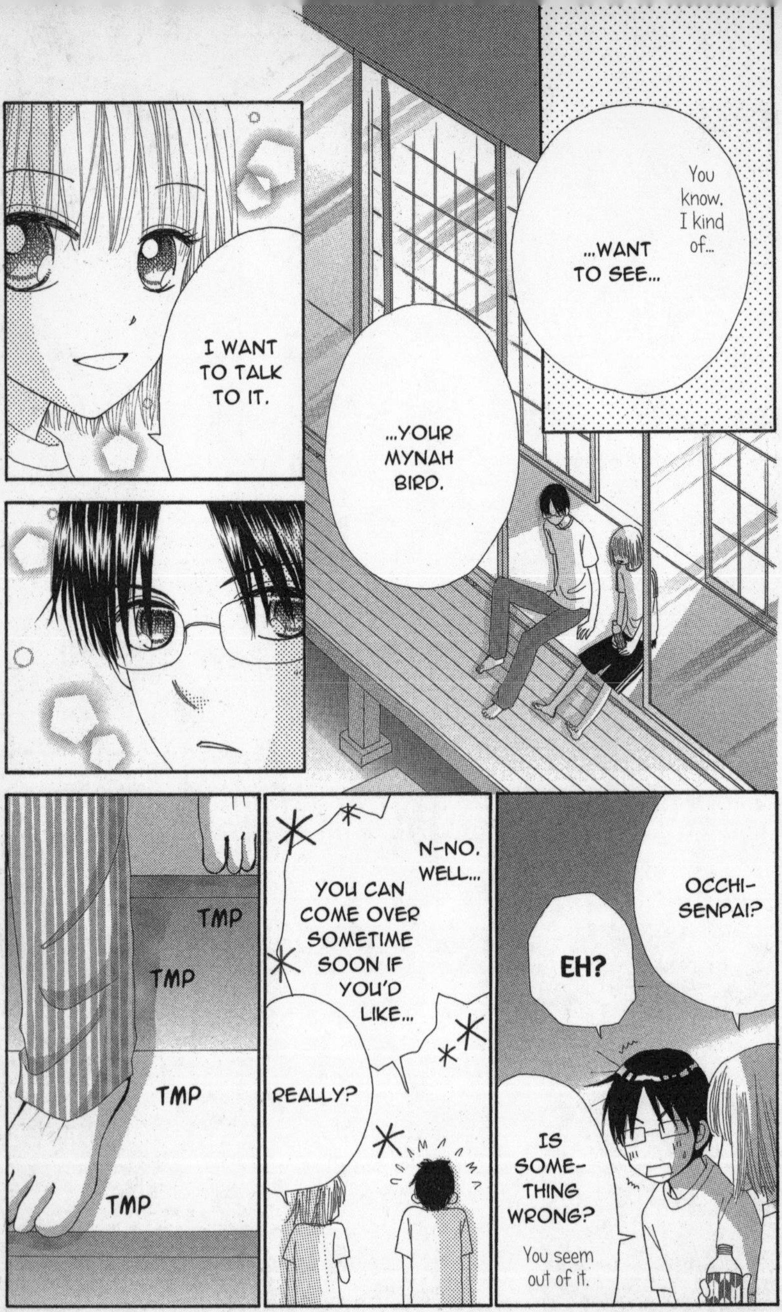
You know. I kind of...
...WANT TO SEE...
...YOUR MYNAH BIRD.
I WANT TO TALK TO IT.
OCCHI-SENPAI?
EH?
IS SOME-THING WRONG?
You seem out of it.
N-NO. WELL...
YOU CAN COME OVER SOMETIME SOON IF YOU'D LIKE...
REALLY?
TMP
TMP
TMP
TMP

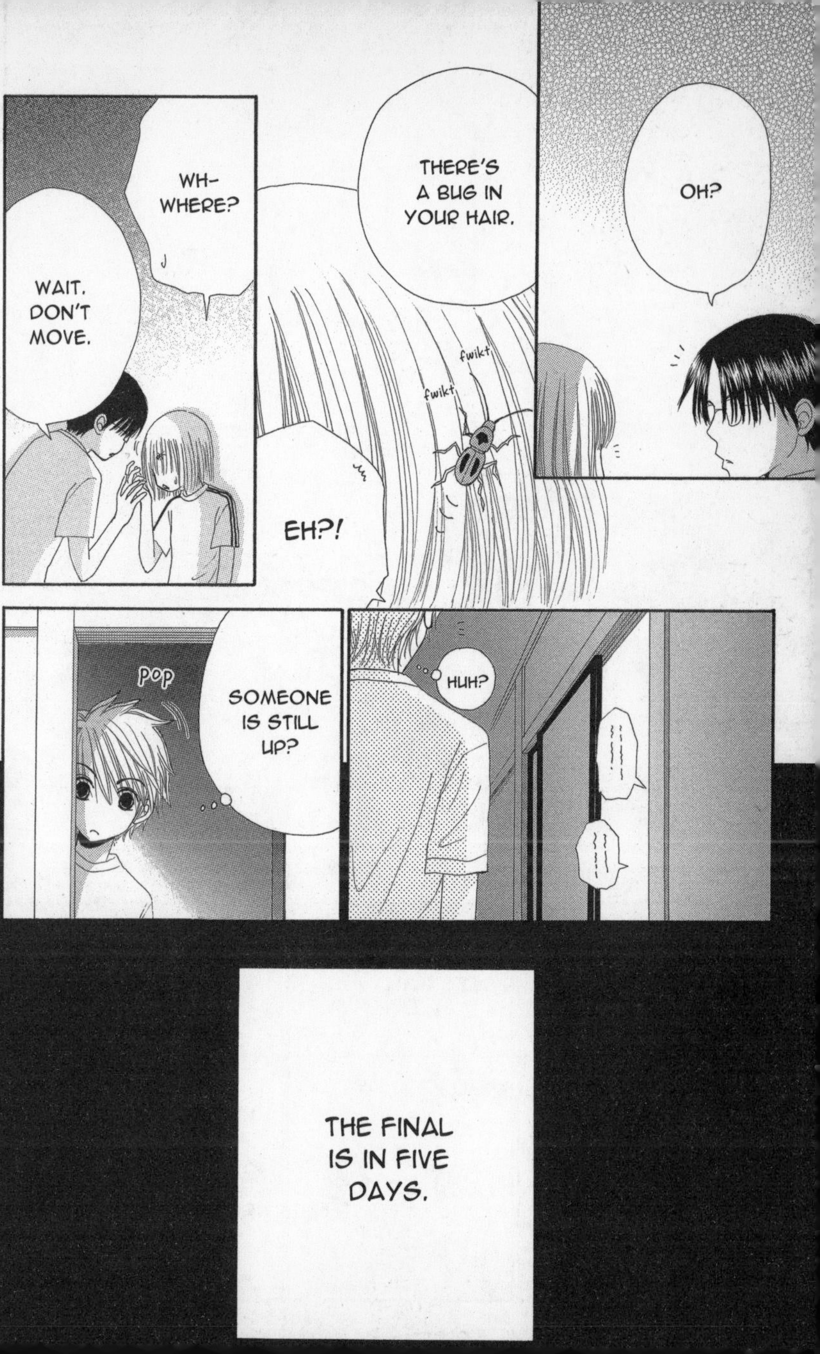
OH?
THERE'S A BUG IN YOUR HAIR.
fwikt
fwikt
EH?!
WH- WHERE?
WAIT. DON'T MOVE.
HUH?
pop
SOMEONE IS STILL UP?
THE FINAL IS IN FIVE DAYS.

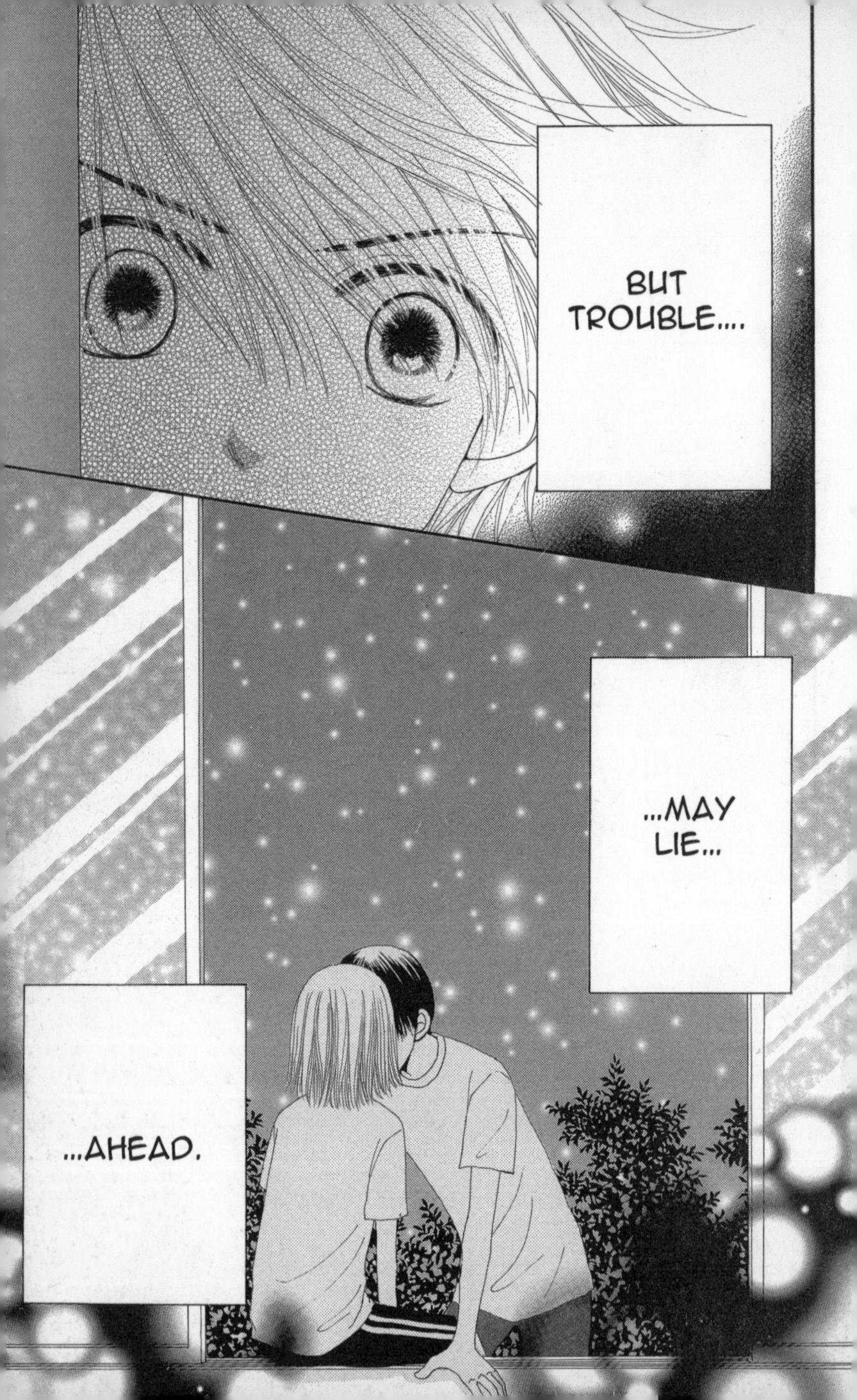
BUT TROUBLE....
...MAY LIE...
...AHEAD.

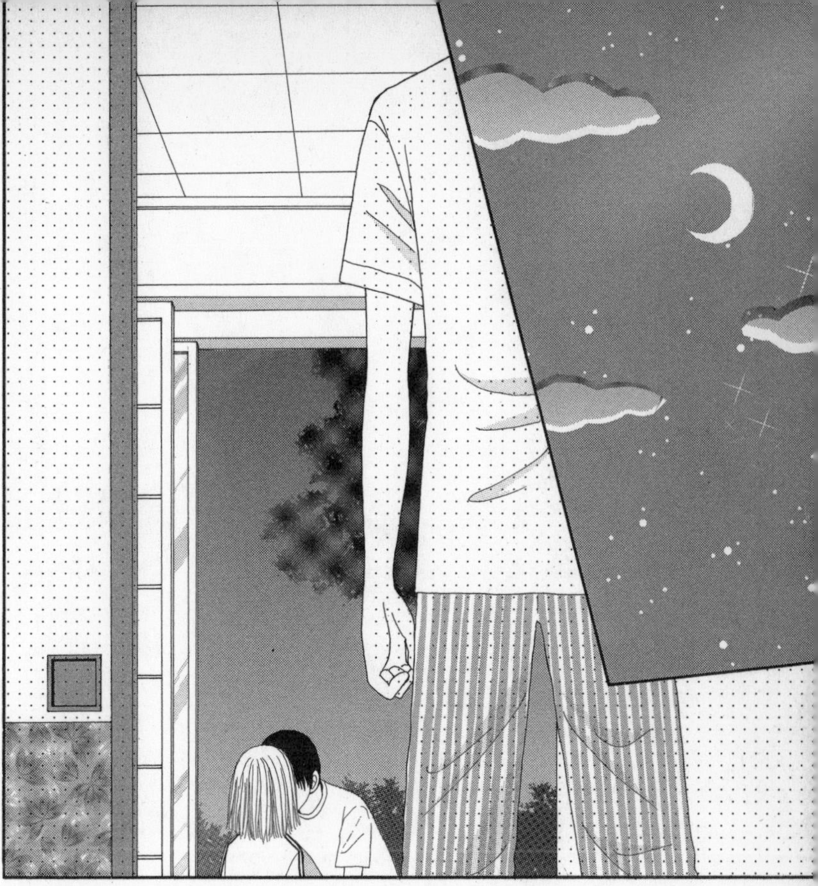

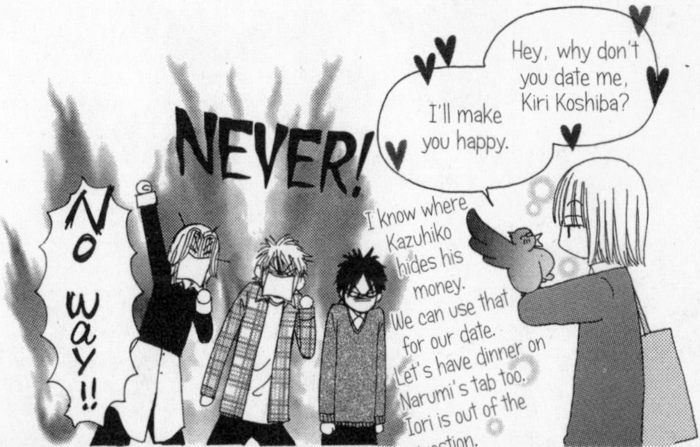
Hey, why don't you date me, Kiri Koshiba?
I'll make you happy.
I know where Kazuhiko hides his money. We can use that for our date. Let's have dinner on Narumi's tab too. Iori is out of the question.
NEVER!
No way!!

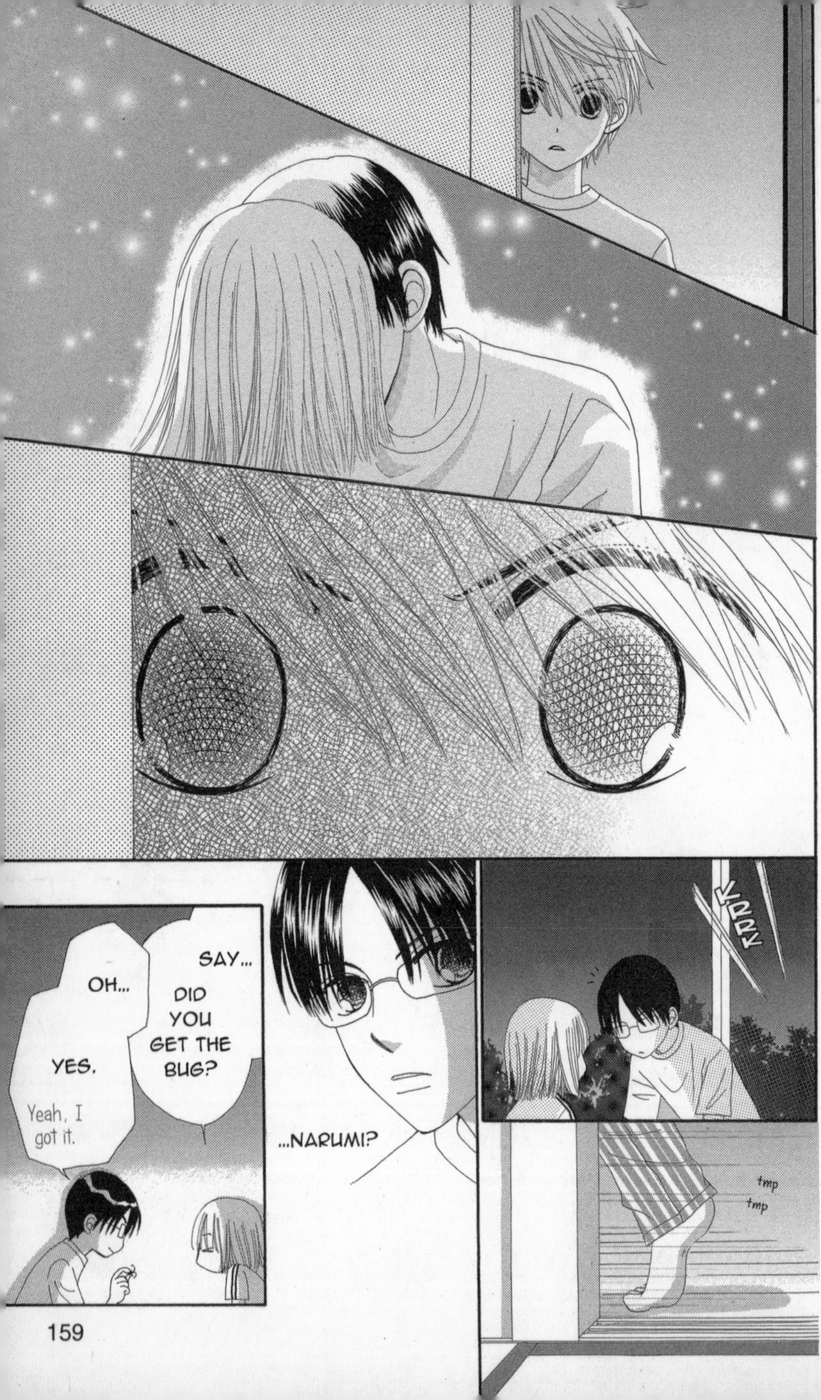
KRRK
tmp
tmp
...NARUMI?
SAY...
DID YOU GET THE BUG?
OH...
YES.
Yeah, I got it.

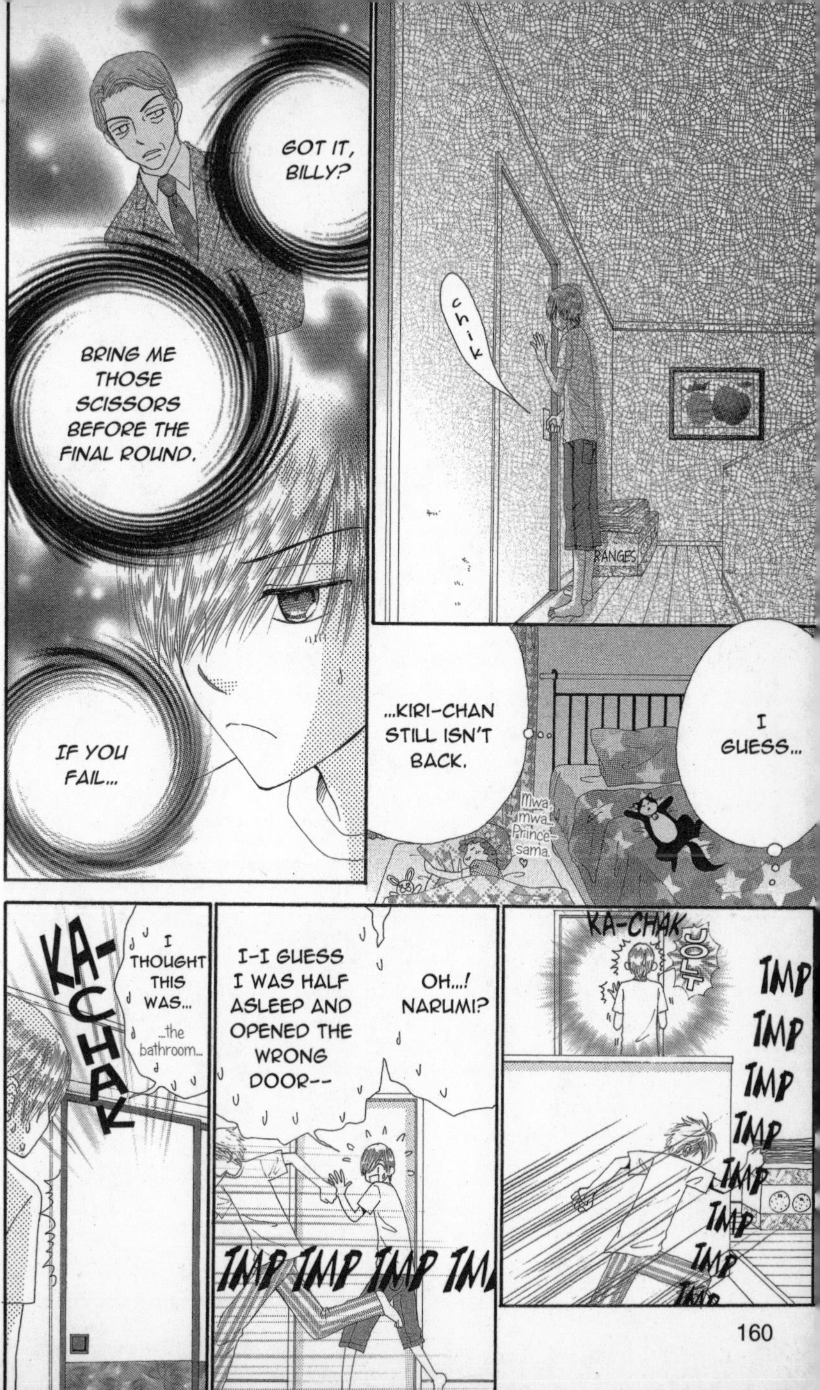
chik
RANGES
I GUESS...
...KIRI-CHAN STILL ISN'T BACK.
Mwa mwa... Prince-sama.
GOT IT, BILLY?
BRING ME THOSE SCISSORS BEFORE THE FINAL ROUND.
IF YOU FAIL...
TMP TMP TMP TMP TMP TMP TMP TMP
KA-CHAK
JOLT
OH...! NARUMI?
I-I GUESS I WAS HALF ASLEEP AND OPENED THE WRONG DOOR--
TMP TMP TMP TM
I THOUGHT THIS WAS...
...the bathroom...
KA-CHAK

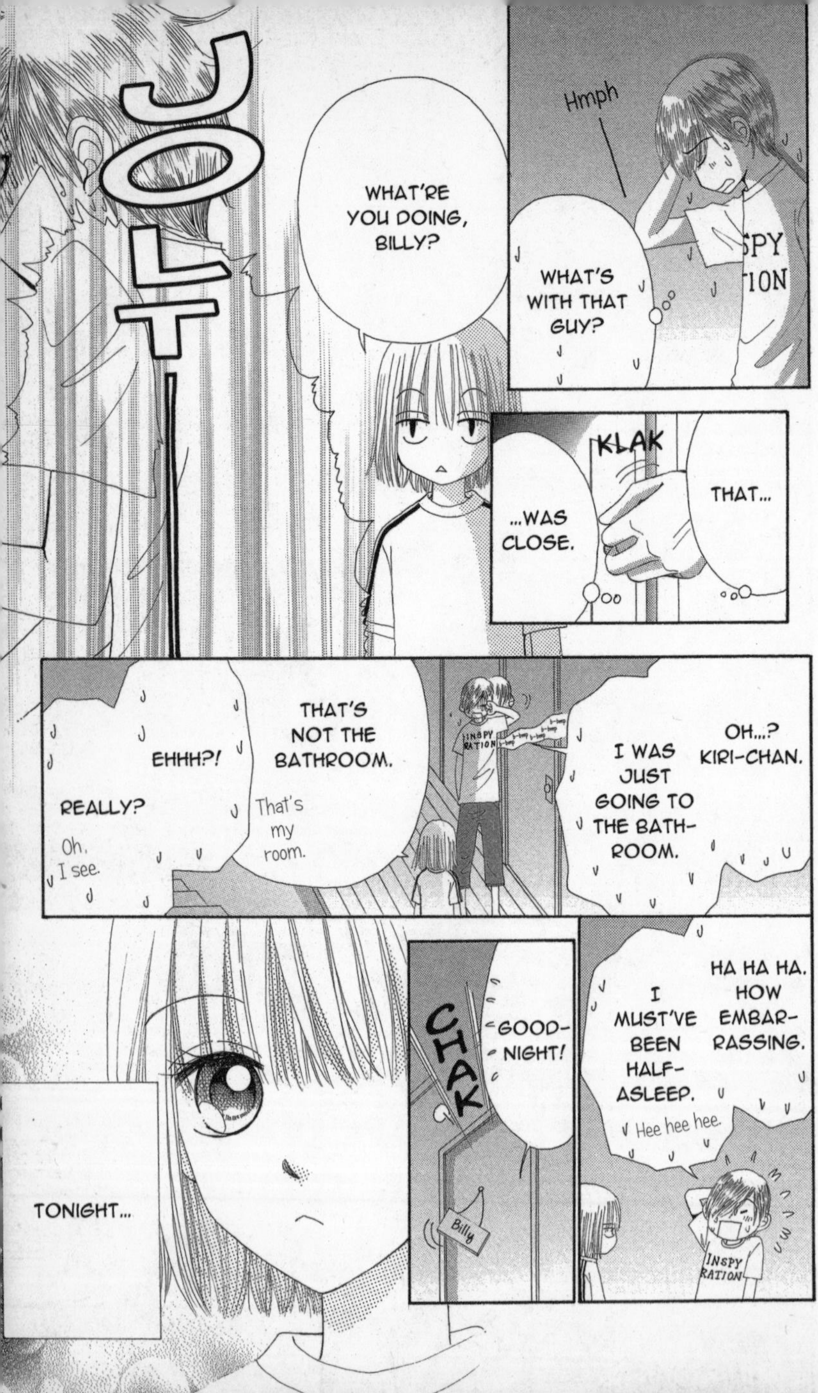
Hmph
WHAT'S WITH THAT GUY?
KLAK
THAT...
...WAS CLOSE.
JOLT
WHAT'RE YOU DOING, BILLY?
OH...? KIRI-CHAN.
I WAS JUST GOING TO THE BATH-ROOM.
THAT'S NOT THE BATHROOM.
That's my room.
EHHH?!
REALLY?
Oh, I see.
HA HA HA. HOW EMBAR-RASSING.
I MUST'VE BEEN HALF-ASLEEP.
Hee hee hee.
GOOD-NIGHT!
CHAK
Billy
TONIGHT...

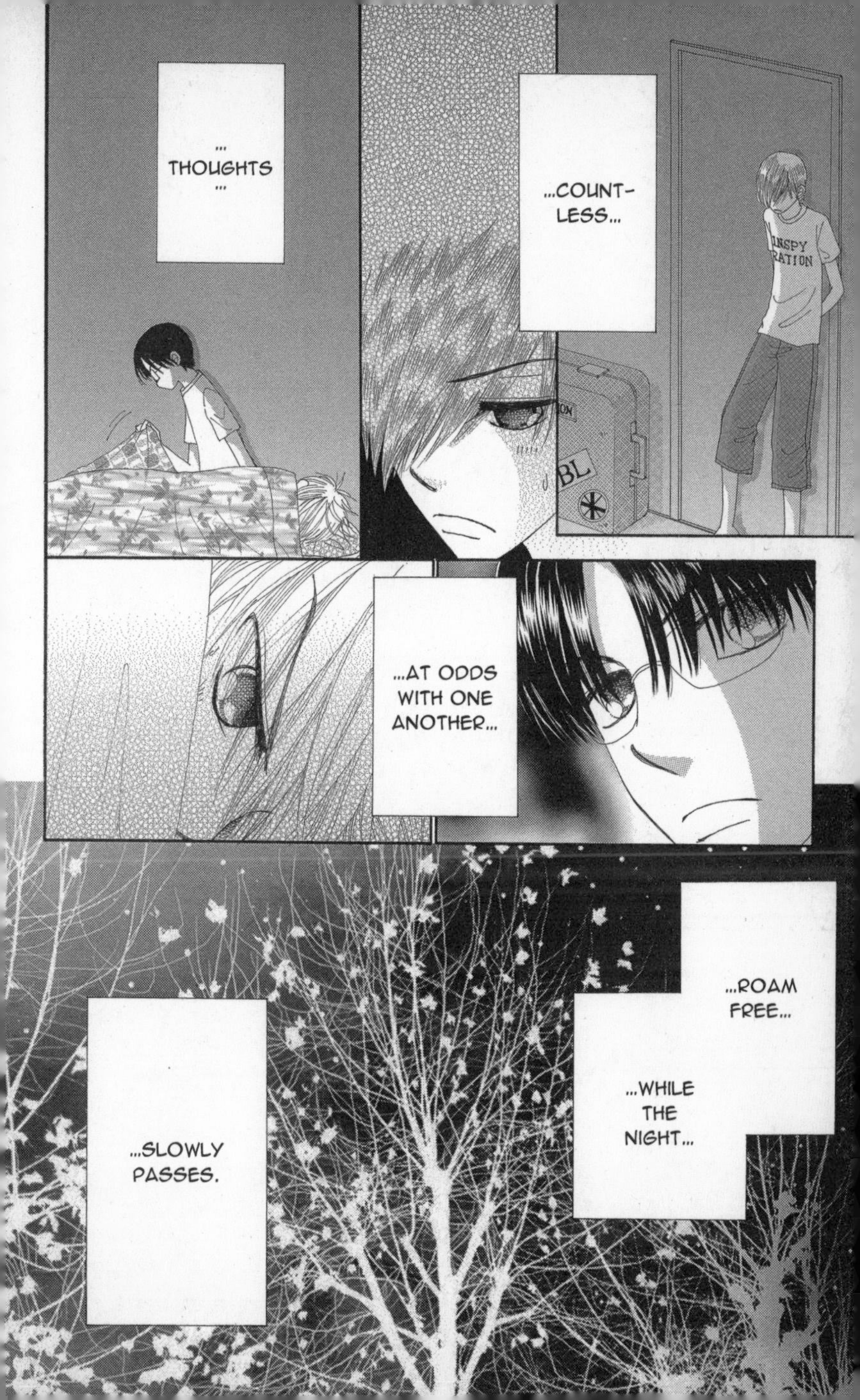
...COUNT-
LESS...
INSPY
RATION
...
THOUGHTS
...
...AT ODDS
WITH ONE
ANOTHER...
...ROAM
FREE...
...WHILE
THE
NIGHT...
...SLOWLY
PASSES.

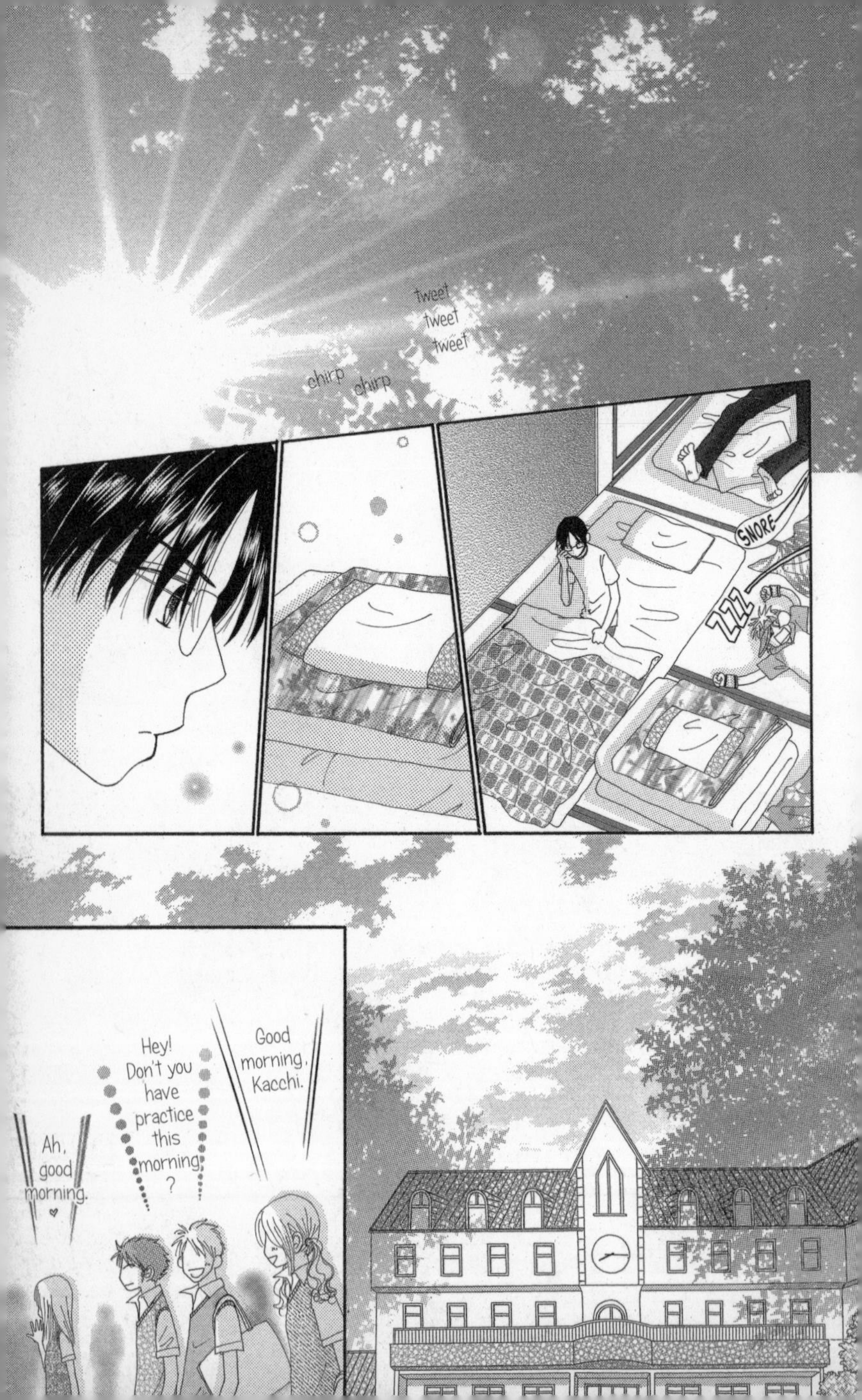
tweet tweet tweet
chirp chirp
SNORE
ZZZZ
Good morning, Kacchi.
Hey! Don't you have practice this morning?
Ah, good morning. ♥

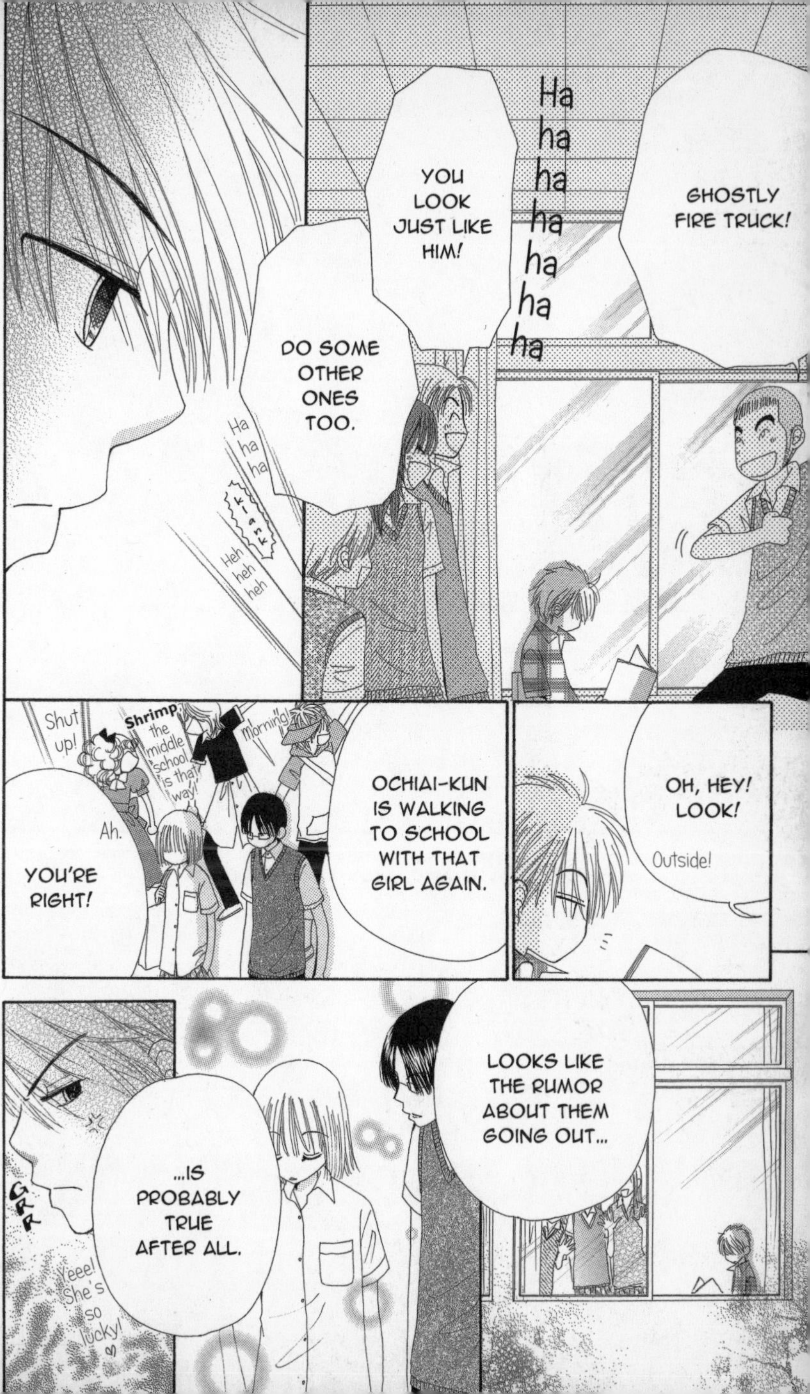
GHOSTLY FIRE TRUCK!
Ha ha ha ha ha ha ha
YOU LOOK JUST LIKE HIM!
DO SOME OTHER ONES TOO.
Ha ha ha
klank
Heh heh heh
OH, HEY! LOOK!
Outside!
OCHIAI-KUN IS WALKING TO SCHOOL WITH THAT GIRL AGAIN.
Morning!
Shrimp the middle school is that way!
Shut up!
Ah.
YOU'RE RIGHT!
LOOKS LIKE THE RUMOR ABOUT THEM GOING OUT...
...IS PROBABLY TRUE AFTER ALL.
GRR
Yeee! She's so lucky!

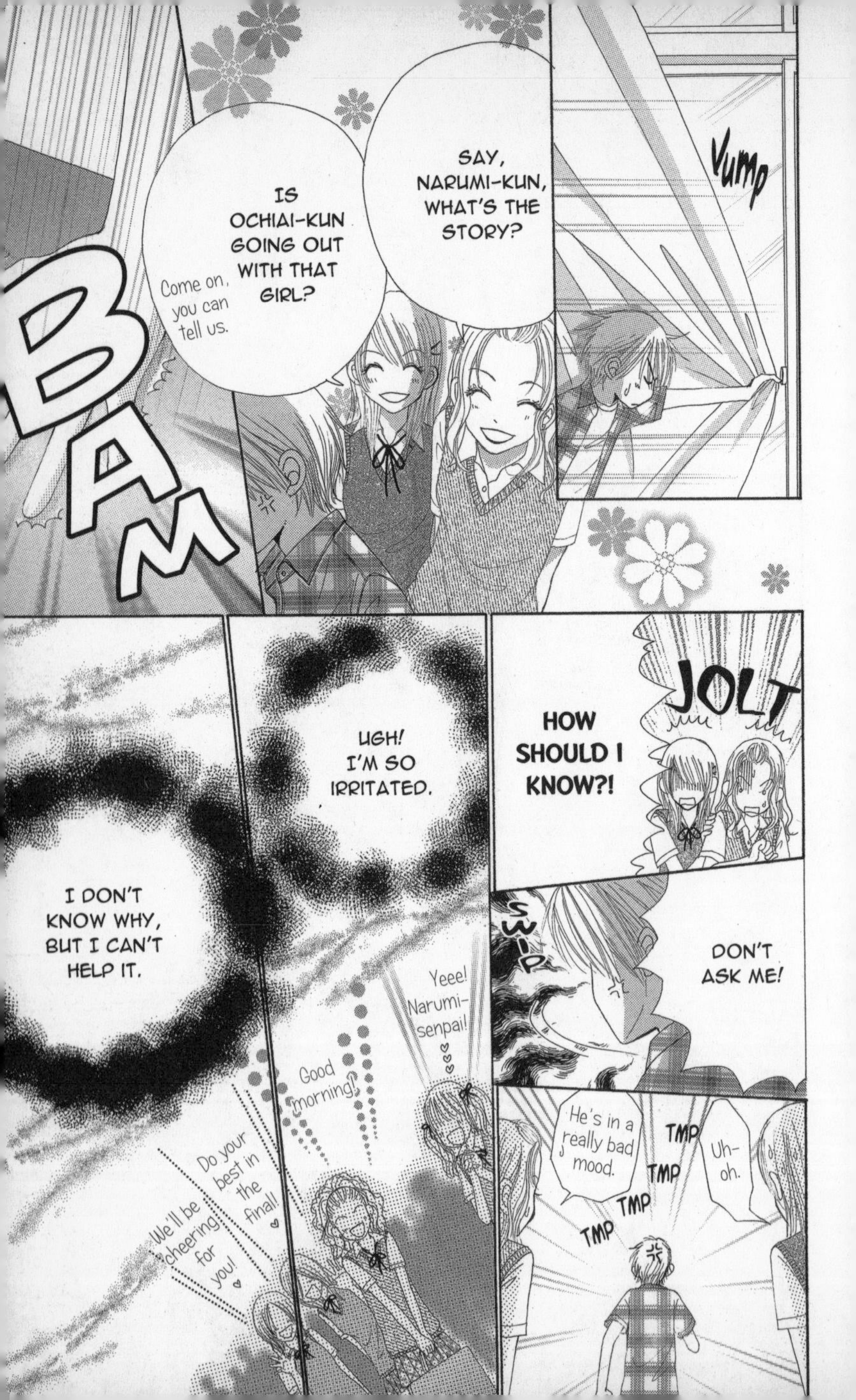
Vump
SAY, NARUMI-KUN, WHAT'S THE STORY?
IS OCHIAI-KUN GOING OUT WITH THAT GIRL?
Come on, you can tell us.
BAM
JOLT
HOW SHOULD I KNOW?!
SWIP
DON'T ASK ME!
Uh-oh.
TMP
TMP
TMP
TMP
He's in a really bad mood.
UGH! I'M SO IRRITATED.
Yeee! Narumi-senpai!
Good morning!
Do your best in the final!
We'll be cheering for you!
I DON'T KNOW WHY, BUT I CAN'T HELP IT.

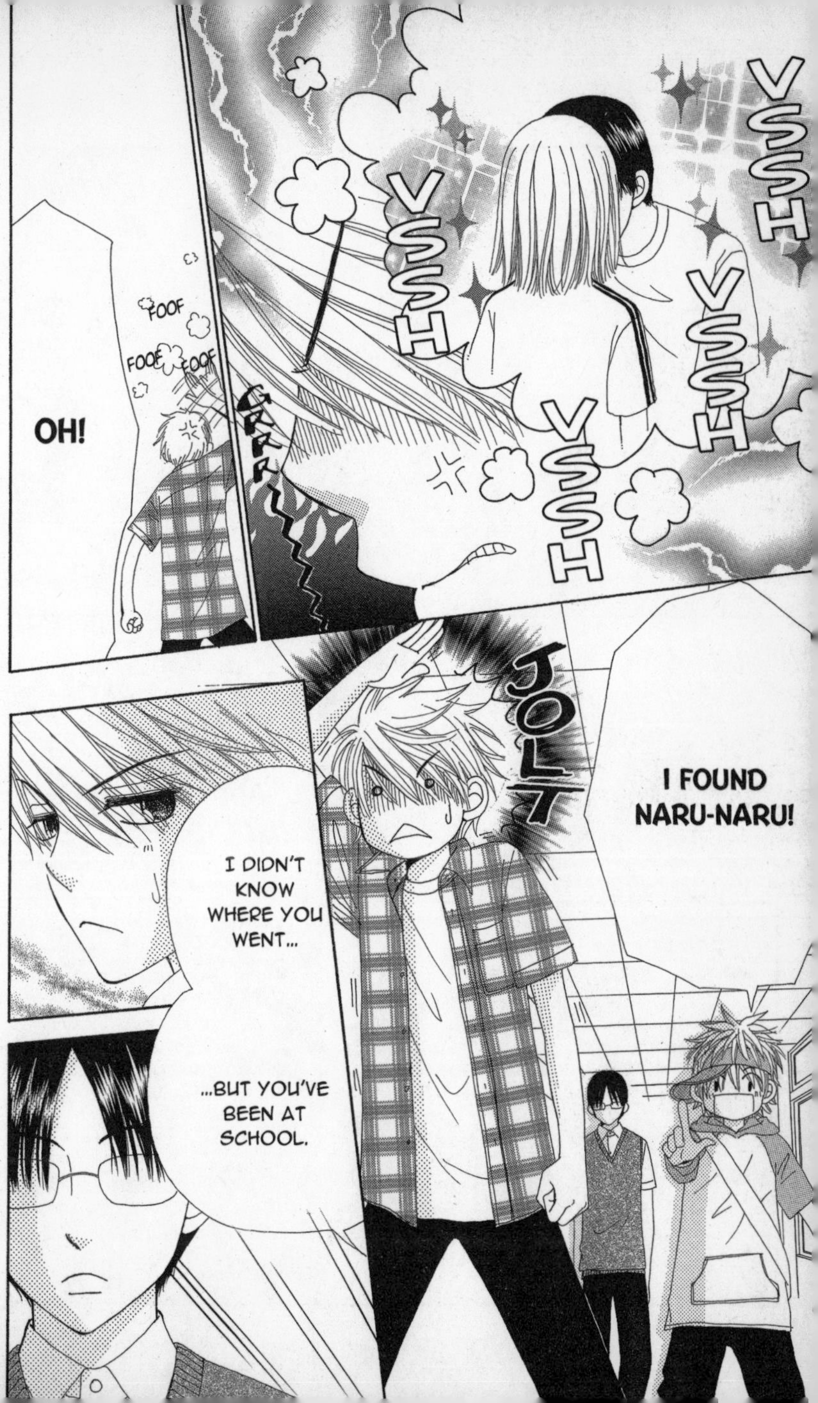
VSSH
VSSH
VSSH
VSSH
GRRR
FOOF
FOOF
FOOF
OH!
I FOUND NARU-NARU!
JOLT
I DIDN'T KNOW WHERE YOU WENT...
...BUT YOU'VE BEEN AT SCHOOL.

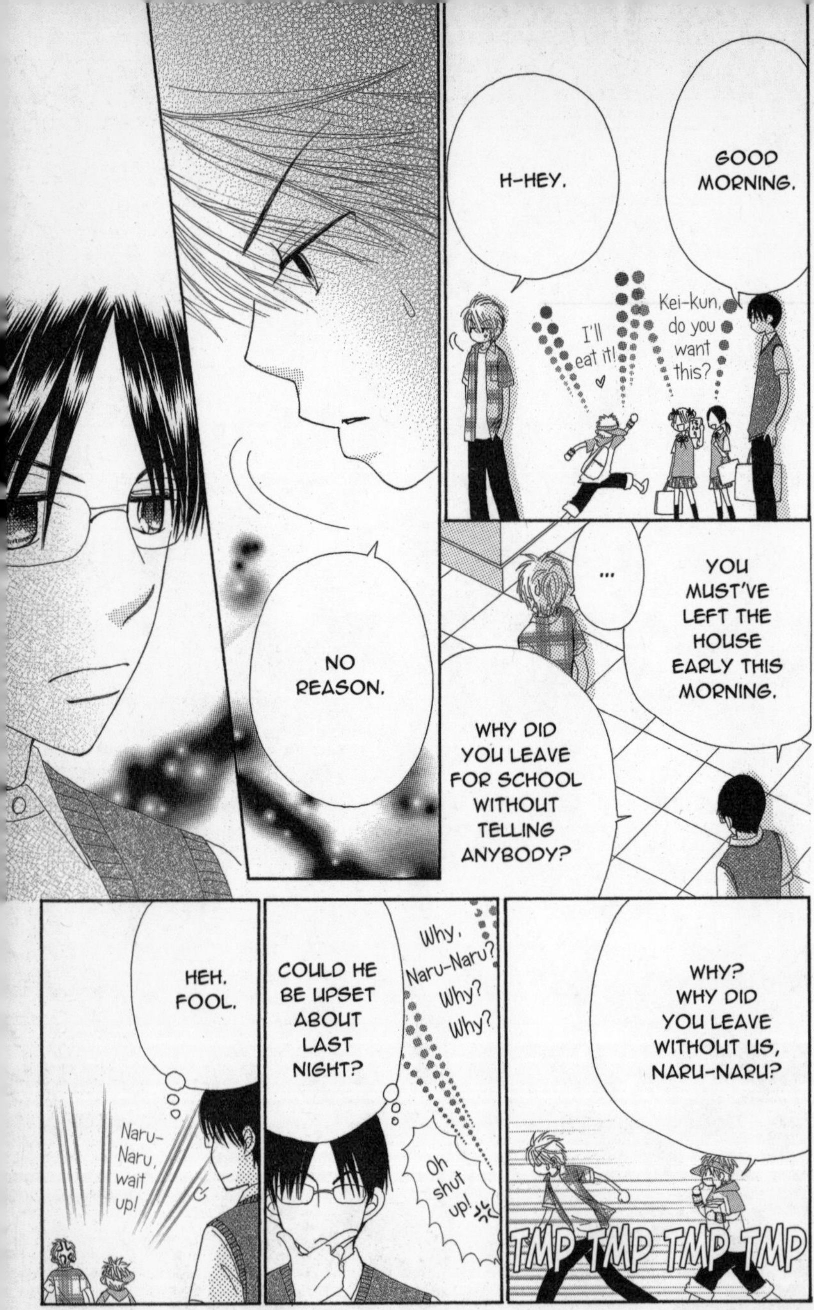
GOOD MORNING.
H-HEY.
Kei-kun, do you want this?
I'll eat it! ♡
YOU MUST'VE LEFT THE HOUSE EARLY THIS MORNING.
...
WHY DID YOU LEAVE FOR SCHOOL WITHOUT TELLING ANYBODY?
NO REASON.
WHY? WHY DID YOU LEAVE WITHOUT US, NARU-NARU?
TMP TMP TMP TMP
Why, Naru-Naru? Why? Why?
COULD HE BE UPSET ABOUT LAST NIGHT?
Oh shut up!
HEH. FOOL.
Naru-Naru, wait up!

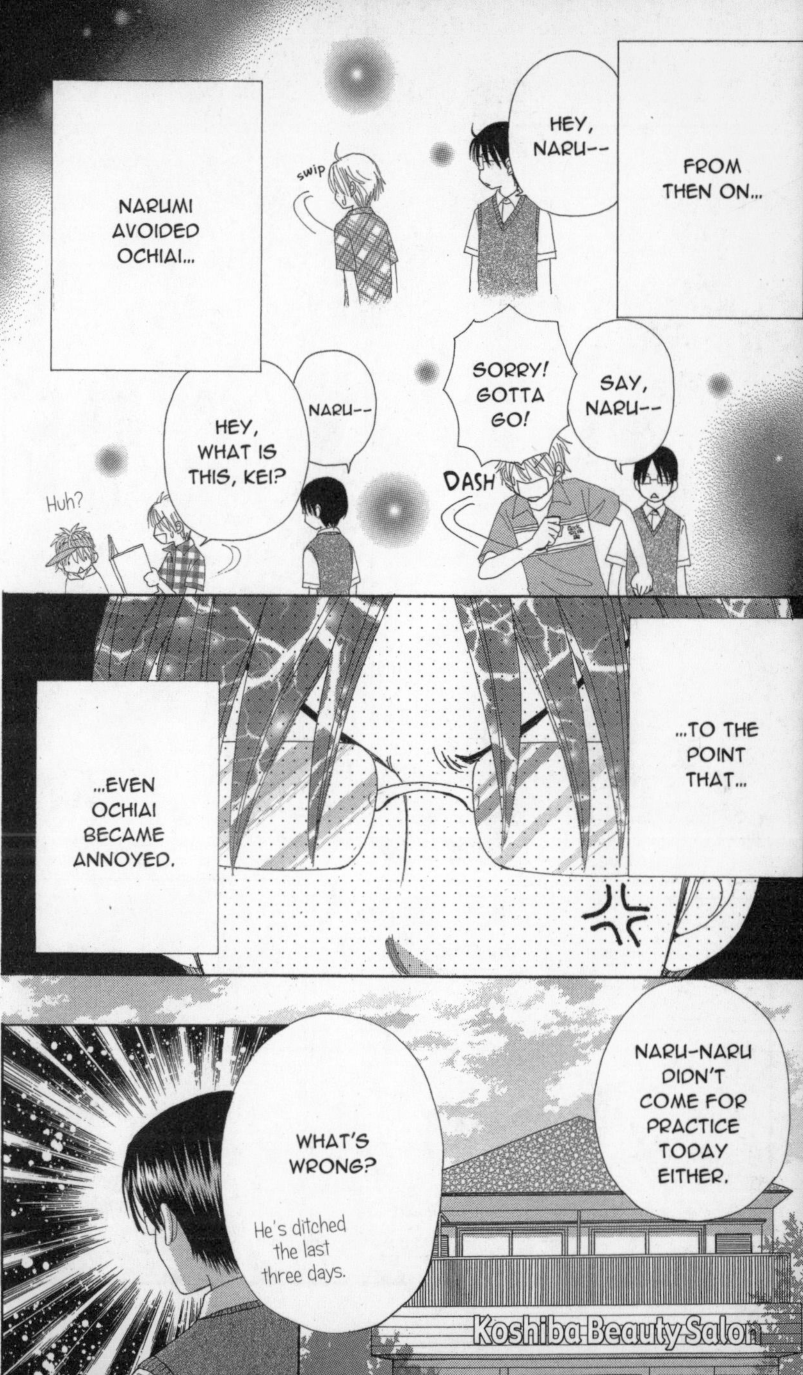
FROM THEN ON...
HEY, NARU--
swip
NARUMI AVOIDED OCHIAI...
SAY, NARU--
SORRY! GOTTA GO!
DASH
NARU--
HEY, WHAT IS THIS, KEI?
Huh?
...TO THE POINT THAT...
...EVEN OCHIAI BECAME ANNOYED.
NARU-NARU DIDN'T COME FOR PRACTICE TODAY EITHER.
He's ditched the last three days.
WHAT'S WRONG?
Koshiba Beauty Salon

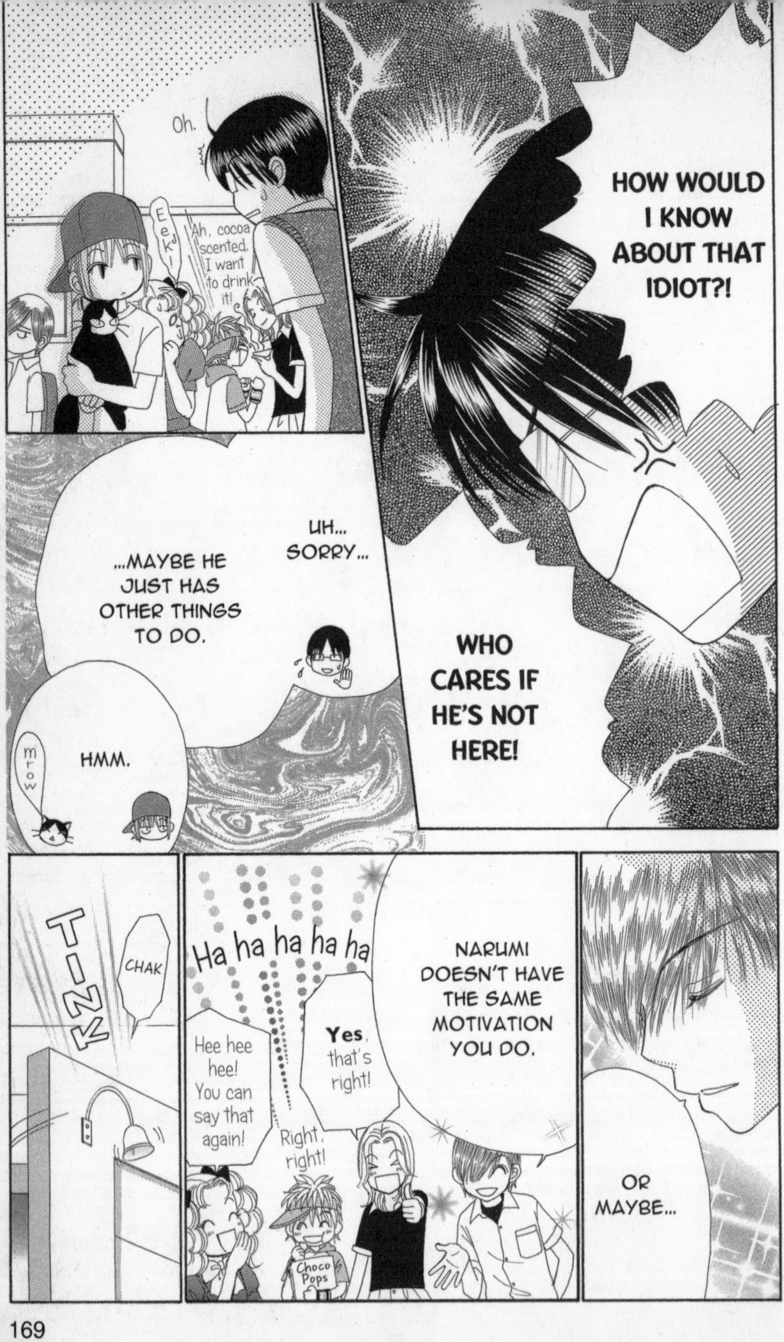
HOW WOULD I KNOW ABOUT THAT IDIOT?!
WHO CARES IF HE'S NOT HERE!
Oh.
Ah, cocoa scented. I want to drink it!
Eek!
UH... SORRY...
...MAYBE HE JUST HAS OTHER THINGS TO DO.
HMM.
mrow
OR MAYBE...
NARUMI DOESN'T HAVE THE SAME MOTIVATION YOU DO.
Ha ha ha ha ha
Yes, that's right!
Hee hee hee! You can say that again!
Right, right!
Choco Pops
CHAK
TINK

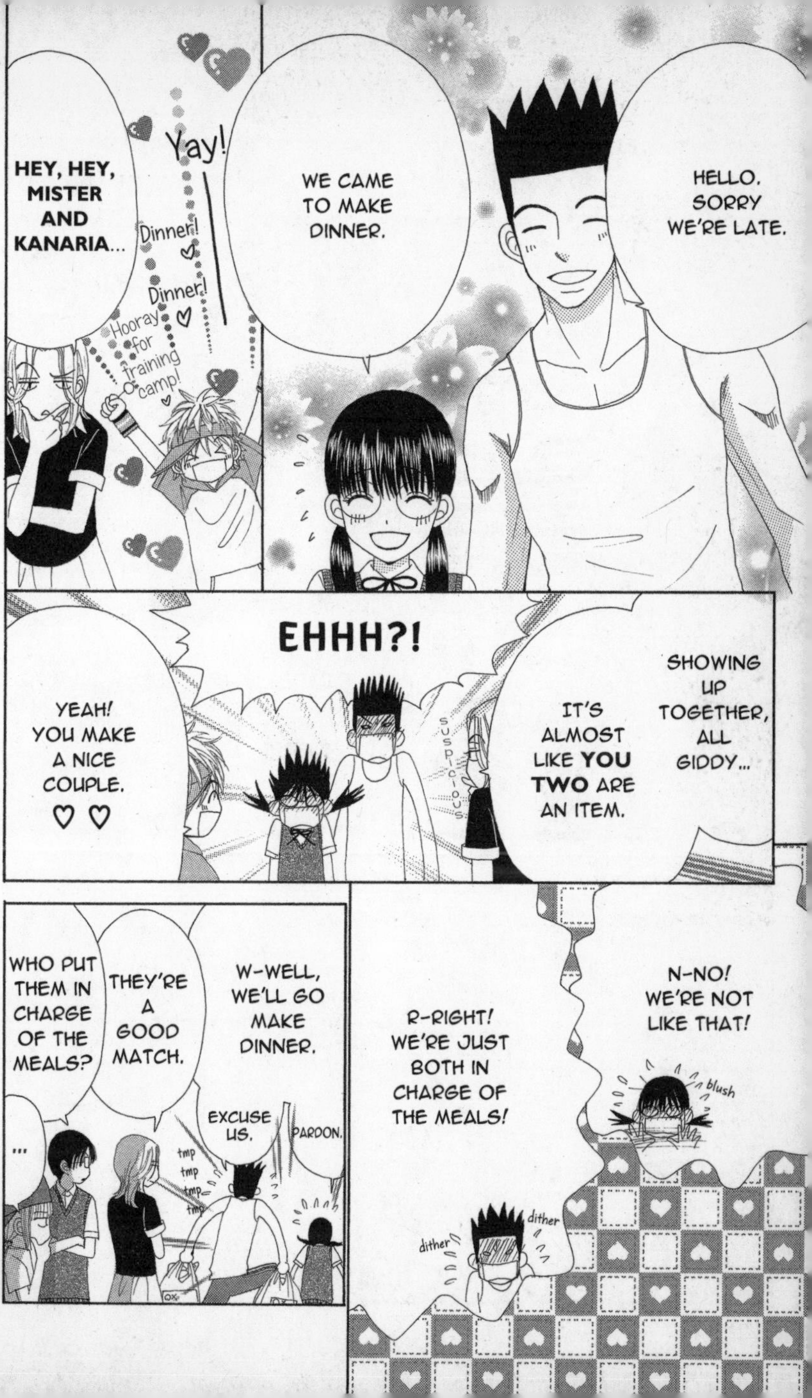
HELLO. SORRY WE'RE LATE.
WE CAME TO MAKE DINNER.
Yay!
Dinner! ♡
Dinner! ♡
Hooray for training camp! ♡
HEY, HEY, MISTER AND KANARIA...
EHHH?!
SHOWING UP TOGETHER, ALL GIDDY...
IT'S ALMOST LIKE **YOU TWO** ARE AN ITEM.
SUSPICIOUS
YEAH! YOU MAKE A NICE COUPLE. ♡ ♡
N-NO! WE'RE NOT LIKE THAT!
blush
R-RIGHT! WE'RE JUST BOTH IN CHARGE OF THE MEALS!
dither
dither
W-WELL, WE'LL GO MAKE DINNER.
THEY'RE A GOOD MATCH.
WHO PUT THEM IN CHARGE OF THE MEALS?
PARDON.
EXCUSE US.
tmp tmp tmp tmp
...

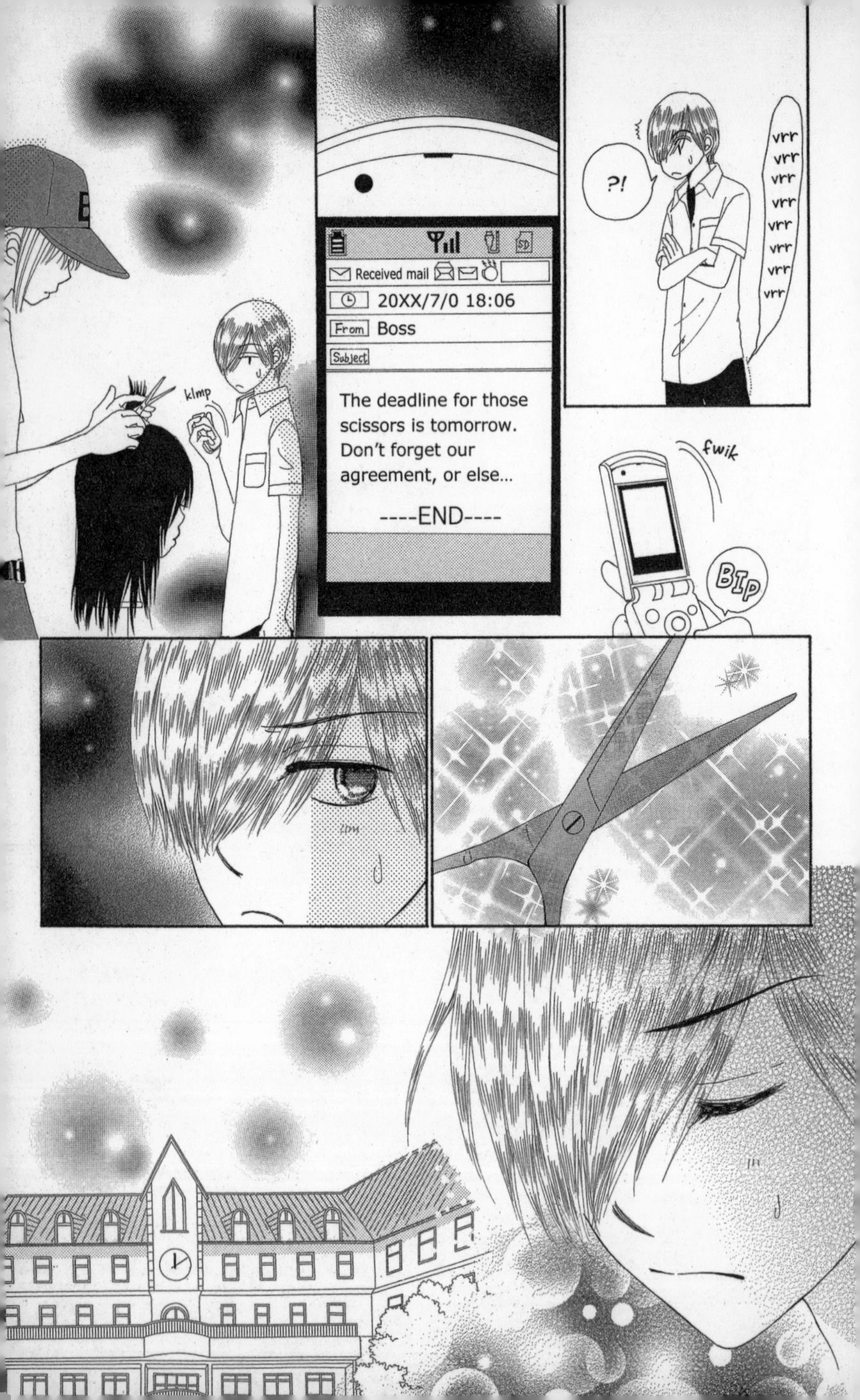
vrr vrr vrr vrr vrr vrr vrr vrr
?!
fwik
BIP
Received mail
20XX/7/0 18:06
From Boss
Subject
The deadline for those scissors is tomorrow. Don't forget our agreement, or else...
----END----
klmp

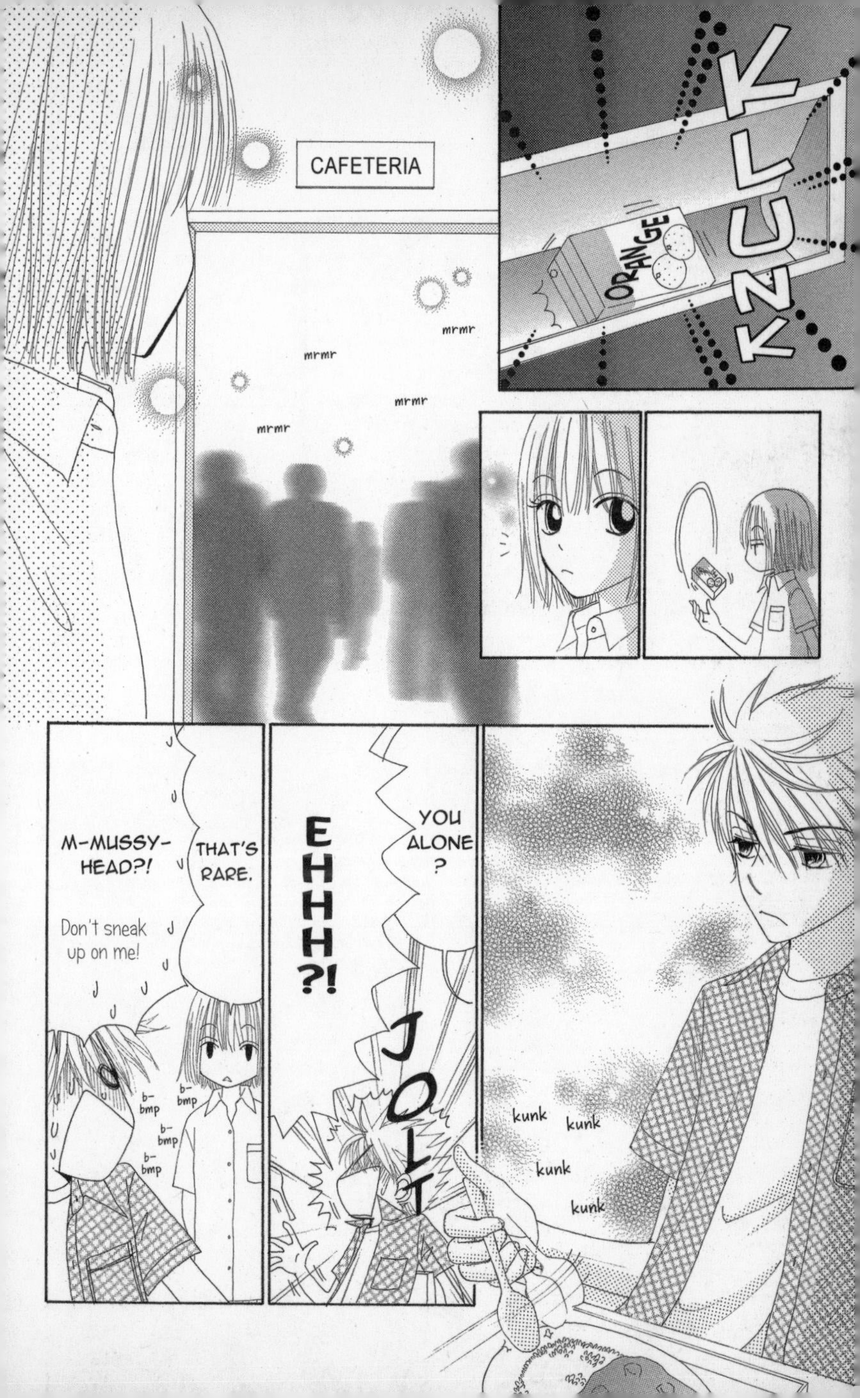
KLUNK
ORANGE
CAFETERIA
mrmr
mrmr
mrmr
mrmr
kunk
kunk
kunk
kunk
YOU ALONE?
EHHHH?!
JOLT
THAT'S RARE.
M-MUSSY-HEAD?!
Don't sneak up on me!
b-bmp
b-bmp
b-bmp
b-bmp

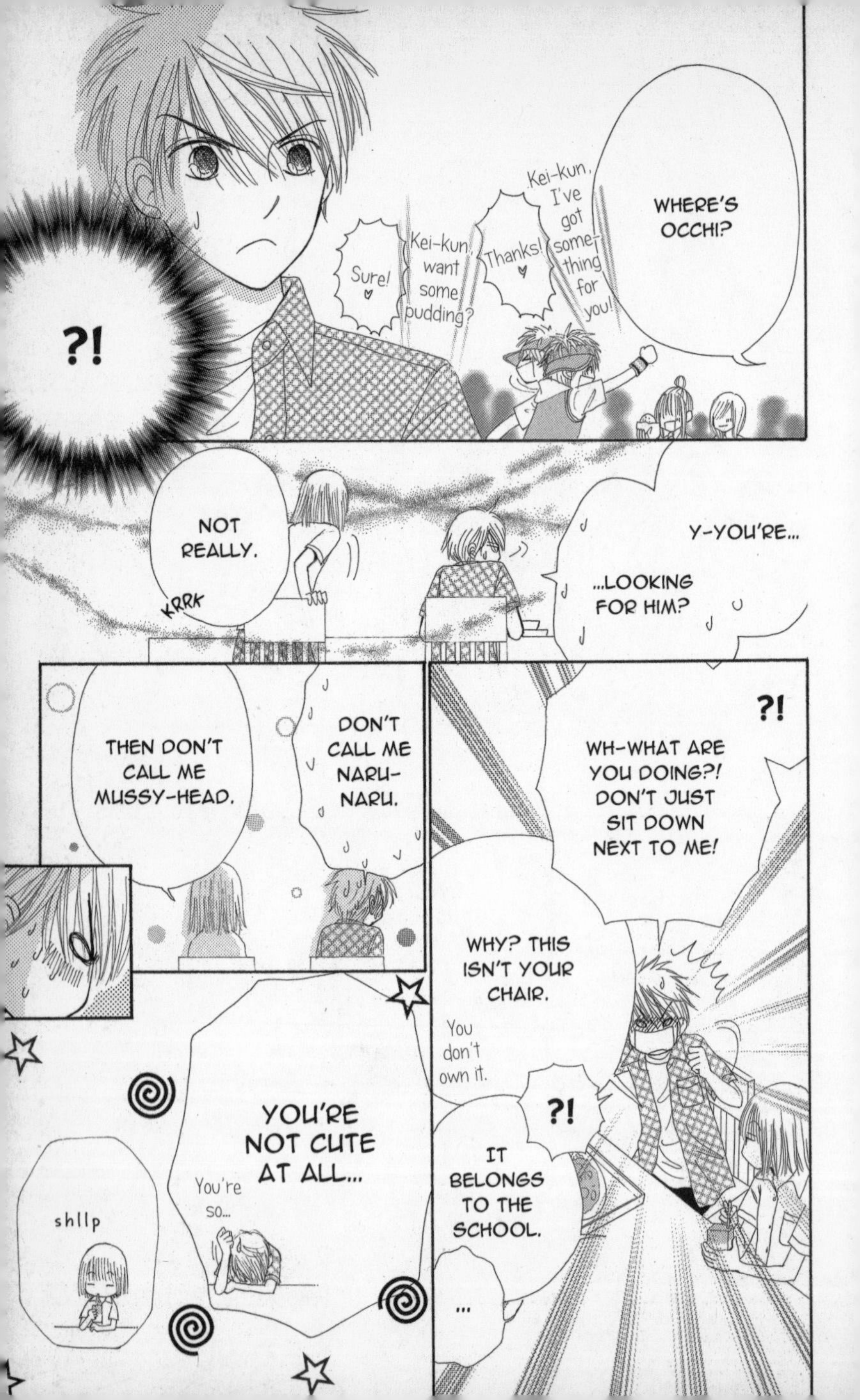
WHERE'S OCCHI?
Kei-kun, I've got something for you!
Thanks! ♥
Kei-kun, want some pudding?
Sure! ♥
?!
Y-YOU'RE...
...LOOKING FOR HIM?
NOT REALLY.
KRRK
?!
WH-WHAT ARE YOU DOING?! DON'T JUST SIT DOWN NEXT TO ME!
WHY? THIS ISN'T YOUR CHAIR.
You don't own it.
?!
IT BELONGS TO THE SCHOOL.
...
DON'T CALL ME NARU-NARU.
THEN DON'T CALL ME MUSSY-HEAD.
YOU'RE NOT CUTE AT ALL...
You're so...
shllp

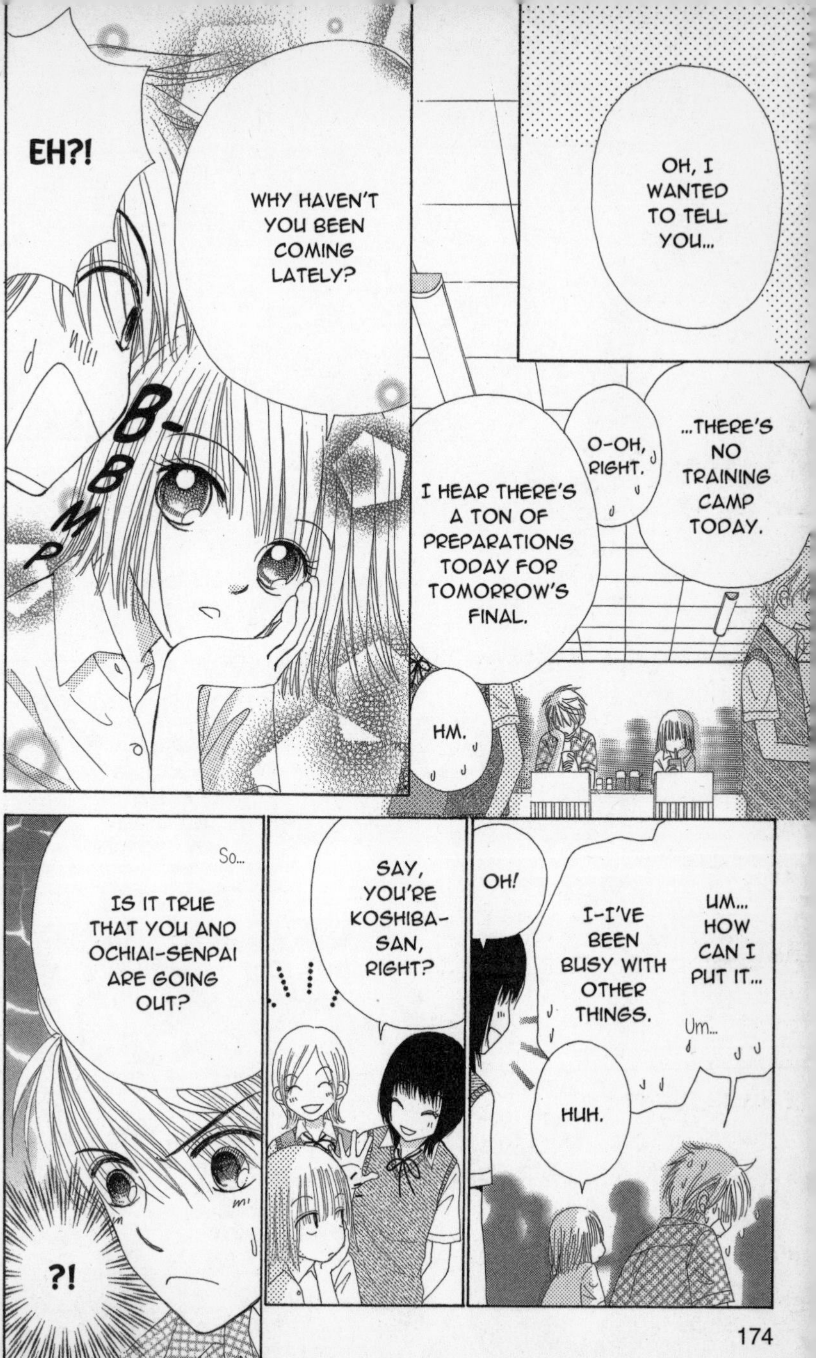
OH, I WANTED TO TELL YOU...
...THERE'S NO TRAINING CAMP TODAY.
O-OH, RIGHT.
I HEAR THERE'S A TON OF PREPARATIONS TODAY FOR TOMORROW'S FINAL.
HM.
WHY HAVEN'T YOU BEEN COMING LATELY?
EH?!
B-BMP
UM... HOW CAN I PUT IT...
Um...
I-I'VE BEEN BUSY WITH OTHER THINGS.
OH!
HUH.
SAY, YOU'RE KOSHIBA-SAN, RIGHT?
So...
IS IT TRUE THAT YOU AND OCHIAI-SENPAI ARE GOING OUT?
?!

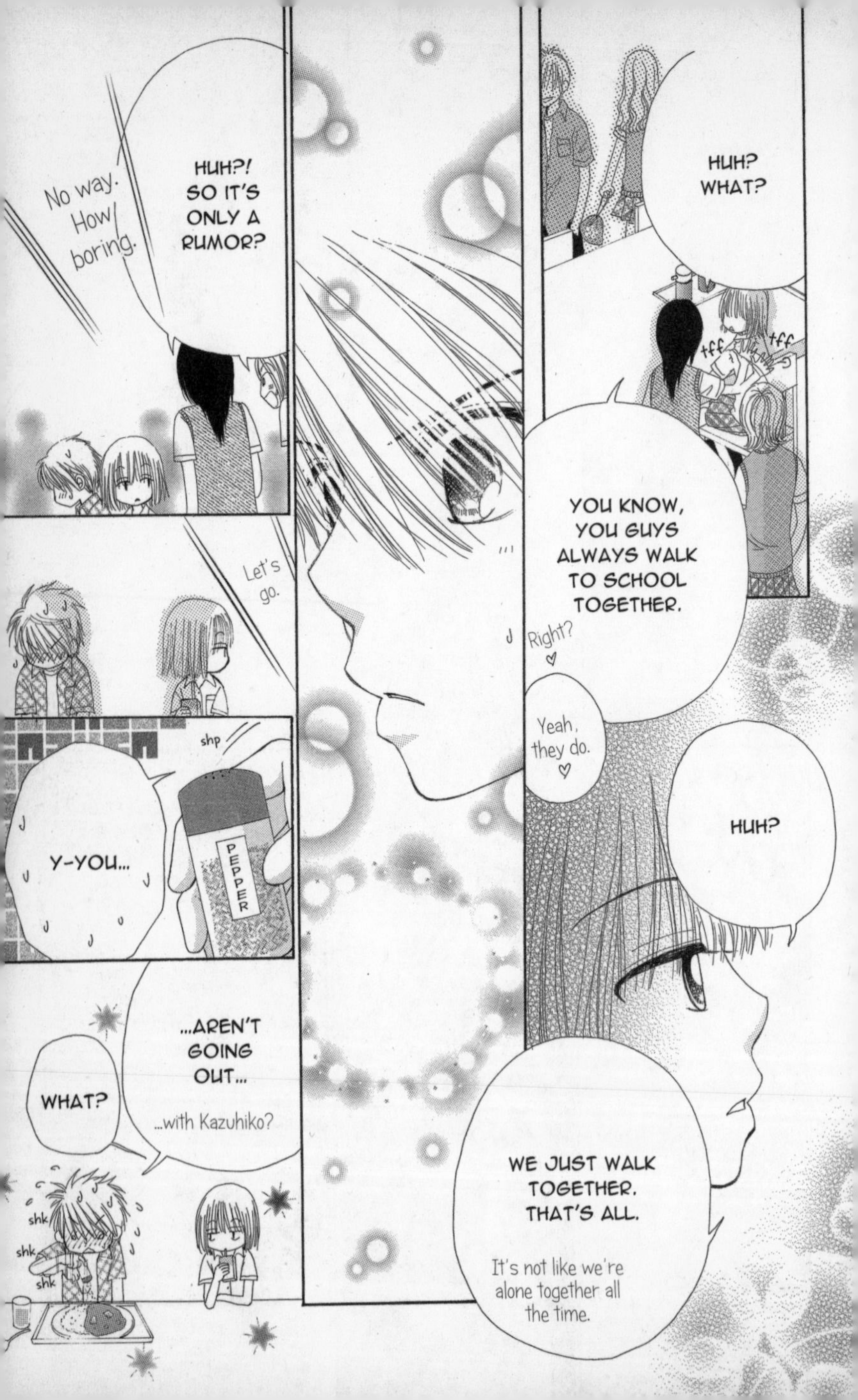
HUH? WHAT?
tff
tff
YOU KNOW, YOU GUYS ALWAYS WALK TO SCHOOL TOGETHER.
Right?
Yeah, they do.
HUH?
WE JUST WALK TOGETHER. THAT'S ALL.
It's not like we're alone together all the time.
HUH?! SO IT'S ONLY A RUMOR?
No way. How boring.
Let's go.
shp
PEPPER
Y-YOU...
...AREN'T GOING OUT...
...with Kazuhiko?
WHAT?
shk
shk
shk

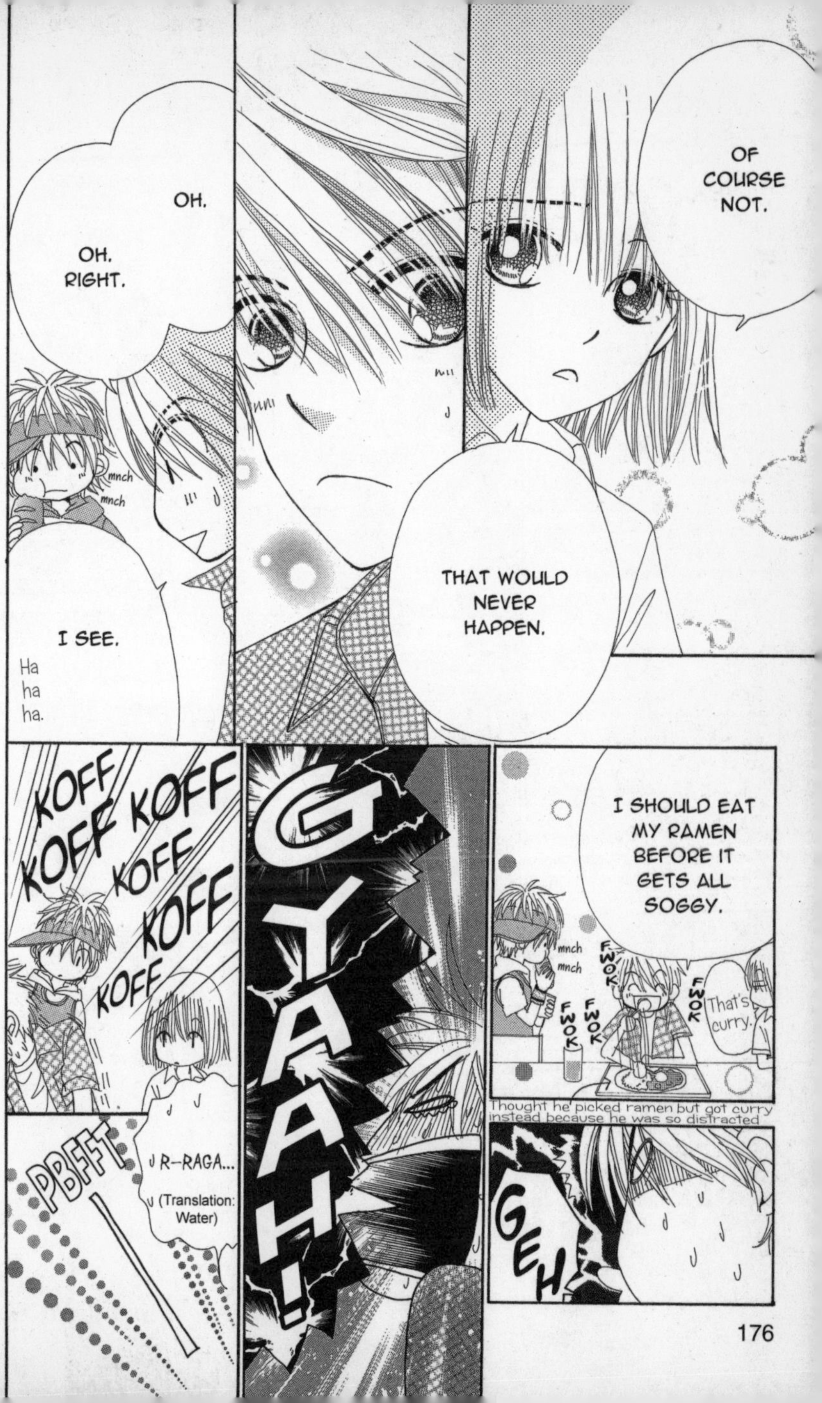
OF COURSE NOT.
THAT WOULD NEVER HAPPEN.
OH.
OH. RIGHT.
mnch mnch
I SEE.
Ha ha ha.
I SHOULD EAT MY RAMEN BEFORE IT GETS ALL SOGGY.
That's curry.
FWOK FWOK FWOK FWOK
mnch mnch
Thought he picked ramen but got curry instead because he was so distracted
GEH.
GYAAAH!
KOFF KOFF KOFF KOFF KOFF KOFF
PBFFT
R-RAGA...
(Translation: Water)

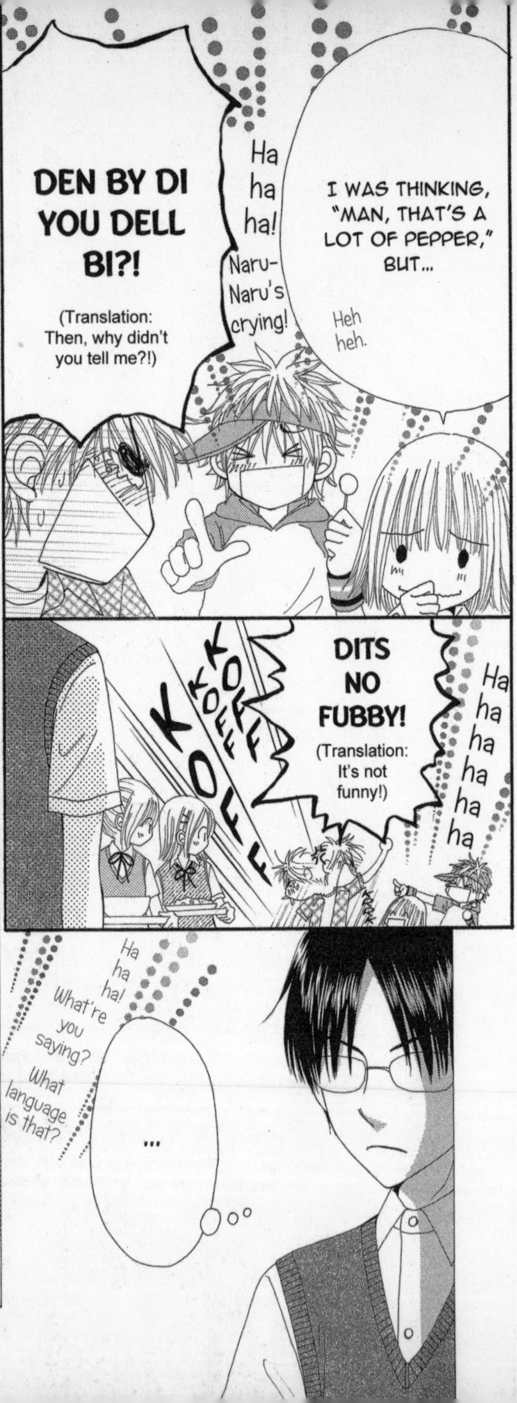
I WAS THINKING, "MAN, THAT'S A LOT OF PEPPER," BUT...
Heh heh.
Ha ha ha! Naru-Naru's crying!
DEN BY DI YOU DELL BI?!
(Translation: Then, why didn't you tell me?!)
Ha ha ha ha ha ha
DITS NO FUBBY!
(Translation: It's not funny!)
KOFF KOFF KOFF
K
KOFF
Ha ha ha!
What're you saying?
What language is that?
...

K's Club Talk

At the Summer Festival in Fukuoka in August 2007, I held a signing session! Thank you to everyone who came in such hot weather! Thank you to everyone who gave me presents and letters!! There was even someone who came all the way from Shizuoka prefecture--I'm filled with so much gratitude! ♡♡♡
I got to talk with the readers while I was signing, though I had very little time. There were comments like "Everyone in my family is reading it," "I'm reading it with my mother," and "My mother is a bigger B.P. fan than me!" All that really made me happy.
Thank you to all the readers, families, and mothers throughout the country!
That reminds me, sometimes I receive letters from the mothers of the readers! (Thank you!) Mothers, which character in B.P. do you like best?

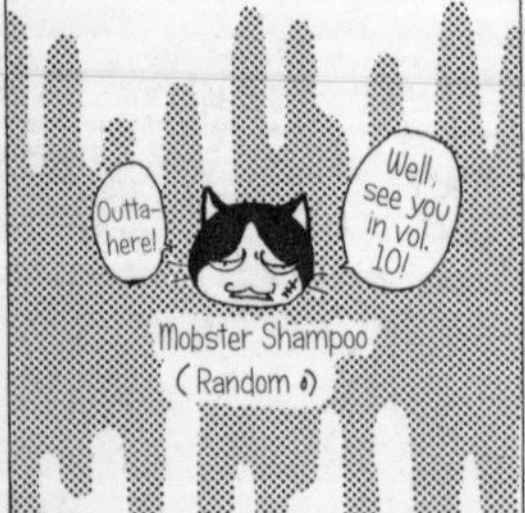
Well, see you in vol. 10!
Outta-here!
Mobster Shampoo
(Random ♪)

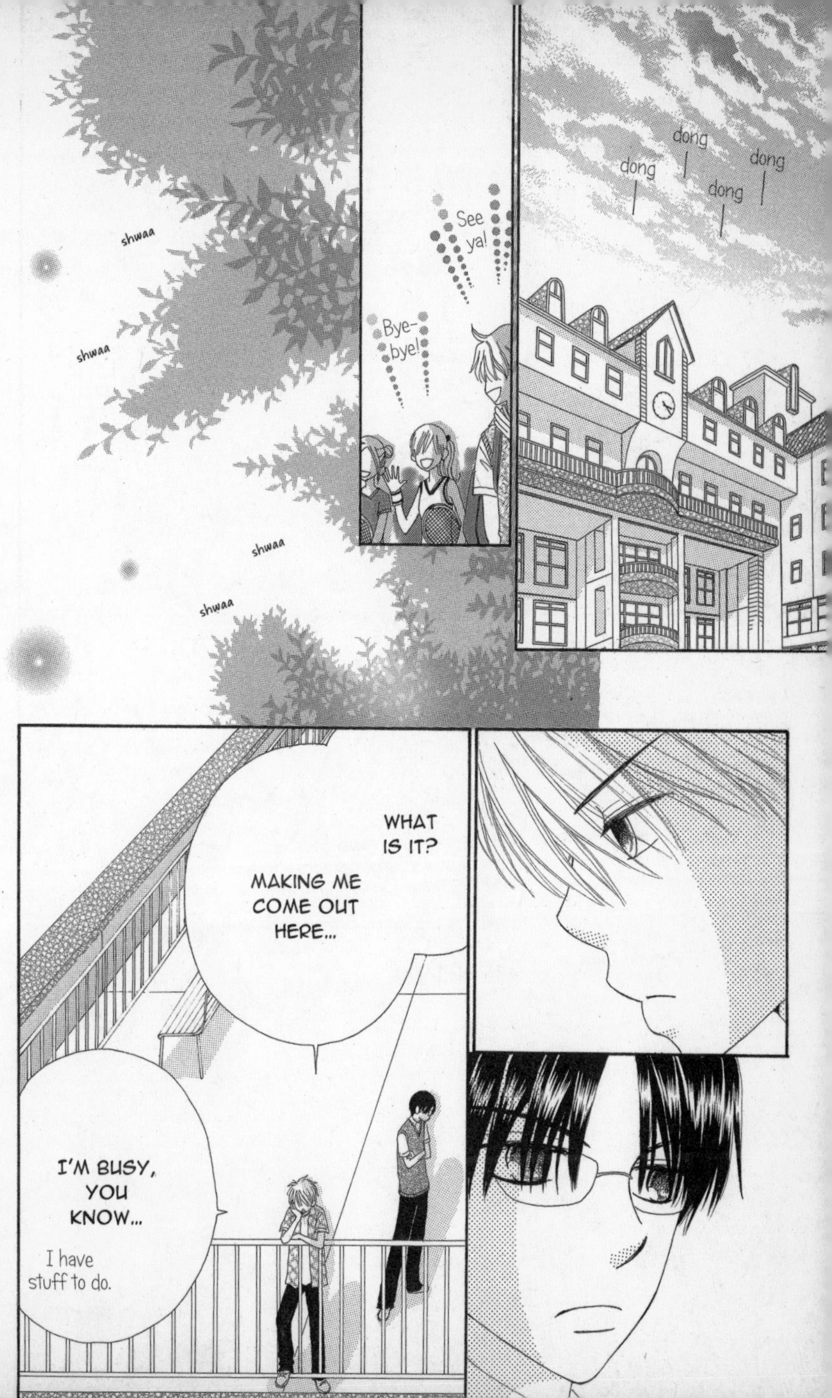
dong
dong
dong
dong
See ya!
Bye-bye!
shwaa
shwaa
shwaa
shwaa
WHAT IS IT?
MAKING ME COME OUT HERE...
I'M BUSY, YOU KNOW...
I have stuff to do.

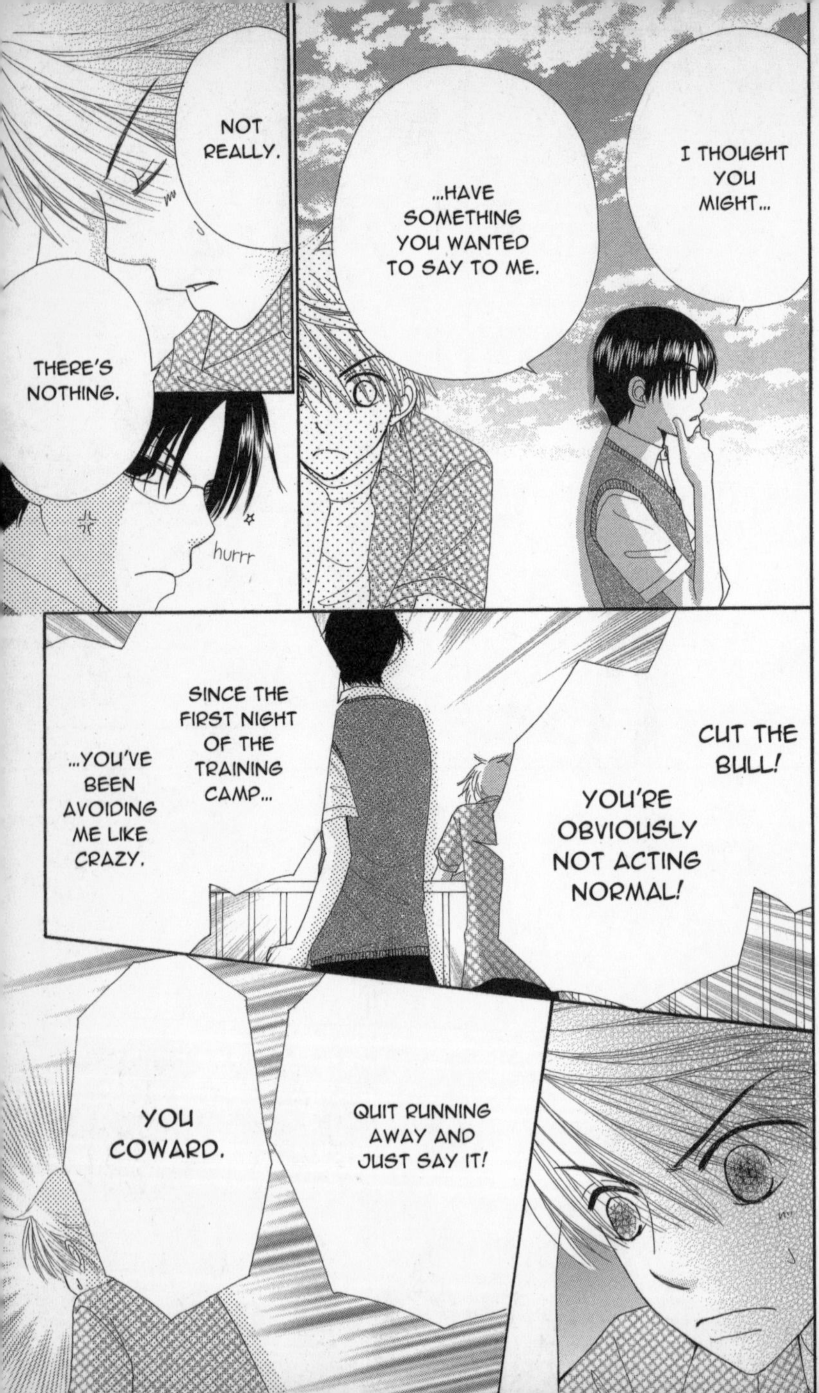
I THOUGHT YOU MIGHT...
...HAVE SOMETHING YOU WANTED TO SAY TO ME.
NOT REALLY.
THERE'S NOTHING.
hurrr
CUT THE BULL!
YOU'RE OBVIOUSLY NOT ACTING NORMAL!
SINCE THE FIRST NIGHT OF THE TRAINING CAMP...
...YOU'VE BEEN AVOIDING ME LIKE CRAZY.
QUIT RUNNING AWAY AND JUST SAY IT!
YOU COWARD.

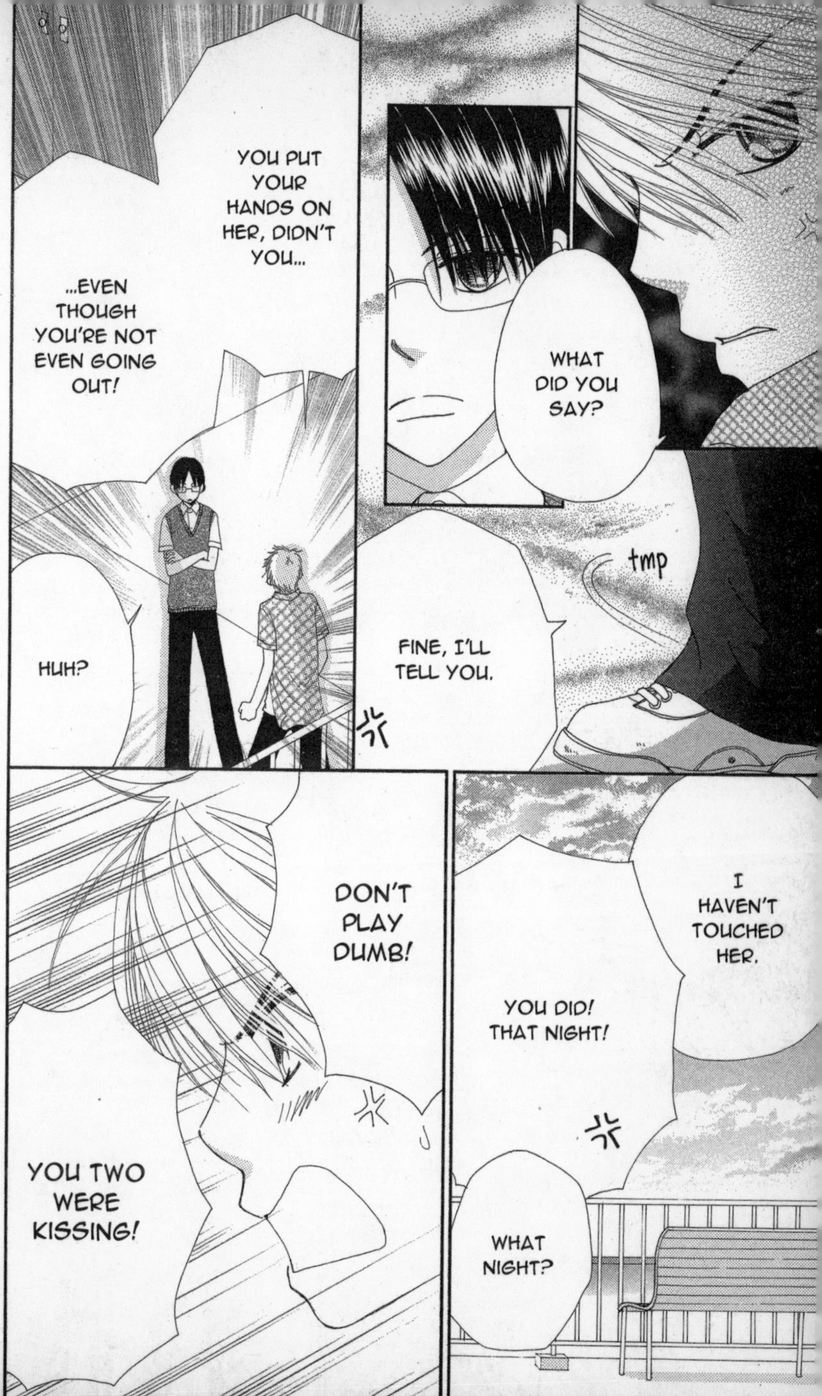
WHAT DID YOU SAY?
tmp
FINE, I'LL TELL YOU.
YOU PUT YOUR HANDS ON HER, DIDN'T YOU...
...EVEN THOUGH YOU'RE NOT EVEN GOING OUT!
HUH?
I HAVEN'T TOUCHED HER.
YOU DID! THAT NIGHT!
WHAT NIGHT?
DON'T PLAY DUMB!
YOU TWO WERE KISSING!

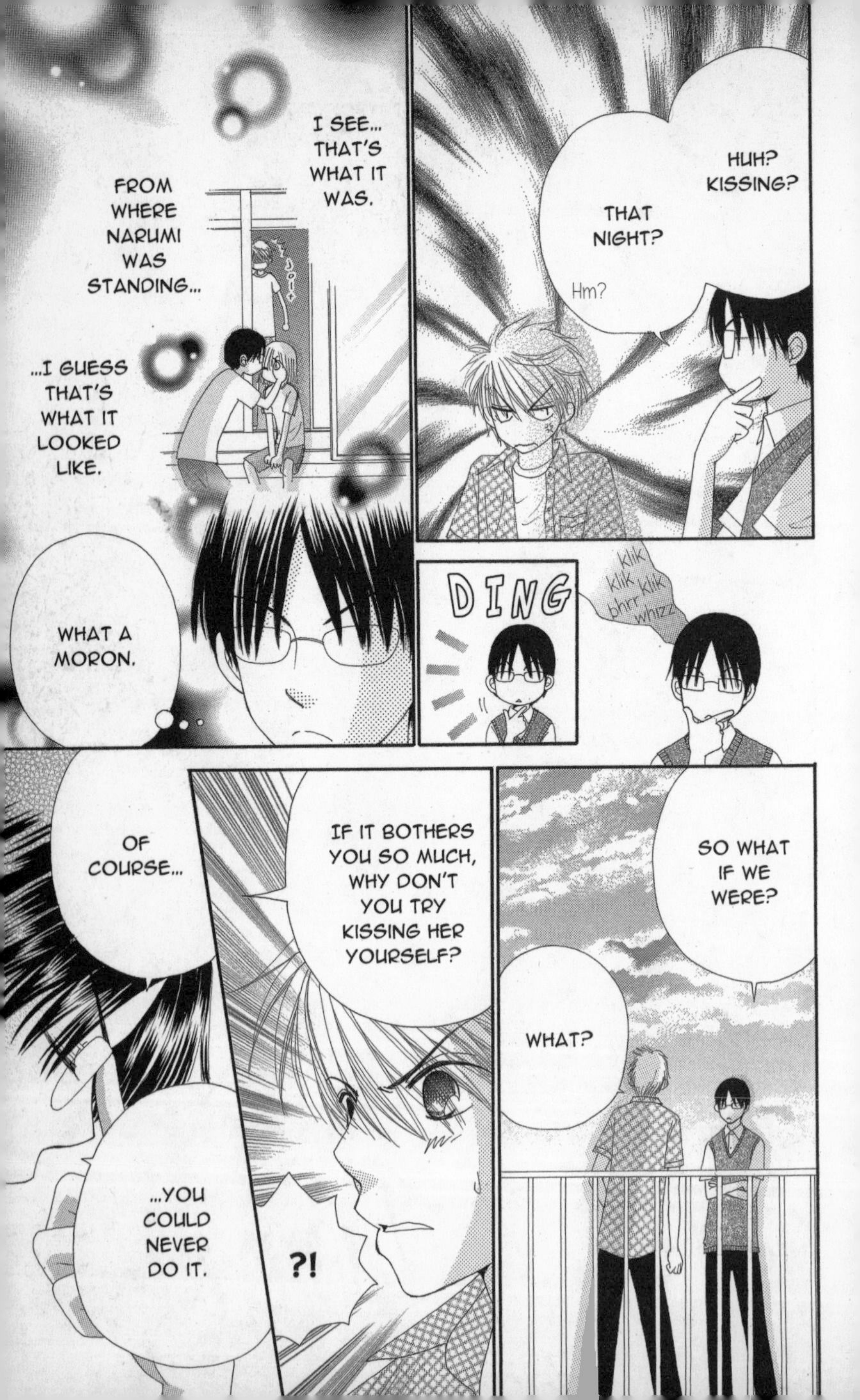
HUH? KISSING?
THAT NIGHT?
Hm?
klik klik klik bhrr whizz
DING
I SEE... THAT'S WHAT IT WAS.
FROM WHERE NARUMI WAS STANDING...
...I GUESS THAT'S WHAT IT LOOKED LIKE.
WHAT A MORON.
SO WHAT IF WE WERE?
WHAT?
IF IT BOTHERS YOU SO MUCH, WHY DON'T YOU TRY KISSING HER YOURSELF?
?!
OF COURSE...
...YOU COULD NEVER DO IT.

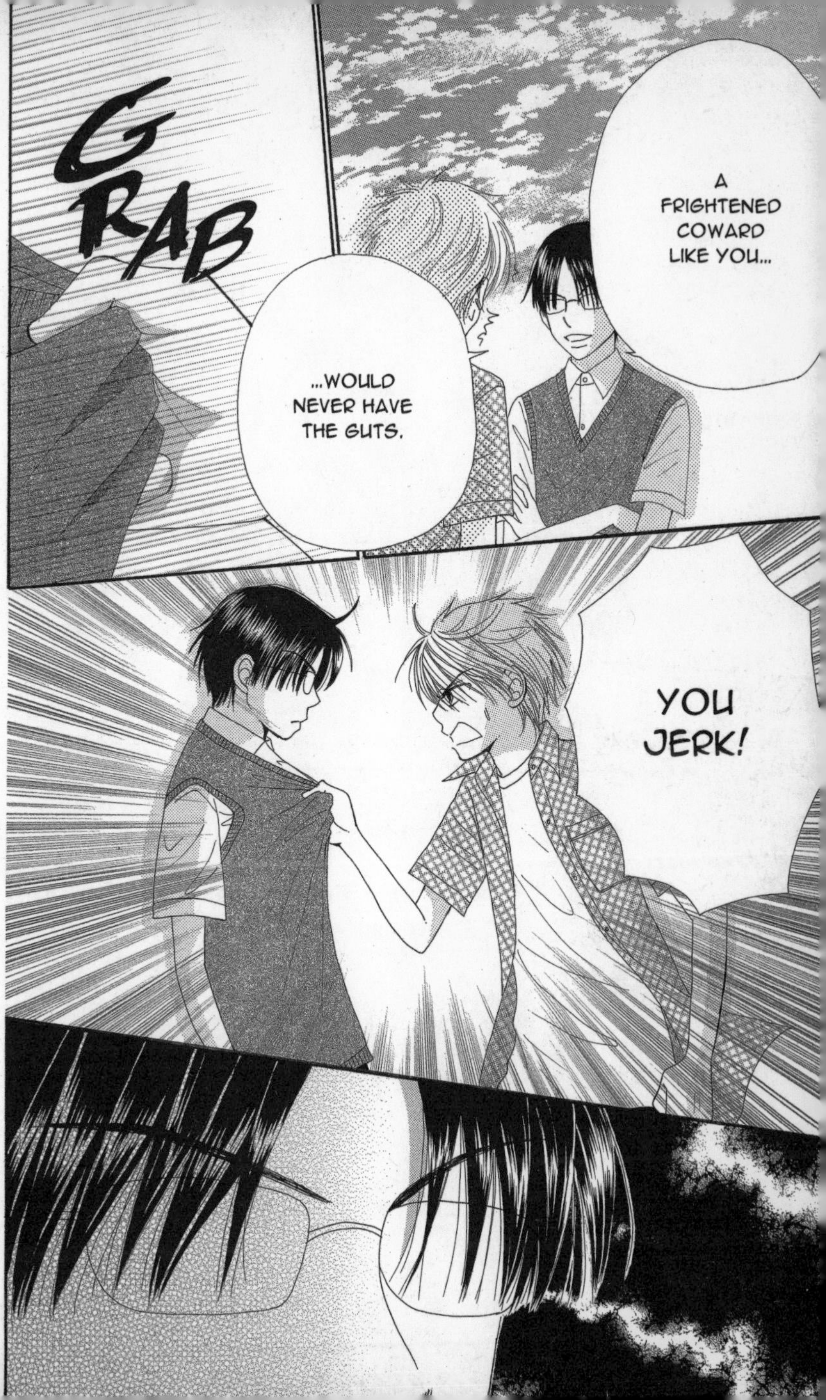
A FRIGHTENED COWARD LIKE YOU...
...WOULD NEVER HAVE THE GUTS.
GRAB
YOU JERK!

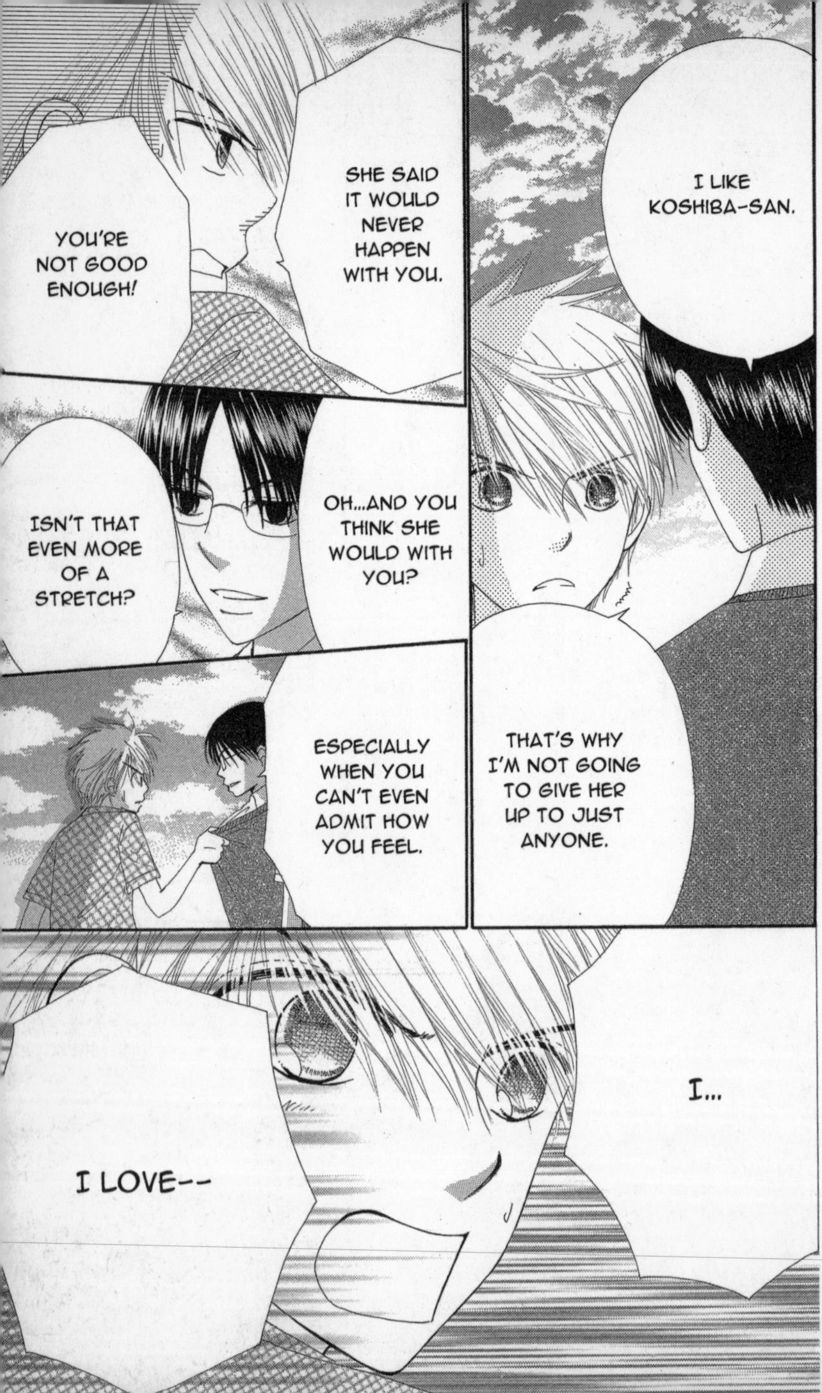
I LIKE KOSHIBA-SAN.
THAT'S WHY I'M NOT GOING TO GIVE HER UP TO JUST ANYONE.
SHE SAID IT WOULD NEVER HAPPEN WITH YOU.
YOU'RE NOT GOOD ENOUGH!
OH...AND YOU THINK SHE WOULD WITH YOU?
ISN'T THAT EVEN MORE OF A STRETCH?
ESPECIALLY WHEN YOU CAN'T EVEN ADMIT HOW YOU FEEL.
I...
I LOVE--

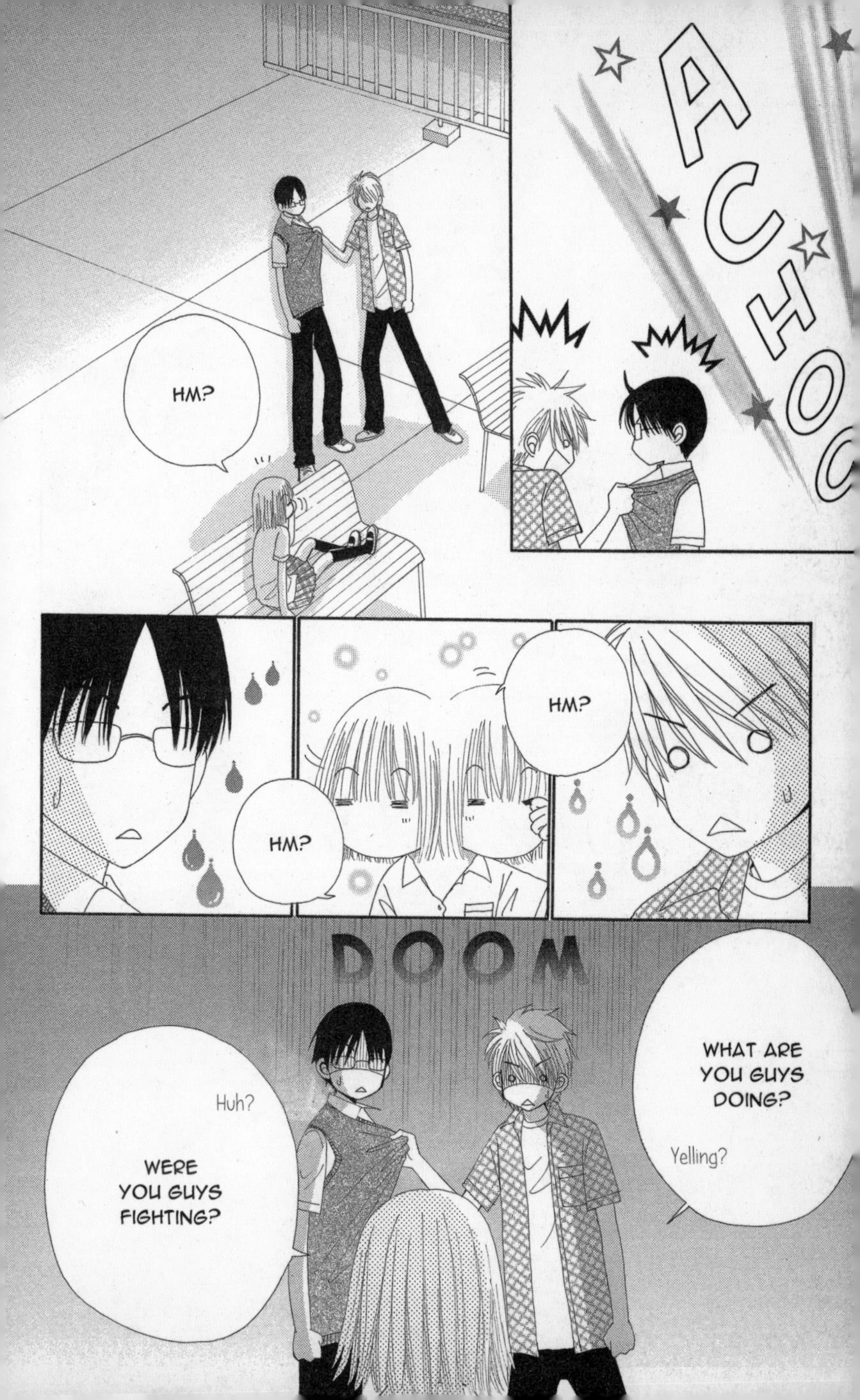
ACHOO
HM?
HM?
HM?
DOOM
WHAT ARE YOU GUYS DOING?
Yelling?
Huh?
WERE YOU GUYS FIGHTING?

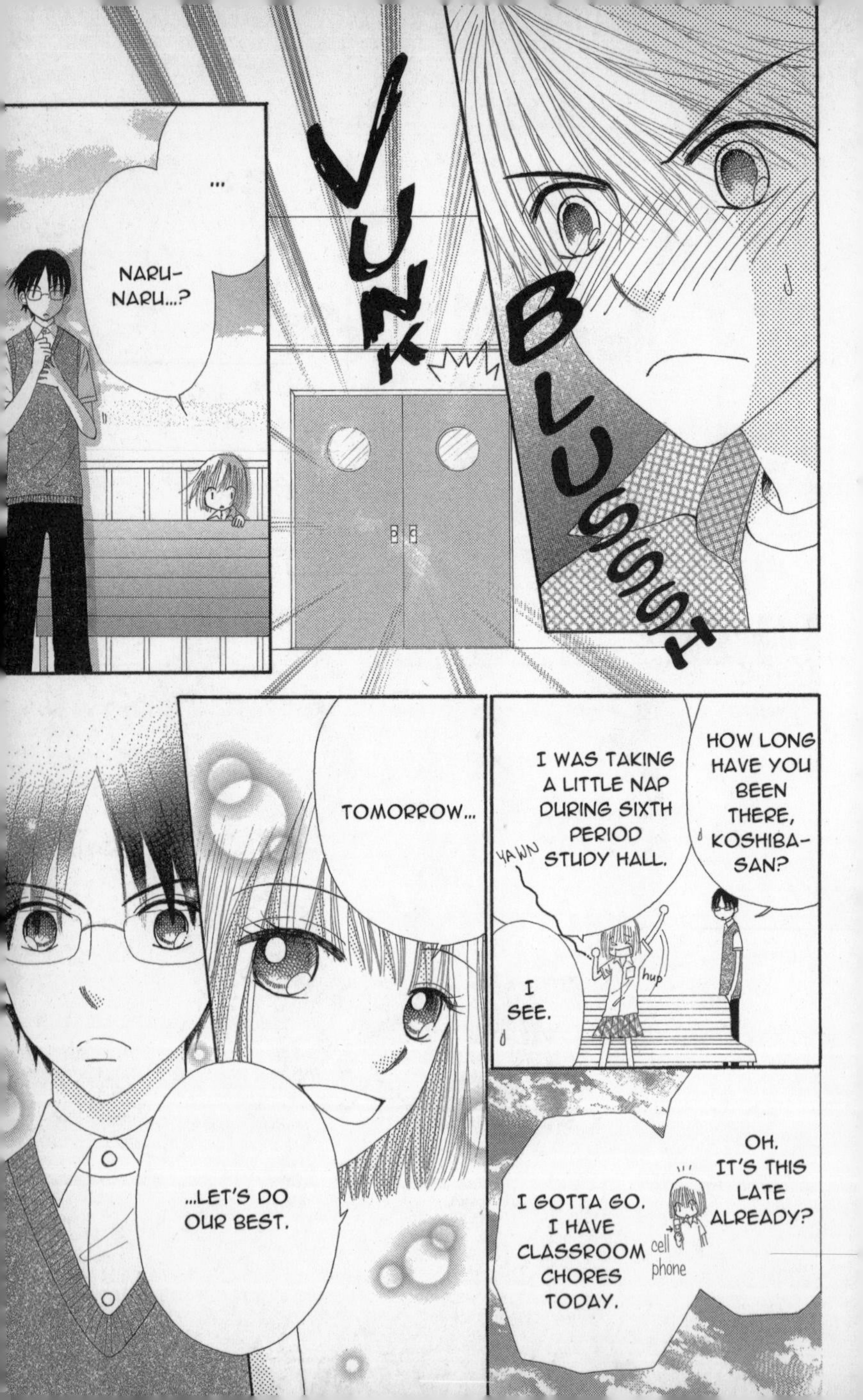
BLUSSSH
VUNK
...
NARU-NARU...?
HOW LONG HAVE YOU BEEN THERE, KOSHIBA-SAN?
I WAS TAKING A LITTLE NAP DURING SIXTH PERIOD STUDY HALL.
YAWN
hup
I SEE.
OH. IT'S THIS LATE ALREADY?
I GOTTA GO. I HAVE CLASSROOM CHORES TODAY.
cell phone
TOMORROW...
...LET'S DO OUR BEST.

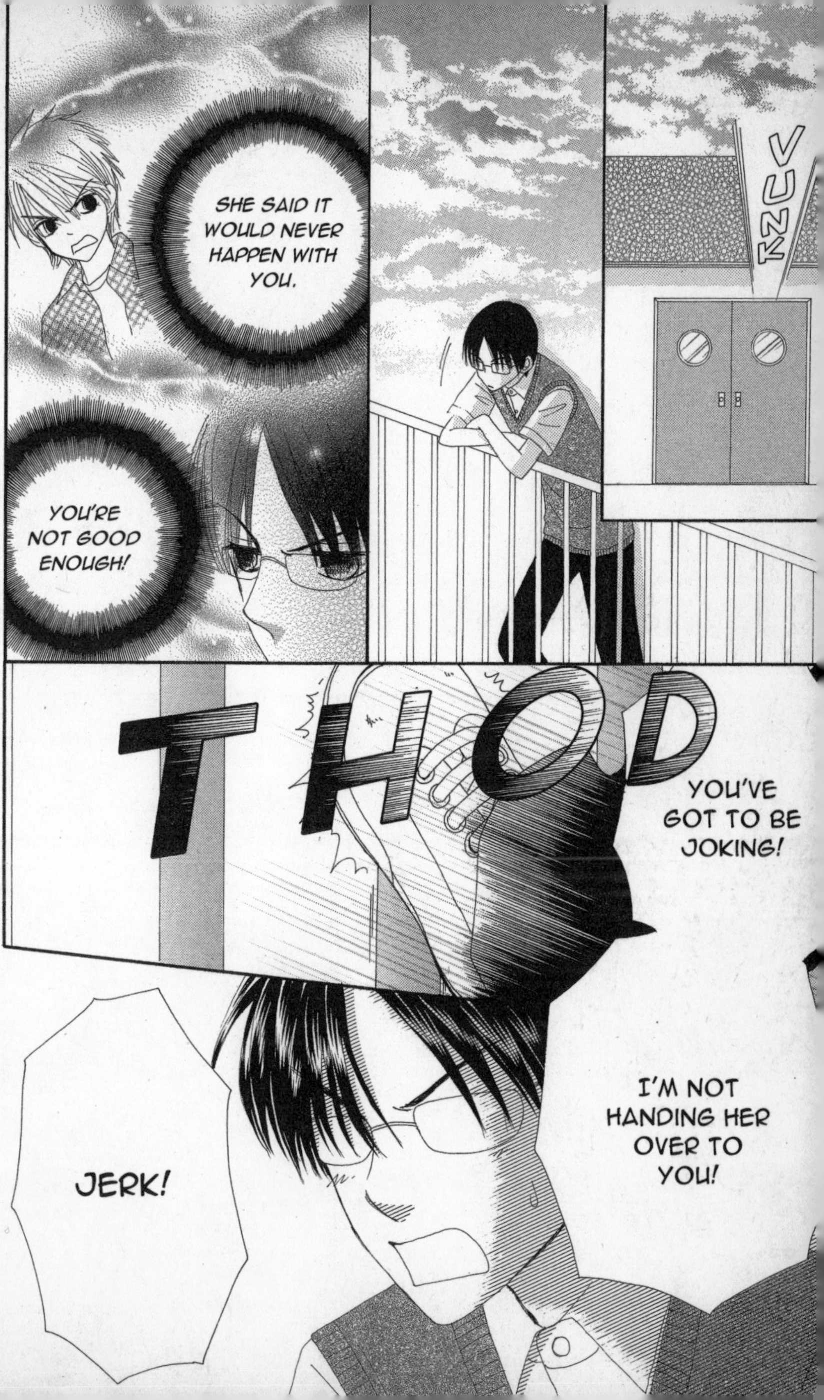
KNUV
SHE SAID IT WOULD NEVER HAPPEN WITH YOU.
YOU'RE NOT GOOD ENOUGH!
THOD
YOU'VE GOT TO BE JOKING!
I'M NOT HANDING HER OVER TO YOU!
JERK!

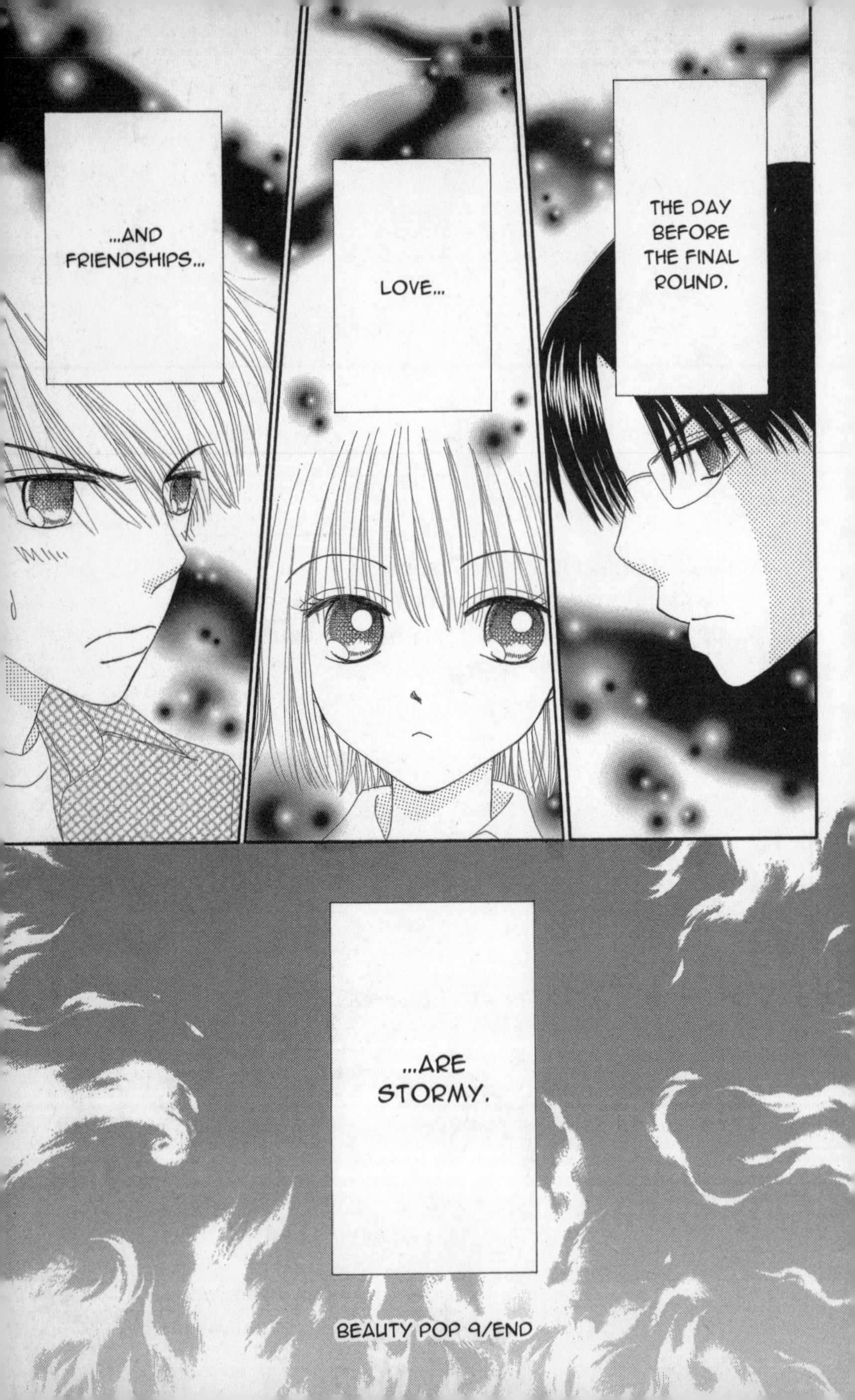
THE DAY BEFORE THE FINAL ROUND.
LOVE...
...AND FRIENDSHIPS...
...ARE STORMY.
BEAUTY POP 9/END

Honorifics

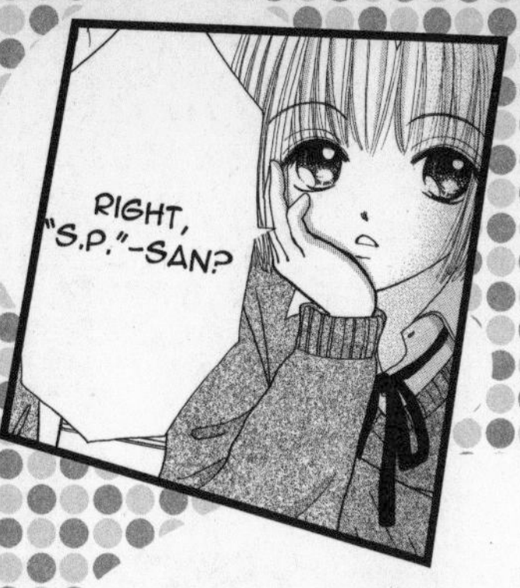
RIGHT, "S.P."-SAN?

In Japan, people are usually addressed by their name followed by a suffix. The suffix shows familiarity or respect, depending on the relationship.

Male (familiar): first or last name + kun
Female (familiar): first or last name + chan
Upperclassman (polite): last name + senpai
Adult (polite): last name + san

+ sama: A deferential suffix that is also used by fan girls when referring to the object of their adoration.

+ sensei: A suffix used for respected professionals, such as teachers, doctors, and mangaka.

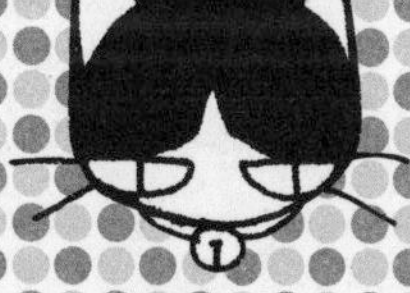

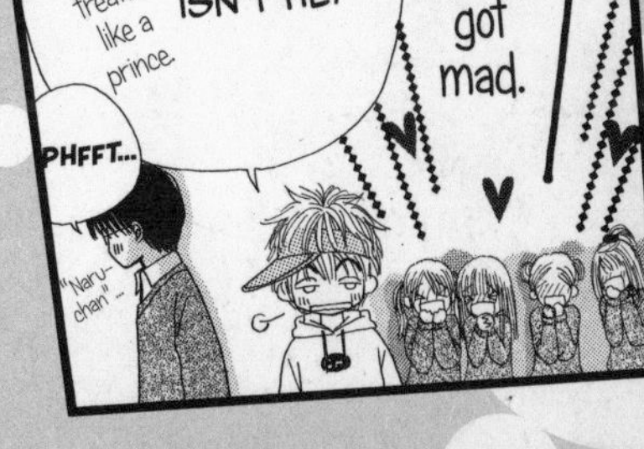
Yeee!
Narumi-senpai got mad.
NARU-CHAN'S FUSSY, ISN'T HE?
Because he's used to being treated like a prince.
PHFFT...
"Naru-chan"...

Author's Note

The Shampoo pouch that Kiri is wearing on the front cover is just like the one that was a prize in the toy crane machines last year. I decided to make the pouch her coin purse in the drawing. I often use this pouch too for carrying small things. ♥

Kiyoko Arai was born in Tokyo and now resides in Chiba Prefecture. In 1999, she received the prestigious Shogakukan Manga Award for *Angel Lip*. The popular *Dr. Rin ni Kiitemite!* (Ask Dr. Rin!) was made into an animated TV show.

Beauty Pop
Vol. 9
The Shojo Beat Manga Edition

STORY AND ART BY
KIYOKO ARAI

English Adaptation/Amanda Hubbard
Translation/Miho Nishida
Touch-up Art & Lettering/Inori Fukuda Trant
Design/Izumi Hirayama
Editor/Nancy Thistlethwaite

Editor in Chief, Books/Alvin Lu
Editor in Chief, Magazines/Marc Weidenbaum
VP of Publishing Licensing/Rika Inouye
VP of Sales/Gonzalo Ferreyra
Sr. VP of Marketing/Liza Coppola
Publisher/Hyoe Narita

Printed in Canada

Published by VIZ Media, LLC
P.O. Box 77010
San Francisco, CA 94107

Shojo Beat Manga Edition
10 9 8 7 6 5 4 3 2 1
First printing, October 2008

www.viz.com

RATED T FOR TEEN
PARENTAL ADVISORY
BEAUTY POP is rated T for Teen and is recommeded for ages 13 and up. This volume contains violence and suggestive themes.
ratings.viz.com

store.viz.com